The Jewish Jesus

The Jewish Jesus

HOW JUDAISM AND CHRISTIANITY SHAPED EACH OTHER

Peter Schäfer

Princeton University Press
Princeton & Oxford

Copyright © 2012 by Princeton University Press
Published by Princeton University Press,
41 William Street, Princeton, New Jersey 08540
In the United Kingdom: Princeton University Press, 6 Oxford Street,
Woodstock, Oxfordshire OX20 1TW

press.princeton.edu

Jacket illustration: *David Anoints Samuel,* paint on plaster.
WC3 1936.127.14. Courtesy of Yale University Art Gallery,
Dura-Europos Collection.

All Rights Reserved

LIBRARY OF CONGRESS CATALOGING-IN-PUBLICATION DATA
Schäfer, Peter.
The Jewish Jesus : how Judaism and Christianity
shaped each other / Peter Schäfer.
p. cm.
Includes bibliographical references and index.
ISBN: 978-0-691-15390-2 (hardcover : alk. paper) 1. Judaism—Relations—
Christianity—History. 2. Christianity and other religions—Judaism—
History. 3. Messiah—History of doctrines. I. Title.
BM535.S26 2012
232.9'0609015—dc23   2011035535
British Library Cataloging-in-Publication Data is available

This book has been composed in Adobe Garamond Pro

Printed on acid-free paper. ∞

Printed in the United States of America

1 2 3 4 5 6 7 8 9 10

For Lily, Sebastian, Maximilian, Otto, Marie, and Sophia

Contents

LIST OF FIGURES   IX

ACKNOWLEDGMENTS   XI

ABBREVIATIONS   XIII

Introduction   1

1. Different Names of God   21
  Offerings   22
  Creation   24
  R. Simlai's Collection of Dangerous Bible Verses   27
  The Bavli Collection   37
  R. Simlai and Christianity   42

2. The Young and the Old God   55

3. God and David   68
  Aqiva in the Bavli   70
  The David Apocalypse   85
  David in Dura Europos   94

4. God and Metatron   103
  Rav Idith and the Heretics   104
  Metatron the Great Scribe   115
  The Celestial High Priest   116
  The Prince of the World   123
  The Instructor of Schoolchildren in Heaven   125
  Two Powers in Heaven   127
  Akatriel   131
  Metatron in Babylonia   138
  Metatron and Christianity   141

5. Has God a Father, a Son, or a Brother?   150

6. The Angels   160
   When Were the Angels Created?   160
   God's Consultation with the Angels   165
   Angels and Revelation   179
   Veneration of Angels   188

7. Adam   197

8. The Birth of the Messiah, or Why Did Baby
   Messiah Disappear?   214
   The Arab   220
   Elijah   222
   The Messiah   223
   The Mother of the Messiah   227
   Christianity   228

9. The Suffering Messiah Ephraim   236
   Pisqa 34   238
   Pisqa 36   242
   Pisqa 37   261
   Christianity   264

NOTES   273

BIBLIOGRAPHY   329

INDEX   343

Figures

1. Western wall of the Dura Europos synagogue   96
2. Original tree design, with objects to its left and right, painted on the two panels above the Torah shrine   97
3. Decorations painted later on the upper part of the original tree design   98
4. Decorations painted later on the lower part of the original tree design   99
5. Edgings added later divide the two main parts of the tree design   100

Acknowledgments

THE BULK OF THIS BOOK WAS WRITTEN DURING MY tenure at the Wissenschaftskolleg / Institute for Advanced Study at Berlin during the academic year 2007–8. A much shorter version in the form of five lectures, delivered in German at Jena University as part of its Tria Corda lecture cycle, was published in 2010 under the provocative title *Die Geburt des Judentums aus dem Geist des Christentums* (The Birth of Judaism from the Spirit of Christianity) by Mohr Siebeck at Tübingen.

My special thanks go to the Wissenschaftskolleg for granting me an unforgettable year of research in my own field and informal exchange with co-fellows in a great variety of other disciplines; what has become chapter 8 of this book was presented as my contribution to the memorable Tuesday colloquium, at which each of us had to make his or her research accessible to our curious and critical co-fellows.

Philip Alexander and Burt Visotzky—the two readers for the press, who graciously chose to reveal their identity—provided me with many important suggestions not just about details but also about the book's larger structure. My former student Moulie Vidas, now a professor at UC Davis, discussed the entire manuscript with me and helped me clarify my ideas. Christoph Markschies was kind enough to read the German version and to enlighten me on matters of early Church history. As always, Brigitta van Rheinberg, Editor in Chief at Princeton University Press, supported me in every possible way. Kevin McAllen, the Wissenschaftskolleg's English-language editor, again took on the task of style-editing the entire manuscript, Will Hively was the perfect professional copy editor for the preparation of the manuscript's final version, and Geoffrey Smith kindly compiled the index. I am enormously grateful to all of them, and it goes without saying that the remaining defects are not their fault.

I dedicate this book, with gratitude and love, to the youngest generation of my family, to my grandchildren Lily, Sebastian, Maximilian, Otto, Marie, and Sophia.

ad loc.	ad locum
Ant.	Josephus, Antiquitates
Apoc. Zeph.	Apocalypse of Zephaniah
ARN	Avot de-Rabbi Nathan
ArOr	Archiv Orientální
Asc. Isa.	Ascension of Isaiah
AZ	Tractate Avodah Zarah
b	Babylonian Talmud (Bavli)
b.	ben ("son of")
BamR	Bamidbar Rabba
BB	Tractate Bava Batra
B.C.E.	Before the Christian Era
Bell.	Josephus, Bellum
Ber	Tractate Berakhot
BerR	Midrash Bereshit Rabba
BSOAS	Bulletin of the School of Oriental and African Studies
BZ	Biblische Zeitschrift
Cant.	Canticum Canticorum (Song of Songs)
CBQ	Catholic Biblical Quarterly
CBR	Currents in Biblical Research
C.E.	Christian Era
ch.	chapter
CN	Codex Neofiti
col.	column
Col.	Letter to the Colossians
1 Cor.	First Letter to the Corinthians
2 Cor.	Second Letter to the Corinthians

Dan.	Daniel
Deut.	Deuteronomy
DevR	Devarim Rabba
ead.	eadem
Eccl.	Ecclesiastes
ed./eds.	editor/editors
EkhaR	Ekha Rabba
1 En.	First Book of Enoch
2 En.	Second Book of Enoch
Eph.	Letter to the Ephesians
EsthR	Midrash Esther Rabba
Ex.	Exodus
Ezek.	Ezekiel
f./ff.	and the following page/pages
FJB	Frankfurter Judaistische Beiträge
fol.	folio or folios
Gal.	Letter to the Galatians
Gen.	Genesis
Hag	Tractate Hagigah
Heb.	Letter to the Hebrews
HTR	Harvard Theological Review
HUCA	Hebrew Union College Annual
Hul	Tractate Hullin
ibid.	ibidem
id.	idem
Isa.	Isaiah
JANES	Journal of the Ancient Near Eastern Society
JBL	Journal of Biblical Literature
Jer.	Jeremiah
JJS	Journal of Jewish Studies
Josh.	Joshua
JQR	Jewish Quarterly Review

JSHRZ	Jüdische Schriften aus hellenistisch-römischer Zeit
JSJ	Journal for the Study of Judaism
Jub.	Jubilees
JWCI	Journal of the Warburg and Courtauld Institute
l.	line
Lam.	Lamentations
LeqT	Midrash Leqah Tov
Lk.	Gospel of Luke
m	Mishna
MekhS	Mekhilta de-Rabbi Shimʿon b. Yohai
MekhY	Mekhilta de-Rabbi Yishmaʿel
MHG	Midrash ha-gadol
MidrHakh	Midrash Hakhamim
MidrTann	Midrash Tannaim
MidrTeh	Midrash Tehillim
MJTh	Marburger Jahrbuch Theologie
Mk.	Gospel of Mark
Ms./Mss.	Manuscript/Manuscripts
MT	Masoretic text of the Hebrew Bible
Mt.	Gospel of Matthew
n.	note
Niddah	Tractate Niddah
NF	Neue Folge
NRSV	New Revised Standard Version
N.S.	New Series
Num.	Numbers
OTP	The Old Testament Pseudepigrapha
p./pp.	page/pages
PesK	Pesiqta de-Rav Kahana
PesR	Pesiqta Rabbati
1 Petr.	First Letter of Peter
Phil.	Letter to the Philippians

PRE	Pirqei de-Rabbi Eli'ezer
Prov.	Proverbs
Ps.	Psalms
Qid	Tractate Qiddushin
QohR	Qohelet Rabba
R.	Rabbi
RB	Revue Biblique
RdQ	Revue des Qumran
REJ	Revue des études juives
Rev.	Revelation
RHR	Revue de l'histoire des religions
Rom.	Letter to the Romans
RRJ	Review of Rabbinic Judaism
RSV	Revised Standard Version
2 Sam.	Second Book of Samuel
Sanh	Tractate Sanhedrin
SekhT	Midrash Sekhel Tov
Shab	Tractate Shabbat
ShemR	Midrash Shemot Rabba
ShirR	Shir ha-Shirim Rabba
SifBam	Sifre Bamidbar (Sifre on Numbers)
SifDev	Sifre Devarim (Sifre on Deuteronomy)
SifZut	Sifre Zuta
Sir.	Jesus Sirach
Sot	Tractate Sotah
Suk	Tractate Sukkah
t	Tosefta
Taan	Tractate Ta'anit
Tan	Midrash Tanhuma
TanB	Midrash Tanhuma Buber
TJ	Targum Jonathan
TO	Targum Onkelos
TPsJ	Targum Pseudo-Jonathan

USQR	Union Seminary Quarterly Review
v./vv.	verse/verses
VigChr	Vigiliae Christianae
vol./vols.	volume/volumes
WaR	Wayyiqra Rabba
y	Jerusalem Talmud (Yerushalmi)
Yalq	Yalqut Shim'oni
Yev	Tractate Yevamot
Zech.	Zechariah
Zeph.	Zephaniah

Introduction

THIS IS A BOOK ABOUT THE EMERGENCE OF RABBINIC
Judaism, that momentous manifestation of Judaism after the destruction of the Temple, under the impact of the rise of Christianity in the first centuries C.E. It is about identities and boundaries, boundaries between religions and boundaries within
religions; about the fluidity of boundaries and the demarcation
of boundaries—identities that are less stable and boundaries that
are more permeable than has been previously thought and yet
increasingly demarcated in order to occupy territories. It is about
the fluidity of categories such as "inside" and "outside," "orthodoxy" and "heresy," not least "Judaism" and "Christianity," shifting paradigms that depend on literary and historical contexts
and do not allow of an easy "either/or." It is a book by a historian
who is deeply convinced that differences matter and must not be
dissolved in overarching ideas void of any attempt to anchor
them in time and place. Its main thesis is that not only the emerging Christianity drew on contemporary Judaism but that rabbinic Judaism, too, tapped into ideas and concepts of Christianity to shape its own identity; that, far from being forever frozen
in ingrained hostility, the two sister religions engaged in a pro-
found interaction during late antiquity. Even more, it posits that

in certain cases the rabbis appropriated Christian ideas that the Christians had inherited from the Jews, hence that rabbinic Judaism *re*appropriated originally Jewish ideas that were usurped by Christianity.

Common wisdom has it that belief in the unity and uniqueness of God has been one of the firmly established principles of Jewish faith since time immemorial. This belief is considered to be forever recorded in the solemn beginning of the biblical *Shemaʿ*, one of the daily prayers in Jewish worship: "Hear, O Israel, the Lord is our God, the Lord alone (*YHWH ehad*)" (Deut. 6:4). Since the latter part of this declaration can also be translated as "the Lord is one," it contains *in nuce* an acknowledgment of Israel's God as the one and only God, with no other gods beside him, and is simultaneously a recognition of him as the one and undivided God, that is, not consisting of multiple personalities. This peculiar character of the Jewish God is generally captured under the rubric "monotheism"—although the view is becoming ever more accepted that such a category is highly problematic for the biblical period, let alone for those periods coming after the closure of the Hebrew Bible. The authors of the Hebrew Bible no doubt tried very hard to implement and enforce the belief in the one God in its double sense, but they also faced considerable resistance and were constantly fighting off attempts to thwart their efforts and—inspired by the customs of Israel's neighbors—to sneak in ideas that ran counter to any strict interpretation of monotheism. Thus it appears that the very notion of monotheism as a monolithic and stable entity is misleading and that we need to distinguish between the rigid and programmatic *rhetoric* of monotheism as opposed to its much less rigorous *practice*.

The rabbis of the talmudic period after 70 C.E. encountered an even more complex environment. Regardless of how much they assumed and insisted on their God's unity and uniqueness, they were surrounded by people—their affiliation with different religious and social groups notwithstanding—for whom such an idea was highly contested territory. The Greeks and Romans were amazed by the notion of a God reserved solely for the Jews, this exclusivity underscored by the Jewish God's strict aniconic character and a complete lack of images depicting him. The well-meaning among them nevertheless tried to integrate this elusive God into their pantheon as some form of *summum deum* or "highest heaven," whereas the mean-spirited parodied the Jewish beliefs or plainly concluded that the Jews must have been the worst of atheists.[1] The emerging Christian sect set out to elaborate the notion of the one and only God in terms of first a binitarian and then a trinitarian theology—that is, they took the decisive step to include God's Son in the godhead, this followed by the inclusion of a third divine figure, the Holy Spirit. And the various groups that are commonly subsumed under the label "Gnosis" embraced the Neo-Platonic distinction between the absolutely and uniquely transcendent God (the first and highest principle) and the demiurge (the second principle) responsible for the mundane creation, which could easily (and derogatorily) be identified with the Jewish creator God.

The rabbis were certainly aware of such developments and responded to them. The rabbinic literature has preserved a wealth of sources that portray the rabbis as engaged in a dialogue, or rather debate, with people who present views that run counter to the accepted or imagined rabbinic norm system. Generally, these dialogue partners—commonly subsumed under the category *minim*, literally "kinds (of belief),"[2] that is, all kinds of people with divergent beliefs—are presented as opponents whose ideas need to be refuted and warded off; hence the customary translation of *minim* as "heretics" (because their ideas deviate from the norm established by the rabbinic majority). It goes without saying that these "heretics" did not escape the attention of modern scholarly research, which, from its inception, was focused on—if not outright obsessed with—identifying this elusive group of people that caused the rabbis so much trouble. The respective sources have been collected and exhaustively analyzed, more often than not with the explicit goal of identifying *the* particular and peculiar heretical "sect" behind each and every individual source. In other words, it was the implicit and unquestioned assumption of most of the relevant scholarship that within the wide spectrum of rabbinic sources we are indeed dealing with clearly defined boundaries between what was regarded as an accepted set of ideas and what was not regarded as such—hence, with boundaries between "orthodoxy" and "heresy"—and that almost all the varieties of heresies can in fact be identified as belonging to this or that heretical group.

The scholarly standard, still largely valid today, has been set by two major works: Travers Herford's *Christianity in Talmud and Midrash*[3] and Alan Segal's *Two Powers in Heaven: Early Rabbinic Reports about Christianity and Gnosticism*.[4] Quite distant in time and methodology, both nevertheless share—in retrospect—a rather naïve confidence in our ability to pin down the heretical "sects" addressed in the sources. Herford arrived at "Christianity" as the main target of rabbinical ire in a relatively effortless fashion, whereas Segal, with his more sophisticated methodological equipment and a much broader perspective, tried to mark out the full range of possibilities—from "paganism" in all its varieties through a more differentiated "Christianity" (Jewish Christians, gentile Christians, God-Fearers, Hellenized Jews) to "Gnosticism," this latter (in the vein of Hans Jonas) in still quite undifferentiated form. Despite its undoubtedly great progress in both methodology and results, *Two Powers in Heaven* remains trapped in that all too rigid straitjacket of definable "religions," "sects," and "heresies" that know and fight each other with an equally well-defined set of ideas and beliefs.

This impasse was readdressed only recently, thanks above all to the work of Daniel Boyarin. In his book *Border Lines: The Partition of Judaeo-Christianity*[5] as well as in a series of articles,[6] Boyarin repeatedly and forcefully maintains that not only is the effort to identify the various heretical "sects" a vain one; moreover, and more importantly, he holds that there were no such heretical groups as well-defined entities distinct from the rabbis. In fact, when exposed to Christian ideas in particular, the rabbis were arguing not against an enemy from the outside but rather from within, that is, against their own colleagues who seemed unduly impressed with certain Christian views. He even goes so far as to suggest that we regard Christianity not as a "sect" within ancient Judaism against which the rabbis fought but as an integral part of the rabbinic mind-set. Much as I agree with the proposition (no well-defined heretical "sects" as opposed to "rabbinic Judaism"), I will demonstrate that Boyarin grossly overshoots the mark with respect to the conclusions he draws. In his desire to integrate Christianity into rabbinic Judaism he in fact blurs the boundaries and cavalierly disregards chronological and geographical (Palestinian versus Babylonian) distinctions (this becoming particularly obvious in his dealing with the Enoch-Metatron traditions).

But still, Boyarin has opened a window and allowed a fresh breeze to reinvigorate the scholarly debate about the *minim*. Indeed, it remains an important question as to what extent the rabbis were active partners in these discussions with the *minim*, that is, whether our rabbinic sources only reflect the fending off and repulse of such "heretical" propositions or whether they reveal hints that the (or rather some) rabbis were actively engaged in expanding the borderlines and softening the all too rigid idea of the one and only God. Phrased this way, the question does not assume that the discussions preserved in our rabbinic sources reflect the controversy of firmly established "religions"—"Jewish," "pagan," "Christian," "gnostic," or other—but allow for still fluid boundaries within (and beyond) which a variety of groups were competing with each other in shaping their identities. From this follows of necessity that the rabbis, in arguing against "heretics," were not always and automatically quarreling with enemies from the outside—however hard they may have tried to give precisely this impression—but also with enemies from within, that is, with colleagues who entertained ideas that the rabbis were fighting against.

A peculiar case is Moshe Idel's book *Ben: Sonship and Jewish Mysticism*.[7] Although Idel does not deal with *minim* in the full sense of this term, his book is nevertheless important for our subject since, in surveying the concept of sonship (the Son of God in particular) in Judaism from antiquity to the modern period, Idel refers to a number of sources also discussed in this present book. In terms of methodology, he typically follows his "phenomenological" approach—an approach that scorns both unilinear histories of Jewish mysticism as well as homogeneous interpretations focusing on the theosophical strand of Kabbalah (as opposed to the ecstatic strand), the latter demonized as Gershom-Scholem-and-His-School.[8] Such an approach leads to a highly idiosyncratic mixture of sources that deliberately ignores the constraints of time and place, advocating instead a synchronic reading of the respective literatures that moves effortlessly back and forth between antiquity, the Middle Ages, and the modern period. The reader who doesn't want to follow Idel's presupposition is confronted with a hodgepodge of sources and impressions that—although often interesting and illuminating—defy any serious source-critical analysis and chronological classification and are therefore, from a historical point of view, worthless.[9] Even at the risk of being suspected of historicism, I prefer a sober historical evaluation to one of impressionistic ideas, brilliant as they might be.

Yet even Idel cannot completely ignore chronology and source criticism. A case in point is his treatment of the antediluvian patriarch Enoch who, according to the Third Book of Enoch (which is part of the Hekhalot literature), was transformed into the highest angel Metatron and called the "Lesser God" (*YHWH ha-qatan*) and who will play a prominent role in the pages of this book. For Idel it is a matter of course that this "Lesser God" of 3 Enoch stands in unbroken continuity with and in fact forms the climax of a much earlier development that started with the First (Ethiopic) and the Second (Slavonic) Book of Enoch.[10] Without taking the trouble of descending into the lowly sphere of source criticism, and with no attempt to date 1 and 2 Enoch,[11] let alone 3 Enoch, which most likely represents the latest of all the Hekhalot writings and belongs to the late or even postrabbinic period,[12] Idel simply declares that the Enoch-Metatron passages in 3 Enoch are among the "early themes in this book."[13] And it is through the use of this artifice that Metatron, the "Lesser God" of 3 Enoch, is read back into much earlier sources and an unbroken chain of tradition is established.[14] As opposed to this mashing together of sources I posit that distinctions are indeed relevant, for they lead us in this case, as I will demonstrate, not into the realm of Palestinian but rather Babylonian Judaism and, chronologically speaking, into a relatively late period.

The most recent attempt to come to terms with the rabbinic heretics is Adiel Schremer's monograph *Brothers Estranged: Heresy, Christianity, and Jewish Identity in Late Antiquity*.[15] Schremer's main thesis is that the attempt by Herford and his new supporters (Boyarin in particular) to see in the rabbinic debates first and foremost a reflection of theological, that is, Christological, themes narrows the complexity of the sources to a single and in fact secondary aspect. The real issue, he maintains, is not theology but social history, namely, the identity crisis Palestinian Jewish society faced after the destruction of the Second Temple in 70 C.E. and the failure of the Bar Kokhba revolt in 135 C.E., which cemented the oppressive power of the Roman Empire. Even the Christianization of the Roman Empire after Constantine's conversion, he suggests, was of little significance: "Palestinian rabbis of late antiquity continued to view Rome as a powerful oppressor, without paying much attention to its new religious character."[16] He even goes so far as to claim that the scholarly bias in favor of Christian themes as being at the center of the debate about heretics ultimately results in suppressing rabbinic Judaism and painting it with Christian colors—hence in "Christianizing" and "colonizing" it.[17]

These are strong words. Much as I agree with Schremer's emphasis on the political and social-historical implications of the rabbis' encounter with the heretics, it seems to me that with his stark contrast of "theological" versus "political" he has set up a straw man that may be useful for developing a new theory but woefully fails to correspond to the historical reality. After all, it is a futile and naïve undertaking to attempt to separate neatly "theology" from "politics," and this is certainly true for late antiquity, the period in question. Schremer is clearly aware of this basic principle,[18] but it appears that he keeps forgetting it and repeatedly lapses into the black-and-white picture of politics and history as something that can and should be separated from and contrasted with theology. This, I am afraid, reveals a rather inadequate conception of theology, not to mention politics.

In what follows I will survey the rabbinic literature for the rabbis' discussions with all kinds of "heretics." I do not claim, however, to do full justice to this subject in all its complexity, that is, to write a new Herford; rather, I will focus on debates about the rabbinic concept of God, his unity and uniqueness, and his relationship with other (prospective) divine powers. In so doing I will start with the assumption that the boundaries between "orthodoxy" and "heresy" have been fluid for a long time or, to put it differently, that the impact of the various "heresies" was crucial to the rabbis in shaping their own identity. With regard to the "heresies," a picture will emerge that is much more diffuse than has been previously thought—with fluid boundaries even between the heretical groups and sects—and that renders fruitless any attempt to delineate these boundaries more sharply. Yet it seems safe to say that the main "opponents" of the rabbis were "pagans" on the one hand (that is, Greco-Roman polytheism in all its diversity) and "Christians" on the other (again, in all its heretical variety and with its own struggle to define its identity).[19] This means that, whereas the emerging Christianity defined itself by making recourse to contemporary Judaism as well as to all kinds of groups and movements within itself, the emerging rabbinic Judaism defined itself by making recourse to *Christianity* (as well as to all kinds of groups and movements within itself). To be more precise: even the phrase "within itself" is ultimately misleading, since this "itself," far from being a stable entity, is the unknown quantity that we aim to describe. In other words, the paradigm of our unknown quantity is in constant flux and not always the same (i.e., not always either a straight "Judaism" or a straight "Christianity"). Depending on the context, it sometimes *is* "Christianity," and sometimes it is *inside* "Judaism"—with the "inside" and "outside" categories becoming ever more blurred.

If we take paganism and in particular Christianity as the most common determiner of those heresies confronting and shaping rabbinic Judaism, we find that the rabbis reacted in two ways: repulsion and attraction. Many of the debates between the rabbis and the heretics betray a sharp and furious rejection of ideas about God that smack of polytheism in its pagan or Christian guise, the latter making do with just two or three gods—that is, developing a binitarian or trinitarian theology. But since such ideas were by no means alien to ancient Judaism—the frequent attacks against polytheistic tendencies in the Hebrew Bible forcefully demonstrate that the authors of the biblical books had good reason to attack polytheism; and the biblical and postbiblical speculations about "Wisdom" (*hokhmah*) and the "Word" (*logos*) prove beyond any doubt that Judaism was open to ideas that accepted divine or semidivine powers next to God—one could regard their elimination with mixed feelings. Hence, some rabbis were resistant to the Christian usurpation of their ideas and insisted that not only did they *originally* belong to them but that they *still* belonged to them. I will demonstrate that this re-appropriation of originally Jewish ideas about God and (semi-) divine powers apart from him took two forms. First, certain Jewish groups elevated figures such as Adam, the angels, David, and above all Metatron to divine status, responding, I posit, to the Christian elevation of Jesus; and second, other groups revived the idea of the suffering servant/Messiah and his vicarious suffering despite (or because of) its Christian appropriation.

Concerning the relevant sources, I will pay due heed to the traditional distinction between earlier tannaitic sources (that is, sources ascribed to the rabbis of the first and second centuries) and later amoraic ones (that is, sources ascribed to rabbis of the third through the sixth centuries). Moreover and most importantly, as I did in my book *Jesus in the Talmud*,[20] I will again be placing great emphasis on the geographical distinction between Palestine and Babylonia; as in *Jesus in the Talmud* it turns out that this distinction is crucial for some of the major texts dealing with the elevation of divine or semidivine figures.

I begin with a chapter ("Different Names of God") addressing a problem that must have plagued the rabbis a great deal: the undeniable fact that the Hebrew Bible uses various names for God, most prominent among them *Elohim* and the tetragrammaton *YHWH*. Both names attracted the attention and curiosity of Gentiles, the latter because of the mystery surrounding it—it was originally used only by the High Priest entering the Holy of Holies of the Temple, and its proper pronunciation was deemed lost—and the former because it is grammatically a plural and hence could easily give rise to the idea that the Jews worshiped not just one God but several gods. The "heretics" apparently knew enough Hebrew to seize the opportunity and insinuate that the Jews were no different in this regard than the pagans and indeed accepted the notion of a pantheon of various gods. Many rabbinic sources prove that the rabbis were frequently exposed to such arguments on the part of the "heretics," who bombarded them with Bible verses in which the name *Elohim* could be interpreted as referring to a variety of gods. The rabbinic literature preserves several collections of such dangerous verses that clearly demonstrate how well-known and widespread this problem must have been.

One such debate, attributed to R. Simlai, a Palestinian amora of the late third/early fourth century, is of particular importance to our subject. I will argue that to a certain degree it presupposes and reflects Diocletian's reform of the Roman Empire toward the end of the third century—a reform that also affected Palestine as belonging to the eastern part of the empire. I posit that the notion of a diarchy of emperors (one Augustus and one Caesar, subordinate to the Augustus) followed by a tetrarchy (two Augusti with equal rights and two subordinate Caesares) gave rise to rabbinic reflections about the nature of their God: attacked by "heretics" insinuating that their *Elohim* mirrored a hierarchy of divine powers similar to the hierarchical structure of the Roman Empire, these rabbis insisted that their God still remained one and the same. Since this more complex power structure of the Roman Empire apparently influenced the evolving theological debate in Christianity about the nature of God (two or even three divine powers), and since both are mutually illuminating developments, I will argue that the rabbis were engaged in discourse not just with the Romans but also with the Christians. I will discuss the impact of this discourse on rabbinic Judaism and demonstrate that the rabbis—familiar with the Christological debate about the Son of God in particular and perceiving it as simultaneously tempting and threatening—ultimately rejected its implications out of hand.

The rabbis not only were aware (and were made aware) that the God of the Hebrew Bible is addressed by different names—sometimes, to complicate matters, even in the plural—they also were confronted with the fact that this God assumes various guises. Here, too, they had to answer impertinent questions from the heretics. The second chapter ("The Young and the Old God") will turn to this problem, using the example of a relatively early (third century) Palestinian midrash. There, the heretics take advantage of the fact that God is sometimes portrayed as a young war hero (most prominently when he redeems his people of Israel from Egypt and drowns the Pharaoh and his army in the Red Sea) and sometimes as a merciful old man (when he gives the Torah to his people at Mount Sinai). Countering the heretics' argument that these various manifestations point to two divine powers of equal right in heaven, one old and one young, the rabbis insist that their God, despite his varying appearances, nevertheless is always one and the same—never changing and never growing old.

The danger evoked by such an interpretation of the Hebrew Bible is obvious: one immediately thinks of the Christian notion of the old and young God—God-Father and God-Son. Although such associations cannot be completely ruled out, I urge caution and argue against a trend in modern scholarship (Boyarin) of reading back into this midrash later Babylonian ideas. The distinction between Palestine and Babylonia is crucial: whereas the later Babylonian rabbis, as I will argue in the next chapter, were indeed exposed to the growing attraction of two divine figures, the situation in third-century Palestine remains different. The early Palestinian amoraim did indeed witness the nascent Christianity, but they were still quite "innocent," with regard both to recognizing the developing theological intricacies of Christianity and to being drawn into them.

A much different picture emerges when we turn our attention to Babylonia. The third chapter ("God and David") deals with an exegesis of Daniel 7:9, found only in the Babylonian Talmud, which boldly assigns the Messiah–King David a throne in heaven, next to that of God. Here we have for the first time clear evidence that certain rabbis felt attracted to the idea of a second divine figure, enjoying equal rights with God. The angry rejection of this idea by other rabbis—and the editor of the Bavli—demonstrates that such "heretical" ideas gained a foothold within the rabbinic fold of Babylonian Jewry. The Bavli's Daniel exegesis finds its counterpart in the David Apocalypse, which gives an elaborate description of the elevated David and his worship in heaven. I posit that this unique piece is structurally similar to the elevation of the Lamb (that is, Jesus Christ) in the New Testament Book of Revelation and can be interpreted as a response to the New Testament. We don't know the time and place of origin of the David Apocalypse, but the fact that it is transmitted as part of the Hekhalot literature and develops ideas known only from the Bavli makes it probable that it indeed belongs to the realm of Babylonian Judaism. The Babylonian context is corroborated by the depiction of the Messiah–King David on the frescoes of the Dura Europos synagogue.

With the fourth chapter ("God and Metatron") we remain largely in Babylonia. The hero now is finally Metatron, that enigmatic figure assuming the title "Lesser God." I begin with an analysis of a midrash transmitted again only in the Bavli, in which Rav Idith (a Babylonian amora of the fourth or fifth century) deflects the fierce attacks of certain heretics who insist on assigning Metatron divine status. The structure of the midrash reveals not only that the heretics have the better arguments; it also becomes clear that the neat distinction between "rabbis" and "heretics" simply doesn't work here, and that we must reckon with the possibility that the clever biblical exegesis of the "heretics" in fact reflects ideas entertained by certain rabbis. No doubt, the notion of a second divine power alongside that of God has gained followers among the Babylonian Jews.

In order to substantiate this claim I survey all the relevant Metatron passages preserved in rabbinic literature. It turns out that almost all of them are found either in the Babylonian Talmud or in the Hekhalot literature, most notably in 3 Enoch; the few Palestinian examples are very late or originally refer to the angel Michael who was later identified with Metatron. Because 3 Enoch and presumably much of the Hekhalot literature if not originated in Babylonia at least received its definite literary form there, I conclude that Enoch-Metatron's elevation to a (semi)divine figure is part and parcel of Babylonian, not Palestinian, Judaism. This Babylonian context is again corroborated by extraliterary evidence, this time the Babylonian incantation bowls where Metatron plays a prominent role. I conclude this chapter with a comparison between Metatron's elevation in our rabbinic sources and Jesus' elevation in the New Testament. Again I posit that the Metatron of the Bavli and the Hekhalot literature is a deliberate response on the part of the Babylonian Jews to the challenges posed by Christianity.[21]

The fifth chapter ("Has God a Father, a Son, or a Brother?") returns to the realm of Palestinian Judaism and analyzes midrashim referring to God's family background. They again reflect the power structure of the Roman Empire with the emperor's dynasty (father, brother, son, probably also adoptive son). Since, as we have repeatedly seen, this hierarchy forms the backdrop of the nascent Christological speculations, it appears that it is the relationship between God and his Son in particular that is at stake in these sources. Additionally, some of these midrashim hint at the increasingly heated debate between Jews and Christians over the question of who is true heir to the Land of Israel.

Enoch-Metatron, being transformed into the highest of all angels and becoming a divine figure next to God, stands at the extreme (Babylonian) end of a much larger spectrum of rabbinic attitudes toward the angels. If we survey the full evidence (chapter 6), it turns out that the earlier Palestinian sources were vehemently opposed to any such possibility of the angels being granted a role transcending their traditional task of praising God and acting as his messengers. This is particularly true for the creation story and the revelation of the Torah on Mount Sinai. With regard to the former, the rabbis set great store in pointing out that the angels were *not* created on the first day of creation—to make sure that nobody should arrive at the dangerous idea that these angels *participated* in the act of creation (as their opponents obviously held). The rabbis had enough trouble with the plural of "Let us make man" in Genesis 1:26—although they opted for the interpretation that God consulted with his angels (the lesser evil in view of the Christian claim that he consulted with his Son), they immediately played down the inherent danger by maintaining that God did not follow the advice of his angels (who were against the creation of man) or by arguing that God did not in fact take this consultation very seriously; and it is left to the Bavli to come up with the most radical solution to this problem—having God burn the stubborn angels with his little finger, clear evidence again that the editors of the Bavli had to deal with groups advocating a more active role being played by the angels. In order to evaluate the dangers inherent in such ideas, I briefly analyze the place assigned to the angels in Philo's sophisticated system of carefully graded divine powers.

Similarly, the rabbis took great care in not granting the angels too active a role during the revelation of the Torah on Mount Sinai. Again, they had every reason for this restraint—cast in the formula that God revealed his Torah "not through the medium of an angel or a messenger"—since the alleged Jewish belief in the angels as mediators of revelation was used by no less a person than Paul to conclude that the Jewish "Law" was inferior to the new Christian interpretation of the Torah. Clearly, the rabbis were vulnerable here because some among them advocated just such ideas. Further indication of this problem is the fact that the rabbis felt compelled to parry attempts to venerate the angels (prominent among them Michael). Hence I posit that ancient Judaism was indeed on its way to introducing an intermediate level of angelic powers and that the rabbis tried very hard to counter such efforts—with more success in Palestine than in Babylonia.

It is not only the angels who are perceived as dangerous competitors with God—the same holds true for Adam, the first man, who, according to some midrashim, was originally created with enormous bodily dimensions (a *makro-anthropos*); one midrash even goes so far as to suggest that God decided to make him mortal only when he realized that the angels made an attempt to worship him (chapter 7). Refuting those scholars who try to locate this midrash within the realm of some vaguely defined "Gnosticism," I suggest that it much better reflects the period after Diocletian's reform—and with all that it implies for the Christological debate. This interpretation is corroborated again by Philo and the New Testament: while Philo identifies the (ideal) heavenly Adam with the Logos, Paul takes the next step and identifies this Logos-Adam with Jesus Christ. So my conclusion is very similar to the one regarding the angels: the rabbis polemicized against attempts to elevate Adam to a supernatural and (semi)divine being because they were aware of the possible

Christological interpretations and, not least, because such ideas had gained followers among the rabbis themselves. The Adam myth is but another example of the theological possibilities inherent in ancient Judaism—possibilities that were developed further by circles that would be labeled "Christian" yet could still remain, to a certain degree, within what would be called "rabbinic Judaism." In distancing themselves from such tendencies the rabbis ultimately aimed to shape their own (rabbinic) identity.

The last two chapters return to the Messiah, a subject already addressed in the chapters on David and Metatron. But the focus here is quite different. In examining a famous midrash in the Jerusalem Talmud about the disappearance of the newborn Messiah, the eighth chapter leads us into that very moment when "Christianity" sprang from the loins of "Judaism." Instead of tracking the more elaborate efforts of differentiation and demarcation (with its aspects of both repulsion and attraction), we now witness an early and archaic attempt to excrete "Christianity" from "Judaism"—yet this is a Christianity that is still regarded as part and parcel of Judaism and at the same time recognized as something that will become Judaism's worst enemy. Hence, this Baby Messiah is simultaneously the Jewish *and* Christian Messiah, caught at that tragic moment when Judaism was desperately trying to retain the Messiah within its fold but was also vaguely sensing that it would ultimately fail and that a new religion had already been born.

With the ninth and last chapter ("The Suffering Messiah Ephraim") we turn to the seemingly traditional task of the Messiah as the redeemer of Israel at the end of time. But what pretends to be traditional emerges as something radically new within the context of rabbinic Judaism or, more precisely, as something originally and inherently Jewish that (1) was usurped by Christianity; as a result of this (2) was suppressed by Judaism;

and then, as the return of the suppressed, (3) was later making its way back ever more forcefully to rabbinic Judaism. I am referring to the idea of the suffering Messiah that evolved from the suffering servant in Isaiah, which was in turn adopted by the New Testament and expanded to include the notion of the Messiah's vicarious expiatory suffering—and was therefore completely ignored by the rabbis. It returns in a series of midrashim (dated presumably to the first half of the seventh century) in the collection Pesiqta Rabbati—just as if nothing had happened, as if the New Testament usurpation of this idea had never occurred. Appearing there is a Messiah named Ephraim of whom God demands that he take upon himself the sins of the people of Israel; only after the Messiah accepts this strange request does God agree to create humankind. Hence, it is ultimately the Messiah's expiatory suffering that guarantees creation and redemption.

With this we come full circle. We have followed the heretics' claim that the different names used for God in the Hebrew Bible point to a variety of deities and similarly that God's different manifestations as a young war hero and an old man lead to the inevitable conclusion that there are at least two gods in Judaism. We have seen that the rabbis virulently rejected such claims, apparently aware of their Christological implications, because they found followers within their own ranks. The latter appeared to be particularly true of the Jews of Babylonia with their bold ideas about David and Metatron as (semi)divine figures elevated to the heavenly Messiah-King and the highest angel respectively. More than anything else it seems to have been the notion of God's Son that bothered the rabbis, a problem coming to the fore also in texts dealing with the imperial-divine family and Adam as a supernatural being in competition with God. Other competitors deemed dangerous were the angels—because they diminished God's creative and revelatory power and could be used as ammunition for the Christian claim that the new covenant had superseded the old covenant.

Most of the sources analyzed in this book touch on Christianity as the major subject of the debates between rabbis and heretics, simultaneously perceived as a threat against which the rabbis' own identity needed to be defined and as a temptation triggering ideas that came dangerously close to the message of the New Testament. In contrast, the midrashim about the birth of the Messiah and the suffering Messiah Ephraim are not instigated by probing questions on the part of the heretics; rather, they lead us into the very heart of Judaism's multifarious and conflict-ridden relationship with Christianity—the birth of Christianity from the loins of Judaism and the bold reappropriation of originally Jewish ideas that had become the main markers of the new Christian religion.

The publisher and I have thought extensively about an appropriate title for this book. The German version was provocatively called *The Birth of Judaism from the Spirit of Christianity*, meant as a deliberate inversion of the much more common *The Birth of Christianity from the Spirit of Judaism*. Whereas the latter phrase expresses the truism that Christianity wouldn't have become possible without Judaism, that is, presupposes and continues Judaism, the former takes a different perspective: what we call Judaism—more precisely rabbinic Judaism—emerged in constant exchange with and differentiation from Christianity (or rather, from what, during this mutual process, became Christianity). It goes without saying that this title is an allusion to Friedrich Nietzsche's famous *The Birth of Tragedy from the Spirit of Music*: just as "music" was the midwife that brought "tragedy" to life, so "Christianity" was necessary to give life to "Judaism."

The present title, *The Jewish Jesus*, looks at the same phenomenon from a different angle. It is inspired by Geza Vermes' classic

Jesus the Jew:[22] whereas Vermes aimed at reclaiming Jesus for the Jews, arguing that the historical Jesus was essentially Jewish and belongs to the Jewish fold, this book is not concerned with the historical Jesus but claims that certain figures within rabbinic Judaism (such as David, Metatron, the Messiah, the angels, Adam) have been assigned a place within Judaism similar to the role Jesus played in Christianity. In other words, such figures— whether adopted or rejected—are attempts to incorporate into or repel from Judaism (semi)divine powers that enhance or threaten the divinity of the Jewish God. I am aware that this title is no less provocative than the earlier one, but I am confident that it will be assessed as an attempt to cast a fresh look at the origins of rabbinic Judaism in conjunction with the emergence of Christianity.

1

Different Names of God

EVEN IF ONE RUNS ONLY A CURSORY CHECK OF THE BIBLE (in the original as well as in translations), it becomes immediately obvious that it uses several names and not just a single appellation to designate God. The two most common names are the tetragrammaton *YHWH* and *Elohim*. Whereas the former has notoriously resisted not only its translation but also its proper pronunciation, the latter is grammatically a plural and literally means "gods." The rabbis of the talmudic period solved the problem of these two names by assigning them to two attributes of God—the one (*YHWH*) to the divine attribute of mercy (*rahamim*) and the other (*Elohim*) to the attribute of God's justice (*din*)—clearly aiming at preserving and maintaining the unity of the one and only God.[1] For modern, post-Enlightenment scholarship the two names served as the main indicator of what in German is called *Quellenscheidung* and as verification of two major layers in the text of the Pentateuch, the "Yahwist" and the "Elohist."[2]

Much as the rabbis were not bothered by various layers of the biblical text but took its unity for granted—an assessment that was shared by most people in antiquity, their affiliation with divergent religious and social groups notwithstanding—their ingenious solution of assigning the two major names of God to two different attributes did not meet with general approval. On the contrary, the fact that in the Hebrew Bible God is assigned different names apparently gave rise to speculation about the nature of God and allowed certain people to question the ideal of the one and only God.

OFFERINGS

I begin my survey with a midrash that addresses the question of offerings presented to God in the Hebrew Bible: which name of God, among the various options, is used when the Bible refers to offerings? The midrash is tannaitic, that is, relatively early, preserved in Sifre Numbers and in Sifra:

> [The other lamb you shall offer at twilight, preparing the same meal offering and libation as in the morning]—an offering by fire of pleasing odor to the Lord (*YHWH*) (Num. 28:8). . . .
>
> Shim'on b. Azzai says: Come and see: In all the offerings [mentioned] in the Torah, it is not said regarding them either "God" (*Elohim*) or "your God" (*Elohekha*) or "*Shaddai*" or "(of) Hosts" (*tzeva'ot*) but "*YH*," the singular/special name (*shem ha-meyuhad*), so as not to give the heretics (*minim*) an occasion to rebel (*lirdot*).[3]

Judging from the names of the rabbis to which this tradition is attributed—Shim'on b. Azzai, a tanna of the second generation and a contemporary of R. Aqiva; and R. Yose, a tanna of the third generation and student of R. Aqiva—this text leads us into the first half of the second century C.E. Its meaning is quite straightforward: although the Bible uses several names for God (*Elohim*, *Shaddai*, Hosts, *YHWH*), when it comes to offerings, it confines itself to the tetragrammaton *YHWH*. This name is explicitly called *shem ha-meyuhad*, which means the singular or special name of God, that is, the name reserved for the one and only Jewish God (alluding to the *YHWH ehad* in Deut. 6:4). Moreover, since the name *YHWH* is also grammatically singular, it is the perfect counterpart to the names *Elohim* and Hosts, which are grammatically plural.[4] Hence, in deliberately using the name *YHWH*, the Bible seeks to avoid leaving its readers with the impression that offerings were made to a plurality of gods.

The addressees of this tradition are unspecified heretics (with the exception of the Bavli parallel, which speaks of *ba'al din*—literally a "legal adversary"), and their reaction is labeled in both Sifre and Sifra as "rebellion" (in the Bavli as *lahaloq*—"to object, to oppose, to utter a different opinion," a term that is also used for rabbinic disputes). From this terminology it would seem that the midrashim have some kind of open apostasy from the (rabbinically defined) Jewish religion in mind, whereas the Bavli conceives a legal dispute—within the realm of the Jewish tradition or with some "outsider." This leaves us with a wide range of possibilities among which, of course, "Gnostics," "Christians," and "pagans" are the usual suspects. Bacher saw here a barb directed against the Gnostics, who allegedly claimed that the laws concerning offerings were given by the demiurge, the secondary creator God (called by the names *Elohim*, *Shaddai*, and Hosts), not by the good and superior God, and that our rabbis, in referring to *YHWH*, wished to argue that *YHWH* was indeed that superior God deserving of offerings.[5] This is quite a far-fetched interpretation. With almost the same right one could claim that the names *Elohim*, *Shaddai*, and Hosts imply a triad and hence refer to the Christian trinity, which the rabbis counter with *YHWH* as the name for the one and only (Jewish) God.

Neither of these options makes much sense. The only conspicuous element in the statement that might serve as a clue for its context is the fact that it explicitly refers to "all the offerings mentioned in the Torah," that is, it is specifically concerned with sacrifices. Offering sacrifices to an extensive pantheon of deities was not only an issue in the biblical framework but also in connection with the daily life of the rabbis in the Greco-Roman world. So one can easily imagine certain Jews or Greek/Roman neighbors of the Jews suggesting to the rabbis that, since the Bible uses different names for God and even certain names in the plural, it would be acceptable or even logical to offer sacrifices to a variety of gods. The rabbis' answer to this imposition is unambiguous: in using only the name *YHWH* for offerings, the Bible makes clear that we Jews worship only one God and not a plurality of deities.

CREATION

The rabbis were well aware of the philological crux implied in the plural form of *Elohim* as God's name (as opposed to the singular *YHWH*). A large number of midrashim address this problem, in particular midrashim dealing with the exegesis of Genesis, since the name *Elohim* appears in the very first verse of the Bible ("In the beginning God [*Elohim*] created . . ."). A case in point is the midrash in Bereshit Rabba:

> R. Yitzhaq commenced with: "The beginning (*rosh*) of your word is truth; and all your righteous ordinance(s) endure[6] forever" (Ps. 119:160).
>
> Said R. Yitzhaq: From the very commencement of the world's creation, "The beginning of your word is truth" (Ps.

ibid.). [Thus:] "In the beginning God (*Elohim*) created" (Gen. 1:1) [corroborates the statement:] "The Lord God (*YHWH Elohim*) is truth" (Jer. 10:10). Therefore: "And all your righteous ordinance endures forever" (Ps. ibid.).

For, in regard to every single decree which you promulgate concerning your creatures, they affirm the righteousness of your judgment and accept it with faith. And no person can dispute (*haluqah*) and maintain that two powers (*shetei rashuyyot*) gave the Torah or two powers created the world. For "And the Gods spoke (*wa-yedabberu Elohim*)" is not written here, but: "And God spoke (*wa-yedabber Elohim*) all these words" (Ex. 20:1). "In the beginning the gods created (*bar'u*)" is not written here, but: "In the beginning God created (*bara*)."[7]

This midrash is a Petiha, transmitted in the name of R. Yitzhaq (presumably R. Yitzhaq b. Nappaha, the late third-/early fourth-century Palestinian amora of the third generation and student of R. Yohanan b. Nappaha, who taught in Tiberias and Caesarea), which explains Genesis 1:1 through Psalms 119:160. In opening his Torah with "in the beginning" (*bereshit*), R. Yitzhaq argues, God has made clear that, from the very beginning, he, God himself, speaks truth; that is, the divinity declares that it is the one and only God who created the world. The biblical verse Jeremiah 10:10, which contains both names for God (*YHWH* and *Elohim*), reveals the "truth" that both names refer to the same God. Moreover, God's righteous ordinances endure "forever" (*le-'olam*), that is, from the beginning of the creation of the world until the present time as well as "for the (whole) world" (*le-'olam*),[8] that is, for all of God's creatures. Temporally and spatially, everybody is included and expected to accept his righteous ordinances: the midrash speaks explicitly of God's "creatures" (*beriyyot*) and not just of "Israel."[9] In particular, no creature is allowed to deviate from the basic truth that there is only one God and that this one and the same God created the world and bestowed the Torah. Despite the plural of *Elohim*, the midrash concludes, the verb attached to it is always in the singular—for example, "God spoke" (sing.) in Exodus 20:1 instead of "gods spoke" (pl.), and "God created" (sing.) in our Seder verse Genesis 1:1 instead of "gods created" (pl.).

The heresy that deviates from the basic truth of the one and only God is called the heresy of the "two powers"—a heresy which maintains that neither a sole God nor a multiplicity of gods are responsible for the creation and the revelation of the Torah but precisely two divine powers. This midrash is relatively late, and there are other and earlier midrashim referring to the heresy of "two powers," which will be discussed in due course. What becomes clear from this context, however, is the fact that the heresy must concern creation in particular, with the revelation of the Torah being a secondary amplification. It presumes that two divine powers—that is, two deities—were responsible for the creation of the world. Whether these deities were equal or whether one of them was subordinate to the other is not entirely clear, although the way the midrash is formulated suggests that they are regarded as equal. If this assumption is correct, a reference to one of the gnostic systems as the alleged heresy seems to be less likely, since all the gnostic systems presuppose a strict separation between a supreme (hidden and unattainable) God and an inferior (even evil) creator god—the Demiurge. Hence, a "two powers" heresy in the sense of a dualistic (gnostic) theology would not appear to be the most obvious option, as has often been proposed.[10] The more likely option, therefore, is a "binitarian" theology, according to which two more or less equal deities are held jointly responsible for the creation of the world. What this precisely means cannot be determined from our present midrash alone—it is presupposed here rather than explained—and needs to be discussed in view of the full rabbinic evidence.

R. SIMLAI'S COLLECTION OF DANGEROUS BIBLE VERSES

A midrash preserved in Bereshit Rabba and in the Yerushalmi presents a comprehensive collection of dangerous questions relating to God's names as they appear in certain biblical verses. It is cast in the form of a debate between R. Simlai and the heretics, with R. Simlai's students present, these demanding a better answer than the one the rabbi has given to the heretics. Beginning with the well-known problem of Genesis 1, discussed above, it continues with an exegesis of Genesis 1:26 and 27 in which—unfortunately for the standard rabbinic argument—the plural of *Elohim* is coupled with a verb that is likewise in the plural:

> The heretics (*minim*) asked R. Simlai: "How many gods created the world?"
>
> He said to them: "I and you must inquire of the first days, for it is written: 'Ask now the former days [which were before you,] since God created (*bara Elohim*) man upon the earth' (Deut. 4:32). It is not written here: 'since they [the gods] created (*bar'u*),'[11] but 'since he [God] created (*bara*).'"[12]
>
> They asked him a second time and said to him: "Why is it written: 'In the beginning God [*Elohim* in the plural] created' (Gen. 1:1)?"
>
> He answered: "'The gods created (*bar'u*)'[13] is not written here, but 'God created (*bara*).'"[14]
>
> R. Simlai said: "In every passage where you find a point (apparently) supporting the heretics (*minin*),[15] you find the refutation at its side."

They asked him again and said to him: "Why is it written: '[And God (*Elohim*) said:] Let us make (*na'aśeh*)[16] a man in our image, after our likeness' (Gen. 1:26)?"

He answered them: "Read what follows—'and the gods created (*wa-yivre'u Elohim*)[17] man in their image' is not written (in the Bible), but 'and God created (*wa-yivra Elohim*)[18] man in his image' (Gen. 1:27)."

When they left, his disciples said to him: "Rabbi, them you have dismissed with a reed, but what will you answer to us?"

He said to them: "In the past Adam was created from dust, and Eve was created from Adam, but henceforth: 'in our image, after our likeness' (Gen. 1:26). Neither man without woman nor woman without man, and neither of them without the Shekhinah."[19]

R. Simlai was a second-generation Palestinian amora of the late third/early fourth century, who spent most of his time in Lydda and Sepphoris; he was a student of R. Yohanan (b. Nappaha), who flourished in Sepphoris, Tiberias, and (later) in Caesarea.[20] Again, the Bible-verses battle that he fights with the heretics focuses on creation. Its starting point is two almost classical verses (Deut. 4:32 and Gen. 1:1) in which the name of God in the plural is combined with a verb in the singular, taken as proof by the rabbis that *Elohim* refers to one God and not a plurality of gods. It is from this that R. Simlai concludes there are many more such pseudo-problematic cases in the Bible, and he adds a comprehensive list that moves to another example from Genesis—that exceptional case in which "*Elohim*" is indeed coupled with a verb in the plural (Gen. 1:26: "let *us* make man, in *our* image and *our* likeness"), running counter to the main rabbinical argument that the plural of *Elohim* is always matched with a verb in the singular.

This answer to the heretics is augmented with an additional discourse among the rabbi and his students,[21] another rabbinic pattern, which obviously seeks to demonstrate that the "real" questions emerge only in the internal setting of the rabbinic academies and not among "rabbis" and "heretics." But the answer to his students in this particular case is odd. It shifts the emphasis from the plural "let *us* make a man" in Genesis 1:26 to the plural "in *our* image, after *our* likeness" in the same verse and apparently argues: whereas the first couple, Adam and Eve, was created solely from dust (Adam) and from Adam (Eve), it is only their descendants that are created in "our image, after our likeness," that is, from their human parents in collaboration with the She-khinah (God). In other words, the plural of "in our image, after our likeness" refers to the cooperation of the human parents as equal partners with God in the act of procreation and has nothing to do with a multiplicity of gods. This response clearly does not address the problem of the two contradictory Bible verses Genesis 1:26 and 1:27 (Why then does Genesis 1:27 say explicitly, "And God created man in *his* image, in the image of God he created *him*; male and female he created *them*"?) and could, moreover, provide the heretics with additional ammunition—namely, that Adam and Eve were created exclusively from matter and that only their descendants have the privilege of being created in the image of God.

It has long been observed that R. Simlai's answer to his students comes surprisingly close to an argument that Paul makes in his first letter to the Corinthians,[22] where he discusses the relationship between man, woman, and God, together with the custom of covering one's head:

(11:2) I commend you because you remember me in everything and maintain the traditions even as I have delivered them to you. (3) But I want you to understand that the head of every man is Christ, the head of a woman is her husband, and the head of Christ is God. (4) Any man who prays or prophesies with his head covered dishonors his head, (5) but any woman who prays or prophesies with her head unveiled dishonors her head—it is the same as if her head were shaven. (6) For if a woman will not veil herself, then she should cut off her hair; but if it is disgraceful for a woman to be shorn or shaven, let her wear a veil. (7) For a man ought not to cover his head, since he is the image (*eikōn*) and glory (*doxa*) of God; but woman is the glory (*doxa*) of man. (8) For man was not made from woman, but woman from man. (9) Neither was man created for (the sake of) woman, but woman for (the sake of) man. (10) That is why woman ought to have a veil[23] on her head, because of the angels. (11) Nevertheless, in the Lord (*en kyriō*) woman is not independent of man nor man of woman; (12) for as woman was made from man, so man is also[24] born of woman. And all things are from God. (13) Judge for yourselves; is it proper for a woman to pray to God with her head uncovered?[25]

Whether this passage[26] is from Paul or—because it interrupts the flow of his argument—a later interpolation resembling the style of the deutero-Pauline letters is not our concern here. Paul justifies the custom of women covering their heads by establishing a hierarchy (in descending order) of Christ/God—man—woman: as man is the "image" and "glory" of God, whereas woman is the "glory" of man, it is not the man but the woman whose head should be covered. This strange logic seems to follow the literal meaning of Genesis 1:27: "And God created *man* in his image, in the image of God he created *him*,"[27] which so conspicuously refers to the man (Adam) alone and not the woman (Eve) as created in God's image. The somewhat lamely appended "male and

female he created *them*" (ibid.)[28] intensifies the impression that
Eve wasn't created in God's image but was rather just a facsimile
of Adam. However, in verses 11 and 12, Paul softens this harsh
verdict and emphasizes that "in the Lord" woman and man are
not independent of each other but equal, since they are both in-
dispensable to the process of procreation. Here Paul suddenly
shifts the argument away from Eve's unique creation from Adam
("as woman was made from man") to the creation of all subsequent human generations involving man and woman ("so man is
born of woman") and ultimately God.

This line of argument is indeed very similar to the one developed by R. Simlai. Like Paul, R. Simlai refers first to the unique
creation of Adam (out of dust) and Eve (from Adam) and then
turns to the creation of Adam and Eve's offspring—all subsequent human generations—which involve man, woman, and
God as equal partners. In particular the midrash sentence "Neither man without woman (*ish be-lo ishah*) nor woman without
man (*ishah be-lo ish*)" is almost literally identical with Paul's (v.
11) "neither woman without man (*gynē chōris andros*) nor man
without woman (*anēr chōris gynaikos*)."[29] However, R. Simlai appears to be much less misogynic than Paul—according to him it
is not just Eve who was not created in God's image: he clearly
implies that both Adam and Eve were not created in the image of
God, and he reserves the honor of being created in the image of
God for those future generations stemming from the primeval
couple.

What we obviously have here is a tradition concerning Genesis 1:26f. that is shared by Paul and a late third-/early fourth-
century rabbi. Where does this lead us? Scholars are divided
about the relationship between these two manifestations of a
similar tradition. Whereas earlier scholars were inclined to see in
R. Simlai's exegesis an example of the (in)famous "Rabbinic
background" of the New Testament, Burton Visotzky has made

a case for the opposite possibility—a rabbinic midrash in fact quoting Paul.[30] This is a tempting proposition, all the more so as it takes into consideration the large chronological gap between Paul and R. Simlai. But it is by no means conclusive. For what then would the polemical barb of R. Simlai's answer be to his students—provided that he wishes to polemicize against Paul. That he is less misogynic than Paul? Hardly a convincing answer. Visotzky does not entertain the possibility—which in my view is more likely—that Paul and his later rabbinic colleague are not dependent on each other (in whatever respect) and accordingly are not in a direct dialogue with each other but rather draw on a common Jewish source that they employ with slightly different emphases. Paul, therefore, does not help us to better understand R. Simlai's argument.

But the heretics don't give up. Knowing the Hebrew Bible quite well, they discover that the idea of more than one divinity (not necessarily just *two* divine powers) is not limited to the grammatical plural of the word *Elohim* or the verb attached to it. Nor is it limited to the problem of creation, as the continuation of their debate with R. Simlai demonstrates.[31] What about the fact, they ask now, that the Bible sometimes mentions various divine names in a single verse: why would it do so if there is only one God as the rabbis maintain? And here we get into really dangerous territory:

> They [the *minim*] asked him [R. Simlai] again: "What is that which is written: 'God (*El*), God (*Elohim*), the Lord (*YHWH*), God (*el*), God (*Elohim*), the Lord (*YHWH*), he knows' (Josh. 22:22)?"
>
> He said to them: "'they know' is not written here, but it is written: 'he knows.'"
>
> His disciples said to him: "Rabbi, them you have dismissed with a reed, but what will you answer to us?"

He said to them: "The three [names] are [but] one name,[32] just as a man says: 'Basileus, Caesar, Augustus.'"

They [the *minim*] asked him [R. Simlai] again: "What is that which is written: 'God (*El*), God (*Elohim*), the Lord (*YHWH*) spoke and called the earth' (Ps. 50:1)?"

He said to them: "Is it written here: 'they spoke and called'? No, it is only written: 'he spoke and called the earth.'"

His disciples said to him: "Rabbi, them you have dismissed with a reed, but what will you answer to us?"

He said to them: "The three [names] are [but] one name,[33] just as a man says: 'Craftsmen, masons, architects.'"[34]

These exegeses of Joshua 22:22 and Psalms 50:1 are constructed almost identically and very much in a similar vein to the midrashim discussed thus far. Despite the multiplicity of divine names sometimes used in the Hebrew Bible, R. Simlai answers the heretics, the verb attached to the names is again in the singular, hence referring to one deity. This is routine; but what is conspicuous here is the answer the rabbi gives to his students, arguing that when we refer to the emperor as "Basileus," "Caesar," and "Augustus," or when we refer to "craftsmen," "masons," and "architects," we always mean one and the same person, not different persons. This argument is odd because neither are craftsmen, masons, and architects the same (they refer to quite different professions in the building trade) nor are Basileus, Caesar, and Augustus necessarily the same. "Basileus," a more general designation for "king," is not particularly meaningful, but the titles "Caesar" and "Augustus" are.[35] The rabbis of the late third and early fourth centuries could hardly have been unaware of Diocletian's reform of the Roman Empire: first the concept of dual leadership, when he installed, in 285 C.E., his fellow officer Maximian as Caesar—with himself retaining the title Augustus (only in 286 was Maximian elevated to the position of Augustus)—and in a second step the concept of the tetrarchy ("rule of four"), with two Augusti and two Caesares, when both Diocletian and Maximian appointed a Caesar (in 293 C.E.) destined to become their successors as Augusti. According to this hierarchical system, the Caesar is clearly subordinate to the Augustus, and since this arrangement held for both the western and eastern parts of the empire—with one Augustus (Maximian) and Caesar (Constantius) ruling the West and the other pair (Diocletian and Galerius) ruling the East—it is virtually impossible that the rabbis should have been unaware of the distinction between Augustus and Caesar. We even know from another midrash that they used this distinction for their own purposes.[36]

At first sight, then, the answer R. Simlai gives his students (that there is no distinction between Basileus, Caesar, and Augustus) would seem to be rather vague or even to gloss over the real problem. If we use the terms *El*, *Elohim*, and *YHWH* for God, he seems to argue, we nevertheless have in mind one and the same God—precisely as the Romans using the terms Basileus, Caesar, and Augustus have one and the same ruler in mind. But this simple answer makes little sense against the backdrop of the Roman Empire, implemented at R. Simlai's time. If we take seriously the issue of the diarchy of Augustus and Caesar and the tetrarchy of two Augusti and two Caesares, we find ourselves in the hierarchy of competing imperial powers in the Roman Empire, which becomes even more relevant to our discussion if we take into consideration that this competition also had religious implications. Not surprisingly, in assuming (in 287 C.E.) the title *Iovius* while granting Maximian the title *Herculius*, Diocletian made clear who was the superior and who the subordinate ruler. This changed when Maximian was elevated to the position of co-Augustus: the triumphal arch of Galerius in Thessaloniki (between 298 and 304) depicts the two Augusti enthroned above the vault of heaven and with the earth as their footstool, obviously on an equal footing with each other.[37] The same is true for coins of the late fourth century, portraying the two Augusti— Valentinian I and his brother Valens—seated on the same imperial throne (*bisellium*).[38]

From this perspective, R. Simlai's answer becomes much less innocent than it appears. Following the translation "The three [names] are the name of one [and the same deity]," it could mean just the opposite of what it pretends to say, namely, *in contrast to* the Roman Empire with its superior Augustus and subordinate Caesar, we, the Jews, have only one Augustus and not the diarchy of an Augustus and a Caesar. Nor do we have a diarchy of two Augusti with equal imperial rights and powers (let alone a tetrarchy of two Augusti and two Caesares). As far as our God is concerned, different divine names do not express a hierarchical structure between a superior and a subordinate God; nor do they allude to two gods enjoying equal rights. The latter option would seem less likely in view of the explicit mention of Caesar next to Augustus in the rabbi's response—but it could be derived from the fact that in the biblical verses the first two names are almost identical, namely *El* and *Elohim* (both translated with "God"). Hence, the possibility cannot be excluded that the cosovereignty of the two Augusti—who represent the undivided unity of the Roman Empire (the *maiestas totius imperii* or *totius orbis*) both together and separately[39]—is also addressed in our midrash.

Taken altogether, it is highly probable that the Roman Empire's distinctive and sophisticated ideas about the rulership and sovereignty of the emperor served as background for our rabbis' debate with the heretics—much more, at all events, than certain alleged gnostic doctrines. But we may go even another step further. Since we know that in the third and fourth centuries the

Christians fervently discussed the relationship of Jesus with his divine Father, it may well be that this problem is also alluded to in our midrash. There is nothing to substantiate such a suspicion, but it gains in probability if we take into consideration that the Christian theological debate was informed and influenced by contemporaneous developments regarding the imperial hierarchy (in other words, that the theological discourse must not be seen independently of the secular power balance).[40] This question can be discussed only in a larger context, and I will return to it at the end of this chapter.

Observing another peculiarity of the Hebrew language, the debate continues with two more examples, from Joshua 24:19 and Deuteronomy 4:7:

> They [the *minim*] asked him [R. Simlai] again: "What is that which is written: 'For he is a holy God (*Elohim qedoshim*)' (Josh. 24:19)?"
>
> He said to them: "'they are holy' is not written here, but: 'he (is holy), he is a jealous God.'"
>
> His disciples said to him: "Rabbi, them you have dismissed with a reed, but what will you answer to us?"
>
> R. Yitzhaq said: "He is holy in every form of holiness." ...
>
> They [the *minim*] asked him [R. Simlai] again: "What is that which is written: 'For what (other) great nation is there that has a God so near (*Elohim qerovim*) to it, [as the Lord our God, whenever we call upon him]?' (Deut. 4:7)." He said to them: "'as the Lord our God, whenever we call upon them' is not written, but 'whenever we call upon him.'"
>
> His disciples said to him: "Rabbi, them you have dismissed with a reed, but what will you answer to us?"
>
> He said to them: "He is near in every manner of nearness."[41]

In these verses the grammatical problem is that the plural of *Elohim* is combined with an adjective also in the plural ("holy" and "near"), hence again suggesting a plurality of gods. But R. Simlai makes clear that in the first case the corresponding verb and in the second case the object (referring to God) appears in the singular, appropriately addressing one God. This is again routine and could easily be applied to many more examples in the Hebrew Bible. The rabbi's answer to his students is more sophisticated and clearly not meant for the ears of the heretics: while *Elohim qedoshim* certainly does not mean "holy gods," the plural of *qedoshim* nevertheless refers to different forms of God's "holiness"; in other words, it expresses a multitude of divine attributes captured under the epithet "holy." Similarly, the plural of *qerovim* refers to the fact that God is near to his people not just in one form of "nearness" but in a variety of forms.

THE BAVLI COLLECTION

The most complete offshoot of such collections of controversial biblical verses appears in the Bavli in the name of R. Yohanan, R. Simlai's teacher (second half of the third century C.E.).[42] In addition to the verses we know from R. Simlai, R. Yohanan adds Genesis 11:7 versus Genesis 11:5 (*YHWH* with a verb in the plural and the singular respectively), Genesis 35:7 versus Genesis 35:3 (*Elohim/El* with a verb in the plural and the singular respectively), 2 Samuel 7:23 (*Elohim* with a verb in the plural but an object referring to God in the singular), and Daniel 7:9.[43] The last example is very different from the previous ones—although thrones (in the plural) are placed in heaven, just one person (the "Ancient of Days") takes a seat—and I will return to it.[44]

The version of our midrash in the Bavli is supplemented by yet another twist of the problem posited by the name(s) of God:

> A heretic (*mina*) once said to R. Ishmael b. R. Yose: "It is written: 'Then the Lord (*YHWH*) caused to rain upon Sodom and Gomorrah sulfur and fire from the Lord (*YHWH*)' (Gen. 19:24)—but 'from him' should have been written!"
>
> A certain fuller said: "Leave him to me, I will answer him."
>
> [He then proceeded:] "It is written: 'And Lamech said to his wives, Ada and Zillah, Hear my voice, you wives of Lamech' (Gen. 4:23)—but he should have said: 'my wives'! Yet such is the Scriptural idiom—so here too, it is the Scriptural idiom."[45]

This exegesis is attributed to a tanna of the second half of the second century—as the continuation makes clear, a contemporary of R. Meir (a third-generation tanna)[46]—hence presenting itself as a tannaitic tradition. Whether it is indeed earlier than R. Simlai's collection—owing to, as Alan Segal suggests, its rather "naïve" approach[47]—or whether it is in fact a later adaptation, put into the mouth of a tanna,[48] must remain an open question (although I tend to the latter possibility).[49] In any case, the problem here is the awkward phrase that "the Lord" causes to rain from "the Lord," insinuating that actually two Lords (gods) are addressed. The proverbial fuller solves this problem with reference to a similar phrase in Genesis 4:23, which does not afford the possibility of two different persons (since two Lamechs do not make any sense). So here the heretic's attack is fended off not on grammatical but on purely stylistic grounds.

Finally, a midrash—also in the Bavli—needs to be discussed in which the problem depends not on different names for God but hinges on different verbs used for the same action carried out by God:

A certain heretic[50] once said to Rabbi: "He who formed (*yatzar*) the mountains did not create (*bara*) the wind, and he who created the wind did not form the mountains, for it is written: 'For, lo, he who forms (*yotzer*) the mountains and creates (*bore*) the wind' (Amos 4:13)."

He replied: "You fool, turn to the end of the verse: 'The Lord, [the God] of hosts (*YHWH Elohei-tzeva'ot*), is his name.'"

He [the heretic] said to him [Rabbi]: "Give me three days' time and I will bring back an answer to you."

Rabbi spent those three days in fasting; thereafter, as he was about to say the Benedictions, he was told: "There is a heretic waiting at the door." [Rabbi] exclaimed: "Yea they put poison into my food!" (Ps. 69:22).[51] Said he [the heretic]: "My Master, I bring you good tidings; your opponent could find no answer and so threw himself down from the roof and died."[52] He [Rabbi] said: "Would you dine with me?" He replied: "Yes." After they had eaten and drunk, he [Rabbi] said to him: "Will you drink the cup of wine over which the Benedictions of the Grace [after meals] have been said, or would you rather have forty gold coins?" He replied: "I would rather drink the cup of wine." Thereupon a heavenly voice (*bat qol*) came forth and said: "The cup of wine over [which] the Benedictions [of Grace have been said] is worth forty gold coins."

R. Yitzhaq said: "The family [of that heretic] is still to be found amongst the notables of Rome and is called the family of Bar Luianus."[53]

The subject here is again the creation, and the heretic concludes from the fact that two different verbs are used for the creation of the mountains and the wind (*yatzar* and *bara* respectively) that two different creators were at work. The rabbi counters with reference to the end of the same biblical verse in which the Lord, the God of Hosts, is identified as the subject of the two verbs, hence as one and the same person who created both the mountains and the wind. The poor heretic finds no response to the rabbi's solution and commits suicide. Other heretics are more forthcoming, the story continues, since the heretic who bears the good tidings of the rabbi's opponent's suicide not only dines with the rabbi but even prefers to participate in the ritual of the Benedictions of the Grace (instead of accepting money). This second heretic, we may gather, is close to converting to Judaism (R. Yitzhaq locates him in a noble Roman family, presumably a family favorably inclined toward the Jews).

This moving story attributed to Rabbi (that is, Rabbi Yehudah ha-Naśi, late second century C.E.) is much less convincing than it would appear. Despite its happy ending (for the rabbis) and its somewhat obtrusive morale, it cannot belie the fact that Rabbi fends the heretic off with an argument that could have easily been turned around and used against him—namely the plurality of God's names (*YHWH*, *Elohim*, and Hosts). As we have seen, it was precisely these names that were used by the heretics as evidence of more than one God. The poor heretic in our story would have been better off consulting his cleverer colleagues instead of committing suicide. Whether this story again presents, in a rather crude and naïve way, what becomes later, in the third century, a much more refined argument, is not so difficult to determine.[54] It seems to me that what we are encountering here is merely a poor example of a typically more sophisticated genre.[55]

To sum up, a considerable number of rabbinic texts take certain grammatical and stylistic characteristics of the Hebrew Bible as a starting point for debates between the rabbis and unspecified heretics: a variety of names used for God (*YHWH, Elohim, Shaddai*, Hosts) and sometimes even in the same biblical verse; the fact that *Elohim* in particular is grammatically plural or that the name *Elohim* is even coupled with a verb or an adjective in the plural; the strange phenomenon that "God" causes something to happen "from God"; and, finally, the use of two different verbs for allegedly the same divine action. All these examples presuppose a firm knowledge of the Hebrew text on the part of the heretics. Most of the midrashim discussed so far address matters of creation, with other subjects (the Torah in particular) presumably being added at a later stage. The heresy/heresies in question seem to focus primarily on a plurality of divine powers, that is, a multiplicity of gods (hence a "pagan" pantheon), but we can observe a tendency to limit the divine powers to two. In the latter case the discussion was obviously informed by contemporary developments in the Roman Empire, namely the implementation of the diarchy of one Augustus and one Caesar and the tetrarchy of two Augusti and two Caesares. These developments—which, of course, are grounded in the earlier system of an emperor "adopting" his successor—in turn may have influenced analogous Christian debates about the relationship between God and his Son, Jesus, so that our rabbinic conflict with the heretics may well reflect both contemporary "pagan" *and* Christian ideas. The bulk of the rabbinic texts analyzed in this chapter are from third and early fourth-century Palestine, a circumstance that fits in well with contemporaneous debates in the Roman Empire. In the following I will discuss the possible Christian implications of R. Simlai's midrash.

R. SIMLAI AND CHRISTIANITY

Recent research has drawn our attention to the fact that the heretics in R. Simlai's midrash[56] refer to precisely *three* names of God (*El, Elohim, YHWH*), which R. Simlai contrasts with three *titles* of secular rulers (Basileus, Caesar, Augustus). This number, Burt Visotzky in particular claims, is not accidental but in fact refers to precisely three deities, that is, not to pagan pantheism in general but to the Christian trinity. Hence, R. Simlai's opponents are Christians who wish to read into the three biblical names of God (*El, Elohim, YHWH*) an allusion to the Christian trinity. Moreover, Visotzky argues further, it is no accident that R. Simlai—immediately before discussing the three names of God—refers to Genesis 1:26 ("*Let us* make a man in *our* image, after *our* likeness"), a verse that plays a crucial role in the trinitarian debate.[57] The earliest proof Visotzky provides for this assumption is the Church Father Irenaeus of Lugdunum in Gaul, who in his polemical masterpiece *Adversus haereses* (written around 180 C.E.) "gave the verse [Gen. 1:26] a Trinitarian reading"[58] following the—not yet trinitarian—exegesis of the Apostolic Father Barnabas.[59] Let us take a closer look at the passage in Irenaeus:

> It was not angels, therefore, who made us nor they who formed us; neither had angels power to make an image of God, nor anyone else, except the word of the Lord, nor any power remotely distant from the father of all things. For God did not stand in need of these [beings] in order that the accomplishing of what he had himself determined with himself beforehand should be done, as if he did not possess his own hands. For with him were always present the word and wisdom, the son and the spirit, by whom and in whom, freely and spontaneously, he made all things, to whom also

he speaks, saying, "Let us make man after our image and likeness" (Gen. 1:26).[60]

Irenaeus polemicizes here against the Jewish-rabbinic interpretation of the plural "Let us make man" as God's question addressed to the angels: shall we make man? This question, of course, is not meant to be understood in the sense that Irenaeus insinuates, namely, that God asks the angels whether they want to create man together with him; rather, the rabbinic exegesis presupposes that God (using the *pluralis maiestatis*) consults with the angels whether he (alone) should indeed create man. (As a rule, the angels' answer is "no"—because, as they remind God, humans are prone to sin—but God doesn't follow their advice: ultimately he creates man, against the advice of his angels.)[61] Irenaeus contrasts this rabbinic exegesis with his Christian interpretation that the plural "let us make" refers to God, the Word, and Wisdom, identifying the Word with the Son and Wisdom with the Spirit. It is, however, questionable as to whether Irenaeus understood Word/Son and Wisdom/Spirit here in any technical dogmatic-trinitarian sense. "Word" (*logos*) and Wisdom (*hokhmah* in Hebrew and *sophia* in Greek) are biblical terms that can be applied to the "Son" and the "Spirit"—but not necessarily so and certainly not automatically to the trinity as defined by the First Council of Nicaea (see below). Using the same logic, one could likewise argue that Philo, with his elaborated system of God, his Logos, and his Sophia, also promoted a trinitarian theology.[62] And one wonders why Christian theologians as late as the fourth century prosecuted such grim and acrimonious debates regarding the precise nature of the trinity if it had indeed all been clarified by Irenaeus in the second half of the second century C.E.

Visotzky's further examples derive from Augustine (354–430), the Latin Father and Bishop of Hippo in Algeria, and Gregory of Nazianzus, the fourth-century Church Father and

Bishop of Constantinople (379–381). With regard to Augustine, Visotzky quotes a passage in which he tries to reconcile Paul's statement in 1 Corinthians 11:7 that "not the woman but the man is the image of God" with Genesis 1:27 ("And God created *man* in his image, in the image of God he created *him*; male and female he created *them*").[63] Augustine's answer: when the woman is referred to separately, "then she is not the image of God," but together with her husband the woman is indeed the image of God.[64] This has nothing to do with the trinity, and the fact that Augustine elsewhere uses Genesis 1:26 as "latently" alluding to the trinity[65] provides little backing for R. Simlai's midrash.

Nor particularly helpful is the passage Visotzky quotes from Gregory of Nazianzus' Fifth Theological Oration, "On the Holy Spirit." It is here that Gregory compares the relationship between God the Father, the Son, and the Spirit with that between Adam, Eve, and their offspring Seth: just as Adam, Eve, and Seth are different persons—but, as human beings, have the same substance (are consubstantial)—so too are the Father, the Son, and the Holy Spirit three separate persons and yet still consubstantial.[66] Since the divinity of the Holy Spirit and his consubstantiality with the Father and Son is the point of Gregory's statement, Visotzky wishes to conclude from Gregory (and also from Augustine) that in fact it is the Holy Spirit, as the weakest point in the trinitarian position, whom R. Simlai attacks in reply to his students:

> [W]e see by his [R. Simlai's] answer to his students that if one really wishes to get embroiled in debate about the Trinity, one must attack the heretics at the weak points in their belief. It is not enough merely to trot out Trinitarian testimonies, suggests our Rabbi; if one wishes to accept the divinity of the Trinity, then one must be prepared to ac-

cept the Holy Spirit as craftsman, builder and architect of
the Universe. One must revere the Spirit as *Basileus*, *Kai-
sar*, *Augustus*. In the privacy of the academy, our Rabbi is
not having a joke at his students' expense, he is instructing
them to engage in *reductio ad absurdum* arguments with
the heretics. If you wish to debate heretics, he tells them,
then know the details of their beliefs and press them hard-
est where they are weakest.[67]

Whether the weakest link in the chain of the trinitarian testimonies or not, it is true that the Holy Spirit is definitely the most
controversial link and the one that was added last in the long evo-
lution of trinitarian belief—but it is an entirely different question whether R. Simlai, in his response to the heretics, alludes to
the position of the Holy Spirit. If we briefly review the history of
trinitarian theology, it becomes immediately clear that for quite
a while the discussions were primarily shaped by the relationship
between Jesus (the Logos) and his divine Father.[68] Whereas the
early Logos theology of Justin Martyr and the apologists regarded the Logos/Jesus as divine—Justin calls Jesus "another
(that is, second) God"[69]—yet clearly subordinate to his Father,
followers of the doctrine called "monarchianism" defended the
"monarchy" of the one and only God as the ruler of his kingdom
against all kinds of "polytheism" or polytheistic tendencies.
These "monarchians" were by no means a uniform movement.
Historians of the ancient Church distinguish between "adoptianist" or "dynamic monarchians"—that is, those who deny
Jesus co–eternal divinity but grant him a kind of "adopted" divinity at the time of his baptism or his ascension—and "strict" or
"modalist monarchians," who consider the Father and the Son as
one and the same person, that is, only one hypostasis, who, however, appears in different "modes": when God created the world
he acted as the Father, but when he set about redeeming the

world he acted as the Son.[70] This latter monarchian doctrine was also called "Sabellianism," named after Sabellius, its main proponent.[71]

Monarchians of whatever stripe were doomed to be eliminated as heretics, and it was the Logos theology with its focus on Jesus and its strong "subordinationist" tendency that would set the parameters of the debate until the Council of Nicaea. This was true of Tertullian (d. ca. 225), the Father of the Latin Church, as well as Origen (d. ca. 254), the distinguished Father of the Eastern Church, who as of 231 lived in Caesarea. When the Holy Spirit comes into play—Tertullian was in fact the first to use the term *trinitas*[72]—he, like Jesus, is clearly subordinate to the Father. Only Origen, as Christoph Markschies has demonstrated, seems to imply an early, not yet fully developed notion of three consubstantial divine hypostases, thus making a breach in the all too rigid schema of a strict subordinationist theology.[73]

But it was not until the First Council of Nicaea (325 C.E.) that the Fathers of the Church, fending off the extreme subordinationist theology of Arius, officially broke with the concept of a trinity in which the Son and Holy Spirit were subordinate to the Father. Yet still, the Council was much more concerned with the relationship of Jesus to his divine Father than with the Holy Spirit. The Nicene Creed determined that Jesus was "God from God, Light from Light, true God from true God," that he was co-eternal with God, and that he was *homoousios*, or consubstantial, with the Father (*homoousios tō patri*). The Holy Spirit is mentioned in the Nicene Creed, but only at the end and almost in passing ("and [we believe] in the Holy Spirit"). It was only after much further theological clarification provided mainly by the Cappadocian Fathers Basil of Caesarea (ca. 330–379 C.E.), Gregory of Nazianzus (329/30–ca. 390), and Gregory of Nyssa (ca. 335–394)—who applied the Nicene formula regarding the Son as consubstantial with the Father to all three divine hypostases (aptly summarized in the phrase *mia ousia—treis hypostaseis*) including the Holy Spirit[74]—that the Council of Constantinople (381 C.E.) expanded the article of the Nicene Creed referring to the Holy Spirit. The Creed of 381 resolved that the Holy Spirit was indeed the "Lord and Giver of life, who proceeds from the Father, who with the Father and the Son together is worshiped and glorified": if the Holy Spirit proceeds from the Father, he must be of the same essence (*ousia*) as God the Father and the Son.

Returning now, after this dogmatic digression, to our R. Simlai and his answer to his students, I find it quite audacious to read into it an echo of the trinitarian debate regarding the Holy Spirit. To begin with, the implicit logic of Visotzky's argument would be that R. Simlai, attacking the Christian heretics at their weakest point (the Holy Spirit), was much less worried about the Son, that is, Christology. His message then would be: we, the Jews, can live with your claim regarding Jesus (that he is a second God, the Son of his divine Father, whatever the precise relationship might be), but what you tell us about the third partner of the divine duality, the Holy Spirit, claiming that the duality is in fact a trinity—this is really all nonsense. Such would have been a very dangerous answer, to say the least. Moreover, if we take the extremely complicated and elongated trinitarian debate into account—with the relatively late clarification regarding the Holy Spirit (namely in the second half of the fourth century)—R. Simlai (late third/early fourth century) would seem a much too early candidate for a rabbinic intervention into the sophisticated debate about the Holy Spirit, which was carried out primarily by the Cappadocian Fathers. One could, of course, argue that R. Simlai is only a symbol of such rabbinic intervention, that the dates of his lifetime don't really matter, and that, if we instead focus on the period of the Talmud Yerushalmi's final editing (end of the fourth or beginning of the fifth century), we come much closer to the epicenter of the trinitarian debate regarding the Holy Spirit. But this, too, is a weak argument because nothing speaks in favor of shifting the exchange between R. Simlai, the heretics, and R. Simlai's students to the final editor of the Yerushalmi (if indeed there ever was one). The collection of cases in the Yerushalmi concerned with certain difficult Bible verses regarding the name(s) of God is too firmly connected with R. Simlai to justify such a drastic move.

I would therefore propose—with Visotzky—that R. Simlai's answers to his students may well have to do with a trinitarian debate but—pace Visotzky—with a yet crude and unsophisticated debate (in comparison with the formulations developed by the Cappadocian Fathers and the Council of Constantinople). It was still a debate that was primarily concerned with the relationship between the Father and the Son, not yet the Holy Spirit, despite the fact that it was aware of and concerned about the problems caused by the inclusion of the Holy Spirit. In other words, despite the three names of God explained by three imperial titles and three related occupations, R. Simlai's main concern is about God and Jesus, not about the Holy Spirit, and hence about the implications of a binitarian and not (yet) a trinitarian theology in the strict sense of the term. On the secular level this fits in very well, as we have observed above, with the reform implemented by Diocletian toward the end of the third century: the diarchy, first, of a senior and junior emperor (Augustus and Caesar) and, second, of two senior emperors (two Augusti), followed by the tetrarchy of two Augusti and two Caesares. Within this hierarchical structure of the Roman Empire there is no room for a trinity. And on the theological level this fits well with the emphasis placed on the relationship between God and Jesus by all Christian theologians up until approximately the middle of the fourth century. Whether or not Origen of Caesarea (Maritima), R. Simlai's younger contemporary, can be rightly called a binitarian rather than a trinitarian theologian,[75] there can be no doubt that in his numerous writings he was much more preoccupied with Jesus than with the Holy Spirit. Quite remarkably, even Basil of Caesarea (Mazaca in Cappadocia)—the oldest of the three Cappadocian Fathers, who so successfully helped pave the way for the Creed of Constantinople[76]— could discuss Genesis 1:26f. without including the Holy Spirit:

> "Let us make (*poiēsōmen*) man" (Gen. 1:26). You hear, fighter against Christ, that he [God] is talking to his companion (*tō koinōnō*) in the work of creation [Jesus], "through whom he also created the worlds, who sustains all things by his powerful word" (Heb. 1:2f.). . . .
>
> According to them [the Jews] it is to the angels that stand around him that he says: "Let us make man" (Gen. 1:26). This is a Jewish fiction (*plasma*), a mythical tale (*mythologēma*) which reveals their contentedness. In order not to have to accept a single addressee (*ton hena*), they introduce a multiplicity. In rejecting the Son, they confer on servants the dignity of being counselors. . . .
>
> "And God created (*epoiēsen*)[77] man" (Gen. 1:27) [says the Bible] and not "[and the gods] created (*epoiēsan*)."[78] [Scripture] refrains here from a pluralization of persons (*ton plēthysmon tōn prosōpōn*). By means of these [words: "Let us make man" (Gen. 1:26)] it teaches the Jew, and by means of these [words: "And God created"[79] (Gen. 1:27)], it blocks off the route to Hellenism (*ton hellēnismon*) and safely reverts to the One (*tēn monada*) so that you know that the Son is with the Father and will be saved from the danger of polytheism (*tēs polytheias*).

> "In the image of God he created him" (Gen. 1:27): Once again [Scripture] reintroduces the person of his [God's] partner (*tou synergou to prosōpon*) [Jesus]. For it does not say: "in his own image," but "in the image of God."[80]

This is an intriguing exegesis of Genesis 1:26f., which takes up elements that are well known from the rabbinic midrash but explains them in a completely different manner. Killing two birds with one stone, as it were, Basil first makes clear that the plural of "Let us make man" refers to God and Jesus, not God and the angels, as the Jews maintain. Then he confronts the plural of "Let us make man" with the singular "And God created": the Jews are instructed, following the plural of "Let us make man," that God is more than just one; and the pagans are instructed, following the singular of "And God created," that the plural of *Elohim* has nothing to do with their pantheon of many gods. The simultaneous use of plural and singular in the biblical text, Basil argues, beats back the rigid and inflexible monotheism of the Jews as well as the naïve polytheism of the pagans.

The third paragraph of this exegesis goes one step further and defines the precise relationship between God-Father and God-Son. By explicitly saying "In the image of *God* he created him [man]" instead of "in his own image," Scripture rules out that "man" was created solely by the Father. "God" means Father and Son, not just the Father. The title "God" makes clear that the Son is included in the act of creation, that he is the partner (*synergos*) in the divine act of creation. Basil clearly presupposes here the theological clarification of the relationship between God-Father and God-Son. With his Son Jesus, God is "One" (*monos*), but both are two hypostases (*hypostaseis*) of the same substance (*ousia*), the only difference between the Son and the Father being that the Son is "begotten" (*gennētos*), whereas the Father is "unbegotten" (*agennētos*). Obviously taking up the Nicene

Creed, Basil elsewhere clarifies the nature of "begotten" versus "unbegotten" by pointing out that "the substance (*ousia*) of the Father is spiritual, eternal, *unbegotten* light," whereas the substance (*ousia*) of the Son is "spiritual, eternal, *begotten* light."[81] Conspicuously, the Holy Spirit plays no role in Basil's exegesis of Genesis 1:26f.

Seen against the backdrop of the trinitarian debate, it seems likely that R. Simlai, in his answer to his students, did indeed address this debate. But were we to argue that the focus is on the Holy Spirit as the weakest member of the divine trinity, then we would be presuming too much sophistication on both the part of contemporaneous Christian theologians and certainly on the part of the rabbi. It was Christology that most occupied the Fathers of the Church during the first centuries C.E. (up until the mid-fourth century)—and thus worried their rabbinic colleagues. R. Simlai and the majority of the rabbis not only knew these debates but referred to and grappled with them.[82] And this is hardly surprising, for reflections about the form and essence of its God were certainly not alien to prerabbinic and rabbinic Judaism. A classical example is the Wisdom theology as developed in the biblical book of Proverbs and in the noncanonical books Jesus Sirach (Ecclesiasticus) and Wisdom of Solomon. In Proverbs (third century B.C.E.?) we are told of Wisdom (*hokhmah*) that she was created before the creation of the world and was with God as his "confidante" or his "master worker" when "he assigned to the sea its limit" and "marked out the foundations of the earth."[83] What I have translated as "confidante" or "master worker" is in Hebrew *amon*, a word whose precise meaning was debated by even the ancient translators. The Septuagint translates *amon* with *harmōzousa*, the "fitting" or "appropriate" (sc. helper), the one who "arranges" everything, that is, it apparently affirms the meaning "master worker" (although in the feminine); and similarly and even more clearly, the Wisdom of Solomon refers to *technītis*, that is, "artist" or "craftsman." Aquila, on the other hand, suggests a very different meaning when he translates *amon* with *tithenoumenē*—that is, "foster child" or "darling." Both translations are possible, but the context clearly speaks in favor of the latter: Wisdom as God's little child, more precisely his little daughter, who was witness of his creation and the source of his delight, "always playing before him," as Proverbs 8:30 explicitly states. In the Wisdom of Solomon (first century B.C.E.) the same Wisdom is described as "a clear effluence from the glory of the Almighty," the "radiance (*apaugasma*) that streams from everlasting light, the flawless mirror of the active power of God, and the image (*eikōn*) of his goodness."[84]

It would therefore not seem a difficult task to develop from such initial stages the idea of a second divine power next to and with God—as indeed Philo did with his comprehensive Wisdom and Logos theology. Judaism did not choose to go this route—at any rate not the variety of Judaism that would gain acceptance in the centuries to come. Jesus Sirach—written about 190 B.C.E. in Hebrew, translated ca. 132 B.C.E. into Greek, but never accepted as part of the official canon of the Hebrew Bible (although highly regarded by the rabbis)—applies Wisdom of Solomon's wisdom to the Torah: "All this [that has been told about wisdom] is the book of the covenant (*biblos diathēkēs*) of the Most High God, the law (*nomos*) that Moses commanded us as an inheritance for the congregations of Jacob."[85] Hence, wisdom in Judaism becomes synonymous with the *book* of the Torah and loses its concrete personal existence. Accordingly, the rabbis understand *bereshit* in Genesis 1:1 not as "*in the beginning* God created the heaven and the earth" but as "*by means of wisdom* (that is, the Torah) God created the heaven and the earth":[86] when God created his world he used the book of the Torah as his architectural "blueprint."

Unlike Judaism, the emerging Christianity retained the particular character of those powers next to God and strengthened that character while yet shifting the main focus from Wisdom to Logos, the "Word" of God. Hence the prologue of the Gospel of John solemnly proclaims (with clear reference to Gen. 1:1, Prov. 8, and Sir. 24):[87]

(1:1) In the beginning was the Word, and the Word was with God, and the Word was God.
(2) It[88] was in the beginning with God.
(3) All things came into being through it [the Word], and without it was not anything that was made.
(4) In it was life, and the life was the light of men.

But that which begins here in the Gospel of John and would be developed further in Christology had its origin in Judaism. Judaism's ever increasing identification of wisdom with the written Torah was clearly related to the dogmatic unfolding of the Logos theology in Christianity. Yet we must not see this development all too one-sidedly as a predetermined and eternally codified process of demarcation. To be sure, R. Simlai distinguishes himself from the heretics, but this differentiation is a vital and mutual activity whose outcome has not been determined in advance. His response to his students demonstrates that the questions raised were taken very seriously *within the rabbinic academy*, since certain rabbis knew only too well that these questions could strike at the very heart of (rabbinic) Judaism. Judaism, too, could have carried on with the ideas of Wisdom and Logos—it is precisely for this reason that the rabbis perceived the developments within Christianity as simultaneously tempting and threatening—it decided, however, under the impact of Christian theology (or rather, under the impact of what would ever more forcefully become the trademark of Christianity), against this option. It would take until the Middle Ages—until the emergence of the Kabbalah as the climax of Jewish mysticism toward the end of the twelfth century—for Wisdom as a person to find her way back into Judaism.[89]

2

The Young and the Old God

GOD APPEARS IN THE HEBREW BIBLE NOT ONLY UNDER different names; he even takes on different guises or, as it were, assumes different incarnations. This phenomenon also did not escape the attention of the rabbis; or, rather, the rabbis could not miss it, because it was used by their heretical opponents in quite obvious ways and gave rise to debates between them. Speaking of rabbinic "opponents," I again leave it an open question as to whether we are dealing with opponents from within, that is, within rabbinic Judaism, or opponents from the outside, that is, groups or rather certain individuals that were on the verge of dissociating themselves from the rabbis as they were increasingly defining themselves.

We encounter the earliest and most famous instance of such a debate in the Mekhilta, a midrash on the biblical book of Exodus. The dating of this midrash is controversial, although most experts tend now to an earlier dating, placing its final redaction sometime in the second half of the third century C.E. The midrash in question is an exegesis of Exodus 20:2: "I am the Lord, your God, who brought you out of the land of Egypt." This exegesis is preserved in many parallels, but I quote it according to the version of the Mekhilta:[1]

> "I am the Lord, your God (*YHWH Elohekha*)" (Ex. 20:2). Why is this said?
>
> For this reason. At the sea he [God] appeared (to them) as a mighty hero (*gibbor*) doing battle, as it is said: "The Lord (*YHWH*) is a man of war" (Ex. 15:3).
>
> At Sinai he appeared (to them) as an old man (*zaqen*) full of mercy, as it is said: "And they saw the God of Israel, etc." (Ex. 24:10). And of the time after they had been redeemed, what does it say? "And the like of the very heaven for clearness" (ibid.). Again it says: "I beheld till thrones were placed" (Dan. 7:9). And it also says: "A fiery stream issued and came forth from before him, etc." (Dan. 7:10).
>
> (Scripture, therefore,) would not let the nations of the world have an excuse for saying that there are two powers (*shetei rashuyyot*), but declares: "I am the Lord, your God" (Ex. 20:2)—
>
> I am he who was in Egypt and I am he who was at the sea. I am he who was at Sinai.[2]
>
> I am he who was in the past and I am he who will be in the future.
>
> I am he who is in this world and I am he who will be in the world to come, as it is said: "See now that I, even I, am he, etc." (Deut. 32:39). And it says: "Even to old age I am the same" (Isa. 46:4). And it says: "Thus said the Lord (*YHWH*), the King of Israel, and his redeemer, the Lord of Hosts (*YHWH tzeva'ot*): I am the first, and I am the last" (Isa. 44:6). And it says: "Who has wrought and done it? He that called the generations from the beginning. I, the

Lord, who am the first, etc. [and with the last I am as well]"
(Isa. 41:4).

R. Nathan says: "From here one can give an answer to
the heretics (*minin*) who say: 'There are two powers (*shetei
rashuyyot*).' For when the Holy One, blessed be he, stood
up and exclaimed: 'I am the Lord, your God' (Ex. 20:2),
was there any one who stood up to protest against him?"

If you should say that it was done in secret—has it not
been said: "I have not spoken in secret, etc." (Isa. 45:19)?
"I said not to the seed of Jacob" (ibid.), (that is), to these
(alone) will I give it. Rather, "they sought me in the desert"
(ibid.). Did I not give it in broad daylight (*pangas*)? And
thus it says: "I the Lord (*YHWH*) speak righteousness, I
declare things that are right" (ibid.).

This midrash is part of a well-structured collection of exegeses
on Exodus 20:2, the very beginning of the Decalogue. I have argued elsewhere that this collection, focusing on Israel's competition with other nations concerning the revelation of the Torah,
bursts the narrow confines of the so-called exegetical midrash
—of which the Mekhilta is a prime example—and borders on
what is soon to become the so-called homiletical midrash.[3] One
needs a precise knowledge not only of the midrash's way of arguing but also of the presupposed exegeses that are only alluded to.
Our midrash begins with a question that makes sense only if we
quote Exodus 20:2 in full: "I am the Lord your God (*YHWH
Elohekha*), who brought you out of the land of Egypt," literally
"*I*, who brought you out (*asher hotzetikha*)"—in the singular.
Hence the real question is: why is the verb attached to "I am the
Lord, your God" (again, *Elohim* being grammatically a plural
and hence prone to the dangerous translation "your gods") ex-
plicitly put in the singular? Answer: the singular "*I* brought you

out" ensures that the plural *Elohim* refers not to two or more gods but to one God only. So far the argument follows the familiar pattern.

But, as the continuation shows, the problem goes deeper. Now our anonymous rabbinic author admits that God in fact does make different and conflicting appearances in the Bible, most commonly as a warrior and as an old man: at the sea—which, of course, refers to the Red Sea (Ex. 13:18ff.)—God appeared to his people as a war hero, and on Mount Sinai he appeared as an old man. By implication, the warrior is a young man—as opposed to the old man on Mount Sinai.[4] These two manifestations of God are documented by appropriate biblical proof texts—Exodus 15:3 for the warrior and Exodus 24:10 with Daniel 7:9f. for the old man.

Exodus 15:3 as proof text for the young warrior is straightforward and poses no problem: after God had killed Pharaoh and his troops in the Red Sea, Moses and the people of Israel praised the divine war hero for his victory over the Egyptians. But what about Exodus 24:10 as proof text for the old man? Here again we need the full biblical text to understand the proof:

> (24:10) And they saw the God of Israel: under his feet there was something like the work of sapphire stone (*livnat ha-sappir*, literally: sapphire brick), like the very heaven for clearness.

This verse can serve as proof text for God being an old man only if we take it to literally mean that the enigmatic "work of sapphire stone" under God's feet—which has worried many exegetes—was in fact his footstool, that is, a footstool needed by an old man.[5] And indeed, Targum Pseudo-Jonathan, translating the verse Exodus 24:10, explicitly refers to the "work of sapphire stone" as the footstool (*hypopodion*) under God's feet.[6]

Why the sapphire stone (or rather, brick) was used as God's footstool—merely alluded to in our midrash (because it isn't crucial for our midrash's argument)—is explained in another midrash; in fact, the footstool is completely incomprehensible in our midrash and probably alluded to only because it is directly linked to the sapphire brick and serves here to illustrate that God, in the guise of an old man, is full of mercy.[7] The starting point of this midrash is the odd "sapphire *brick*" in the biblical proof text—after all, the sapphire is a precious stone and not a precious brick. Targum Pseudo-Jonathan on Exodus 24:10 gives the following explanation:

> Nadab and Abihu lifted up their eyes, and they saw the glory of the God of Israel; and in place of[8] the footstool (*hypopodion*) of his feet which was placed beneath his throne (they saw) something like the work of sapphire stone—a memorial of the servitude with which the Egyptians had oppressed the children of Israel to serve in clay and bricks. There were (Israelite) women treading clay with their husbands, and (among them) was a delicate young woman, who was pregnant and lost her fetus, and (the fetus) was crushed with the clay. Thereof Gabriel descended, made a brick of it [the embryo], lifted it up to the highest heavens and put it as a footstool (*gelugdaq*) in place of the *hypopodion* of the Lord of the world.

So now we know why the sapphire in Exodus 24:10 is called sapphire brick and not sapphire stone, and how it got into heaven—it was actually a brick containing the miscarried fetus of an Israelite woman in Egypt, hence not just any brick but a very precious brick. God used it as his footstool, presumably as a constant reminder of Israel's forced labor in Egypt. It is only against this background that the no less enigmatic continuation of our midrash makes sense: "And of the time after they had been redeemed, what does it say? 'And the like of the very heaven for clearness' (Ex. ibid.)." After Israel was redeemed from Egypt, that is, after *God* had redeemed his people from Egypt, he no longer needed the "sapphire brick" as a memento of his people's slavery—the sapphire brick disappeared, and the heavens were shining again in their original clearness.[9] The editor of our midrash is not bothered by the fact that God, along with the disappearance of the sapphire brick, also loses his footstool. He uses the midrash of the sapphire brick only to prove that God, as an old man, needed a footstool and that this God, in the guise of an old man, has proven to be "full of mercy": he has exchanged his royal footstool for a sapphire brick so as to be permanently reminded of his people's forced labor, in need of his mercy and of redemption. Nor is the editor bothered by the fact that the footstool of sapphire brick had actually disappeared at the revelation on Mount Sinai, since by then God had already redeemed his people from Egypt. For him it is important only to demonstrate that, in contrast to the young warrior at the Red Sea, the God who revealed himself on Mount Sinai was a merciful old man.

The second proof text for God being an old man (Dan. 7:9f.) is again easier to understand if we quote it in full:

> (7:9) I beheld till thrones were set in place, and the Ancient of Days took his seat. His garment was like white snow, and the hair of his head was like pure wool. His throne was fiery flames, and its wheels were blazing fire. (10) A river of fire streamed forth from before him; thousands upon thousands served him, and myriads upon myriads stood attending him. The court sat down and the books were opened.

This couldn't be clearer: God, the "Ancient of Days," taking his seat on his heavenly throne is graphically described as having white hair (pure wool is white), that is, as an old man. We don't need the explicit mention of a footstool here; the image is clear. And actually verse 10, too, is superfluous, unless the emphasis isn't placed on the river of fire that streams from and before the throne (the only part of the verse quoted in the midrash) but on the innumerable servants of the Ancient of Days: the divine king has attained an advanced age, for he requires many servants. But this isn't very likely, particularly since the ending of verse 10 with the heavenly court does not go well with our midrash, which wishes to underscore God's mercy. The emphasis clearly lies on verse 9—the Ancient of Days with white hair—and not on the river of fire and the heavenly court in verse 10.

Having proven that God indeed takes on the appearance of both a young and old man, the editor returns to the initial verse Exodus 20:2: despite his different incarnations—Scripture clarifies this point against the objection of the nations of the world—God always remains one and the same. The young warrior God in Egypt and at the Red Sea is the same as the old and merciful God on Mount Sinai; the God of Israel's past is the same as the God of Israel's future; and the God of this world is the same as the God of the world to come (the eschaton). God in fact does not even grow old; he remains the same—at the beginning of his history with his people Israel, as well as its end.[10] Different manifestations of God do not mean that there are different gods.

Whereas this first part of the midrash comes along anonymously and is directed at the "nations of the world," that is, all those nations *not* Israel, the second section is attributed to R. Nathan (a fourth-generation tanna and contemporary of Rabbi) and explicitly addresses the heretics. The heresy in question is in both sections the heresy of the "two powers," that is, the belief in just two (and not multiple) deities. Unlike the problem of God's different names discussed in the previous chapter, where most of the respective midrashim were connected with the act of creation, here the heresy of two powers raises its seductive head at the very moment when God revealed himself as "the Lord, your God" on Mount Sinai. R. Nathan's midrash presupposes, therefore, that the nations of the world[11] were present, together with Israel, when God revealed himself as the Lord. The nations (this is R. Nathan's argument) were given the chance to protest God's claim to being the one and single God not only for Israel but for all nations—but they were cowards and did not dare seize the opportunity. Since they did not veto God's claim when they had their chance, they implicitly accepted it and shouldn't now pretend that they had always been against it.[12]

The third and last section of our midrash (it is unclear whether or not it is part of R. Nathan's exegesis, but I would opt for the latter, namely, that it is an addition to R. Nathan) responds to and expands R. Nathan's argument. First, it counters the possibility that God made his claim secretly—and that the other nations could not therefore protest against it. Isaiah 45:19 states explicitly, it argues, that God did not speak "secretly, in a land of darkness." But then, second, the midrash moves to another subject that is not necessarily implied in the previous exposition of Exodus 20:2. That is to say, whereas the gist of our midrash on Exodus 20:2 centers on God's proclamation to all the nations that he is the one and only God, now the emphasis shifts to the related but different question of whether God offered the Torah to Israel alone or to the other nations as well.[13] The answer is given in a complicated—and probably even slightly corrupt[14]— exegesis of the last part of Isaiah 45:19. The verse, typically translated as "I did not say to the seed of Jacob: seek me in chaos (*tohu baqqshuni*)," is here broken down into two sections: the first part, "I did not say to the seed of Jacob," is understood as "I did not say to the people of Israel that I will offer the Torah only to them"; and in the second part *tohu* is interpreted not as "chaos" but as "desert," and the verse is decoded as meaning "they (that is, the people of Israel) sought me (God) in the desert," in other words: Israel asked me to give the Torah to them—and I complied with their desire and gave them the Torah, however, in broad daylight and not in the dark of night. The other nations had ample time and opportunity to intervene and make their claim; that they didn't is their fault and gives them no right to lay claim to the Torah now.

Is it possible to determine more precisely the heresy in question and the group(s) behind it—beyond what we have noticed so far? Both parts of this question are of course closely related. As to the kind of heresy, the midrash clearly has two *complementary* powers in mind, not two *opposing* powers. This rules out, as Segal has correctly observed, any gnostic system that relies on two opposing deities—one supreme and one inferior god.[15] But when Segal goes on to discuss, over many pages, all the possible options for the heretical groups involved (Hellenistic Jews, Gentiles, gentile Christians, "God-Fearers," Jewish Christians, etc.), one cannot help but think that he overshoots the mark. Such an extremely differentiated demarcation of the various groups is prima facie highly problematic; or, to put it differently and more pointedly, the search for neatly differentiated groups is in itself misguided, since it acts on assumptions that are anything but self-evident. Segal published his book in 1977, and more than thirty years on we now know that the static picture of early consolidated groups or sects competing with and fighting each other should be abandoned in favor of a more dynamic image of yet undefined and fluent clusters that were constantly changing, overlapping, and influencing each other. It becomes increasingly clear, however, that the notion of two complementary powers (either with one subordinate to the other or with both on an equal footing), which seems to lie at the heart of the matter, leads us into the imperial structure of the Roman Empire and its repercussions on the development of a binitarian and trinitarian Christian theology.

Yet Segal proposes to go a step further, wishing to demonstrate that in fact the quotation from Daniel, if taken seriously in all its implications, presents the real core of the midrash—namely, that we need to take into consideration not only the quoted verses Daniel 7:9f. but also Daniel 7:13f. (the verses speaking of the "one like a human being," traditionally translated as "Son of Man"):

> (7:13) As I watched in the night visions,
> I saw one like a human being,[16]
> coming with the clouds of heaven.
> And he came to the Ancient One (*'atiq yomayya*)
> and was presented before him.
> (14) And to him was given dominion and glory and
>   kingship,
> that all peoples, nations, and languages should serve him.
> His dominion is an everlasting dominion
> that shall not pass away,
> and his kingship is one
> that shall never be destroyed.

Since the Daniel passage, including the verses 13 and 14, may be understood as referring to two separate divine figures (the "Ancient of Days" and the "Son of Man"), Segal argues, it is this possible interpretation that poses the real danger not made explicit but only alluded to in our midrash.[17] Daniel Boyarin has taken up this line of argument[18] in a number of recent articles[19] and contends:

It is the passage from Daniel that is alluded to, *but not cited* in the anti-"heretical" discourse [in our Mekhilta midrash], the "Son of Man" passage so pivotal for the development of early Christology, that is the real point of contention here and the reason for the citation of the verse Exodus 20,2.... The text portentously *avoids* citing the Daniel verse[s] most difficult for rabbinic Judaism, [Dan. 7] vv. 13–14.[20]

Boyarin goes on to insinuate that from the full Daniel quotation (Dan 7:9f. and 7:13f.) it becomes clear that the real issue in our midrash is "the doubling of descriptions of God as *senex* (judge) and *puer* (man of war) and the correlation of those two descriptions with the divine figures of Ancient of Days and Son of Man from Daniel." When the two divine (!) figures swiftly mutate to "a Father-person and a Son-person," the desired Christological implications—spiced up with oblique references to the prologue in the Gospel of John, the Memra theology of the Targumim, and subtle terminological distinctions in the Christological discourse—become only too obvious.[21]

This is quite a creative interpretation of our midrash. True, the young and old dichotomy is crucial to the midrash, and it rests on the juxtaposition of Exodus 15:3 (man of war = young man) and Exodus 24:10 plus Daniel 7:9f. (old man). But Daniel 7:9f. is quoted for no other reason than to prove that God can and sometimes does manifest himself as an old man—the same reason why Exodus 24:10 is quoted (as well as Exodus 15:3, namely, to prove that God sometimes manifests himself as a young man)—and it is pure speculation that the Mekhilta, in quoting Daniel 7:9f., wishes to allude to another midrash on Daniel. 7:9f. *and* 7:13f.[22] As a matter of fact, with the exception of one sugya in the Babylonian Talmud (to which I will turn in the next chapter) there exists no such midrash unequivocally juxtaposing Daniel's "Ancient of Days" and "Son of Man" in such a way as to insinuate or attack the idea of an old and a young deity.[23] To be sure, the rabbinic midrash frequently fails to quote explicitly the part of the biblical proof text crucial to its interpretation (because it presupposes that every reader or listener knows the Bible by heart and can easily complement the part that is not quoted), but in our case the whole midrash revolves around the problem of two deities, and it would be more than odd if the author quoted Dan. 7:9 in order to prove that God manifests himself as an old man, while at the same time leaving it to the ingenuity of the reader or listener to complement this proof text with yet another one that implies the manifestation of a "young God" (the Son of Man of Dan. 7:13f.). More precisely, if the author of our midrash had wanted to use Daniel 7:13f. as proof text for a "young god" as opposed to an "old god," the appropriate (and easy) place would have been immediately after the quotation of Exodus 15:3—but this is what he did *not* do.

Boyarin is certainly right in referring to the *puer senex* typology; in his eagerness, however, to apply it to the Ancient of Days and Son of Man typology in Daniel, he fails to explain it in its own terms. The *puer senex* motif is well known in the Greek and Roman literature; its main purpose is to advocate an ideal according to which a young man presents himself (e.g., in court) as an experienced and merciful (!) senior judge (*puer senilis*), whereas an old man—despite the limitations of old age—proves his juvenile spirit.[24] The person who achieves the *puer senex* ideal is one and the same individual, not split into two personae. As employed by our midrash, this motif means that the Jewish God embodies the ideal of the *puer senex*—the young and simultaneously wise and serene old man—yet the "nations" (i.e., the Greeks and Romans) should not mistake this classical ideal and split these qualities of God into different divine personae. Moreover, since the emphasis in the midrash is placed not just on the juxtaposition of "young" and "old" but also of "war hero" and "merciful judge," the "nations" may be tempted to abolish the *puer senex* equilibrium and to divide the one and only Jewish God into two gods or even—according to the various tasks assigned to them— into a pantheon of multiple gods.

Thus does it appear that in our midrash the cultural and religious context of the Roman Empire once more comes to the fore—although Christian theological implications cannot be completely ruled out. As we have seen, this context and theological considerations are inextricably linked, but in our Mekhilta midrash they remain in the background. The Daniel exegesis may well lead to Christological reflections, but the Mekhilta certainly does not (yet) presuppose speculations about Daniel's Ancient of Days and Son of Man in the sense of a Christian Father-God and Son-God; to discover the imprint of such reflections in the Mekhilta means to misconceive the exegetical structure of the midrash. This is not to say, however, that Daniel 7 played no role in the discussion of two possible powers in heaven. As the next chapter will demonstrate, it did; yet we need to pay close attention not only to how the sources develop their ideas about the unity and diversity of God but also to the provenance of our sources. With the Mekhilta we are no doubt in Palestine and probably as early as the second half of the third century. The evidence to be discussed in the following chapter will lead us into the realm of Babylonian Jewry, a very different world, with all its distinctive characteristics and peculiarities.

God and David

The collection of problematic Bible verses
referring to the name of God in the plural or to the different
names of God that the Bavli transmits in the name of R. Yohanan (R. Simlai's teacher) climaxes with Daniel 7:9 ("I beheld
till thrones were placed"),[1] the verse quoted but not discussed in
the Mekhilta. This verse deviates from the other verses in R. Yohanan's collection in that the problem it poses does not relate to
God's names and to the question of whether the verb coupled
with them is in the singular or plural. What then is its problem?
Let us take another look at the Daniel verse:

> (7:9) I beheld till *thrones* were set in place, and the Ancient
> of Days (*'atiq yomin*) took his seat. His garment was like
> white snow, and the hair of his head was like pure wool.
> *His throne* was fiery flames, and its wheels were blazing fire.

If we read this verse with the rabbis' eyes, the problem posed by
it is obvious: why were thrones (in the plural) set in place when
only one person (the Ancient of Days) takes his seat?[2] Would he

sit on several thrones? Hardly, since "*his throne* was fiery flames." What then about the other thrones? The easiest answer to this question (which in all likelihood is presupposed in the biblical text) would be that the other thrones were prepared for the members of the heavenly court—since the continuation in verse 10 explicitly states that the court sits down (presumably on the other thrones):

> (7:10) A river of fire streamed forth from before him; thousands upon thousands served him, and myriads upon myriads stood attending him. The court sat down and the books were opened.

Yet this seemingly simple solution to the problem is not the one the rabbis propose. In fact, it is explicitly refuted in our case. When the anonymous Bavli editor asks, "Why were these (verbs in the plural, in R. Yohanan's collection)[3] necessary," he answers:

> To follow the argument of R. Yohanan, who said: The Holy One, blessed be he, does nothing without consulting the heavenly family [his angels],[4] as it is written: "The sentence is by the decree of the Watchers, and the decision by the word of the holy ones" (Dan. 4:14).
>
> Now, that is satisfactory for all (the other verses mentioned by R. Yohanan), but how do we explain "till thrones were set in place" (Dan. 7:9)?
>
> One (throne) was for him [God] and the other one was for David.[5]

So the Bavli editor refers to R. Yohanan, who argues that the verbs in the plural coupled with a name of God in the singular are meant to underscore that God, before he undertakes an important decision (and in particular before he passes a sentence), always consults his angels. This follows the standard argument in such cases as discussed in the first chapter. But the Bavli editor sees clearly that Daniel 7:9 is out of place here since it is quite different from the other verses presented by R. Yohanan. Ironically, he apparently maintains that even if the heavenly court (the court consisting of God's angels) is explicitly mentioned in Daniel 7:10, our problem isn't solved by simply assigning the other thrones to the angels that God is about to consult. For the tension between the thrones in the plural and the one throne of the Ancient of Days remains, as it is only the one throne of the Ancient of Days that is emphasized (a river of fire streams forth from it)[6] and, moreover, as it is not explicitly said of the members of the heavenly court that they sit on thrones. Therefore, the Bavli editor concludes, we are dealing with two thrones, one for God and one for David.

Aqiva in the Bavli

With this solution the Bavli editor follows a Baraitha transmitted in the name of R. Aqiva:

> As it has been taught [in a Baraitha]: One was for him [God] and the other one was for David—these are the words of R. Aqiva.
> R. Yose said to him: "Aqiva, how long will you make the Shekhinah profane?! Rather, one (throne) was for justice (*din*) and the other one was for mercy (*tzedaqah*)."
> Did he [Aqiva] accept this answer from him [Yose] or not?
> Come and hear! For it has been taught [in another Baraitha]: One is for justice and the other one is for mercy—these are the words of R. Aqiva.

Said R. Eleazar b. Azariah to him [Aqiva]: "Aqiva, what have you to do with the Aggadah?! Confine yourself to the (study of) Nega'im and Ohalot! Rather, one was a throne and the other one was a footstool: a throne to take his seat on it, and a footstool in support of his feet."[7]

This is a remarkable exchange, put into the mouth of three second-generation tannaim of the early second century C.E.—R. Aqiva, R. Yose (the Galilean), and their slightly older contemporary Eleazar b. Azariah. The sugya begins with a Baraitha attributed to R. Aqiva that takes the plural of "thrones" in Daniel 7:9 literally and argues that if thrones were set up, then we are dealing with at least two thrones, that is, in addition to the throne for the Ancient of Days there must have been another throne for someone else, and this someone else was David. In other words, from Daniel 7:9 we learn that in fact one throne in heaven was set up for God and another for David. R. Yose vehemently disagrees with this exegesis proposed by Aqiva. He doesn't tell us what it is that he disapproves of, but we can guess at it. No, he argues, this evokes dangers that we would do best to avoid: the two thrones are not, God forbid, for God and David; rather, they are for two different attributes of the same God—the divine attributes of justice and mercy.

The ascription of different attributes to God—in particular the two most important attributes of justice and mercy[8]—is classical rabbinic theology.[9] These two attributes are also inferred from the doubling of the divine names (*YHWH* and *Elohim*); accordingly, a midrash on Genesis 2:4 ("in the day that the Lord God [*YHWH Elohim*] made the earth and the heavens") expounds:

This may be compared to a king who had some empty glasses. Said the king: "If I pour hot water into them, they will burst; if cold, they will contract [and snap]." What then did the king do? He mixed hot and cold water and poured it into them, and so they remained (unbroken).

Even so, said the Holy one, blessed be he: "If I create the world on the basis of mercy (*rahamim*) alone, its sins will get out of hand; (if I create it) on the basis of judgment (*din*) alone, the world cannot exist. Rather, I will create it [the world] (simultaneously) on the basis of judgment and of mercy—hopefully it will then stand!"[10]

Since it would not have been viable with just a single attribute, God created the world with a well-balanced mixture of justice and mercy. R. Yose prefers applying this doctrine of God's two attributes to the two thrones in Daniel: God actually did take his seat, so to speak, on two thrones, each for one of his two attributes. At least R. Yose apparently believes that this exegesis is less dangerous than R. Aqiva's reference to a second person next to God (David) who also takes his place on a heavenly throne. R. Aqiva takes R. Yose's objection to heart and accepts his toned-down interpretation. At any rate, this is what the second Baraitha maintains, where R. Aqiva is mentioned as the author of the exegesis aiming at the divine attributes.

Unfortunately this concession is of no avail to Aqiva, since another rabbi (Eleazar b. Azariah) immediately rebukes him, making it unambiguously clear that he had better keep his hands off the Aggadah and stick to what he knows best—Halakhah![11] The plural of "thrones," Eleazar argues, does not refer to two different attributes of God but, quite concretely, to God's throne proper and its accompanying footstool. This interpretation is indeed much more harmless—everything remains within the realm of the one and only God, without evoking the threat of a second deity. So the ultimate message of the Bavli sugya is that explanations broaching the possibility of two deities—God and

David as well as the divine attributes of justice and mercy—are dangerous and must be debarred: Daniel speaks of a *single* divine figure seated on his throne and resting his feet on a footstool.[12]

But why David in Aqiva's first answer? As I said above, the sugya expounds Daniel 7:9, but there is a conspicuous lack of reference to the "Son of Man" of Daniel 7:13f.; yet here, unlike in the Mekhilta,[13] the reference to David makes sense only if we include the Son of Man. For who is David here? Certainly not the earthly King David, highly respected as he was by the rabbis, but the Davidic Messiah. And whatever or whomever the "Son of Man" in Daniel might have originally meant—most likely the angel Michael as the heavenly counterpart of the people of Israel on earth[14]—he was most definitely regarded as a messianic figure. So, what Aqiva is actually saying with his first exegesis is that the thrones emplaced in heaven were reserved for God and the Messiah-King David. Although Daniel mentions God (the "Ancient of Days") only as taking his seat, we must infer from the plural of "thrones" that David also took his seat on the throne reserved for him. If David is in fact the "Son of Man" of Daniel 7:13f., appearing on the clouds of heaven and being presented to the "Ancient of Days," we must assume that he took his place on a throne next to that of God. To be sure, the Bavli does not explicitly state that the Messiah David is "young"—in contrast to the "Ancient of Days"—but he is clearly elevated to a divine or at least semidivine status, seated on a throne next to that of God and, as Israel's redeemer, embodying God's salvific power.

This is undoubtedly a powerful—and extremely dangerous—solution to the problem raised by the plural of "thrones." Its implications become apparent if we briefly recall the history of the idea of the Son of Man in ancient Judaism. It begins with Daniel and finds its first striking continuation in the so-called Similitudes of the First (Ethiopic) Book of Enoch (chapters 37–71), which most scholars date to the end of the first century B.C.E. or more precisely to the turn of that century.[15] There, the Son of Man, together with the Ancient of Days, is described as follows:

(1) And there I saw One who had a head of days,
and his head was white like wool,
and with him was another,
whose countenance had the appearance of a man,
and his face was full of graciousness, like one of the angels.
(2) And I asked the angel who went with me
and showed me all the secret things,
concerning yonder Son of Man, who he was,
and whence he was,
(and) why he went with the Chief of Days.
(3) And he answered and said to me:
"This is the Son of Man, to whom belongs righteousness,
and righteousness dwells with him;
and all the treasures of that which is hidden he reveals
because the Lord of spirits has chosen him,
and whose cause before the Lord of spirits triumphs by
    uprightness for ever.
(4) And the Son of Man whom you have seen
shall rouse up the kings and the mighty from their
    couches
and the strong from their thrones,
and he shall loosen the loins of the powerful
and break the teeth of sinners.
(5) And he shall cast down the kings from their thrones
    and kingdoms
because they do not extol and praise him,
nor with humble gratitude acknowledge
whence the sovereignty was bestowed on them.[16]

The visionary here is the patriarch Enoch who has ascended to heaven, where he is granted a vision. This vision clearly refers back to Daniel 7: the "Chief of Days" of course is the "Ancient of Days" in Daniel 7:9, and the "other one" who is with him and looks like a human being is the Son of Man (*bar enash*), who comes with the clouds of heaven and to whom is given dominion, glory, and kingship (Dan. 7:13f.). The Son of Man's personality, however, is here described more colorfully than in Daniel—his justice and uprightness exceed everything, and he knows all the secrets (obviously in both heaven *and* earth). Although he looks human, he resembles an angel and is, evidently, hence an angelic being (as is likely also the case in Daniel). His task is to carry out the divine judgment at the end of time: he will topple the kings of the earth from their thrones (i.e., all the rulers of the nations that are ill-disposed toward Israel), destroy all sinners, and—as is further explained in the continuation (ch. 47)—help the righteous to achieve their final victory. Thus, the Son of Man of the Similitudes is no doubt a semidivine figure who performs the task of the Messiah.

The most dramatic appearance of the Son of Man is reserved for the Similitudes' last chapter (ch. 71). It describes Enoch's return to heaven, where he first sees the holy angels, among them the archangel Michael, who introduces him into all the secrets of heaven and earth (71:4). Finally he sees in the highest heaven the heavenly Temple with the innumerable angels who serve in the Temple and guard the divine throne (71:7); prominent among these angels are the four archangels Michael, Gabriel, Raphael, and Phanuel (71:8). And then comes the climax of the vision:[17]

(9) And Michael, and Gabriel, Raphael and Phanuel,
and many holy angels without number,

came forth from that house.
(10) And with them the Chief of Days,
His head was white and pure as wool,
and his raiment indescribable.
(11) And I fell on my face,
and my whole body became weak from fear,
and my spirit was transformed;
and I cried with a loud voice,
with the spirit of power,
and blessed and glorified and extolled.

What happens here is unheard of in the ascent apocalypses. While the visionary usually approaches the Holy of Holies, with the divine throne in its midst, in a state of shaking and trembling (or rather, as in the older Book of the Watchers of the Ethiopic Enoch, stops in the entrance to the Holy of Holies and prostrates himself there),[18] here it is not only the four archangels but also God himself (Daniel's Ancient of Days) who come to meet the visionary (Enoch). Enoch, seeing the divine procession marching toward him, prostrates himself and is apparently transformed into an angelic being (v. 11). He responds by praising God, and then he finally learns the reason for this highly unusual heavenly activity:

(12) And these blessings which went forth out of my
        mouth
were well pleasing before the Chief of Days.
(13) And the Chief of Days came with Michael and
        Gabriel, Raphael and Phanuel,
and thousands and myriads of angels without number.
(14) And that angel [Michael] came to me,
greeted me with his voice and said to me:
"You are the Son of Man who is born for righteousness;

and righteousness abides upon you,
and the righteousness of the Chief of Days forsakes you
  not."
(15) And then he [Michael] said to me:
"He proclaims to you peace in the name of the world to
  come;
for from hence has proceeded peace since the creation of
  the world,
and so shall it be to you for ever and for ever and ever.[19]

The climax and crucial message of Enoch's vision is the revelation that Enoch himself is the Son of Man, the chosen, the embodiment of righteousness. The man Enoch who ascended to heaven couldn't remain a human being but had to be transformed into an angel in order to fulfill his task, namely, to lead—as Israel's Messiah and redeemer –God's people into a period of perpetual peace. All his followers, concludes the vision, will live together with him in this eternal bliss:

(16) And all shall walk in your ways,
since righteousness never forsakes you:
With you will be their dwelling places,
and with you their inheritance,
and they shall not be separated from you for ever and ever.
(17) And so there shall be length of days with the Son of
  Man,
and the righteous shall have peace and an upright way
in the name of the Lord of spirits for ever and ever."[20]

The Son of Man of the Similitudes is the Messiah, whose just rule will mean never-ending bliss for the people of Israel. That Enoch, the human being transformed into an angel, proves to be this very Messiah is a peculiarity of the Similitudes; but this is of course neither intended in Daniel nor does it find its immediate continuation in the respective literature. As will be seen in the next chapter, this idea re-emerges much later in Judaism.

Also the Fourth Book of Ezra—originating after 70 C.E., more precisely around 100 C.E.—harks back to the Son of Man of Daniel 7. In one of its visions (ch. 13) Ezra beholds "something like the figure of a man come up out of the heart of the sea: And I looked, and behold, that man flew with the clouds of heaven."[21] An innumerable multitude of men gather from the four corners of the earth to wage war against the "man," yet he destroys them—not with weapons of war but with a stream of fire sent forth from his mouth.[22] Afterward, God explains the vision to Ezra: the "man" is "he whom the Most High has been keeping for many ages, who will himself deliver his creation."[23] When the predestined signs of the end have come to pass, "then my Son will be revealed, whom you saw as a man coming up from the sea."[24] This "Son" will destroy the nations waging war against him with the stream of fire coming forth from his mouth, that is, as God explains, with the Law that is symbolized by the fire.[25]

No doubt, the "man" here is again the Messiah who will lead the eschatological war against the sinners and nations of the world. It is difficult to decide, however, whether the designation of the Messiah as "son" goes back to a Christian revision of the book or is in fact part of the Jewish original. The Fourth Book of Ezra is preserved only in translations that are likely to stem from a Greek text, which, in turn, would seem to depend on a Hebrew or Aramaic original. The Latin translation has here *filius*, whereas one of the two Arabic translations probably goes back to the Hebrew *'avdi* ("my servant"), and the other Arabic translation ("my youth") can be traced back to the Greek *pais*.[26] Elsewhere this Messiah is explicitly called "my Son the Messiah," rendered in the Latin translation with *filius meus Jesus*[27]—at least "Jesus" is here a clear Christian interpolation. But the "servant," if indeed he appeared in the Hebrew original, goes back to the "Servant of the Lord" of Isaiah,[28] and even the "son" need not be Christian: Psalm 2 addresses the Davidic king as God's Son ("You are my Son; today I have begotten you");[29] and according to 2 Samuel, God orders the prophet Nathan to declare to David: "I [God] will be a father to him, and he [David] shall be a Son to me."[30] The Messiah in the Fourth Book of Ezra is obviously God's Son—indeed a younger God—and the addition "Jesus" allows a Christian reader to easily grasp that this Messiah is a reference to Jesus Christ.

And therewith we have arrived at Christianity—the reappropriation and adaptation of the idea of the Son of Man as presented in the New Testament. Geza Vermes has carefully analyzed the Son of Man references in the New Testament and distinguished between those that refer directly or indirectly to Daniel 7:13 and those that are independent of Daniel, the latter being by far the most common.[31] We are interested only in references that refer directly to Daniel. The first of a total of two references can be found in Jesus' eschatological speech—recorded in all three synoptic Gospels—in which he predicts the destruction of the Temple and the end of time that it will initiate. At the peak of destruction, when sun and moon are darkened and the stars commence to fall from heaven, the Son of Man will arrive with the clouds of heaven, wreathed in great power and glory, and he will dispatch the angels to gather Israel's elect from the four corners of the earth.[32] This apparently alludes to the return of Jesus the Messiah after his resurrection and ascent to heaven.

The other reference relates to the High Priest's solemn question to Jesus as to whether or not he is the Messiah, to which Jesus gives the ambiguous answer: "You have said so."[33] Only in Mark does he give the straightforward answer: "I am." And immediately thereafter he adds:

> And you will see the Son of Man
> seated at the right hand of the Power
> and coming with the clouds of heaven.[34]

Jesus—whether it be the historical Jesus or Mark's Jesus is irrelevant for our purpose—candidly identifies himself here with the Son of Man of Daniel, explicitly referring to Daniel 7:13. The "Power" (*dynamis*) is a designation for God—in rabbinic Judaism the power or authority of the God who reveals himself (*gevurah* in Hebrew).[35] Yet unlike Daniel, he refers to another biblical verse, namely, Psalms 110:1, where it says:

> The Lord (*YHWH*) says to my lord (*adoni*):[36] "Sit at my right hand, until I make your enemies your footstool."

This is the famous psalm verse that would become part and parcel of the Christian doctrine of the *sessio ad dexteram*.[37] The speaker, of course, is God, and the addressee is David, originally the Davidic king or a descendent of the Davidic dynasty. Yet what is at stake here is not some Davidic king but the Messiah as the descendant of David, that is, the Davidic Messiah. Among the various messianic expectations of ancient Judaism, the Messiah from the house of David definitely embodies that which would become the most important one[38]—certainly in the New Testament. The complicated genealogy of Matthew 1 makes it unambiguously clear that Jesus, the Messiah, is a descendant of the house of David,[39] and a number of passages in the New Testament explicitly refer to our psalm verse in connection with the resurrected Jesus.[40] No doubt then, it is the Messiah Jesus, the offspring of David, who is portrayed as the "other" lord who takes his seat at God's right hand in heaven.

With this we come full circle. The Son-of-Man expectation of Second Temple Judaism is eminently messianic—from Daniel through to the Similitudes of the Ethiopic Book of Enoch and the Son of Man vision of the Fourth Book of Ezra to its climax in the New Testament, where Jesus is identified as the Son of Man who, as the Davidic Messiah, takes his seat on the throne reserved for him at God's right hand. It is highly probable that R. Aqiva in the Bavli knows of this *Jewish* chain of tradition and refers to it (yet of course without its Christian implications). And it is little wonder that R. Yose and, even more so, R. Eleazar b. Azariah, both aware of the Christian ramifications, try to immediately defuse any such implications in R. Aqiva's exegesis, seeing as how they threaten to evoke (in their view) that most dangerous and detested of all heresies—Christianity—and in its most provocative form. Both Jews and Christians shared a belief in the Davidic Messiah, and when Aqiva has his Messiah take his seat next to God in heaven, all rabbinic fences erected against this particular heresy are pulled down—with incalculable consequences for rabbinic Judaism.

So I wish to argue that in our Bavli sugya we are indeed confronted with rabbinic polemics against Christianity, that is, Christianity in its very essence, with the Messiah Jesus competing with the Jewish Messiah. But crucial for a *historical* interpretation of this evidence is the fact that this unequivocal tradition—and related traditions to be discussed in the chapter to follow—are limited to the Bavli and do not appear in Palestinian sources. Here I disagree with Boyarin, who, as we have seen, seeks to transport the Babylonian debate back into the Mekhilta. The Bavli, I posit, clearly reflects not just a dispute with Christian doctrines but most likely even presupposes knowledge of the New Testament as a canonic text,[41] whereas the Mekhilta (discussed above) and most other Palestinian sources are dealing with less specified and more amorphous ideas that are still emerging and have not yet crystallized into their final form.

One might object that the Bavli presents his discourse in terms of Baraithot, that is, as tannaitic and by definition *Palestinian* traditions. But I do not think this is a valid objection. To begin with, not all Baraithot quoted in the Bavli are original, tannaitic Baraithot. Furthermore, the fact that a messianic interpretation of Daniel 7:9 is attributed to Aqiva—of all rabbis—is by no means surprising since it was none but Aqiva who was believed to have enthusiastically acclaimed Bar Kokhba as the Messiah—and who was then immediately rebuked by his contemporary Yohanan b. Torta.[42] The Bavli sugya follows exactly the same discursive pattern: Aqiva sticks his neck out too far—and a colleague immediately calls him off. Hence, the conspicuous fact remains that our highly charged dispute appears to be a genuine Babylonian tradition, reflecting a distinct Babylonian cultural context. Boyarin got this right, for he emphasizes that we are not dealing here with allusions to early Palestinian rabbinic traditions but with ideas that "were formed in late antiquity and in Babylonia, [attributable] not to the Rabbis who are told about but to the Rabbis who did the telling."[43] And Boyarin is also right in assuming that Son-of-Man traditions such as those preserved in our Bavli sugya must have been "extant within the circles that produced rabbinic literature itself and that the 3 *Enoch* and the *Hekalot* cannot be neatly separated from those circles at all."[44] I presume that this is a little swipe being taken at my dating of the Hekhalot literature as late rabbinic or even postrabbinic—but I agree: the Hekhalot literature and 3 Enoch as part of the Hekhalot literature "cannot be neatly separated from those circles that produced rabbinic literature itself" (and that stand behind the Son-of-Man or similar traditions). The nub of the matter, however, is what precisely we mean here by "rabbinic literature"—and my answer is: most definitely not all of rabbinic literature, but only the Babylonian Talmud! As I have always argued—and as more recent research confirms[45]—it was the spiritual milieu of Babylonia, not Palestine, in which most of what we call Hekhalot literature took shape, and this is certainly and exceptionally true for the book titled 3 Enoch, the last one in the distinguished line of Hekhalot writings both chronologically and conceptually. It is no coincidence that there exists here a strong spiritual and cultural affinity between certain ideas expressed in the Bavli and in the Hekhalot literature, in particular in 3 Enoch. But Boyarin's attempt to transport Babylonian concepts and ideas back into Palestinian sources (Mekhilta) blurs the boundaries and ignores important distinctions between Palestine and Babylonia.[46]

Thus, in contrast to the Palestinian sources, in the Babylonian Talmud we are confronted with Christianity as a religion in the process of establishing itself. The order of battle is now more clearly recognizable and more uniform than in the Palestinian sources—the opponent's contours have become more visible: it is no longer the Son of Man of Daniel, the Ethiopic Book of Enoch, and the Fourth Book of Ezra but the Son of Man Jesus Christ who, as God's Son, has returned to his father in heaven. *Jewish* circles in Babylonia were apparently impressed by such a "heresy" and found the idea of a Messiah, enthroned next to God in heaven, to be an attractive one—despite or probably even because of its so obvious Christian implications.

What, then, does this mean with respect to the question of the group(s) behind our Bavli sugya? Boyarin correctly and successfully liberates the debate from Segal's well nigh desperate attempt to pinpoint the identity of the specific groups about which the rabbis were so concerned; instead, he emphatically argues that any such attempt is intrinsically misguided because in fact there were no real groups of external heretics; rather, "the Rabbis are effectively expelling the Two-Powers heresy from within themselves," and this, in his view, holds particularly for the Enoch traditions and everything connected with "Christianity":

> The Enoch traditions were indeed, and continued to be right into and through late antiquity, the province of Israel *simpliciter* (including much of the Christian communities) and not of a sect within Israel (of course this doesn't mean that they were of interest to all Jews or all Jewish groups)....
> Once we fully take in that "Christianity" is simply part and parcel of ancient Judaism, this very way of posing the issue becomes immaterial, in my humble opinion.[47]

I will turn to the Enoch traditions in the next chapter, but so much has become clear: the harmonious picture Boyarin draws of an unbroken continuity of Enochic and Christian traditions *within* rabbinic Judaism overshoots the mark. True, we have all learned by now that the old model of the "parting of the ways" of Judaism and Christianity needs to be abandoned in favor of a much more differentiated and sophisticated model, taking into consideration a long process of mutual demarcation *and* absorption;[48] but to maintain that "'Christianity' is simply [!] part and parcel of ancient Judaism" means to replace one evil with another. True, the fact that the rabbis reject the notion of two powers—and that they reject in particular "Aqiva's" proposal to assign the "thrones" in Daniel 7:9 to God and David—does not necessarily imply that such ideas were restricted to "outsiders" against whom the rabbis exclusively argue. To the contrary, they also clearly argue against the enemy from within, that is, against followers of these heresies within their own fold (otherwise they would not have put the "heresy" in the mouth of R. Aqiva). Yet this insight does not necessarily imply that all these debates were *always* inner-Jewish debates and that *all* the "heretics," with *all* their contested ideas, must be led back to the lap of Judaism—

that everything, through late antiquity (!), takes place *within the same* Judaism. If I might employ a mixed metaphor here, this misguided attempt to harmonize the historical dissonances—ignoring all geographical (Palestine and Babylonia) and chronological boundaries—in my humble view means throwing out the baby with the bathwater.

THE DAVID APOCALYPSE

Not surprisingly, the second major text dealing with the elevation of the Messiah-King David has been preserved in the Hekhalot literature. This so-called David Apocalypse is most likely an independent literary unit of unknown provenance that was integrated primarily in Hekhalot Rabbati.[49] It bears all the characteristics of the classical apocalypse; and I have argued elsewhere that, together with two other apocalyptic units, it was inserted into Hekhalot Rabbati by an editor who was dissatisfied with Hekhalot Rabbati's messianic message (the Merkavah mystic as a quasi-messianic figure who makes the Messiah superfluous) and wished to counterbalance it with a more traditional messianic outlook.[50]

It begins with the angel Sasangiel—presumably identical with Metatron[51]—revealing to R. Ishmael, one of the heroes of the Hekhalot literature, Israel's gloomy future, the nation being chastised by one terrible punishment after the other and climaxing in the destruction of the Temple and Jerusalem. R. Ishmael, dismayed at this news, faints and needs to be revived by the angel Hadarniel (another name for Metatron). Hadarniel shows Ishmael the treasuries of consolation and redemption, where numerous angels weave garments of redemption and crowns of life. One of these crowns—a particularly magnificent crown with sun, moon, and the twelve constellations attached to it—is prepared for David, the king of Israel. When Ishmael begs the angel to show him the glory of David, the angel asks him to be patient and wait just three more hours to see him. After three hours he finally has a vision of David and the heavenly court:

He [Hadarniel] sat me [Ishmael] upon his lap,
saying to me: "What do you see?"
    I[52] answered him:
"I see seven bolts of lightning that flash[53] like one."
    He said to me: "Squeeze your eyes (tightly) so that you
        do not shudder before those,
who went forth toward my beloved one."[54]
    Immediately all the Ofannim and Serafim[55]
        approached,[56]
stores of snow and stores of hail,
clouds of glory,
constellations and stars,
ministering angels and the flares of the *zevul*.[57]
    They say: "For the leader, a psalm of David. The
        heavens are telling [the glory of God]" (Ps. 19:1).
    Then I heard a voice of great tumult that came from
        Eden[58] saying:
"The Lord will be king for ever" (Ps. 146:10).[59]
    And behold, David, the king of Israel, came at the
        head.
And I saw all the kings[60] of the house of David behind
    him.
Each one (was wearing) his crown upon his head,
but the crown of David was brighter and more special
    than all (the other) crowns.
Its splendor reaches from one end of the world to the
    other.
    When David, the king of Israel, ascended to the

Temple[61] that is in the *raqia*,[62]
there was prepared for him a throne of fire
that is forty parasangs high
and twice as long and twice as wide.

When David came and sat himself down upon his
throne,
prepared opposite[63] the throne of his creator,
and all the kings of the house of David sat down before
him,
and the kings of the house of Israel behind him,
David immediately recited hymns and praises
that no ear had ever heard.

When David began and said:
"The Lord will be king for ever, your God, O Zion, for all
generations, Hallelujah!" (Ps. 146:10),

Metatron and all the constellations[64] began and said:
"Holy, holy, holy is the Lord of hosts,
the whole earth is full of his glory" (Isa. 6:3).

The *hayyot ha-qodesh*[65] (also) praise and say:
"Blessed is the glory of the Lord from his place" (Ezek.
3:12).

And the *reqi'im*[66] say:
"The Lord will be king, etc." (Ps. 146:10).

And the earth says: "The Lord was king (Ps. 93:1),[67]
the Lord is king (Ps. 10:16),
the Lord will be king for ever and ever" (Ex. 15:8).

And all the kings of the house of David say:
"The Lord will be king over the entire earth" (Zech.
14:9).[68]

Ishmael's vision opens with mighty and frightening apparitions of light, "bolts of lightning (*beraqim*) that flash (*ratzin*) like one." This is reminiscent of Ezekiel's four creatures (*hayyot*) that have the appearance of fire from which "lightning (*baraq*) flashed."[69] Of these creatures it is said that they "darted to and fro" (*ratzo wa-shov*),[70] using the same Hebrew root (*rutz*) as the David Apocalypse. Moreover, Ezekiel puts great emphasis on the fact that the movement of the four creatures is in unison and in complete harmony. These bolts of lightning (seven in number)[71] are directed "toward my beloved one" (*dodi*), and here we move from the realm of Ezekiel to the beloved of Song of Songs. This, however, is a most remarkable and unheard-of statement, since, as the context makes clear, the "beloved" is David, the Messiah-King.[72] Yet we know very well that according to the standard rabbinic interpretation the beloved in Song of Songs is none but God himself, certainly not David. So what is going on here? Does the Messiah-King absorb characteristics that were originally reserved for God? This is precisely what I believe our apocalypse seeks to convey and what I will further demonstrate.

David's epiphany begins with his heavenly entourage—Ofannim and Serafim as two classes of high angels (according to the classical rabbinic taxonomy located, together with the four creatures, in the seventh heaven, *'aravot*, where God also is seated on his throne); snow and hail as two major forces of nature (traditionally located in the sixth heaven, *makhon*); the constellations and stars (traditionally located in the second heaven, *raqia'*); and the ministering angels (located in the fifth heaven, *ma'on*). *Zevul*, which is here reserved for the ministering angels, is traditionally the fourth heaven where Jerusalem and the Temple are located and where Michael, the heavenly High Priest, offers his sacrifices.[73]

This phalanx of heavenly forces bursts out quoting Psalms 19:1, which, under the heading "For the leader, a psalm of

David," opens with the heavens proclaiming God's glory. This is clear enough: the heavenly forces tell of God's glory and, as the continuation with the voice from Eden makes clear, praise God as divine king. The "voice of great tumult" (or, less literally, "a great roaring noise") is the sound of the four departing creatures carrying God on his heavenly throne, which Ezekiel hears when he, after having seen God and received God's message, is brought back to Tel Aviv.[74] So the obvious message would be that although David is a king—and a very special king indeed, namely the Messiah-King—the true king is and remains God. But is this really what our apocalypse wants to convey? For, strangely enough, the heading of Psalms 19:1 could just as easily be translated "*For* the leader, a psalm *for* David," and the continuation would be "the heavens are telling the glory"—not of God, but of David! Accordingly, the "voice of great tumult" would then be announcing not God's eternal kingship but rather—in his capacity as Messiah-King—that of David. This, of course, is a very different and daring reading of the heavenly forces' praise.

It jibes, however, very well with the next stage in our apocalyptic narrative: David's appearance, after having been greeted and acclaimed by the heavenly forces, at the top of the procession of the kings of Israel entering the heavenly Temple. From among these kings he is singled out by virtue of a unique crown that is more magnificent than all the other crowns and whose splendor reaches from one end of the world to the other. This is reminiscent of Metatron, the "Lesser God" in 3 Enoch, who receives not only a majestic robe but also a crown with refulgent stones whose brilliance shines into the four quarters of the heaven 'aravot, into the seven heavens, and into the four quarters of the world.[75] Furthermore, David is seated on a "throne of fire" that is opposite the throne of God. The throne of fire clearly alludes to the throne of the Ancient of Days in Daniel, that is, God's throne (!), which consists of "fiery flames";[76] and that it is located opposite God's throne—obviously in the seventh heaven—reminds us of Aqiva's interpretation of Daniel 7:9 with God's and David's throne in close proximity to each other. David's throne even outshines that of Metatron, which looks "like the throne of glory" (i.e., God's throne) but is explicitly located at the *entrance* of the seventh palace and not in its midst, a location reserved for God's throne alone.[77] Hence, our David here is very much modeled along the lines of Metatron, the "Lesser God," and even outdoes him to some degree.

Now David takes his seat on his throne of fire, surrounded by the kings of the house of David (= Judah) and the house of Israel. His enthronement initiates some kind of heavenly worship or ritual, led by David himself, a series of hymns and praises that "no ear had ever heard." To be sure, it is not the content of the hymns that have never been heard—they consist of well-known Bible verses—but rather the structure and setup of the worship: an antiphonal chant between David, Metatron, the holy creatures, the *reqi'im* (that is, presumably the seven heavens), the earth, and finally the kings of the house of David. The antiphon begins with David praising God with Psalms 146:10 as king forever; followed by Metatron and his angelic host singing the trisagion of Isaiah 6:3 and the holy creatures responding with Ezekiel 3:12; the heavens repeating Psalms 146:10; the earth answering with a mélange of Bible verses emphasizing God's kingdom in the past, present, and future; and the kings of the house of David concluding with Zechariah 14:9. So the subject of the heavenly antiphon is God as eternal king, appropriately praised by the trisagion and the response from Ezekiel 3:12. Interestingly enough, this more intimate praise is uttered by Metatron and the holy creatures, whereas David, the heavens, the earth, and the Davidic kings focus on God's kingdom.

There is no doubt that David, the elevated Messiah-King, enthroned in the heavenly Temple, is here praising God as his king (together with the heavens, the earth, and his fellow kings)—but where in fact *is* God during all this? Presumably on his throne opposite that of David in the heavenly Temple. Yet the apocalypse doesn't really talk about God, nor does the visionary (R. Ishmael) see God. That God resides in the heavenly Temple, seated on his throne, is merely presupposed: David enters the Temple, in which God is apparently already present, takes his seat on his throne opposite God's throne, and praises God as king.

The purpose of this heavenly ritual is clearly eschatological, since R. Ishmael witnesses it in response to his concern about Israel's future. Hence the message is that God—Israel's past, present, and future king—will ultimately redeem his people. Regardless of the horrible events that may befall Israel, God will remain their king—and what is more, as Zechariah 14:19 would have it, he "will be king over the entire earth." Zechariah 14 is an apocalypse describing the day of the Lord, that is, the end of the world—the nations will conquer Jerusalem and destroy the Temple, but God, standing on the Mount of Olives, will do battle with the nations; Israel will be rescued, and the time of redemption will dawn, with neither cold nor frost nor night, but accompanied solely by living waters flowing out from Jerusalem.

It is here, at very latest, that a strange tension becomes apparent. The Messiah-King David and his heavenly entourage praise God as king, culminating in the verse from Zechariah in which God is Israel's redeemer, but there is no Messiah mentioned. So we have a Messiah-King (David) and God functioning as the Messiah (if we take Zechariah seriously), and both seated on thrones in the midst of the heavenly Temple. Quite an odd scenario, if taken literally. Yet I believe that this is precisely what we are expected to do, and what we end up with are two competing divine figures—God and David. Not only is David seated on a throne similar to God's and located opposite it, he and God facing one another, but he is evidently the main figure in this heavenly scenario. He is elevated to the highest possible position in heaven, praised like God, and although he duly praises God as his king and Israel's redeemer, it is he who is the Messiah revealed to R. Ishmael.

In searching for parallels that might help to explain this unique position of David, Anna Maria Schwemer (in her detailed analysis of the David Apocalypse)[78] has drawn our attention to the fact that Psalm 146, one of the key texts used in the apocalypse, is closely related to Psalm 22, and that Psalm 22 (according to the Letter to the Hebrews) is in turn the psalm that Jesus intones after his entry into the heavenly Temple.[79] This seems to me rather far-fetched. A much closer—and much neglected—parallel can be found in the Book of Revelation, where the visionary enters heaven and sees both God seated on his heavenly throne and the enigmatic figure of the Lamb that is identified with the Son of Man = the Messiah = Jesus.[80] Here we are mainly interested in the relationship between God and the Son of Man–Lamb. The Son of Man appears first in the introduction, described as clothed in a long robe with hair as "white as white wool, white as snow," feet like "burnished bronze," and a voice "like the sound of many waters."[81] These epithets are clearly taken from Daniel 7 and Ezekiel 1, where they refer to God and not to the Son of Man; hence, our Son of Man is from the very beginning identified as someone who looks like God. Furthermore, the last message Revelation's Son of Man orders the visionary to write down concludes with the statement, mentioned only in passing, that the Son of Man sits together with his Father on his throne: "To the one who conquers I will give a place with me on my throne, just as I myself conquered and sat down with my Father on his throne."[82] These are not two thrones next to or opposite one another; rather, God and the Son of Man sit together on a single throne, clearly the *bisellium* that we know from the Roman emperors.[83]

Yet what the visionary then sees doesn't describe the Son of Man as sitting on his throne together with God; it first depicts God alone on his throne and surrounded by twenty-four elders seated on their thrones and by the four holy creatures on each side of God's throne. The four creatures, uttering the trisagion of Isaiah 6:3,[84] initiate an antiphonal chant with the twenty-four elders responding and praising God as the creator of all things.[85] The similarities to the Apocalypse of David are striking. First, there is the very fact of the antiphonal chant (which continues in Revelation as well as in the Apocalypse), then the trisagion, which in the Apocalypse is uttered by Metatron but then followed by the holy creatures responding with Ezekiel 3:12. And Revelation's version of the trisagion is remarkable—not only because it doesn't quote Isaiah 6:3 literally (unlike the Apocalypse) but also because it adds "who was and is and is to come." This formula may indeed allude to other verses from Isaiah,[86] but it may equally well refer to God's kingship—the Lord was king, the Lord is king, and the Lord will be king forever and ever—as in the David Apocalypse.

Now finally the Lamb comes to the fore, standing between the holy creatures and the elders. Both the holy creatures and the elders prostrate themselves before the Lamb and sing a "new song," praising the Lamb and not God, followed by another song uttered by the angels, the holy creatures, and the elders, and again praising the Lamb. It not only bestows upon the Lamb the same epithets that had been reserved for God in the first song[87]—namely glory, honor, and power—it even adds four more: wealth, wisdom, might, and blessing.[88] And then the antiphonal chant concludes with a song uttered by all the creatures in heaven and on earth, under the earth, and in the sea (compare the songs uttered by the heavens and the earth in the Apocalypse of David) and which addresses God and the Lamb together, with the four creatures responding "Amen" and the elders prostrating themselves and worshipping—God and the Lamb![89]

There can be no doubt that Revelation elevates the Son of Man/the Lamb/Jesus to a position that equals God's—meaning that he becomes a second divine power in heaven. And this is precisely what happens with David, the Messiah-King, in the Apocalypse of David. What the rabbis were afraid of in R. Aqiva's interpretation of Daniel 7:9—that David could become a divine figure next to God—has come true in the David Apocalypse. How do we explain this bold step in the Apocalypse? Schwemer wants to see the common features of the Apocalypse and the New Testament—the alleged similarity with the Letter to the Hebrews—as evidence that the traditions in the David Apocalypse are particularly old.[90] I believe that the opposite conclusion is far more likely the case, namely, that the David Apocalypse *responds* to the New Testament, in this case the Book of Revelation. Its author seeks to make clear that the Son of Man–Messiah usurped by the New Testament is in fact the Jewish redeemer who has been elevated by God to heaven; that any attempt on the part of the Christians—the religion that competes with the Jews—to claim this redeemer for themselves is misguided and needs to be countered. As I mentioned above, we know nothing of the origin of the David Apocalypse, but we should register the obvious similarity between certain traditions in the Bavli and the Hekhalot literature, something that we will indeed continue to do.

David in Dura Europos

The importance of David's enthronement as the messianic king in late-antiquity Judaism finds an unexpected confirmation in Jewish visual art. In 1932 the remains of a synagogue were discovered at Dura Europos, with all its walls decorated with colorful frescoes—something unique and until then unheard of. While mosaics are well documented in ancient synagogues, frescoes are the exception, and certainly such early ones. We are also able to precisely date the Dura frescoes: Dura Europos was a Roman frontier town on the Euphrates in today's Syria, at the border of the Sassanian Empire. The frescoes must have been created between 244 and 255 C.E., since after 254 the synagogue, filled with soil and rubble, became part of the city's rampart. This measure, although it did not save Dura from destruction—the city was conquered by the Sassanian king Shapur I in 256/57—would preserve the frescoes for posterity.

The most important wall of the synagogue is the western wall, which faces toward Jerusalem; it contains the niche for the Torah shrine, surrounded by a fresco that is subdivided into panels (see fig. 1). The two panels directly above the Torah shrine, that is, apparently in a central position, are unfortunately very poorly preserved and have been painted over several times. The first stage of painting consists of a large tree spreading over both panels, with two objects to the left and right of the tree's trunk that are difficult to identify (see fig. 2). Then the upper and lower parts of the tree were decorated: the upper part with a figure seated on a throne, flanked by two other figures with a lion below them (see fig. 3) and later supplemented by twelve additional figures (see fig. 5); the lower part of the tree with another seated figure playing the lyre (to the left of the lion) and two scenes below the tree—on the left the dying Jacob, who blesses his twelve sons, and on the right Jacob, who, in the presence of his son Joseph, blesses his grandsons Ephraim and Manasseh (see figs. 4 and 5). Edgings that were added later subdivide and frame the two main parts of the final composition (see fig. 5).

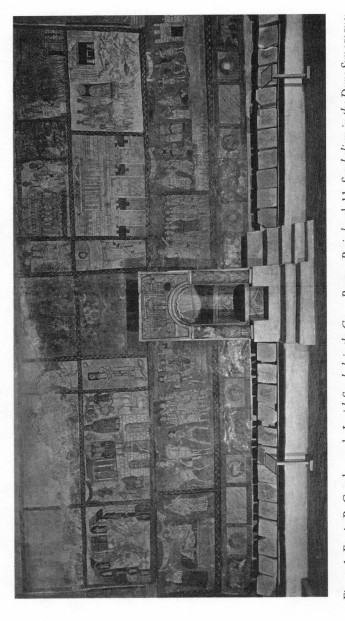

Figure 1. Erwin R. Goodenough, *Jewish Symbols in the Greco-Roman Period*, vol. 11: *Symbolism in the Dura Synagogue: Illustrations*, New York: Pantheon, 1964, Plate West Wall I. Reprinted with permission of Princeton University Press.

Figure 2. Goodenough, *Jewish Symbols*, vol. 11, fig. 76. Reprinted with permission of Princeton University Press.

Figure 3. A. R. Bellinger, F. E. Brown, et al., *The Excavations at Dura Europos: Final Report VIII, Part 1*, New Haven: Yale University Press, 1956, Plate XXXIII. Reprinted with permission of Yale University Press.

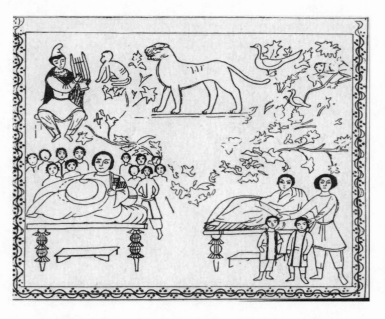

Figure 4. Goodenough, *Jewish Symbols*, vol. 11, fig. 77. Reprinted with permission of Princeton University Press.

Figure 5. Goodenough, *Jewish Symbols*, vol. 11, fig. 323. Reprinted with permission of Princeton University Press.

We are most interested in the two seated figures. Since the excavation of the synagogue, scholars have puzzled over their identification, and I cannot discuss this problem here in detail; however, I still believe that the most plausible supposition is that which identifies the figure enthroned on top of the tree as King David—not the historical King David but David the Messiah-King—and the figure playing the lyre also as David, that is, a David who has adopted traditions of the Greek Orpheus and who is likewise interpreted as a messianic figure.[91] This cluster of references to the Messiah-King David is striking, and all the more so if we pay heed to the overall composition of the fresco with the exalted David enthroned above the Torah shrine and in the treetop; coming immediately to mind is the Davidic Messiah as the last shoot from the stump of Jesse,[92] as a counterimage to the representation of Jesus as the Messiah-King in the apses of Christian churches.[93] The lion, of course, refers to the lion of Judah, another prominent messianic symbol, and the twelve figures (added later) obviously refer to the twelve tribes of Israel, to whom the messianic redemption will be granted.

And what about the two figures on the left and right of David seated on his throne? Most scholars suggest identifying them with prophets who are relevant to David, such as Samuel (who anointed him king) or Nathan (Samuel's successor).[94] Against this, Jonathan Goldstein has proposed that the Dura fresco in fact presents the first known depiction of Moses and Elijah flanking the Messiah-King's throne[95]—similar to later Christian depictions of Jesus with Moses and Elijah (e.g., in the monastery of St. Catherine on Mount Sinai and in the Basilica of San Apollinare in Classe, both dating to the sixth century C.E.). As we know, Moses and Elijah appear together with the transfigured Christ in the New Testament,[96] and this no doubt is the reason why they are depicted with Christ on Christian mosaics. Could it be that in their fresco the Jews of Dura Europos continued an originally Jewish tradition—Moses and Elijah as the companions of the Messiah-King—while being well aware of these Christian connotations? Or might they even have been *responding* to this Christian adaptation or rather usurpation of a Jewish tradition, conveying the message: we know of this Christian connection, and it is precisely for this reason that we are reclaiming our Jewish Messiah along with his companions? The exalted Messiah is enthroned above the Torah shrine because fulfillment of the Torah guarantees the coming of the Messiah and the final redemption—not least a redemption from Christian oppression.

It is no accident that this programmatic message on the western wall of the Dura Europos synagogue appears in a synagogue on the outermost eastern edge of the Roman Empire, at the immediate border of the Sassanian Empire. The frescoes are rife with Persian influence, and even David is depicted in Persian garb. It seems that the Jews of this godforsaken frontier post not only felt free to decorate their synagogues with frescoes and to adopt Persian styles in their artwork but also took the liberty of grappling with Christianity—at a great geographic remove from the constraints imposed by rabbinic Judaism in Palestine and still untouched by the dogmatic definitions of the Christian councils.

4

God and Metatron

IT IS NOT ONLY DAVID, THE KING OF ISRAEL AND ARCHETYPE of the Messiah, whom some rabbis elevated to an outstanding and privileged position in heaven. Some sources, and, as we will see, again the Babylonian Talmud and the Hekhalot literature in particular, single out another human being that they promote to the highest possible position in heaven, namely, the antediluvian patriarch Enoch, whom we have encountered as the hero of the Ethiopic Book of Enoch (1 Enoch). But whereas Enoch is transformed into an angel here and, in the Similitudes, is identified with the Son of Man, in the rabbinic and Hekhalot sources now to be discussed, Enoch becomes the highest angel in heaven and is called Metatron (a name unknown to the earlier apocalyptic sources), even assuming—in the Third Book of Enoch (3 Enoch)—the unique and unheard-of epithet *YHWH ha-qatan*, that is, the "Lesser God."

RAV IDITH AND THE HERETICS

Immediately following the exegesis of the "thrones" in Daniel 7:9, the sugya in the Bavli[1] continues with another midrash referring to Metatron instead of David:

> R. Nahman said: "A person who knows how to answer the heretics (*minim*) as R. Idith, let him answer; and if not, let him not answer."
>
> A certain heretic (*mina*) said to Rav Idith: "It is written: 'And to Moses he [God] said: Come up to the Lord (*YHWH*)' (Ex. 24:1). But surely it should have said: 'Come up to me!'"
>
> He [Rav Idith] said to him [the heretic]: "This was Metatron, whose name is like the name of his master, as it is written: 'for my name is in him' (Ex. 23:21)."
>
> "But if so," [the heretic retorted,] "we should worship him!"
>
> "It is written [in the same passage, however, replied R. Idith]: 'Do not rebel against him (*al-tamer bo*)' (Ex. 23:21), [that is], do not confuse me with him!"[2]
>
> "But if so, why does it say: 'He will not pardon your transgression' (ibid.)?"
>
> He [Rav Idith] answered [the heretic]: "We maintain by oath[3] that we would not receive him even as a guide/messenger (*parwanqa*),[4] for it is written: 'And he [Moses] said to him [God]: If *your* [personal] presence[5] will not go, etc. [do not bring us up from here]' (Ex. 33:15)!"

In order to understand fully this extraordinary midrash,[6] let us first look at the biblical context. The debate is sparked by the verse Exodus 24:1, which indeed poses a problem, for who is the "he" speaking to Moses? Supposedly God, who invites Moses (together with Aaron, Nadab, and Abihu, and the seventy elders) to ascend Mount Sinai and worship him there. But why then does God, addressing Moses in direct speech, say, "Come up *to the Lord* (*YHWH*)" and not "Come up *to me*"? The stylistic problem here is similar to the one discussed above (also in b Sanhedrin), which refers to the awkward phrase that "the Lord" causes rain from "the Lord" (Gen. 19:24)—instead of "from him"—and hence insinuating that two Lords (gods) are actually being addressed.[7] Whereas in the midrash discussed above, this type of misinterpretation is refuted on purely stylistic grounds (such is the idiom of the Bible), here the seemingly simple rabbinic answer to the heretic makes the problem worse and opens a Pandora's box of possible heretical implications. *YHWH* in Exodus 24:1, the rabbi contends, does not apply to God but to his angel: God (*YHWH*) invites Moses to ascend to the angel (*YHWH*), and this is the angel Metatron, both called by the same name *YHWH*.[8] We recognize this angel from the previous chapter in Exodus (Ex. 23:20ff.), though he is still without a name:

> (23:20) I am going to send an angel (*mal'akh*) in front of you, to guard you on the way and to bring you to the place that I have prepared. (21) Be attentive to him and listen to his voice; do not rebel against him (*al-tamer bo*), for he will not pardon your transgression; for my name is in him (*ki shemi be-qirbo*).

Here we learn that God will protect his people of Israel with an angel, who will guard them on their way through the desert until they reach the place that God has prepared for them—the land of Israel. In order to arrive safely at the Promised Land, God admonishes his people to listen to his angel and not rebel against him because, if they do not obey, the angel will not pardon their transgression. The reason for this exceptional position conferred upon the angel is almost casually provided by the enigmatic phrase concluding this passage: "for my [God's] name is in him." The biblical author does not bother to explain what precisely this means, so we can only guess that the angel is somehow meant to be God's agent or deputy and as such represents God's own presence among the people of Israel in the desert.[9] But since the angel does not have a name in the Bible, we cannot say with certainty what the phrase "my name is in him" alludes to *in the Bible*.

The rabbi, however, does know. Since Metatron's name is like the name of God (similar or even identical to God's name), he argues, the angel Metatron could just as well be called by the name *YHWH*. I will return to the premises of this bold identification shortly, but let us first continue to follow the gist of the debate between the rabbi and the heretic. If Metatron is indeed interchangeable with *YHWH*, that is, the angel with God and God with the angel, then the rabbi is in trouble. The heretic immediately seizes his chance and retorts: fair enough, but then we ought also to worship Metatron, as he is God's equal. The rabbi's answer to this very dangerous conclusion is one that resorts to an argument typical of rabbinic exegesis: he maintains that the phrase *al-tamer bo* does not mean, as usually understood, "do not rebel against him [the angel]" but rather "do not exchange me [God] for him [the angel]" or "do not confuse me with him" (from Hif'il *le-hamir*); consequently, Metatron is not God and therefore unworthy of worship. Yet the clever heretic keeps pegging away and points out another weakness in the rabbi's argument: if Metatron is not God's equal, why then does the Bible explicitly state that he will not forgive our sins if we fail to heed him? Isn't forgiveness of sins God's prerogative? The rabbi, instead of referring to the obvious—namely, that his reading "do not confuse me [God] with him [the angel]" fits perfectly well with the continuation "for he [the angel] will not pardon your transgression" (because, being a simple angel, he *cannot* pardon transgressions)—resorts to another biblical verse far removed from the text under discussion: "If *your* [God's] face (that is, your personal presence) will not go (with us), do not bring us up from here" (Ex. 33:15). In other words, we want you, God, and not just a guide or messenger, let alone someone who claims to be a second(ary) God.

No doubt, the heretic in fact has the stronger argument on his side,[10] and this becomes even more obvious when we consider the broader context of the biblical passage Exodus 23:20f. Whereas in Exodus 23:20f. God speaks of himself and his angel, clearly distinguishing between the two, the following verses are less forthright. Verse 22 continues: "But if you listen attentively to *his* [the angel's] voice and do all that *I* say, then *I* will be an enemy to your enemies," and the same is true of verses 23ff., which go on to say: "When *my angel* goes in front of you, and brings you to the Amorites (etc.), and *I* blot them out . . . and *I* will bless your bread and water, etc." (with many "I"s following).[11] When Exodus 24:1 then concludes: "And to Moses he said: Come up to the Lord (*YHWH*)," the reader is totally confused as to who is talking. The biblical text evidently does *not* clearly distinguish between God and his angel, or indeed, to use the rabbi's phrase, confuses the angel with God. In trying to avoid this confusion, the rabbi actually argues against the grain of the biblical text ("do not confuse me with him" instead of "do not rebel against him"). This, to be sure, is something the rabbis do quite often and quite successfully, but in this case the point is not only that the heretic has a strong argument for his interpretation but also that his argument supports the plain meaning of the biblical text against the rabbi's exegesis.

As we turn now to the implications of the rabbi's argument, it is obvious that he follows a tradition according to which the angel Metatron assumes the position of the highest angel in heaven because his name is like the name of his master—God. These two presuppositions need to be unraveled. First Metatron, the highest angel. This tradition is based on the identification of Enoch, the antediluvian patriarch, with Metatron. What the Hebrew Bible recounts of Enoch is relatively meager. It says (Gen. 5:21–24):

> (5:21) When Enoch had lived 65 years, he begot Methuselah. (22) After the birth of Methuselah, Enoch walked with God (*wa-yithalekh Hanokh et-ha-'Elohim*) for (another) 300 years and begot sons and daughters. (23) All the days of Enoch came to 365 years. (24) Enoch walked with God (*wa-yithalekh Hanokh et-ha-'Elohim*); then he was no more (*we-'enennu*), for God had taken him away (*ki-laqah oto Elohim*).

These few enigmatic sentences in the Hebrew Bible became the springboard for much speculation in the postbiblical Jewish and (later) Christian literature. If the Bible twice emphasizes that Enoch walked with God, we must thereby conclude not only that he was the privileged favorite of God among his fellow patriarchs (because he lived an exceptionally ethical life)—and this may well have been the reason why God took him away so early—but also that he was physically, in the literal sense of the word, walking with God. Since, after the expulsion of Adam and Eve from paradise, God no longer walks with human beings on earth, Enoch's walking with God could only have taken place in heaven. Hence, Enoch must have ascended to heaven to visit God; at the relatively young age (in comparison to his fellow patriarchs) of 365 years, he stayed in heaven with God and did not return to earth. This is what the cryptic "then he was no more, for God had taken him away" means: Enoch in fact did not die but was taken up by God to heaven and remained there with him as the highest angel.

That Enoch resides in heaven with God obviously has consequences for his appearance: is he still a human being or an angel or perhaps something in between? For it seems inconceivable that a human being, with his perishable body, can remain (forever?) with God in heaven. But it is not until the Similitudes or Parables of Enoch[12] that Enoch, the human being who ascended to heaven, can no longer remain human and is transformed into an angel[13]—a human-turned-angel, moreover, who, as we have seen, is identified with the Son of Man of Daniel.[14] The Second (Slavonic) Book of Enoch (2 Enoch)—presumably from the first century C.E. in its Greek original—is the first text that explicitly states that Enoch "has become like one of the glorious ones, and there was no observable difference [between him and an angel]."[15]

So far so good. But what about Enoch becoming that specific angel *Metatron* as presupposed by Rav Idith in the Talmud? This identification is exclusively reserved for the Third Book of Enoch (3 Enoch),[16] which in its final redaction belongs to a much later period, namely to the late-rabbinic or even postrabbinic era, that is, somewhere between the completion of the Babylonian Talmud and the Karaite Kirkisani (around 900 C.E.).[17] There, Enoch is taken up into heaven and undergoes a process of transformation that is described in great detail: he is infused with divine wisdom,[18] assumes enormous dimensions, and is equipped with seventy-two wings and 365,000 eyes.[19] Then God provides him with a throne similar to his own throne of glory, placed at the entrance of the seventh palace, and has a herald announce that he is appointed God's servant as prince and ruler over all the heavenly forces.[20] So, in fact, Enoch-Metatron becomes God's representative in heaven, his deputy and viceroy. His transformation not yet complete, God fashions for him a majestic robe and a kingly crown and calls him the "Lesser God (*YHWY ha-qatan*) . . . because it is written: My name is in him (Ex. 23:21)"[21]—using precisely the same biblical proof text as Rav Idith in our Bavli story. Finally, God inscribes on Metatron's crown the letters by which heaven and earth were created,[22] and all the angels in heaven fall prostrate before him upon seeing his majesty and splendor.[23] Then comes the ultimate transformation:

> At once my flesh turned to flame,
> my sinews to blazing fire,
> my bones to juniper coals,
> my eyelashes to lightning flashes,
> my eyeballs to fiery torches,
> the hairs of my head to hot flames,
> all my limbs to wings of burning fire,
> and the trunk of my body to blazing fire.
> On my right—those who cleave flames of fire,
> on my left—burning brands,
> round about me swept wind, tempest, and storm;
> and the roar of earthquake upon earthquake
> (was) before and behind me.[24]

Now Enoch's human existence is completely annihilated and he is turned into Metatron, an angelic being of fiery substance.

Having argued that the identification of the biblical angel in Exodus 23 and 24 with the angel Metatron makes sense only against the backdrop of the Enoch-turned-Metatron tradition in 3 Enoch, we still need to explain the rabbi's second implication—that Metatron is indeed this peculiar angel because his name is like that of God—*YHWH*. What does the name Metatron have in common with the name *YHWH*? Scores of scholars have agonized over the meaning of "Metatron."[25] Among the many suggestions, the one that has probably found the most support derives Metatron from the Greek *metathronos*, translated as "(the one who serves) behind the throne" or "(the one who occupies the throne) next to the divine throne." A slight modification of this option assumes that *metathronos* is equivalent to *synthronos*, meaning "the one enthroned together with (God)."[26] Another derivation that has recently gained momentum is from the Latin *metator* ("leader, guide, measurer, messenger"). Philip Alexander in particular has argued that *metator* can also designate the officer in the Roman army whose task it is to prepare a camp-site and that, more generally, the term can be used for anyone who prepares the way, a forerunner.[27] In support of this etymology one can refer to the fact that *metator* is indeed attested as a loanword in rabbinic literature,[28] whereas *metathronos* does not appear as a regular loanword. Moreover, and quite conspicuously, the only early Palestinian source in which the term Metatron appears, the Midrash Sifre Deuteronomy, points in this direction:

> [On that very day the Lord addressed Moses as follows: "Ascend this mountain of the Abarim, Mount Nebo, which is in the land of Moab, across from Jericho,] and view the land of Canaan, [which I am giving the Israelites for a possession]" (Deut. 32:48f.).
>
> R. Eli'ezer says: "The finger of the Holy One, blessed be he, is what served Moses as *metatron*, pointing out to him all the cities of the land of Israel—this far is Ephraim's territory, this far is the territory of Manasseh."
>
> R. Yehoshua says: "Moses saw it [the land of Canaan] all by himself! How so? He [God] empowered Moses' eyes, and he saw from one end of the world to the other."[29]

Here *metatron* is clearly derived from Latin *metator* or Greek *mētatōr*—"guide." But this guide has nothing to do with an angel; on the contrary, it is not an angel but the "finger" of God himself that serves as guide. Accordingly, the bone of contention between our two rabbis—the second-generation tannaim Eli'ezer b. Hyrkanos and his opponent Yehoshua b. Hananiah —is not the relationship between God and his angel but the theological implications in assigning a finger to God (that is, the problem of anthropomorphism). Since all the manuscripts in Finkelstein's edition have *metatron* instead of *metator* or *mētatōr*, it may be safe to assume that the original term *metator/mētatōr* was replaced by later medieval scribes with *metatron* because of the well-known name of the angel Metatron. It seems to me highly implausible, therefore, to argue conversely that the appellation *metator* "may first have been given to the angel of the Lord [in Ex. 23] who led the Israelites through the wilderness: that angel acted like a Roman army *metator*, guiding the Israelites on their way."[30] There is nothing that leads from the function of the Roman army *metator* to the position of Metatron, the highest angel in heaven.[31]

This interpretation is supported by another Palestinian source, where the name Metatron is used in a very similar way. The Midrash Bereshit Rabba relates God's command in Genesis 1:9 ("Let the waters under the sky be gathered together into one place, and let the dry land appear") to Psalms 104:7 ("At your rebuke they [the waters] flee; at the sound[32] of your thunder they take to flight"). R. Levi expounds God's thundering voice as follows:

> R. Levi said: Some interpreters, e.g., Ben Azzai and Ben Zoma, interpret: The voice of the Lord became a *meta-tron*[33] to the waters, as it is written: "The voice of the Lord is over the waters; [the God of glory thunders, the Lord, over mighty waters]" (Ps. 29:3).[34]

Here it is not the finger but the voice of God that serves as *metatron/metator* for the primordial waters: it tells them where to gather in order to make room for the mainland. This again has nothing to do with the angel Metatron—and, unlike R. Yehoshua in Sifre, R. Levi is unconcerned about anthropomorphic statements about God.

Hence, in my view, the most plausible explanation for the name Metatron is still the one that refers to the enthronement of Metatron as the highest authority in heaven next to God, that is, to his elevation as a kind of co-ruler, albeit subordinate to the supreme God. The fact that none of the etymological derivations is fully satisfactory[35] does not mean much—neat etymological derivations are rare anyway, certainly in the Hekhalot literature. Metatron's enthronement—and the office resulting from it—play such an important role in 3 Enoch and in the sole parallel in the Bavli[36] that the affinity between his name and the heavenly throne can hardly be overlooked.

But why is Metatron's name like the name of his master, as the rabbi in our Bavli sugya claims, and why does Exodus 23:21 ("for my name is in him") prove this assumption? The etymological explanation, proposed by Joseph Dan,[37] that the name Metatron actually refers to the Greek word *tetra* ("four") and alludes to the *tetra*grammaton *YHWH*—hence, that God's name is literally contained in Metatron's name—is not very convincing. Etymologically, the name Metatron has nothing to do with the name of God, *YHWH*. Metatron is not the "Lesser God" (*YHWH ha-qatan*) because the name *YHWH* is part of the name Metatron; rather, it would seem that the Bavli refers to an earlier tradition according to which an angel does bear the name of God in his name, and this is the angel Iaoel or Yaho'el, whom we encounter in the Apocalypse of Abraham[38] as Abraham's heavenly guide and mentor. There, the angel's name is explicitly and correctly identified as the same as God's (10:3): "Iao" is the Greek equivalent of the Hebrew tetragrammaton *YHWH*,[39] coupled with the ending "-el" (literally "God"), the customary theophoric ending of many Hebrew names. Scholars have suggested, correctly in my view, that the Metatron of 3 Enoch absorbed not only earlier Enoch traditions but Iaoel traditions as well and that it is due to this latter that Metatron's name is supposed to be like that of God.[40] It may even be that the appellation *YHWH ha-qatan* was originally that of Iaoel and not Metatron. So, it would seem that Rav Idith's answer in our Bavli sugya presupposes precisely that Iaoel tradition which was merged in 3 Enoch with the figures of Enoch and Metatron into a single Metatron tradition.

This does not mean, however, that we can determine more concretely the form in which our rabbi knew this tradition. Rav Idith, the hero of the Bavli sugya, is difficult to identify. The most plausible candidate would seem to be Rav Idi[41] bar Abin I, a fourth-generation Babylonian amora who lived around 350 C.E.; in this case his source would be Rav Nahman bar Yitzhaq, his contemporary, who died in 356 C.E.[42] Rav Nahman bar Ya'aqov, Nahman bar Yitzhaq's teacher and a third-generation Babylonian amora (d. 320 C.E.), would be too early for Rav Idi bar Abin; and Rav Idi bar Abin II, a seventh-generation Babylonian amora (mid-fifth century), would be too late for any possible Rav Nahman (unless we wish to identify our Rav Nahman with Rav Nahman bar Rav Huna, Idi bar Abin II's alleged successor as head of the academy of Sura). Hence, our earliest option for dating the Bavli tradition according to its attribution would be the mid-fourth century (and the latest option would be the mid-fifth century). Since it is highly unlikely that the composition collected under the title 3 Enoch took shape in the fourth or even fifth century, Rav Idi(th) must refer to a tradition of unknown provenance that was later incorporated into the book of 3 Enoch.

So now we have largely marked out the implications of Rav Idith's Metatron tradition. One of our most important observations is the fact that it again appears in the Babylonian Talmud—and within the classical rabbinic literature *only* in the Babylonian Talmud.[43] The sole parallel to Rav Idi(th)'s midrash in Palestinian sources[44] mentions not Metatron but only "our Prince," that is (presumably) Michael, Israel's guardian angel. In order to better assess this conspicuous finding, we need to evaluate all the relevant Metatron evidence in both the Palestinian and Babylonian sources. This will give us a clearer picture of the characteristics associated with Metatron and the similarities as well as differences between the traditions preserved in Palestine and Babylonia.

Metatron the Great Scribe

The (Palestinian) Targum Pseudo-Jonathan translates Genesis 5:24 as follows:

> Enoch worshiped in truth before the Lord, and behold he was not with the inhabitants of the earth because he was taken away and he ascended to the firmament at the command of the Lord, and he was called Metatron, the Great Scribe (*safra rabba*).[45]

Conspicuous here is the fact that, first, Enoch is explicitly identified with Metatron and, second, that Metatron receives the epithet "the Great Scribe." As to the former, this is the only Palestinian source in which such an identification of Enoch with Metatron is made. But it means little, since Targum Pseudo-Jonathan contains much post-talmudic material (for example, it mentions Fatimah, the daughter of the prophet Muhammad) and it may well be that our passage belongs to a later stratum of targumic traditions.[46] As to the latter, the title "Great Scribe" points to early Enochic traditions that assign Enoch scribal functions. Scholem has already drawn our attention to the Book of Jubilees (4:23), where Enoch is described as "writing condemnation and judgment of the world, and of all the evils of the children of men,"[47] yet there is much more relevant material.[48] In the Book of the Watchers, Enoch is called "scribe of righteousness,"[49] and the same holds true for the Testament of Abraham.[50] According to the Astronomical Book of 1 Enoch, the angel Uriel instructs Enoch to write down the secrets of the movements of the stars;[51] and according to the Second Book of Enoch, Enoch is instructed by the angel Vrevoil to write down 366 books "about his marvelous travels and what the heavens look like."[52] Another honorific title—"the distinguished scribe"—is bestowed on Enoch in the Enochic fragments of the Book of Giants, found in Qumran.[53] Hence, it would seem that this rather late targumic reference has preserved a faint echo of certain Enoch traditions familiar from the pseudepigraphic Enoch literature—through channels unknown to us. But it must be emphasized that this particular tradition is far removed from any notion of Enoch as being elevated above the angels and transformed into a divine co-ruler with God.[54]

THE CELESTIAL HIGH PRIEST

A remarkable tradition concerning a certain "Prince" in heaven is preserved in the enigmatic tractate Re'uyot Yehezqel, which many scholars seek to locate on the periphery of Merkavah mysticism:

> And what is there in [the third heaven] *zevul*?
> R. Levi said in the name of R. Hama bar Uqba, who said [it] in the name of R. Yohanan: The Prince (*ha-śar*) is not

dwelling anywhere but in *zevul*, and he is the very fullness (*melo'o*) of *zevul*.

And before him are thousands of thousands and myriads of myriads who minister to him. Of them it is said by Daniel: As I watched, thrones were set in place, etc. [and the Ancient of Days took his seat. His garment was white as snow, and the hair of his head like pure wool. His throne was fiery flames; its wheels were blazing fire.] A river of fire streamed forth, etc. [from before him. Thousands upon thousands served him; myriads upon myriads stood attending him] (Dan. 7:9f.).

And what is his name?

Kimos (*QYMWS*) is his name.

R. Yitzhaq said: *Me'atah* is his name.

R. Inyanei bar Sasson (Sisson?) said: *Bi-zevul* ("in *zevul*") is his name.

R. Tanhum the Elder said: *Atatyah* is his name.

Eleazar Nadwadya (Nadwad, Narwad, Nedudeya?) said: Metatron (*myttrwn*), like the name of the Power (*gevurah*).

And those who make theurgical use of the name say: Salnas (*SLNS*) is his name, *QS BS BS QBS* is his name, similar to the name of the creator of the world.[55]

This passage is part of a description of the seven heavens and their inventories. It locates a "Prince," whose name is at first not specified, in the third heaven (*zevul*). Of this Prince we learn only that he is the "fullness of *zevul*"—whatever this means: that he represents the "essence" of *zevul* or that he fills it out completely?[56]—and that many angels serve him (with Daniel 7:9f. as proof text). Since his name is not explicitly mentioned, the second section of our passage asks after his name and provides a list of names, most of which are unintelligible *nomina barbara*. Only the name Metatron immediately stands out as an unambiguous identification—all the more so as the author hastens to add that well-known specification that his name is like the name of the Power (which is, of course, God).

The date and provenance of Re'uyot Yehezqel, wherefrom our passage derives, is much debated among scholars. Whereas Scholem (followed by Gruenwald) takes it for granted that the tractate is part and parcel of the Hekhalot literature and hence of Merkavah mysticism,[57] Halperin has conclusively argued that "not only is the *Visions of Ezekiel* not a *Hekhalot* text; it is, by and large, very unlike the *Hekhalot*."[58] This line of reasoning is followed by Goldberg, who—on the basis of a detailed formanalytical analysis—concludes that it is a late rabbinic midrash and definitely not a "mystical text."[59] No one doubts, however, that it is of Palestinian origin. The names of the rabbis quoted are all of Palestinian provenance and, following the framework established by these names (none of which is later than ca. 300 C.E.), Gruenwald has concluded that the tractate must have been written in the fourth or, at very latest, early fifth century.[60] Halperin casts doubt on the usefulness of the rabbinic names for establishing the date of the tractate and raises the possibility that these names are fictitious and lead us nowhere; in fact, he contends, a number of aspects would indicate that the tractate is a late text.[61] But Halperin qualifies this statement with regard to precisely the passage in question, which, he quite rightly observes, is different from the bulk of the material assembled in the tractate and which he identifies as an early Palestinian source or even—because of its affinity with certain Hekhalot texts—an early "proto-*Hekhalot*" composition.[62] Hence, the rationale for dating our particular passage seems to go in circles and ultimately depends on its interpretation (if it be true that it is indeed uncharacteristic of the tractate's gist). What then is the message of our passage?

I will begin by stressing the fact that the Prince dwelling in *zevul* is anonymous: the explanation in the second part, clearly referring to Metatron, may well have been added by an editor who felt it necessary to provide the Prince with a moniker. But application of the name Metatron is by no means imperative— quite the contrary. If we didn't know from the second part of our passage that the Prince was Metatron, we would conceive a very different name, namely, Michael. For we possess a close parallel to Re'uyot Yehezqel's schema of the seven heavens and its inventories in the famous sugya in b Hagiga (12b) and related texts.[63] There it is stated, anonymously:

> *Zevul* is [the heaven] in which [the heavenly] Jerusalem and the Temple and the Altar are built, and Michael, the Great Prince, stands and offers up thereupon an offering.

This is the locus classicus for *zevul*'s inventory: it contains the heavenly Temple with Michael, the celestial High Priest, performing the sacrifice in heaven. Scholem has suggested, therefore, that the Prince in our passage in Re'uyot Yehezqel is indeed Michael, not Metatron, who offers the heavenly sacrifice[64] (the only difference being that according to b Hagiga *zevul* is the fourth heaven, whereas in Re'uyot Yehezqel it is the third heaven)[65] and that our passage reflects a stage in which Michael is identified with Metatron (similar to the identification of Metatron with Iaoel)[66] as made explicit in the second part. The straightforward message of the first part would then be: Michael/Metatron functions as the celestial High Priest in the heaven called *zevul* and, in order to support his duties, he has thousands and myriads of angels at his behest who attend his performance of the heavenly sacrifice (Dan. 7:9f.).

A similar function of Metatron is well known from the He-khalot literature. There, a Tabernacle or Temple of the "Youth" (*mishkan ha-naʿar*) is mentioned, in which the "Youth"—explicitly identified as Metatron—deafens the ears of the holy creatures so that they are unable to listen to the ineffable name of God, which Metatron is about to utter.[67] Metatron clearly does not offer a heavenly sacrifice here, but still there can be no doubt that he is portrayed as serving in the heavenly Temple. The only source in the classical midrash that combines the "Tabernacle of the Youth" and Metatron's heavenly sacrifice is preserved in the late Midrash Numbers Rabba:

> R. Shimʿon expounded: When the Holy One, blessed be he, told Israel to set up the Tabernacle (*mishkan*), he inti-mated to the ministering angels that they should also con-struct a Tabernacle. And when one was erected below, the other was erected on high. The latter was the Tabernacle of the Youth (*mishkan ha-naʿar*), whose name is Metatron, and there he offers up the souls of the righteous to atone for Israel in the days of their exile.[68]

Although this midrash is transmitted in the name of R. Shimʿon (presumably R. Shimʿon b. Pazzi, the Palestinian amora of the third generation, late third century C.E.), its dating on the basis of this attribution is quite problematic. To begin with, Numbers Rabba is not a particularly reliable source;[69] and, second, it is by no means self-evident that the identification of the heavenly Tabernacle as the "Tabernacle of the Youth," that is, of Metatron, is part of R. Shimʿon's interpretation. Just the opposite appears to be the case, namely, that this identification (which presup-poses the identification of Metatron with Michael) was made, at a very late stage, under the influence of the Hekhalot literature—and not the other way around.[70]

Yet the quotation of Daniel 7:9f. in our Re'uyot Yehezqel passage complicates matters. The verse speaks of the "Ancient of
Days," no doubt God, who takes his seat on his heavenly throne
and has thousands and myriads of angels serving him. Hence, if
we apply this to the Prince in *zevul*, we can only conclude that
the Prince Michael/Metatron is identified with the Ancient of
Days, that is, with God; in other words, that Michael/Metatron
is not only a second divine power next to God but even serves as
God's surrogate. Such a message is unheard of. To be sure, we
know of texts that conceive Metatron as God's viceroy,[71] but nowhere is it said that Metatron (let alone Michael) can be equated
with God. I don't believe, therefore, that such an unduly literal
reading of our passage in Re'uyot Yehezqel makes sense. The
most likely explanation of the text is that the quotation from
Daniel is meant to prove that Michael/Metatron, during his celestial duties, is served by the host of angels—and certainly not
that *he* is the "Ancient of Days."

On this level, therefore, our passage is still quite "innocent." It
is interested in Metatron's function in heaven, clearly as an angel,
and not in his relationship with God. But one can see how it
might give rise to other more dangerous speculations. Once Michael is identified with Metatron and the Metatron traditions
sneak in, a Pandora's box is opened: one might then consider
that the plural of "thrones" in Daniel 7:9f. might refer not just to
God's throne but rather to one throne for the "Ancient of Days"
and another for David/the Son of Man or Metatron;[72] or consider the dangerous implications resulting from the insight that
Metatron's name is like the name of his master.[73] The first implication could easily be read into the quotation of Daniel 7:9f.,
and the second one is even made explicit in the second part of
our midrash.

So what do we make of this interpretation of the Re'uyot Yehezqel passage? Do we have here a relatively early (fourth cen-

tury?) *Palestinian* source, which for the first time more or less openly plays with possibilities regarding Metatron that are made explicit in later and predominantly *Babylonian* sources (Metatron's name like the name of his master in b Sanhedrin 38b and 3 Enoch; Michael/Metatron as the celestial High Priest in b Hagiga 12b and Seder Rabba di-Bereshit)? In other words, does our passage (to be sure, only this particular passage) in Re'uyot Yehezqel provide evidence of a "proto-Hekhalot" composition (Halperin)? I doubt that this is the most plausible explanation. First of all (to reiterate), there is nothing problematic with Michael/Metatron serving in the heavenly Temple; this could well be an earlier Palestinian tradition that simply wasn't followed up in Palestine, while becoming prominent in Babylonia. That Metatron's name is like the name of the divine Power presupposes the identification of Iaoel with Metatron and certainly has the potential for more dangerous complications. Again, if it had its origin in Re'uyot Yehezqel, then it wasn't really followed up in Palestine. But we have already seen that our passage is quite alien to the bulk of Re'uyot Yehezqel. Could it be, therefore, that the explicit explanation of the anonymous Prince's name as Metatron in the second part is indeed a later addition? The theurgical use of the name mentioned at the end of our passage strongly supports such a suspicion: this is uniquely Hekhalot literature and completely alien to the classical rabbinic literature. So what we then encounter here is not a "proto-Hekhalot" composition but, to the contrary, a well-developed Hekhalot composition put into the mouths of Palestinian rabbis and imposed on Re'uyot Yehezqel. Or, to go a step further, could it be that we need to rethink the date and provenance of Re'uyot Yehezqel and consider a later—Babylonian—composition (or a later composition with heavy Babylonian accents) that was pretending to be Palestinian? These questions cannot be conclusively answered, but the framework of predominantly Palestinian rabbis—some of them of quite uncertain provenance[74]—can hardly serve as prime evidence for a Palestinian origin of our text.

The Prince of the World

A number of sources, mainly in the Bavli, mention another anonymous angel bearing the title "Prince of the World" who has also been identified with Metatron:

> R. Shemuel bar Nahmani said in the name of R. Yonathan: The following verse was uttered by the Prince of the World (*śar ha-ʿolam*): "I have been a youth (*naʿar*) and now I am old" (Ps. 37:25). For who else could have said it! If the Holy One, blessed be he, be suggested, is there any old age in his case? Then David must have said it? But was he so old? Consequently it must be concluded that the Prince of the World said it.[75]

Here, R. Shemuel bar Nahmani—a Palestinian amora of the third generation, who flourished in Tiberias but spent some time in Babylonia; his teacher R. Yonathan b. Eleazar, a Palestinian amora of the first generation, flourished in Sepphoris but was born in Babylonia—applies the verse Psalms 37:25 to the "Prince of the World" as its speaker. God cannot be meant, he argues, because God does not grow old. Nor does the verse refer to David, since David wasn't particularly old. Hence, so the rabbi's conclusion, it is the "Prince of the World" who laments his old age.

The identity of this "Prince of the World" is not entirely clear, but it would seem that he is a special angel in charge of the world as a whole, distinct from the guardian angels assigned to the nations; this we can infer from the few rabbinic texts in which he is mentioned. According to the Midrash Shemot Rabba, the Prince of the World uttered the verse "What shall I do when God rises up? When he makes inquiry, what shall I answer him" (Job 31:14) in response to God's plan to smite the Egyptians (Ex. 12:23). The one who is speaking in this verse, the midrash explains, was originally the Prince of the World, although later Job applied the verse to himself.[76] Similarly, R. Hanina b. Papa (a Palestinian amora of the third generation who lived in Caesarea but also in Babylonia) expounds in the Bavli that the verse Psalms 104:31 ("May the glory of the Lord endure forever; let the Lord rejoice in his works") was approvingly pronounced by the Prince of the World when the plants, upon their creation,[77] realized that the specification "after its kind" referred not only to the trees (to which it is attached in the Bible) but to themselves as well.[78] And finally, a midrash again in the Bavli (put in the mouth of R. Tanhum, who identifies the fifth-generation tanna Bar Qappara as its author) has first the earth and then the Prince of the World intervene when God, following his attribute of justice, rescinds his original plan to appoint King Hezekiah as the Messiah (albeit unsuccessfully).[79]

The Prince of the World in our b Yevamot passage makes for a nice fit in this context. Being that special angel set over the world, apparently he was present during the creation of the world and will remain so throughout the world's history until its end (the messianic period)—wherefore he recognizes that he has grown old. But it is in this capacity that he seems to have absorbed features characteristic of Metatron.[80] If we take into consideration the discussion in Sanhedrin 38b about David and Metatron[81]— and the fact that our text explicitly excludes God and David—it becomes probable that Metatron is indeed referred to by this title in our passage. This assumption is supported by the reference to *na'ar* ("youth") in the psalm verse, which is one of the epithets of Metatron in 3 Enoch.[82] Moreover, an angel called "Prince of the World" also appears in 3 Enoch; although he is not explicitly identified with Metatron, the way he is described and the tasks assigned to him nevertheless make such an identification likely.[83]

In any case, whoever the "Prince of the World" might be, our midrash in b Yevamot is conspicuously critical of him and clearly fends off the idea, most prominent in the Bavli and 3 Enoch, of a young divine power next to God. This Prince of the World/Metatron may want to argue, our midrash maintains, that he is a young "god," but alas, he is compelled to realize that he has grown old—something that does not happen to a god. Hence he cannot claim to be a divine power on an equal footing with God.

The Instructor of Schoolchildren in Heaven

The Bavli transmits a brief sugya about God's mourning over the destruction of the Temple, in which Metatron makes an appearance:

> R. Aha said to R. Nahman bar Yitzhaq: Since the day of the destruction of the Temple, there is no laughter for the Holy One, blessed be he.
> Whence do we know that there is not?
> Shall we say from the verse: "And on that day the Lord, the God of hosts, called to weeping and mourning, to baldness, etc. [and putting on sackcloth]" (Isa. 22:12)? But this refers to that [particular] day and no more.
> Shall we then say, from this verse: "If I forget you, O Jerusalem, let my right hand wither! Let my tongue cling to the roof of my mouth if I do not remember you" (Ps. 137:5f.)? This excludes forgetfulness, but not laughter.
> Hence, [it is known] from the verse: "For a long time I have held my peace, I have kept still and restrained myself, etc. [now will I cry out like a woman in labor, I will gasp and pant]" (Isa. 42:14).

What then does God do in the fourth quarter [of the day]?—He sits and teaches the schoolchildren Torah, as it is said: "Whom will he teach knowledge, and to whom will he explain the message? Those who are weaned from the milk, those taken from the breast" (Isa. 28:9).

Who instructed them theretofore?

If you like, you may say Metatron, and if you like, you may say that he [God] did both.[84]

The two Babylonian rabbis Aha (bar Ya'aqov) and Nahman bar Yitzhaq (fourth-generation amoraim, first half of the fourth century C.E.) search for a biblical proof that God stopped laughing after the destruction of the Temple. Having rejected the verses Isaiah 22:12 and Psalms 137:5f., they settle on Isaiah 42:14—obviously undisturbed by the fact that God's crying is compared to that of a woman in labor. But since the Talmud does not want God to spend all day and night crying (the sugya continues with the question of what God does at night), it reserves the fourth quarter of the day for something more productive: the Torah instruction of schoolchildren (presumably the little children in heaven who have died a premature death). This leads to the further problem (typical of the Bavli's reasoning) of who instructed the poor children before God took over, that is, before the destruction of the Temple. Answer: You may wish to assign this task to Metatron—or you may conclude that God himself instructed the schoolchildren before the destruction of the Temple as well as after. Here Metatron enters the discussion almost casually. The answer clearly presupposes his presence as a very high angel in heaven, if not as a second divine power. Hence, the seemingly dispassionate or casual answer (whatever you prefer: Metatron or God) reveals that the Bavli editor doesn't really care and in fact makes Metatron and God interchangeable—as we know by now quite a dangerous attitude.[85]

TWO POWERS IN HEAVEN

The next text to be discussed here, again from the Babylonian Talmud,[86] is the most conspicuous one. It refers to the famous *pardes* story in the Tosefta[87] of the four rabbis (Ben Azzai, Ben Zoma, Aher, and R. Aqiva) whose visit or ascent to the garden (*pardes*)—presumably the heavenly realm[88]—wrought devastation: Ben Azzai died, Ben Zoma suffered harm, and Aher "cut down the shoots"; only R Aqiva emerged from this experience unscathed.[89] Aher, the hero of our story in the Bavli, is the notorious arch-heretic Elisha b. Avuyah, who has been given the epithet Aher, probably meaning "the other," that is, the heretic. In all four cases the Tosefta provides a proof text from the Bible designed to explain what happened to each of the four rabbis. In the case of Aher, the verse Ecclesiastes 5:5 is quoted: "Let not your mouth lead your flesh into sin [and say not before the angel that it was an error]." It is unclear what this verse means in the context of the Tosefta story, and the Bavli sets out to explain why it has been applied to Aher:

What does this [verse] refer to?[90] He [Aher] saw that permission had been given to Metatron to sit[91] and write down the merits of Israel.

He [Aher] said: "It is taught as a tradition that above (*lema'lah*) there is no standing[92] and no sitting, no jealousy[93] and no rivalry, no back and no weariness. Perhaps, God forbid, there are two powers (*rashuyyot*) [in heaven]!?"

[Thereupon] they led Metatron forth and flogged him with sixty fiery lashes. They said to him: "Why, when you saw him [Aher], did you not rise before him?"[94] Permission was [then] given to him [Metatron] to efface the merits of Aher.

A heavenly voice went forth and said: "'Return, back-sliding children' (Jer. 3:14, 22)—except for Aher."

[Thereupon] he [Aher] said: "Since I have been driven forth from that world [the future world], I will go forth and enjoy this world." So Aher fell into bad ways (*tarbut raʿah*).[95]

Aher sees Metatron sitting in heaven, presumably on a throne, and is surprised at this sight because he has learned (in the rabbinic academy) that angels are supposed to have no knee joints and therefore cannot sit: it befits the angels to praise God while they are standing;[96] they don't sit on heavenly thrones. More-over, since the angels have been created as perfect beings and cannot sin, there is no competition among them in heaven—and they certainly don't suffer from physical fatigue since they don't have a human body. That they have "no back" seems to imply that they do not turn their backs to each other, as they have faces in all directions and have no need to turn around.[97] From this, Aher can only conclude that he is not gazing upon an angel but at a divine being and that, accordingly, there are indeed two powers in heaven, not just the one and only God. This is, the anonymous Bavli author argues, what the verse Ecclesiastes 5:5 means: in opening his mouth and suggesting that there might be two powers in heaven, Aher committed a grave sin, which he could not expiate by pretending that it was an error and that in fact he was aware he was seeing just an angel. He was punished by a divine voice that declared that his sin was so grave that he could never atone for it; therefore, he was destined to eternal damnation.

This is clear enough, but our Bavli story oddly and ostenta-tiously has Metatron being punished first, before it is Aher's turn. According to the Bavli, Metatron is clearly the main cul-prit: he is severely flogged because he did not rise before Aher and thus divert him from his fateful mistake. Remaining seated, he neglected to make clear that he wasn't God, seated on his throne, but just an angel, standing around like all the rest. In other words, he deliberately gave Aher the wrong impression that he was a second divine power next to God—therefore he needed to be punished and demoted to his true position as one among many angels.

Quite surprisingly, this Bavli story has a parallel in 3 Enoch (what is surprising is not the fact that the Bavli and 3 Enoch relate a similar story—indeed, this can be expected—but that 3 Enoch conveys this particular Metatron-critical story). Following the description of Enoch's elevation from a human being to the highest angel in heaven—his transformation into Metatron, the "Lesser *YHWH*,"[98] sitting on a throne, similar to God's, at the entrance of the seventh heaven, judging all the angels in heaven and assigning them to their respective angelic rank[99]— 3 Enoch suddenly incorporates the Aher tradition and continues:

But when Aher came to behold the vision of the Merkavah (*bi-tzefiyyat ha-merkavah*) and set eyes upon me [Metatron], he was afraid and trembled before me. His soul was alarmed to the point of leaving him because of his fear, dread, and terror of me, when he saw me seated upon a throne like a king, with ministering angels standing beside me as servants and all the princes of kingdoms crowned with crowns surrounding me.

At that hour he opened his mouth and said: "There are indeed two powers (*rashuyyot*) in heaven!"

Immediately a heavenly voice came out from the presence of the Shekhinah and said: "'Return, backsliding children' (Jer. 3:14, 22)—except for Aher."

Then Anafiel *YWY*,[100] the honored, glorified, beloved, wonderful, terrible, and dreadful Prince, came at the com-

mand of the Holy One, blessed be he, struck me [Meta-
tron] with sixty fiery lashes and made me stand on my
feet.[101]

Here, Aher's misperception of Metatron's role in heaven forms
the climax of Metatron's elevation to the status of "Lesser
YHWH"—or rather, to be more precise, the *anti*climax, for it
precipitates, as in the Bavli, Metatron's punishment. But, in stark
contrast to the Bavli version of our story, it is Aher who is punished first—immediately after he "recognizes" Metatron as a second divinity in heaven—not Metatron. Metatron is punished
after Aher, and we learn now who punishes him: the angel
Anafiel on behalf of God. This version of Aher's vision in heaven
flows more smoothly than the one in the Bavli—which does not
necessarily mean, however, that it takes precedence over the
Bavli version; both versions supplement each other and presumably draw from a common source.[102] Yet above all it is the story's
insertion at precisely this point in 3 Enoch that is so striking:
after all the effort the editor of 3 Enoch has made in elevating
Metatron to the highest possible rank in heaven, almost on a par
with God, he suddenly rescinds his own efforts and demotes
Metatron to the status of an ordinary angel (the highest angel in
heaven seems now to be Anafiel, whom we know also from other
passages in the Hekhalot literature). This clearly runs counter
to 3 Enoch's main message. So ultimately, even the editor of
3 Enoch, like his colleague in the Bavli, feels compelled to tone
down the image of Metatron that he has just rendered.[103] All
things considered, he wishes to make clear, we shouldn't elevate
Metatron to a level that moves him so dangerously close to
God—an insight that does not, however, prevent him from
treating Metatron in the remainder of his book as precisely this:
God's viceroy with almost unlimited power. The Aher episode is

strangely out of place in 3 Enoch, a book dedicated to the fabulous ascent of a human being to the highest power in heaven.

AKATRIEL

Another enigmatic figure, with the name Akatriel, appears only in the Bavli and the Hekhalot literature. The name seems to be derived from *keter*, "crown," but it is unclear whether it refers to God himself or to a high angel. I begin with the version of the Bavli:

> What does he [God] pray?
> Rav Zutra bar Tobi said in the name of Rav: "May it be my will that my mercy may suppress my anger, and that my mercy may prevail over my [other] attributes, so that I may deal with my children according to the attribute of mercy and, on their behalf, stop short of the limit of strict justice."
> It was taught: R. Ishmael b. Elisha said: "I once entered into the innermost part [of the Sanctuary] to offer incense and saw Akatriel *YH*, the Lord of Hosts, seated upon a high and exalted throne."
> He said to me: "Ishmael, my son, praise me!"
> I replied: "May it be your will that your mercy may suppress your anger and your mercy may prevail over your [other] attributes, so that you may deal with your children according to the attribute of mercy and may, on their behalf, stop short of the limit of strict justice!"
> And he nodded to me with his head.[104]

This sugya deals with the question of whether or not God prays. Having answered it affirmatively, it asks what it *is* that God prays. Rav (the well-known Babylonian amora of the first generation) quotes one of God's prayers in which he expresses his hope that his attribute of mercy will prevail over his attribute of justice (both these attributes are said to be in ceaseless conflict with one another within God).[105] This is followed by a Baraitha attributed to R. Ishmael b. Elisha, the no less famous tanna of the second generation who is supposedly of priestly origin (and would become one of the heroes of the Hekhalot literature). In a clearly imagined scene, R. Ishmael acts as the High Priest in the Temple, offering incense in the Holy of Holies (the privilege of the High Priest)—obviously the Temple in Jerusalem, but the text may already be toying with the possibility that he ascended to heaven and in fact entered the Holy of Holies of the heavenly Temple— where he encounters "Akatriel *YH*, the Lord of Hosts, seated upon a high and exalted throne." When Akatriel asks Ishmael to praise him (or to bless him: the Hebrew can mean both), the rabbi/High Priest miraculously repeats the prayer that God himself uses to pray—and Akatriel immediately agrees to accept it.

From the context in which the Baraitha is put, there can be no doubt that for the Bavli editor Akatriel is identical with God: R. Ishmael quotes God's prayer and Akatriel, that is, God, graciously accepts it.[106] At most one could assert that Ishmael's Baraitha is independent of the Bavli's context, which may well be the case. But even then it would be extremely hard to argue in favor of Akatriel as a second divine power in heaven. While one could point to the fact that—at least in the Hekhalot literature— divine epithets such as listed here might be applied to certain particularly high angels, the expression "seated upon a high and exalted throne" is apparently a quotation from Isaiah 6:1 and hence refers to God alone. Furthermore, the divine attributes of mercy and justice are reserved solely for God, and nowhere in the rabbinic and the Hekhalot literature are they applied to certain angels.

The Bavli sugya appears almost verbatim in the Hekhalot literature as part of Hekhalot Rabbati,[107] but only in the New York manuscript and hence is most likely a quotation from the Bavli (and not the Bavli *Vorlage*).[108] That Akatriel is identical with God would also seem to be presupposed, however, in other Hekhalot texts. In the so-called Aggadat R. Ishmael, an originally independent brief apocalypse about Israel's redemption that was integrated in Hekhalot Rabbati,[109] "Akatriel *YH*, the Lord, the God of Hosts" reveals the destiny of Israel to R. Ishmael, and this Akatriel is doubtless God himself and not some angel. In the macroform Hekhalot Zutarti the "Prince of the Countenance" (probably Metatron) is adjured by certain names, among them Akatriel, which are obviously names for God: the name Akatriel is "sealed upon the crown and engraved upon his throne."[110] The same is true of a late appendix to 3 Enoch, which appears in a group of three Ashkenazi manuscripts[111] and is clearly influenced by Eleazar of Worms' Sodei Razayya,[112] as well as in a macroform that has been integrated (under the title *Hilkhot Metatron*) in Sodei Razzaya.[113] It is not published in the *Synopse zur Hekhalot-Literatur* but included in Odeberg's edition and Alexander's translation of 3 Enoch (as ch. 15B).[114] There, it is part of the tradition of Moses' ascent to heaven: the angels, with Metatron, the "Prince of the Countenance" in their vanguard, receive the prayers of Israel and place them as a crown on the head of God. Hearing Israel's prayers, Akatriel *YH* answers and commands Metatron to listen to Moses' prayer and to fulfill every request that he makes "of me"—here, Akatriel is clearly God and at the same time oddly distinct from God.

Yet things become ever more complicated if we consider another version of R. Ishmael's encounter with Akatriel. This version is preserved in a passage appended to the macroform

Ma'aśeh Merkavah under the title "The Mystery of Sandalfon" (*razo shel Sandalfon*):

> Elisha b. Avuyah said: "When I ascended to the *pardes* I beheld Akatriel *YH*, the Lord of Hosts, who sits at the entrance to the *pardes*, and 120 myriads of ministering angels surround him, as it is said: 'Thousands upon thousands served him and myriads upon myriads, etc. [stood attending him]' (Dan. 7:10). When I saw them I was alarmed and startled and pulled myself together and entered before the Holy One, blessed be he."
>
> I said before him: "Lord of the world, you wrote in your Torah: 'Behold, to the Lord, your God, belong heaven and the heaven of heavens, etc.' (Deut. 10:14). And it is written: '[The heavens are telling the glory of God,] and the firmament (*raqia'*) declares the work of his hands' (Ps. 19:2)—one alone!"
>
> He said to me: "Elisha, my son, have you perhaps come in order to reflect upon my mysteries (*middotai*)?[115] Have you not heard the parable that human beings apply?"[116]

This is a unique text. It is clearly an adaptation of Ishmael's encounter with Akatriel, but Ishmael has turned into Elisha b. Avuyah—that is, the arch-heretic Aher—and Akatriel has turned into an angel. In other words, the Ishmael story has emerged as a new version of Aher's ascent to heaven and his encounter with Metatron. There can be no doubt that "Akatriel *YH*, the Lord of Hosts" is now Metatron: he does not sit in the heavenly throne room but at the entrance to the highest heaven (here called *pardes*, alluding to the story of the four rabbis who entered *pardes*), and Aher proceeds from him to the Holy One, blessed be he, namely, God. Hence, God and Akatriel/Metatron are definitely two distinct beings. As in the Aher story, Metatron sits on his throne, but he is quite unapologetic about it here, and there is no hint whatsoever that he is going to be punished for his behavior. On the contrary, he is served by Daniel's thousands and myriads of angels—the same angels that (in Dan. 7) serve the Ancient of Days, that is, God! Hence, the angel Akatriel is endowed with the same attributes that in Daniel and elsewhere are solely reserved for God.

As in the Bavli and the 3 Enoch versions of his ascent,[117] Aher can only conclude from the sight of Akatriel that there are two powers in heaven; but, unlike what happens in the Bavli and 3 Enoch versions, he doesn't approve of this conclusion (and doesn't become a heretic). On the contrary—startled and astonished by what he sees—he bravely reproaches God for provoking, with Akatriel's enthronement, the misleading impression of two powers in heaven, namely, God and Akatriel/Metatron. This impression is misleading and wrong, he argues before God, because it contradicts God's own Torah, which declares that the heavens belong to God and proclaim his glory. The strangely added "one alone" clearly means that there is one God alone and that an observer (such as Aher) would not expect two divinities in heaven. Yet God punishes neither the angel nor Aher; rather, he reproaches Aher by telling him that it is not his business to reflect upon God's mysteries. And that's where the story ends. Unfortunately, both manuscripts break off here (it follows the new macroform Harba de-Moshe, "The Sword of Moses").[118]

So what we have here is a tradition regarding the highest angel Akatriel-Metatron, who sits at the entrance to the divine throne room and conveys the impression of a second divinity. He is most definitely not God, since the Merkavah mystic (Aher) manages to continue his heavenly journey and attain to God himself; but his appearance is powerful enough to confuse Aher and cause him to express his confusion before God, who slaps down his curiosity. Although the parable that God promises to quote is missing—or else deliberately omitted—we are safe to assume that it was meant to illustrate that it is inappropriate for human beings to reflect upon such mysteries. Unfortunately, it is impossible to date this episode; most likely, it is an originally independent microform whose provenance and date of origin are unknown. What we do know, however, is that it is part of the Hekhalot literature and the later Metatron traditions, as we encounter them only in the Bavli and the Hekhalot literature. It offers a radically new interpretation of Aher's ascent to heaven. Whereas the versions in the Bavli and 3 Enoch presuppose yet sharply *criticize* the notion of a second, (quasi-)divine power in heaven, our episode betrays no critique of any such heavenly figure—on the contrary, if my interpretation of God's answer to Elisha b. Avuyah is correct, it *confirms* this idea and repudiates the rabbinic critique. Like 3 Enoch it reflects groups that were apparently drawn into the bold idea of a second (younger?) God next to the God of the Hebrew Bible.

Finally, we must give consideration to a microform, incorporated in Hekhalot Rabbati[119] and Merkavah Rabbah,[120] in which R. Nehunya b. Haqanah adjures R. Ishmael with the "great seal" and the "great oath" to protect him from forgetting the Torah. In sections 279 (Hekhalot Rabbati) and 678 (Merkavah Rabbah) the "great seal" and "great oath" are presented as belonging to

"Zebudiel,[121] the Lord (*YHWH*), the God of Israel, and this is (*we-ze hu*) Metatron, the Lord (*YHWH*), the God of Israel, God of heaven and God of earth, God of gods, God of the sea and God of the mainland."

In the slightly different version in section 309 (Pereq R. Nehunya b. Haqanah) it is said that R. Ishmael is adjured "with his [Nehunya b. Haqanah's] great seal, with Zebudiel, the Lord (*YH*), with Akatriel, the Lord (*YH*) in heaven and on earth," and the following paragraph (§ 310) states explicitly that Metatron bears the names "Ziwutiel, the servant (*'eved*), Zebudiel, the Lord (*YH*), and Akatriel, the Lord (*YWY*), the God of Israel." If one takes this passage at face value, it could easily be argued that Metatron is identified as God; in other words, that Metatron-Akatriel appears here as a second God. But I doubt that things are so simple. First of all, we have seen that Akatriel can be used unequivocally as a name for God; it could be possible, therefore, that Metatron infiltrated the adjuration through Akatriel, which became one of Metatron's names. Second, and more important, what does it mean that certain angelic names receive the divine epithet *YH* or *YHWH* or *YWY*? Does it really mean that these angels are identified with God in the sense that they become divine figures next to and on an equal footing with God? I don't think so. If we take this view, we would perforce need to conclude that wherever in the Hekhalot literature divine epithets are attached to angelic names, these angels are elevated to divine status. But since this is quite common—see, for example, the names of the guardian angels attending the ascent and descent of the Merkavah mystic,[122] which all bear the epithet *YHWH*, or the angels in 3 Enoch,[123] who all bear the epithet *YWY*—we would arrive at an enormous number of deified angels in heaven.

Instead of seeing in the Merkavah Rabbah and Hekhalot Rabbati passages another indication of Metatron-Akatriel's infiltration into the divine realm, it would seem much more plausible to regard the angelic-divine names with divine epithets as just one more indication that the boundaries between God and his angels in the Hekhalot literature—or, to be more precise, in certain strata of the Hekhalot literature—become fluid and that we cannot always decide with certainty whether God or his angels are meant. Yet the fact that names of angels are interchangeable with divine names and vice versa does not mean that the angels *become* God. As the "Mystery of Sandalfon" in particular demonstrates, there is clear evidence indeed that Metatron was on his way to becoming a second divine power—but this development does not hinge on whether he is granted divine epithets or not.[124]

METATRON IN BABYLONIA

Our survey of the Palestinian and Babylonian Metatron traditions yields a very clear finding. First, most if not all of the unquestionable Metatron traditions—that is, traditions referring to the angel Metatron as a potential divine or semidivine being threatening the unique position of God in heaven—appear only in the Bavli and the Hekhalot literature. There may have been certain such ideas in embryo in the Palestinian sources, but these remain vague and obscure—if they are not in fact later Babylonian adaptations of Palestinian traditions that originally had nothing to do with the Bavli's and the Hekhalot literature's Metatron. If this indeed be the case, the traditions that grew up around the angel Metatron lead us unequivocally and conspicuously into the cultural climate of Babylonian Judaism.[125] It is the worldview of Babylonian—not Palestinian—Jewry that casts the idea of a divine vice-regent or co-ruler into the figure of Enoch-Iaoel-Michael-Metatron-Akatriel, that exceptional human being who ascended to heaven and was transformed into the "Lesser *YHWH*."[126]

Evidence for the Babylonian provenance of the Metatron traditions is bolstered by the fact that Metatron is mentioned on quite a surprising number of Babylonian incantation bowls.[127] The incantation bowls are burned from clay with inscriptions in Aramaic that are arranged in a circle on the bowls' inner surface. These inscriptions mention the magical-apotropaic purpose of the bowls; most frequently they are concerned with the protection of the owner's family, his house, or his property, or with fending off demons, sometimes also with the use of love magic, or with just how to inflict damage on an enemy. The bowls were turned upside down (that is, with the opening down) and buried in the ground, or they were set into the foundations of the house—most likely to trap demons and keep them imprisoned in the bowl. Many such bowls were commissioned by Jews in Sassanian Babylonia and can be dated between the sixth and eighth centuries C.E., that is, at the time of the Babylonian Talmud.

The most common title assigned to Metatron on the bowls is "the Great Prince" (*sara rabba* or *iśra rabba*), a title, however, that rarely appears in the Hekhalot literature (most prominently in section 376, where Metatron is called "the beloved servant" [*shamsha rehima*] and "the Great Prince of the testimony" [*sara rabba de-sahaduta*]).[128] This title is frequently augmented with other epithets, such as "the Great Prince of his (that is, God's) throne" (*isra rabba de-kurseh*),[129] "the Great Prince of the entire world" (*isra rabba de-khulleh 'alma*)[130]—which is, of course, reminiscent of the "Prince of the World" in the Bavli[131]—or "the Great Prince (*sara rabba*), who is called the great healer (*asya rabba*) of mercies."[132]

A much-discussed example is a bowl found in Nippur and published for the first time by James Montgomery,[133] who dates all these Nippur bowls to no later than the beginning of the seventh century.[134] There, Metatron appears among certain angels—who are invoked in order to bring healing (*asuta*) to the bowl's clients—and is assigned the epithet *YH*, that is, the (abbreviated) tetragrammaton,[135] similar to Akatriel in the "Mystery of Sandalfon."[136] Rebecca Lesses has argued that the bowl text echoes a "Hekhalot incantation of Metatron embedded within another incantation for healing and protection" and that the "author of this bowl text may have known of the Hekhalot text that explicitly links the names of Metatron with healing."[137] The implicit knowledge of Hekhalot texts by the authors of bowl texts is an intriguing suggestion, but when Lesses (following

Martin Cohen and Philip Alexander) concludes that Metatron is here identified with the God of Israel[138]—owing to the circumstance that the bowl text and the Hekhalot incantation on which it is presumably based attaches the epithet *YH* to Metatron's name—her reach unfortunately exceeds her grasp. As I have demonstrated above, there is nothing uncommon about angelic names (not only the name of Metatron) being coupled with the tetragrammaton; but this can hardly be used as proof that Metatron appears on the bowl as a "second God."[139] The significance of this bowl and the other incantation bowls mentioning Metatron lies in the fact that the bowls apparently draw from the same pool that also feeds the Metatron passages in the Bavli and 3 Enoch or, to put it differently, the ideas inscribed on the incantation bowls, which are criticized in the Bavli and which come to the fore most prominently in 3 Enoch and in the "Mystery of Sandalfon"—these ideas must be seen and evaluated together, since they would seem to be part and parcel of the same circles.

The spiritual home of these circles is Babylonia, not Palestine.[140] We are now in the heartland of Sassanian Mesopotamia and chronologically clearly *after* the dogmatic decisions of Nicaea (325), Constantinople (381), and Chalcedon (451). The Jews of the Babylonian academies of the sixth and seventh centuries lived under completely different conditions than their fellow Jews under Roman and Byzantine dominion. They were a minority in the Sassanian Empire, but—in comparison to the Christians—a rather privileged minority. They could afford, without running the risk of being persecuted by Christian rulers (in the Sassanian Empire Christians, not Jews, were persecuted), to aggressively advocate their faith in opposition to the Christians—and they did indeed exploit this possibility, as we know from other sources.[141]

METATRON AND CHRISTIANITY

The Bavli's and Hekhalot literature's image of Metatron as a potential second divinity is ambiguous, wavering between a highly critical and an affirmative attitude. But even the critical approach can hardly conceal the fact that certain (Jewish) circles in Babylonia must have fancied the idea of a second divine power next to God. More precisely, it appears that with the figure of Metatron certain Jews in Babylonia in particular found a vehicle for entertaining—in a remarkably pronounced and undisguised way—ideas that seem to have been unparalleled in other (Palestinian) sources.[142] Why were these ideas perceived as so dangerous that they needed to be attacked in the Bavli and even toned down in 3 Enoch? In what follows I will attempt to situate these ideas in the context of the intricate tangle of the two sister religions "Judaism" and "Christianity," emerging in the first centuries C.E., interacting with and responding to each other, and gradually becoming ever more differentiated in the course of time.

There can be little doubt that pre-Christian Judaism developed ideas that helped pave the way to a "binitarian" theology—cases in point are speculations about Logos and Wisdom, certain angelic figures, Adam as the original *makro-anthropos*, and other exalted human figures[143]—of which the early New Testament speculations about the Logos Jesus are but one particularly prominent example. The Metatron traditions, as part of the larger Messiah–Son of Man complex, clearly belong to this store of potentially powerful and dangerous ideas, as several scholars have observed. But the problem is where precisely to place them among this illustrious company. Most scholars take it for granted that the Metatron of 3 Enoch—not only with regard to its content but also chronologically—is the legitimate albeit youngest child of the Second Temple Enoch literature. This fateful view was inaugurated when Hugo Odeberg called his influential edition *3 Enoch or The Hebrew Book of Enoch* (published Cambridge 1928), and it was cemented when 3 Enoch was included—as "3 (Hebrew Apocalypse of) Enoch"—in James Charlesworth's *Old Testament Pseudepigrapha*, and there immediately following 1 and 2 Enoch. It is in this scholarly tradition that 3 Enoch can be treated unabashedly and without any further ado *after* 1 and 2 Enoch and *before* the Qumran texts and all the other relevant apocalypses—and as recently as in a book published in 2007, namely, Andrew Chester's *Messiah and Exaltation*. Here is Chester's justification, which deserves to be quoted verbatim:

> Very great caution is needed in discussion of 3 Enoch, of course, not least because of problems with dating and with relating the different pieces of tradition to each other. In contrast to the view that it represents a late stage of the Hekhalot tradition, however, it has been argued with some plausibility that it is in important respects different from the other Hekhalot traditions, and stands much closer to those found in apocalyptic texts.[144]

This is a highly revealing passage. First, Chester makes clear that he is aware of the problems of dating and literary structure of 3 Enoch. But then, with a stroke of the pen, he ignores such reservations and simply declares that 3 Enoch, because it is different from the other Hekhalot traditions and stands closer to the apocalyptic texts, cannot be dated to a late stage of the Hekhalot literature (which, as a footnote discloses, is my position). No one wishes to dispute the latter claim (that 3 Enoch is different from the other Hekhalot writings and has greater affinity with the apocalyptic tradition)—on the contrary; but to conclude from this that 3 Enoch must be early means to confuse arguments of style and content with those of provenance and date. With the same justification, one could claim, for example, that apocalypses such as the apocalypse of Zerubavel or of Elijah need to be integrated into the early Jewish apocalyptic literature.

I have singled out Chester's strategy with regard to 3 Enoch because it is symptomatic of a tendency prevalent in modern scholarship to mix texts and ideas into one big meat loaf just because of some real or imaginary resemblance. After the ingredients are baked—or only half-baked—they all taste the same. Contrary to this trend, I wish to insist on the peculiarities of time and place and assess the specific way in which the Bavli and 3 Enoch conceive the figure of Metatron within the chronological and geographical framework of Babylonian Judaism—that is, in terms of time, of the sixth or seventh century (or even later). At this stage of history the Christian doctrine of the trinity was fully developed—with its last stage coming at the Council of Chalcedon (451 C.E.), which maintained the full humanity and divinity of Jesus (as opposed to ascribing to Jesus just one nature, divine and not human) and which brought about the schism of the so-called Oriental Orthodoxy. Therefore, it seems unlikely that the Jewish concept of Metatron as the *YHWH ha-qatan* exerted any influence on the emergence and crystallization of the Christian doctrine—a possibility that Christoph Markschies recently mapped out as an important avenue of future research;[145] in fact, quite the opposite. Instead of regarding 3 Enoch's Metatron as part of the fabric from which the doctrine of the trinity was woven (and even less so as part of the fabric from which the New Testament Jesus was fashioned), we do better to understand the figure of Metatron as an *answer* to the New Testament's message of Jesus Christ.[146] Not only was the New Testament—presumably in its Syriac translation, the Diatessaron and/or the Syriac Peshitta—in all probability known to the Babylonian Jews;[147] it is moreover quite plausible that the latter, if not fully aware of all the intricacies of the trinitarian debate, were at least familiar with some of its basics. Travers Herford refers to the opening passage of the Epistle to the Hebrews:[148]

> (1:1) Long ago God spoke to our ancestors in many and
>   various ways by the prophets,
> (2) but in these last days he has spoken to us by a/the Son,
> whom he appointed heir of all things,
> through whom he also created the worlds (*epoiēsen tous
>   aiōnas*).
> (3) He is a reflection of God's glory (*apaugasma tēs doxēs*)
> and the exact imprint of God's very being (*charaktēr tēs
>   hypostaseōs autou*),
> and he sustains all things by his powerful word.
> When he had made purification for sins,
> he sat down at the right hand of the majesty on high,
> (4) having become as much superior to angels (*kreittōn
>   genomenos tōn anggelōn*)
> as the name he has inherited is more excellent than
>   theirs.[149]

The Son here is Jesus Christ, who is conceived not only as participating in the creation but also as God's reflection and hypostasis. The language used is reminiscent of the Jewish Wisdom speculation, but whereas Wisdom[150] in Proverbs 8 is just present at the time of creation—yet nevertheless finds "delight with humankind" (Prov. 8:31), and in Sirach 24 is even instructed by God to make her dwelling in Israel (24:8)—the Logos Jesus is the tool through which God created the world: he sustains it and returns to his divine origin after having purified humanity of its sins.[151] That he is the "reflection (*apaugasma*) of God's glory" and the "imprint of his hypostasis" echoes Wisdom of Solomon 7:25–26, where Wisdom is described as "a clear effluence from the glory of the Almighty," the "radiance (*apaugasma*)[152] that streams from everlasting light, the flawless mirror of the active power of God, and the image of his goodness." But at the same time these epithets, in particular the term "hypostasis," foreshadow the Christological debates about the nature of Jesus in relation to his divine Father. Upon his return to heaven, God assigns to Jesus a throne next to him and a special name (presumably the very name of God). Both these qualities mark him as superior to all the angels, and the Epistle to the Hebrews text continues to stress precisely this superiority: God alone calls him "my Son" (v. 5),[153] the angels are asked to worship him (v. 6),[154] his throne is forever (v. 8),[155] he will remain forever (v. 11),[156] and he is asked to sit at God's right hand (v. 13).[157] The similarities of Jesus' exalted position with Metatron's elevation are obvious. What is missing in 3 Enoch, however, is the strong connection with creation. Enoch/Metatron was certainly not created before the creation of the world (as is implied with regard to Jesus in Hebrews), nor was he the tool of God's creation. Yet we should not underestimate the fact that, according to 3 Enoch, God wrote "with his finger, with a pen of flame" on Metatron's crown "the letters by which heaven and earth were created . . . the letters by which all the necessities of the world and all the orders of creation were created."[158] So there is definitely a certain creative power involved in the image of Metatron as well.

Guy Stroumsa has drawn our attention to another notable parallel, the famous hymn in Paul's letter to the Philippians,[159] where it is said of Jesus that he,

> (2:6) though he was in the form of God (*en morphē theou*),
> did not regard equality with God
> as something to be exploited,
> (7) but emptied himself,

taking the form of a servant (*morphēn doulou*),
being born in human likeness.
And being found in human form,
(8) he humbled himself
and became obedient to the point of death—
even death on a cross.
(9) Therefore God also highly exalted him (*hyperypsōsen*)
and bestowed on him the name
that is above every name (*to onoma to hyper pan onoma*),
(10) so that at the name of Jesus
every knee should bend,
in heaven and on earth and under the earth,
(11) and every tongue should confess
that Jesus Christ is Lord,
to the glory of God the father.[160]

If we read this text in light of the Metatron traditions in 3 Enoch, some striking parallels emerge—as well as some differences. Christ, though conceived in the "form of God," did not insist on his equality with God but rather assumed the "form of a servant [or slave]" and hence of a human being. After he died, God exalted him, that is, raised him from the dead, gave him the name "above every name," whereupon all heavenly and earthly beings worshiped him and acknowledged him as the "Lord." The movement here is from the top down (from Christ's divine existence to his human form) and then again from the bottom up (from his human existence back to his original divine form). The latter movement is caused by God, exalting Jesus after his death and bestowing on him the most powerful name, that is, the name of the Lord. In Metatron's case there is only one movement, from the bottom up: he begins as a human being who, however, does not die (and certainly not such a shameful death as Jesus died on the cross) but is exalted by God upward to heaven so as to assume there his angelic and almost divine function as God's deputy and viceroy, appearing in the form and with the attributes of God, bearing God's name, and being worshiped by the angels. Ironically, it is in this state that he is called, together with the name of God (*YHWH ha-qatan*), "servant" (*'eved*). Hence, despite the similarities, the Metatron tradition suggests a dramatic reversal of the New Testament narrative. We do have a Godlike figure, it posits, but this figure did not first originate in heaven and then relinquish his divinity in order to become human; on the contrary, this figure was fully human and was chosen by God to be transformed into a divine being and to assume his function as God's servant and as judge over angels and humans alike.

So, one could ultimately argue that Metatron indeed adopts the role of Jesus Christ, yet without the mythical—and, for the Jewish reader, unacceptable—package deal of Jesus' divine origin and human birth. The savior quality of that divine figure, so dominant in the New Testament, is no doubt also present in the Metatron tradition. The Metatron of 3 Enoch knows, and apparently judges, all the secrets in the hearts of his former fellow humans on earth,[161] and he carries on his crown "the letters by which all the necessities of the world and all the orders of creation were created."[162] And the Metatron of the heretics in the Bavli has the power to pardon human transgression, that is, to forgive sins.[163] This function of Metatron stands in opposition to the traditional pattern of redemption as described in the latter part of 3 Enoch, with God's right arm redeeming Israel and with the appearance of the Messiah.[164] Hence, a certain macroform of 3 Enoch[165] finds it necessary to conclude the book with an account of the traditional messianic expectation, despite the impressive role Metatron plays in it. Yet another macroform, adding paragraphs 71–74,[166] is not content with such an ending and concludes with the seventy names of God[167] that he himself bestows on Metatron:[168]

I [God] took seventy of my names and called him [Metatron] by them, so as to increase his honor. I gave seventy princes into his hand, to issue to them my commandments in every language; to abase the arrogant to the earth at his [Metatron's] word; to elevate the humble to the height at the utterance of his lips; to smite the kings at his command; to subdue rulers and presumptuous men at his bidding; to remove kings from their kingdom, and to exalt rulers over their dominions, as it is written: "He controls the possession of times and seasons; he makes and unmakes kings" (Dan. 2:21).[169]

Here Metatron receives illimitable power on an equal footing with God. This becomes unambiguously clear from the Daniel quotation, where—in the original context—*God* is meant and certainly not an angel. So the anonymous editor who added these paragraphs wished to leave no doubt whatsoever that Metatron assumed the role of co-ruler with God, that he was a second divine figure. When exactly these passages were added is impossible to say (we know very little about the relationship between the macroforms 3 Enoch and Alfa Beta de-Rabbi Aqiva), but even if they are later than some earlier (core) macroform of 3 Enoch, the conspicuous fact remains that someone found it necessary to counterbalance the all too traditional messianic ending of 3 Enoch with this megapowerful Metatron figure.

I conclude by positing that the Metatron of certain circles in the Bavli and in 3 Enoch, against whom the rabbis of the Bavli and the editors of 3 Enoch argue, becomes a Jewish savior figure far beyond the traditional role the Messiah plays in the scenario of redemption and salvation, thus *responding* to the role Jesus plays in Christianity. We do not need Jesus—so contend these circles—and we certainly need not become entangled in that weird and inexplicable net of Christological arcana in which you, the Christians, are caught (although ultimately, this is my argument, they are caught!). Our savior is a human figure who was created but transformed into a divine being,[170] and as such he judges now, together with God (or rather, on his behalf) both heaven and earth. The tension between his task and the task of the traditional Messiah is not really resolved in 3 Enoch, and in a sense one could argue that Metatron has superseded the traditional concept of the Messiah—a result similar to that of the New Testament, where the Messiah has come and yet needs to return. If this interpretation is correct, the new and bold message of 3 Enoch would then be: Our representative in heaven will return to us at the end of time and complete the work of redemption. The ultimate redemption will be accomplished neither by the traditional Messiah nor by God himself but by a savior who is one of us—true man and new God.

5

Has God a Father, a Son, or a Brother?

IF GOD MIGHT HAVE A JUNIOR PARTNER IN HEAVEN, THE question of a divine family arises, one similar to the gods of the Greco-Roman pantheon or, accordingly, the imperial family, with the emperor's son or adoptive son as the most prominent member. Hence it comes as no surprise that a series of midrashim attack the idea that God might be assigned a family and in particular that he should have a son. The most straightforward—and probably earliest—of such exegeses appears in the Yerushalmi:

> [He (King Nebuchadnezzar) answered: "But I see four men unbound, walking in the middle of the fire, and they are not hurt; and the fourth] has the appearance of a divine being (*bar-elahin*, lit. 'son of the gods/God')" (Dan. 3:25).
>
> Reuben said: In that hour, an angel descended and struck that wicked one [Nebuchadnezzar] upon his mouth and said to him: "Amend your words—has he [God] a son (*bar*)?"

He [Nebuchadnezzar] corrected himself and said: "Blessed be the God of Shadrach, Meshach, and Abednego" (Dan. 3:28)—"who has sent his son (*berei*)," is not written here, but "who has sent his angel (*mal'akhei*) and delivered his servants who trusted in him" (Dan. 3:28).[1]

The Reuben who provides this exegesis of Daniel 3:25 seems to be the well-known Aggadah teacher Reuben, a contemporary of Mani I and Yohanan b. Nappaha (second half of the third century C.E.).[2] Its hero is the wicked king Nebuchadnezzar, destroyer of Jerusalem and the First Temple, who mistakes the angel in the furnace—sent by God to protect Shadrach, Meshach, and Abednego—for a divine being (reading *bar-elahin* literally as "son of the gods" or "son of God"). Another angel makes sure that he immediately corrects himself: when the furnace is opened and the three victims of the king's rage leave it unharmed, Nebuchadnezzar himself praises their God (the Jewish God) for sending his angel to protect his servants. Ironically, his praise turns into a proper rabbinic exegesis, correctly arguing that the Bible speaks of God's angel (*mal'akh*) but not his son (*bar*). Accordingly, we cannot conclude from Daniel 3:25 that the Jewish God has a son whom he sends down to earth to protect his followers.

It is no coincidence that Nebuchadnezzar hatches the idea of God having a son. The Aggadah lists him among the infamous kings who, in their hubris, declared themselves god (the other kings are Hiram, Pharaoh, and Sanherib). In Nebuchadnezzar's case, his claim to be like God is derived from Isaiah 14:13f.: "You said in your heart: I will ascend to heaven; I will raise my throne above the stars of God. I will ascend above the heights of the clouds; I will be like the Most High"—whereupon the Bible, that is, God, replies: "Yet you shall be brought down to She'ol, to the uttermost parts of the pit" (Isa. 14:15).[3] It has been argued, quite convincingly, that the midrashim against Nebuchadnezzar's hubris reflect a polemic against Rome, in particular against its cult of the emperor.[4] Then the biblical Nebuchadnezzar would perforce embody and prefigure the hubris of the Roman emperors who, in their vanity, claim to have ascended to heaven and become the deified personification of the empire. Yet our midrash in the Yerushalmi goes in a different direction. It is not concerned with Nebuchadnezzar's claim to divinity but with his misguided attempt to insinuate that God has a son. To be sure, such an idea might also be explained within the context of the Roman imperial system—like any other emperor, God has a son (biological or adopted) who is destined to become his successor—but this hardly accounts for the utter rage entailed in God's reaction to Nebuchadnezzar's misperception. Nebuchadnezzar's insinuation that God might have a son must have struck a more sensitive nerve—and the most likely candidate for this nerve would seem to have been Christianity's Jesus with his claim to be the Son of God and to have ascended to heaven to take his seat on a throne next to that of his Father. Unlike the angel in Daniel, this Son of God has indeed been sent to earth, albeit not to rescue just Shadrach, Meshach, and Abednego from a furnace but the entire people of Israel. In short, it is more likely this Christian claim against which our midrash in the Yerushalmi argues.[5]

A few Palestinian midrashim raise the same issue. The first pertinent midrash can be found in Shemot Rabba on the beginning of the Decalogue (Ex. 20:2):

Another explanation of "I am the Lord your God" (Ex. 20:2).

R. Abbahu said: A parable of a human king—he may rule, but he has a father or a brother; yet the Holy One,

Blessed be he, said: I am not thus; "I am the first" (Isa. 44:6), for I have no father, "and I am the last" (ibid.), for I have no brother, "and besides me there is no God" (ibid.), for I have no son.[6]

R. Abbahu—the Palestinian amora of the third generation and head of the academy of Caesarea, well known for his debates with heretics (d. ca. 300 C.E.)—applies the verse Isaiah 44:6 to God's alleged family. This verse was used in the Mekhilta to prove that God, despite his various manifestations throughout Israel's history, always remained the same.[7] Now it is employed to parry the idea of a divine dynasty, similar to the dynasty of human emperors (no doubt Roman ones). Unlike a human imperial dynasty, R. Abbahu argues, the Jewish God has neither father nor brother nor son; he is not only always the same God but also has no rival—be it brother or son—who might dispute his claim to legitimate sovereignty. Here we find ourselves again within the context of the Roman imperial hierarchy, which could easily be combined with polytheistic as well as Christological ideas. These concepts overlap and influence each other, and hence it is fruitless to play off one against the other.[8] But since R. Abbahu's exegesis of Isaiah 44:6 starts with "father" and climaxes in "son," a Christological tinge to the underlying debate would indeed seem plausible.

A similar interpretation is preserved in the Midrash Deuteronomy Rabba, a homily about Deuteronomy 6:4 and Proverbs 24:21:

Another explanation: "Hear, O Israel, the Lord is our God, the Lord alone (*YHWH ehad*)"[9] (Deut. 6:4). This bears out what Scripture says: "My son, fear the Lord and the king, etc. [and do not associate with those who change (*shonim*)]" (Prov. 24:21). . . .

Another explanation: What is the meaning of: "and the king" (Prov. 24:21)? Make him [God] king over you.

"And do not associate with those who change (*shonim*)" (Prov. ibid.): Do not associate with those who declare that there is a second god (*eloha sheni*).

R. Yehudah bar Shim'on said: [Scripture says:] "In the whole land, says the Lord, two parts (*pi-shenayim*) therein shall be cut off and perish" (Zech. 13:8). [This means:] the mouths (*ha-piyyot*) that declare that there are two powers (*shetei rashuyyot*) shall be cut off and perish.

And who will survive in the future? "And the third (part) shall be left therein" (ibid.). This refers to Israel who are termed "thirds," for they are threefold, (namely,) priests, Levites, and Israelites; and they are descended from three Patriarchs, (namely,) Abraham, Isaac, and Jacob.

Another explanation: Because they praise the Holy One, Blessed be he, with the threefold expression of holiness, "Holy, holy, holy" (Isa. 6:3).

R. Aha said: God was angry with Solomon when he uttered the above verse.

He said to him: Why do you express a thing that concerns the sanctification [of my name] by an obscure allusion (*notariqon*) [in the words:] "And do not associate with those who change (*shonim*)"? (Prov. 24:21). Thereupon [Solomon] immediately expressed it more clearly [in the words:] "There is one that is alone (*ehad*), and he has not a second (*sheni*); he has neither son nor brother" (Eccl. 4:8)—he has neither son nor brother, but: "Hear, O Israel, the Lord is our God, the Lord alone (*YHWH ehad*)"[10] (Deut. 6:4).[11]

This homily plays with the meaning of the word *shonim* in Proverbs 24:21, which—in an anonymous interpretation—is explained as alluding to *sheni*, a "second" divine power. Hence the verse is understood as "Make only God, the Lord, king over you and do not associate (or dally) with those heretics who introduce a second god into the divine pantheon." To this, R. Yehudah bar Shim'on (a Palestinian amora of the fourth generation in Lydda, first half of the fourth century C.E.) adds another exegesis that plays with the same root: *pi-shenayim* in Zechariah 13:8 is translated literally as "the mouth of two," that is, those "mouths" which declare that there are "two" powers in heaven—they shall be cut off from the people of Israel and perish forever. Only the third part—that is, the part that does not propagate the belief in two powers—will remain in the land: the true Israel that is divided into the three groups of priests, Levites, and Israelites and which is the legitimate descendant of Abraham, Isaac, and Jacob (= Israel). Only they, as another anonymous explanation adds, praise God with the genuine trisagion of Isaiah 6:3.

Finally, R. Aha—a contemporary of Yehudah bar Shim'on, who flourished in Lydda and Tiberias—has God rebuke Solomon for producing a verse in the Book of Proverbs that is prone to such a dangerous misreading (that God himself inspired Solomon with the Book of Proverbs does not faze our author). Thereupon Solomon immediately sets the record straight and comes up with a better verse from another divinely inspired book—of all biblical books, the controversial Book of Ecclesiastes—which states unambiguously that God is indeed the one and only God, with no second god (son or brother) beside him. The *ehad* of this verse (Eccl. 4:8) refers perfectly back to the *ehad* of Deuteronomy 6:4.

Again, the heresy of the "second god" (son or brother) can be easily integrated, as scholars have observed, into any kind of "polytheistic," "dualistic," or "Christian" system. Segal, for instance, entertains the possibility of a reference to the Persian religion, "where the good and evil inclinations were sometimes conceived as twin brothers," but ultimately opts for a "response to Christian or gnostic doctrine, even if there is no firm evidence for deciding between the two."[12] Maier, on the other hand, flatly denies any Christological background to our text, a possibility that he wishes to reserve solely for much later midrashim, which, "in their relatively articulate polemics," belong to the early Middle Ages.[13] The dualistic—Persian or gnostic or other—separation between a good and evil god is highly unlikely here, since our midrash does not allude to the question of good and evil; although it makes little sense to try to distinguish neatly between "Christian" and "gnostic" ideas, the dualism between good and evil, so characteristic of gnostic systems, is completely absent here. Within the spectrum of possible references and cross-references, the most plausible one is still that our authors are indeed responding to Christian ideas. This holds true, first of all, for the exposed position of the son in our midrash. (I would posit that the brother is secondary and primarily makes an appearance because he is mentioned, together with the son, in Eccl. 4:8.) But there is more. The quotation of Zechariah 13:8, alluding to the "land" and to the two parts of the people who will be cut off from the land (the heretics) with the third part that will remain (the true Israel), may well indicate the dispute between Christians and Jews regarding the legitimate ownership of the Land of Israel. Against the Christian claim to ownership—as the new covenant, which has superseded the old covenant of the Jews—our midrash makes clear that in fact these Christian heretics, who wish to install Jesus as a second god and who maintain that they have inherited the land from the Jews, will be forever expelled from the land. The Land of Israel belonged to the people of Israel in the past—and it will belong to the true Israel (the remnant of Israel) in the future. The priests, Levites, and Israelites, who constitute this true Israel, are the descendants of Abraham, Isaac, and Jacob, that is, the Israel by blood and not the Israel by faith. Accordingly, it is not the new trisagion of the Christians—the Sanctus—but the old trisagion of the Jews that is the genuine trisagion.

The last relevant example to be discussed in this context is a midrash that expands on the subject of God's various manifestations as a war hero and an old man, as discussed above.[14] A homily in Pesiqta Rabbati combines the verse Exodus 20:2 ("I am the Lord your God") with the verse Deuteronomy 5:4 ("The Lord spoke with you [the people of Israel] face to face at the mountain"). The midrash understands the phrase "face to face" (*panim be-fanim*)—originally referring to a direct, "face to face" encounter between God and his people—as "face after face," that is, in various guises and appearances. First, R. Levi (a third-generation Palestinian amora) applies God's various guises to his appearance as a young man (the war hero at the Red Sea) and an old man (on Mount Sinai when he gave the Torah to Israel). To this familiar interpretation R. Hiyya bar Abba (presumably Hiyya II bar Abba, a contemporary of R. Levi; beginning of the fourth century C.E.) adds the following illustration:[15]

> If the whore's son (*bera di-zeneta*) tells you: "These [different guises] are two gods," answer him:
> "I am the one from the sea, and I am the one from Sinai."

This is followed by another interpretation by R. Levi, which takes "face after face" as literally meaning that God appeared to the people of Israel with many faces: a threatening face, a severe face, an angry face, a joyous face, a laughing face, and a friendly face. And again, R. Hiyya bar Abba adds yet a further clarification:

> If the whore's son tells you: "These [different faces] are two gods," answer him:

"It is not written here [in Deut. 5:4]: 'Gods spoke (*dibberu Elohim*)[16] [to you] face after face,' but 'The Lord spoke (*dibber YHWH*)[17] [to you] face after face on the mountain.'"[18]

R. Hiyya bar Abba's answers are routine: different guises and different faces of God do not imply that there is more than one God; in particular, the recourse to a philological argument (the verb attached to "God" appears in the singular and not in the plural) is standard procedure in such debates. This would suggest that our rabbi is polemicizing against certain polytheistic ideas familiar from the Roman pantheon. But conspicuously, he does not argue against *many* gods but very precisely against *two* gods. The usual suspects for this belief in two gods in the relevant research literature are, as always, Gnosticism and Christianity.[19] Maier, in his attempt to purify the rabbinic tradition of all anti-Christian implications,[20] prefers an antignostic impetus as the lesser evil.[21]

Yet again, I don't find the clear-cut distinction between "Christianity" and "Gnosticism" particularly illuminating. If we want to argue in favor of a peculiarly gnostic brand of Christianity, we would expect at least a hint of the good god versus evil god (the demiurge) dualism, but such a dualistic concept is completely missing. So "Christianity," in the sense of a Father-God and a Son-God, is still the most likely candidate for our rabbi's ire. Moreover, the fact that the heretic is introduced as the "son of a/the whore" sounds, as I have argued elsewhere,[22] suspiciously like Jesus himself is speaking: that Jesus was born of a whore is the notorious rabbinic answer to the Christian claim of his virgin birth.[23] True, as Maier reminds us, the introductory phrase "if the whore's son" (that is, the son of the whore) can also be translated "if a whore's son" (that is, *a* son of *a* whore), hence referring not to Jesus but to any heretic.[24] But the phrase "son of the whore" is so unusual[25]—and the designation of Jesus' mother as a whore so well known—that the attempt to apply it to some heretic instead of to Jesus smacks of apologia. And the fact that the binitarian Christian doctrine of a Father-God and Son-God is placed in the mouth of Jesus himself is certainly not as strange as Maier would have us believe.[26] The New Testament problem of whether or not the *historical* Jesus claimed to be the Son of God is completely irrelevant here. Our rabbinic midrash does not reflect questions of New Testament scholarship—for the rabbis it was doubtless not just some crazy Christian theologians who regarded Jesus as God's Son and hence a second God, but Jesus himself who laid claim to this scandalous privilege.

In sum, the (primarily Palestinian) midrashim discussing God's family background are nevertheless mainly concerned with the relationship between God and his Son. They most likely reflect the rabbinic discourse with the nascent Christology that in turn was informed by the power structure of the Roman Empire, that is, we again encounter the dynamic triangle of "Romans," "Christians," and "rabbis" as mutually overlapping "factors." The Palestinian coloring provides an added dimension in terms of the power struggle over the question as to who is true heir of the Land of Israel—the Christians or the Jews, that is, the people of the new or the old covenant.

The Angels

In analyzing Metatron's peculiar function as a possible younger partner within the divine configuration, we touched upon the relationship between God and his angels. After all, despite—or because of?—his human origin, Metatron became the highest angel in God's celestial household. But the question of how the angels relate to God, their creator, is a much broader one that has been extensively discussed in rabbinic Judaism. In this chapter I will resume a discussion that I began more than thirty years ago in my book *Rivalität zwischen Engeln und Menschen: Untersuchungen zur rabbinischen Engelvorstellung*,[1] with special emphasis, of course, on the problem of how the angels may be regarded as impinging on God's sovereignty.

When Were the Angels Created?

The first question that attracted the attention of the rabbis was that of when precisely the angels were created. The biblical creation story does not bother to include the angels in God's work of creation; as a matter of fact, they make their appearance in the course of the biblical narrative only very gradually, with unclear functions and even an unclear division of labor between God and his angels. It is questionable, for example, who the "sons of God" (*benei ha-Elohim*) were that descended to earth and begat children with the daughters of humans (Gen. 6). And the "angel of the Lord" (*mal'akh YHWH*), who is first mentioned in Genesis 16:7 as appearing to Hagar, seems not to be an angel in the common sense of the word but God himself in his earthly manifestation.[2] Similarly, the identity of the "three men" (*anashim*) appearing to Abraham in Genesis 18 is uncertain. The chapter begins with the unequivocal statement that "the Lord" (*YHWH*) appeared to Abraham by the oaks of Mamre (18:1), but when Abraham looks up, he sees "three men" (18:2). Later in the story "they" not only speak to Abraham (v. 9), but just one of them addresses the patriarch as well, in the singular (v. 10), as does even "the Lord" himself (v. 13). Adding to the confusion, when the punishment of Sodom is effected, "the men" go to Sodom together with Abraham (v. 16), but "the Lord" speaks to him (v. 17)—as if God is one of the three "men,"[3] who, in the next chapter (19:1), to complete our confoundment, become "two angels" (*mal'akhim*). We encountered the same problem in Exodus 23:20ff., where the demarcation between God and his angel is equally unclear.[4]

But the Hebrew Bible is full of angels in the capacity of God's royal household, his messengers, and not least as attendants to his throne (e.g., the Seraphs of Isa. 6:2 and the holy creatures of Ezek. 1, who bear the divine throne). They are physically closest to God, as close as any created being can get—for created they are: the rabbis leave no doubt that the angels are God's creatures and not some preexistent beings on an equal plane with him. The following midrash fills in the lacuna left by the Bible with regard to the day on which the angels were created:

When were the angels created?

R. Yohanan said: They were created on the second day, as it is written: "Who set the beams of his upper chambers in the waters, etc." (Ps. 104:3), followed by: "Who made the winds his angels" (Ps. 104:4).

R. Hanina said: They were created on the fifth day, as it is written: "And let birds fly (*ye'ofef*) above the earth" (Gen. 1:20), and it is written, "And with two he [the Seraph] did fly (*ye'ofef*)" (Isa. 6:2).

R. Luliani b. Tabri said in the name of R. Yitzhaq: Whether we accept the view of R. Hanina or that of R. Yohanan, all agree that none were created on the first day, lest you should say: Michael stretched out [the heaven] in the south and Gabriel in the north, while the Holy One, blessed be he, measured [it] in the middle. Rather, "I am the Lord, who made all things, who alone stretched out the heavens, who by myself (*me-'itti*) spread out the earth" (Isa. 44: 24)—*mi itti* ("who was with me") is written: who was associated with me (*shutaf 'immi*) in the creation of the world?

According to the custom of the world, a mortal king is honored in his state and the great men of the state are honored with him. Why? Because they bear the burden [of state] with him. The Holy One, blessed be he, however, is not so. Rather, he alone created his world; he alone is glorified in his world.

R. Tanhuma said: "For you are great and do wondrous things" (Ps. 86:10.). Why? [Because] "you God are alone" (ibid.)—you alone did create the world: "In the beginning God created" (Gen. 1:1).[5]

Structurally, this midrash is part of a Petiha interpreting Genesis 1:1 (Seder verse) by means of Psalms 86:10 (Petiha verse). In doing great and wondrous things, that is, in creating his world, God was alone (Ps. 86:10)—hence, Genesis 1:1 means that God alone created the world (with the emphasis placed on "God"). This view is defended against the unwelcome possibility that the angels might be seen as participants in the act of creation. This possibility is nullified, first, by R. Yohanan (the well-known second-generation Palestinian amora Yohanan bar Nappaha of Sepphoris and Tiberias), who argues that since the angels were created on the second day, they could not have participated in the creation of heaven and earth, which were created on the first day. His reasoning is as follows: the "beams of his upper chambers" refer to the firmament (*raqia'*),[6] which was created on the second day; since (in Ps. 104:4) the angels are mentioned immediately after the "beams of his upper chambers," we must thereby conclude that they were created on the second day as well. R. Hanina (either the first-generation Palestinian amora Hanina b. Hama, the teacher of R. Yohanan, or Hanina b. Pappos of Caesarea, the third-generation Palestinian amora) even prefers the fifth day of creation, using a *gezerah shawah* argument: since the *ye'ofef* in Isaiah 6:2 refers to the angels, we must conclude that the *ye'ofef* in Genesis 1:20 alludes also to the angels, who, therefore, were created on the same day as the birds, that is, the fifth day.

R. Luliani b. Tabri in the name of R. Yitzhaq (the third-generation Palestinian amora of Tiberias and Caesarea, student of R. Yohanan) harmonizes the two opposing opinions of his colleagues by stressing that it matters little whether the angels were created on the second or fifth day; what matters, he argues, is that they were not created on the *first* day, as such an idea could introduce the dangerous possibility that the angels cooperated with God in creating heaven (and earth). As potential partners of God he singles out Michael and Gabriel; they both might have extended the heavens to the south and north (actually, we would expect four angels, namely two additional angels who spread the heavens to the west and east, thus covering all four directions), while God measured its proper dimensions in the middle—clearly following the pattern of the vault of heaven, resting upon an earth imagined as a disk. The biblical proof text plays with the *ketiv* and *qerei* of *mi itti* versus *me-'itti* in Isaiah 44:24. Whereas the *qerei* reads *me-'itti* ("by myself")—which in fact also excludes the participation of a partner—the *ketiv* allows for an even stronger interpretation: "Who was with me (*mi itti*) when I created heaven and earth; who was my partner?" And the answer to this rhetorical question can only be: nobody, not even an angel. The accompanying parable stresses the difference between the heavenly king and human kings. Whereas human kings share the burden of governing the state with their officials and advisers, God bore the burden of creating the world alone.

A reading of the Book of Jubilees[7] makes clear that it was not the rabbis who invented the question as to the precise day on which the angels were created. There, the "angel of the presence" dictates the course of history to Moses—from the beginning of creation up until the implied present (the revelation of the Torah on Mount Sinai). The creation account begins with the first day, when God "created the heavens, which are above, and the earth, and the waters and all of the spirits which minister before him"— followed by a detailed list of the angels created, including the abysses, darkness, and light.[8] It is obvious that this description summarizes Genesis. 1:1–3 and that the creation of the angels on the very first day is based on the *ruah Elohim* of Genesis 1:2, interpreting *ruah* as "spirits" in the plural. The Book of Jubilees, therefore, had no qualms about placing the creation of the angels on the first day—which is in keeping with the book's general strategy with regard to angels.[9] But the rabbis *did* have qualms since their attitude toward this question is unambiguous.[10] There must have been some kind of dramatic change between the Book of Jubilees and the third century C.E.

Is it possible to determine more closely against whom the polemic of our rabbis was directed? In *Rivalität zwischen Engeln und Menschen*, I have argued that the alternative of external groups/sects versus internal Jewish opponents is not a particularly fruitful framework, since the borders are permeable;[11] moreover, the demarcation of "rabbis" from other well-defined static entities—whether summarized under the label of "Christianity" or "Gnosis" or something else entirely—has since proven to be ever more problematic, not least in the course of our present investigation. What we can say with some degree of confidence is that our rabbis argue against the *differentiation of functions* attributed to God, in this case his function as creator (we will see that other functions may also be involved): when God acts in certain functions—such as creating the world—he does not disintegrate into multiple personae but remains the one and only God, complete and whole. Or, to put it differently, the rabbis don't want to tie God to different functions and fight against tracing different functions of God to different gods. As our midrash demonstrates, God's function as creator was regarded as a particularly sensitive one, since any indication of the angels' participation in the work of creation as divine or semidivine coworkers needed to be scotched.

God's Consultation with the Angels

How very sensitive this issue was is demonstrated by those midrashim dealing with the notoriously difficult question of the plural of Genesis 1:26. As we have seen above, R. Simlai's standard answer to the heretics was: despite the plural of *na'aseh adam* (literally, "let us make a man," or, in form of a question,

"shall we make a man?"), when it comes to Adam's actual creation, in coupling "*Elohim*" with a verb in the singular (Gen.
1:27: "and God created the man"), the Bible makes clear that it
was God alone who performed the act of creation.[12] Yet this
grammatical argument—the plural "let us make man" is quite
simply a *pluralis maiestatis*—fails to answer the question as to
whom precisely God is addressing his statement or query: to
himself or to someone else? The rabbis consider several possibilities—to the "works of heaven and earth," the "works of each day
[of creation]" or indeed "his own heart"[13]—but ultimately they
settle on the angels: before creating Adam, God consulted his
angels as to whether or not he should do so. Understood this
way, the Bible, however, fails to record the angels' response to
God's question. Immediately following the question in verse 26,
in verse 27 God undertakes Adam's creation without any further
ado. Not so the midrash, which sets out to fill the lacuna in the
biblical text:

> R. Hanina did not say thus, but [he said that] when [God]
> came to create the first man, he took counsel with the min-
> istering angels, saying to them: "Shall we make a man?"
> (Gen. 1:26). They said to him: What shall his character be?
>
> He answered: Righteous men shall spring from him,
> as it is written: "For the Lord knows the way of the righ-
> teous," (Ps. 1:6) [which means that] the Lord made known
> the way of the righteous to the ministering angels. "But
> the way of the wicked shall perish" (Ps. ibid.): He hid it
> from them. He revealed to them that the righteous would
> arise from him [Adam], but he did not reveal to them that
> the wicked would spring from him, for had he revealed to
> them that the wicked would spring from him, the quality
> of justice (*middat ha-din*) would not have permitted him
> to be created.

R. Shim'on said: When the Holy One, blessed be he, came to create Adam, the ministering angels formed themselves into groups and parties, some of them saying: Let him be created, whereas others urged: Let him not be created. This is what is written: "Love and Truth fought together (*nifgashu*),[14] Righteousness and Peace combated each other (*nashaqu*)"[15] (Ps. 85:11).

Love said: Let him be created, because he will dispense acts of love, whereas Truth said: Let him not be created, because he is full of falsehood; Righteousness said: Let him be created, because he will perform righteous deeds, whereas Peace said: Let him not be created, because he is full of strife.

What did the Holy One, blessed be he, do? He took Truth and cast it to the ground.[16]

[Thereupon] said the ministering angels before the Holy One, blessed be he: Sovereign of the Universe, how do you despise your Truth?[17] Let Truth arise from the earth, as it is written: "Let truth spring up from the earth" (Ps. 85:12)....

R. Huna Rabba of Sepphoris, said: While the ministering angels were arguing with each other and disputing with each other, the Holy One, blessed be he, created him. He said to them: What can you avail? Man has already been made![18]

This midrash addresses the issue of God's seeking counsel from the angels in a wickedly funny way. Whereas the angels take the question "Shall we make a man?" quite seriously and wish to ponder its pros and cons, it is clear from the outset that God has no intention of taking his angels' advice seriously. He cunningly hides from them the truth that some (in fact most) of Adam's descendants will *not* be righteous, in other words, that human beings will be sinners through and through. Had he revealed this truth to his angels, the "quality of justice"—that is, his own divine justice as opposed to his divine mercy—would have prohibited the creation of man.

Following this initial interpretation by R. Hanina (presumably Hanina b. Papa, the Palestinian amora of the third generation), R. Shim'on (apparently Shim'on b. Pazzi, Hanina b. Papa's contemporary, end of the third century C.E.) takes the irony even further. Although, as we have just heard, God keeps from his angels the negative implications of Adam's creation, the angels are still well aware that human beings will be both righteous and wicked. Accordingly, some argue in favor of Adam's creation, others against it. Hence, although the truth is known, and God ought to conclude that Adam's creation is unwarranted, this is the last thing in the world that God wishes to admit. Like a despotic human ruler he hurls "Truth" (that is, the angelic faction representing truth) down from heaven to earth, an intemperate act that the angels answer with the perfect Bible verse. But God is unimpressed. While the angels still quarrel with each other, God creates facts, that is, he creates Adam.[19]

The unequivocal message of this midrash is that God—although taking counsel with the angels (or, to put it differently, although the strange plural *na'aseh* in Gen. 1:26 forces the rabbis to admit that God took counsel with the angels)—couldn't care less about his angels' input. He knows that the angels will invoke his own divine justice, which does not permit the creation of man; but he chooses *not* to follow his justice, and hence the angels' perfectly proper rejoinder. He wanted man, despite man's inherent inclination to sin, and the implications of this attitude for rabbinic anthropology are quite far-reaching.[20] But for our context it is sufficient to note the highly ironical way in which God's consultation with the angels is played out *ad absurdum*. True, our midrash argues, God took counsel with his angels, but in fact this counsel was a farce. God never meant it to be serious—and he certainly never accepted the angels as equal partners in his act of creation; to the contrary, he exposed the angels as powerless and completely unimportant.

The following midrash demonstrates that the plural of *naʿaseh* was indeed seen as potentially dangerous—that is, as providing ammunition for the "heretics":

R. Shemuel b. Nahman said in the name of R. Yonathan: When Moses was engaged in writing the Torah, he had to write the work of each day [of creation]. When he came to the verse that said: "And God (*Elohim*) said: Let us make a man, etc." (Gen. 1:26), he said: "Master of the Universe! Why do you furnish an excuse to the heretics (*minim*)?" "Write," [God] replied, "whoever wishes to err may err!"

The Holy One, Blessed be he, said to him: "Moses, this man that I create—do I not cause men both great and small to spring from him? Now if a great man comes to obtain permission (for a proposed action) from one that is less than he, he may say, 'Why should I ask permission from my inferior?' Then they will answer him, 'Learn from your creator, who created all that is above and below; yet when he came to create man, he took counsel with the ministering angels.'"

R. Hila said: There is no taking counsel here, but it may be compared to a king who was strolling at the door of his palace when he saw a block of stone[21] lying about. He said: "What shall we do (*naʿaseh*)[22] with it?" Some answered: "[Use it in building] public buildings," whereas others

answered: "private buildings." The king declared: "I will
make a statue of it!"—and who then can hinder him?[23]

Here God gives two answers to Moses' (legitimate) question,
both transmitted by R. Shemuel b. Nahman (a Palestinian amora
of the third generation, who flourished in Tiberias) in the name
of his teacher R. Yonathan b. Eleazar of Sepphoris (a first-
generation Palestinian amora). First he crankily rebuffs Moses'
concern: I couldn't care less, is his initial answer—I cannot gear
my Holy Scripture to avoiding potential misinterpretations by
potential heretics and you shouldn't bother yourself with it either. But then he deigns to give a second answer: the omnipotent
God, who is in no need of any consultation and advice, nevertheless consulted with his angels before he decided to create man.
The clear message of this rather pious answer is that God wished
to give his creatures an object lesson in moral behavior—that
even someone who is superior to his fellow human beings is well
advised to take counsel with them instead of just having things
all his own way. This midrash's message is at loggerheads with the
midrash discussed above.

But R. Hila (a contemporary of Shemuel b. Nahman, early
fourth century) finds the recourse to God-as-role-model-for-
human-behavior rather lame and inadequate, opting instead for
the ironical solution proposed in the first midrash: God did not
really consult with the angels but in fact knew exactly what he
wanted to do; playing the good-natured superior, he simply went
through the motions of consulting with his subordinates. It is
the decision of the divine king that ultimately matters—the angels are mere decorative accessories with no real decision-making
power. In other words, the angels' counsel is toned down, as it
were, lest they come too close to God.

The motif of God's consultation with the angels is developed
further in a series of other midrashim.[24] As a rule, the angels op-

pose the creation of man; yet in several cases God not only responds disrespectfully or even mockingly but counters their opposition with harsh measures. In the following midrash, God exposes the angels as actually inferior to human beings:

What was then the wisdom of the first man [Adam]? When the Holy One, blessed be he, wished to create the first man, he consulted with the ministering angels and said to them: "Shall we make a man?" (Gen. 1:26).

They said to him: "Master of the universe, 'What is man (*enosh*) that you are mindful of him, etc. [and the son of man (*ben adam*) that you care for him?]'" (Ps. 8:5).[25]

He answered them: "This man, whom I wish to create in my world, his wisdom will be greater than yours!"

What did [God] do? He assembled all domestic animals, wild beasts and fowl and made them pass before them [the angels]. He asked them: "What are the names of these [creatures]?" But they [the angels] did not know.[26]

Having created the first man, God asks him the same question that he has addressed to the angels and, lo and behold, Adam rattles off all the appropriate names for the animals (Gen. 2:20). Yet beyond what can be proven from the Bible, Adam knows his own name, Adam—"because I was fashioned out of the earth (*adamah*)"—and even the name of God, the Lord ("because you are Lord [*adon*] over all your works"). To this R. Aha adds:

The Holy One, Blessed be he, said: "I am the Lord (*YHWH*), that is my name" (Isa. 42:8).

"That is my name"—[the name] by which the first man [Adam] called me.

"That is my name"—[the name] that I have agreed with myself to be called by.

"That is my name"—[the name] that I have agreed to be called by when I am with the ministering angels.[27]

So the angels get it all wrong. At first, they try to argue against the creation of man—with a Bible verse that in fact says the opposite of what they wish to read into it, at least if we, following good rabbinic custom, pay due heed to its continuation: "You have made him [man] a little lower than God, and crowned him with glory and honor" (Ps. 8:6). And then they not only fail the test of giving the animals their proper names (which Adam passed with flying colors) but are even forced to call God by the name Adam has given him. Hence, although they were created anterior to Adam (on the second or the fifth day as opposed to the sixth), the angels are indeed much inferior to Adam and the human race inaugurated by him. Human beings, not the angels, are the favored creatures of God; they are the summit of all creation.

The Bavli's version of God's consultation with the angels goes furthest in its antiangelic tendency:

Rav Yehudah said in the name of Rav: When the Holy One, blessed be he, wished to create the [first] man, he [first] created a class of ministering angels and said to them: "Is it your desire that we make a man in our image" (cf. Gen. 1:26)?

They answered before him: "Sovereign of the universe, what will be his deeds?" He replied: "Such and such will be his deeds."

[Thereupon] they said before him: "Sovereign of the universe, 'What is man (*enosh*) that you are mindful of him, etc. [and the son of man (*ben adam*) that you care for him?]'" (Ps. 8:5).

[Immediately] he stretched out his little finger among them and consumed them with fire.

The same thing happened with a second class [of angels]. The third class said to him: "Sovereign of the universe, what did it avail the first [class of angels] that they spoke to you [as they did]? The whole world is yours, and whatever you wish to do in your world—do it!"

When he came to the generation of the flood and of the division [of tongues] whose deeds were corrupt, they [the angels] said before him: "Sovereign of the universe, did not the first [class of angels] speak right before you?" He answered them: "Even to old age I am the same, and even to grey hairs I will bear, [I have made, and I will carry; I will bear and I will save]" (Isa. 46:4).[28]

According to Rav (the well-known Babylonian amora of the first generation, first half of the third century C.E.), the opposing angels are not just humiliated but annihilated. Only the third class of angels learn their lesson, that is, not to mistake their master's question for an invitation to serious dialogue but simply to tell him what he wishes to hear. I see no basis here for the claim that "the angels share in the creation of man in this story."[29] To the contrary, as in comparable stories, the plural is a *pluralis maiestatis*[30] and the question purely rhetorical. God does not ask the angels to participate in his creation of man; he is not in earnest with his question. All he wants is that they confirm his decision— and those angels stupid enough to misunderstand the rules of this game are severely punished (even though they were in fact right in arguing that human beings are prone to sin). God simply does not accept man's sinfulness as an argument against his creation. Some midrashim even regard man's sinfulness as an advantage he has over the angels, for man has the choice between good and evil, whereas the poor angels are sinless—not because they have so chosen but because they are incapable of sin.[31] So ultimately, while many rabbis follow the interpretation of the plural "Shall we make a man?" as a question addressed to the angels, they do everything to play down the possible implications of involving the angels in the act of creation.

In search of a possible reason for the rabbis' ire against the angels as potential participants in the creation of man, scholars have directed our attention to Philo's interpretation of Genesis. 1:26.[32] According to Philo, the great first-century C.E. Hellenistic-Jewish philosopher, the angels are the "viceroys" of God, his "his ears and eyes, so to speak," his messengers and mediators.[33] In particular, Philo attaches great importance to emphasizing how silly it would be to assume that God, "the original and perfect Lawgiver," punishes by his own hands; rather, he uses "those [hands] of others who act as his ministers" and reserves to himself only the bestowal of "boons, gifts, and benefits."[34] It is on the basis of this important distinction that Philo discusses Genesis 1:26:

> It is for this reason, I imagine, that Moses, when treating in his lessons of wisdom of the creation of the world, after having said of all other things that they were made by God, described man alone as having been fashioned with the cooperation of others (*meta synergōn heterōn*). His words are: "God said, let us make man after our image" (Gen. 1:26), "let us make" indicating more than one. So the Father of all things is holding parley with his powers (*tais heautou dynamesin*), whom he allowed to fashion the mortal portion of our soul by imitating the skill shown by him when he was forming that in us which is rational, since he deemed it right that by the Sovereign should be wrought the sovereign faculty in the soul, the subject part being wrought by

subjects. And he employed the powers that are associated with him (*tais meth' heautou dynamesin*) not only for the reason mentioned, but because, alone among created beings, the soul was to be susceptible of conceptions of evil things and good things, and to use one sort or the other, since it is impossible for him to use both [at the same time]. Therefore God deemed it necessary to assign the creation of evil things to other makers (*dēmiourgois*), reserving that of good things to himself alone.[35]

Philo clearly distinguishes here between two parts of the human soul, one rational (immortal) and susceptible to good things and the other one irrational (mortal) and susceptible to evil. Since God can be held responsible only for the creation of good things, he delegated the creation of the irrational and mortal part of the human soul to his "powers" and "demiurges." Hence, man is the only creature—because of his peculiar makeup—that required the cooperation of "others as fellow-workers (*synergōn*)."[36] Elsewhere, Philo calls these assistants in the creation of man "lieutenants" (*hyparchoi*), again "demiurges," and "angels" (*anggeloi*).[37] The generic term for all these assistants seems to be "powers":

Now the King may fitly hold converse with his powers (*tais heautou dynamesin*) and employ them to serve in matters which should not be consummated by God alone. It is true that the Father of All has no need of aught, so that he should require the co-operation of others, if he wills some creative work, yet seeing what was fitting to himself and the world which was coming into being, he allowed his subject powers to have the fashioning of some things, though he did not give them sovereign and independent knowledge for completion of the task, lest aught of what was coming into being should be miscreated.[38]

Jarl Fossum would conclude from this and similar passages that the "powers" are synonymous with "angels" in Philo,[39] but the matter is more complicated than that. Philo employs a highly complex and sophisticated hierarchy of "powers" emanating from God, chief among them the "Word" (*logos*) and "Wisdom" (*sophia*).[40] It is true that the Logos is also identified with the "principal angel," as Fossum puts it.[41] He is unambiguously called God's "chief messenger" or "archangel" (*archanggelos*), "highest in age and honor,"[42] his "Firstborn Son," "viceroy of the great king,"[43] "the most senior among the angels, their ruler (*archanggelos*) as it were,"[44] and the "charioteer of the powers (*tōn dynameōn*).[45] As such, the Logos is explicitly matched with the angel of Exodus 23:20, who also plays such a prominent role in the rabbinic literature.[46] But this does not mean that the "powers" are completely identical with the angels. They are, in terms of Philo's Platonic philosophy, facets of the unknowable, unattainable, transcendent God; as such, they are (at least in their essence) unknowable as well but nevertheless embody and enable the transition from the transcendent God (through many stages) down to our visible world. They embody those divine activities that lead to the world of ideas and ultimately to the created world perceptible to our senses:

> God is one, but he has around him numberless powers (*dynameis*), which all assist and protect created being, and among them are the powers of chastisement. . . . Through these powers (*dia toutōn tōn dynameōn*) the incorporeal and intelligible world was framed, the archetype (*to archetypon*) of this phenomenal world, that [incorporeal world] being a system of invisible ideal forms (*ideais aoratois*), as this [the phenomenal world] is of visible material bodies.[47]

Philo is obviously using the term "angels" in an ambiguous way. On the one hand the angels are part of the divine powers (in particular as "archangels"), but on the other they are inferior to these and rank low in the hierarchy of heavenly beings; in this latter sense, Philo explicitly states that they "wait upon these heavenly powers."[48]

Yet what is striking in Philo's description of the creation of the world is the very fact that the invisible and transcendent God unfolds in a rich hierarchy of divine powers, from Logos and Wisdom down to the lowest angels, who all assume their ordered place in the process of creation. It is within this context that Philo assigns to the "angels" their specific task of creating the mortal part of the human soul, explaining the difficult verse Genesis 1:26. In its capacity for generating evil things, the human soul cannot have been created by God himself; the creation of this part of the soul was left to inferior powers.

Philo is well aware of the potential danger that he evokes with his system of divine powers, including the participation of the angels in the creation of man. Having described the origins of the two worlds, the incorporeal and the visible world, he seems startled by the possible implications:

> Now the nature of these two worlds has so struck with awe the minds of some, that they have deified (*exetheiōsan*) not merely each of them as a whole, but also their fairest parts, the sun, the moon and the whole sky, and have felt no shame in calling them gods.[49]

Philo admits here that the differentiation and diversification of God in divine potencies, according to the Platonic model, could lead certain uncouth and unenlightened people to the wrong conclusion, namely, that even the heavenly bodies at the bottom of emanation are independent deities. Philo does not quote the Bible here, but one can easily assume that he had verses such as Deuteronomy 4:19 and Exodus 20:4f./Deuteronomy 5:8f. in mind. Deuteronomy 4:19 in particular mentions—together with the sun, the moon, and the stars—the "host of heaven," that is, the angels that one should not worship, and the Decalogue verses Exodus 20:4f./Deuteronomy 5:8f. play a crucial role in the rabbinic discussion of the veneration of angels.[50] It is unlikely that the Palestinian rabbis who demoted the angels and argued against their participation in the creation of man knew Philo's writings and were in dialogue with him. But still, it is highly probable that they were indeed aware of Platonic/Philonic attempts to manifest God within a complex system of divine powers and potencies as well as of the fact that the biblical angels in particular could be easily integrated into such a system. In relegating the angels' creation to the second or fifth day of creation and in downplaying the angels' role in the creation of man, the rabbis were clearly trying to draw a strict line between their concept of God as sole creator and any attempt to distinguish between divine powers and to diversify God's functions—let alone to elevate the various powers to deities. It is also certainly no accident that they felt compelled to stress time and again that everything God had created was intrinsically good[51]—obviously so as to fend off the idea (inherent not only in Philo's notion of creation but also in the concept that would be labeled "gnostic" in the modern scholarly discourse) that certain inferior powers were involved in and responsible for the creation of the evil part of man.

ANGELS AND REVELATION

The angels play no particular role in the biblical account of the revelation on Mount Sinai (Ex. 19f.). But there are certain difficult verses in the Bible, such as Deuteronomy 33:2f. and Psalms 68:18, which might be understood as referring to the angels in conjunction with the revelation. Using these verses, the rabbis took it for granted that the angels were present when God revealed the Torah on Mount Sinai. The enigmatic phrase "at his right *esh dat lamo*" in Deuteronomy 33:2 is translated in the Septuagint as "at his right [there were] angels with him," and the no less enigmatic *me-rivavot qodesh* in the same verse is understood as myriads of holy angels in the Targumim.[52] Similarly, what is usually translated as "God's chariots are myriads upon myriads, thousands upon thousands" in Psalms 68:18 is understood by the rabbis as large numbers of angels accompanying God upon his descent to Mount Sinai.[53] The angels here are mainly decorative; but the following midrashim show that this ornamental role of the angels could become so prominent that God would be in danger of disappearing in the angelic multitude:

> "I will sing to the Lord" (Ex. 15:1). For he is excellent, he is majestic, he is praiseworthy, and there is none to compare with him, as it is said: "For who in the skies can be compared to the Lord, etc. [who among the heavenly beings (*benei elim*) is like the Lord]?" (Ps. 89:7). And [Scripture] says: "A God feared in the great council of the holy ones" (ibid. v. 8). And it says: "O Lord, God of hosts (*tzeva'ot*), who is as mighty as you, O Lord?" (ibid. v. 9).
>
> What is the meaning of *tzeva'ot*? He is the ensign (*ot*) among his host (*tzava*).[54] And likewise, when it [Scripture]

says: "And he came (*ata*) from the myriads [of] holy [ones] (*me-rivavot qodesh*)" (Deut. 33:2), [it means that] he is the ensign (*ot*) among his holy myriads.[55] And so also David says: "There is none like you among the gods (*elohim*), O Lord, etc." (Ps. 86:8). And [Scripture] also says: "My beloved is radiant and ruddy, etc. [distinguished among myriads (*dagul me-revavah*)" (Cant. 5:10).[56]

Using Psalms 89:7–9 as proof text, this midrash makes clear that the angels, who descended with God to Mount Sinai, cannot be compared with him: none of the heavenly beings is like the Lord (v. 7), the holy ones even fear him (v. 8), and none of the angelic host is as mighty as God (v. 9). Accordingly, the difficult *ata me-rivavot qodesh* in Deuteronomy 33:2 is explained as meaning that God stands out as the ensign (*ot*) among his angels, with Psalms 86:8 and Canticum Canticorum 5:10 as further proof texts: whereas *elohim* in Psalms 86:8 is understood as angels, Canticum Canticorum 5:10 brilliantly takes up the "myriads" (*rivavot*) of Deuteronomy 33:2 and stresses that God is "distinguished" (*dagul*) among the myriads (*revavah*) of his angels. In other words, although God's heavenly court is magnificent and mighty, it is nothing in comparison to God himself. And this is also true with regard to the revelation on Mount Sinai, when the angels descended together with God to bestow the Torah on his people of Israel. As another midrash explains, God took even the most beautiful and magnificent angels with him when he descended to Mount Sinai, but he is nevertheless distinct from them and is to be identified as such.[57] A parallel to this midrash recognizes the most beautiful and powerful angels as Michael with his group and Gabriel with his group. When Israel becomes frightened at the overwhelming sight of them, God reminds his people:

Don't go astray after one of these angels, who descended with me. They all are my servants, (but) I am the Lord, your God: "I am the Lord, your God" (Ex. 20:2). From this moment they acknowledged the kingship of the Holy One, blessed be he, upon them (*yihadu*) and said to each other: "Hear, O Israel, [the Lord is our God, the Lord alone (*YHWH ehad*)]" (Deut. 6:4).[58]

This midrash plays with the word *ehad* in Deuteronomy 6:4. In acknowledging God's kingship, Israel "unites" him—that is, makes him one (this is what the root *yahad*, Pi'el *yihed*, literally means)—and accepts him as the one and only God for them. But the angels' appearance on Mount Sinai comes dangerously close to infringing on God's sovereignty, and God needs to remind his people that the angels are nothing but his servants and that he alone is Israel's God.

This also holds true for the second part of the verse Psalms 68:18, used to prove the angels' presence at the revelation on Mount Sinai. Its meaning is unclear, but literally translated it might be understood as: "the Lord (*adonai*) is among them [the angels], [on Mount] Sinai, at the holy place." Again, the rabbis need to make clear that God takes a special place among his angels:

Note that in the words "The Lord (*adonai*) is among them" (Ps. 68:18), the name of God is not spelled with a Yod [*YHWH*] but with an Aleph and a Dalet [*adonai*]—[to show that] the Lord of the whole world was among them [the angels]. . . .

Another explanation of "The Lord is among them": The Sages say: The name of God was joined with the name of each [angel], [such as] Micha*el* and Gabri*el*.

> The Holy One, blessed be he, said to Israel: Do not imagine that because you have seen so many faces, therefore there are many deities in heaven. Know that I am the only God, as it is written: "I am the Lord (*YHWH*), your God (*Elohekha*)" (Ex. 20:2).[59]

This midrash first interprets the fact that Psalms 68:18 uses the word *adonai* for God (which is understood as meaning "Lord, Master")—instead of the tetragrammaton *YHWH* or the name *Elohim*—as proof that God presented himself to his angels as the Lord of the universe. By contrast, the Sages (that is, the rabbis) prefer the more dangerous explanation that God had joined his name with the names of the angels (by adding the theophoric element *-el* to their angelic names: Micha-el, Gabri-el, etc.)—which, philologically speaking, is certainly correct but somewhat careless since it could be perceived as elevating the Mount Sinai angels to a divine or semidivine status. God, therefore, needs to immediately clarify the situation and explain to Israel that, although they see many faces resembling divine figures, the angels are no gods, and he remains the only real God in heaven (as he declared at the beginning of the Decalogue).

Nevertheless, some midrashim continue to play with fire and assign the angels a particular function in the course of revelation. A midrash in Pesiqta de-Rav Kahana is still relatively harmless. Interpreting Lamentations 2:13, the midrash explains that the Israelites, when receiving the Torah, were adorned with magnificent jewelry: sixty myriads of angels descended with God and bestowed upon each and every one of them a glorious crown.[60] The following midrash on Canticum Canticorum 1:2, however, goes much further:

> Another explanation: "Let him kiss me with the kisses of his mouth" (Cant. 1:2).

R. Yohanan said: An angel carried the utterances (*dibbur*) [at Mount Sinai] from before the Holy One, blessed be he, each one in turn, and brought it to each of the Israelites and said to him: "Do you take upon yourself this utterance (*dibbur*)? So-and-so many rules are attached to it, so-and-so many penalties are attached to it, so-and-so many precautionary measures are attached to it, so many precepts and so many lenient and strict applications are attached to it; such-and-such a reward is attached to it."

The Israelite would answer him: "Yes!" He [the angel] then said: "Do you accept the divinity (*elohut*) of the Holy One, blessed be he?," and he [the Israelite] answered: "Yes, yes!"

Thereupon [the angel] kissed him on his mouth; this is what is written: "To you it was shown so that you might know [that the Lord is God]" (Deut. 4:35), namely, by an [angelic] messenger.[61]

Here the angels play an active role in bestowing the Torah on Israel. They take each and every word issuing from the mouth of God—obviously of the Ten Commandments—and bring it to each of the Israelites asking them whether they accept it. When, in a second step, the Israelites also accept the divinity of God—that is, God as their one and only God—the angels kiss them as a sign of approval. Hence, according to R. Yohanan's interpretation (presumably Yohanan bar Nappaha, the second-generation Palestinian amora of the second half of the third century), the kisses of Canticum Canticorum 1:2 are not the kisses of God—as the lover of Canticum is usually understood—but the kisses of his angels. Thus does R. Yohanan conclude that the words of the Ten Commandments—whose acceptance in turn leads to cognizance of God's divinity—were "shown" to the Israelites by a messenger and not by God himself. The angels are clearly presented here as the mediators of revelation. But this is not the only possible explanation. Immediately following R. Yohanan's interpretation, the midrash states that according to "the rabbis" it wasn't the angels who went to the Israelites but the "words" themselves, asking for their acceptance; and an anonymous explanation even suggests that the Israelites heard the words directly from God's mouth. In other words, the idea of the angels' mediation was by no means undisputed. Some rabbis apparently preferred to personify the words of revelation—or even dared to imagine God in anthropomorphic form—rather than risk attributing to the angels the role of mediators between God and Israel.

The attempt to deflect the angels' mediation in the course of bestowing the Torah on Israel finds its most explicit expression in the frequently repeated formula "not through the medium of an angel or a messenger."[62] Interpreting the verse Exodus 31:12, "And the Lord spoke to Moses," the Mekhilta categorically states: "[Directly] and not through the medium of an angel or through the medium of a messenger."[63] This is clear from the Bible itself, since the text continues: "You [Moses] yourself are to speak to the Israelites" (Ex. 31:13)—but the fact that the midrash feels compelled to emphasize it, and exclude the angels' mediation, is conspicuous. The version preserved in Avot de-Rabbi Nathan is even more outspoken:

> Moses received [the] Torah from Mount Sinai—not through the mouth of an angel and not through the mouth of a Seraf but through the mouth of the King of Kings, the Holy One, blessed be he, as it is said: "These are the statutes and ordinances and laws [that the Lord established between himself and the sons of Israel on Mount Sinai through the hand of Moses]" (Lev. 26:46).[64]

The first part of the first sentence of this midrash is a quotation from Pirqe Avot,[65] and Avot de-Rabbi Nathan's commentary attempts to make clear that it was God himself who gave the Torah to Israel and not an angel. This seems to have become standard rabbinic theology and was extended, beyond the subject of revelation, to other crucial areas as well, such as smiting the Egyptian firstborn,[66] the exodus from Egypt,[67] or the gift of rain to the land of Israel in its season.[68] In all these cases the formula wishes to stress that God did not need mediators to carry out his acts of revelation and salvation.

It is no coincidence that the rabbis were particularly concerned about the angels' possible participation in the revelation of the Torah. We have already seen that the Book of Jubilees has no problem whatsoever with the angels being created on the first day of the work of creation. Most conspicuously, it is also the "Angel of the Presence" who is employed as mediator between God and Moses: when Moses is summoned by God to Mount Sinai to receive the Torah, God asks the Angel of the Presence to dictate to Moses the course of history from the beginning of creation until his own present, the revelation on Mount Sinai.[69] Hence, although the revelation originates with God, the angel takes God's place as the mediator of revelation—and in the continuation of the book the boundaries between God and his Angel of Presence are constantly blurred.[70] This approach seems to have been quite common in the Second Temple period. Josephus has Herod, in a speech addressing his troops, compare the Greek "heralds" to the Jewish "angels":

For those things which are admitted by both Greeks and barbarians to be most lawless, these men have done to our envoys and have cut their throats, although the Greeks

have declared heralds (*tous kērykas*) to be sacred and invio-
lable, and we have learned the noblest of our doctrines and
the holiest of our laws from the angels (*di' anggelōn*) sent
by God.[71]

It has been suggested that *anggeloi* should be understood
here—in accord with the literal meaning "messengers"—as
prophets or priests and not as "angels" in the technical sense of
the word.[72] But those messengers par excellence are the angels,
and I find it hard to imagine Josephus arguing that "the noblest of our doctrines and the holiest of our laws" were indeed
revealed and communicated by prophets or priests and not
by angels.

The most explicit reference to angels as mediators of the "law"
can be found in the New Testament. When Stephen—accused
of "blasphemous words against Moses and God"[73]—is brought
before the council of elders, scribes, and High Priests, he too refers in his long speech to Moses as the "one who was in the con-
gregation in the wilderness with the angel (*meta tou anggelou*)
who spoke to him at Mount Sinai, and with our ancestors."[74] His
speech climaxes in the following accusation against the Jews:

> (7:51) You stiff-necked people, uncircumcised in heart and
> ears, you are forever opposing the Holy Spirit, just as your
> ancestors used to do. (52) Which of the prophets did your
> ancestors not persecute? They killed those who foretold
> the coming of the Righteous One, and now you have be-
> come his betrayers and murderers. (53) You are the ones
> that received the law as ordained by angels (*eis diatagas
> anggelōn*), and yet you have not kept it.[75]

The Jews, hearing these words, "became enraged and ground
their teeth at Stephen" (7:54)—clearly not because he has told

them that they received the law through angels but because he has blamed them for not adhering to it. That the Torah was mediated by angels is implied as a matter of course. Paul uses precisely this tradition as an argument to prove that the "law" is secondary:

> Why then the law? It was added because of transgressions, until the "seed" would come to whom the promise had been made; and it was ordained through angels (*diatageis di' anggelōn*) by a mediator.[76]

Here the "law" is clearly something preliminary, namely, a tool to help bridge the time span between the covenant with Abraham and his "seed" until the arrival of the ultimate "seed," that is, Jesus (Galatians 3:16 identifies the "seed" as Jesus Christ). It is this preliminary law that was "ordained through angels" by using a mediator (Moses). Or to put it differently, because this law was delivered on Sinai by angels and not directly by God, it is in fact not only preliminary but also inferior—inferior to the new law inaugurating the new covenant and embodied in Jesus. Only this new law was ordained directly through God and not through his messengers. A similar argument is made by the author of the Letter to the Hebrews. Having explained that Jesus is superior to the angels (Heb. 1:4) and that the angels are nothing but "spirits in the divine service, sent for the sake of those who are to inherit salvation (*sōtēria*),"[77] he continues:

> (2:1) Therefore we must pay greater attention to what we have heard, so that we do not drift away from it. (2) For if the message declared through angels (*ho di' anggelōn lalētheis logos*) was valid, and every transgression and disobedience received a just penalty, (3) how can we escape if we neglect so great a salvation (*sōtēria*)?[78]

This statement juxtaposes the angels with their message (the Law of Moses) and Jesus with his (salvation)—just as Jesus is superior to the angels, so is his salvation superior to the law brought by the angels. Again, the offense is not the claim that the Law of Moses was ordained by angels but that Jesus' salvation superseded the Law of Moses. Since Paul and the author of the Letter to the Hebrews are definitely arguing with Jews, we can take it for granted that the "law ordained or declared through angels" reflects a common Jewish standpoint. Hence, when the rabbis of rabbinic Judaism contest this standpoint and claim that God neither needed nor used the angels to carry out his revelation on Mount Sinai and the subsequent salvation history, they are obviously arguing against a (Jewish) view introduced during the Second Temple period and taken up in the New Testament.[79] One could even go a step further and argue that they contested this standpoint and insisted on God's direct involvement *because* the New Testament used it to propagate the inferiority of the Law of Moses and its abolition by Jesus Christ. Confronted with such a claim, the rabbis could not but insist that the law was given by God himself and that God remains the master of history, including the ultimate salvation of his people—or to put it another way, that the old covenant was still valid and there was no need for a new one.

Veneration of Angels

Rabbinic literature provides clear evidence that the rabbis were even concerned about the possible veneration of angels. Such an attempt again has its roots in the earlier apocalyptic literature. For example, when the seer in the Apocalypse of Zephaniah (end of the first or beginning of the second century C.E.)[80] encounters "a great angel standing before me with his face shining like the rays of the sun in its glory,"[81] he falls on his face and worships

him, and the angel must explain to him that he is not "the Lord
Almighty" but "the great angel Eremiel."[82] Similarly, the prophet
Isaiah in the Ascension of Isaiah[83] falls prostrate and attempts to
worship the angel on the throne of the second heaven; here, too,
his angelic guide needs to explain to him that he must worship
only the figure he will be seeing in the seventh heaven (that is,
God).[84] The same pattern is followed in the Apocalypse of John,
an indubitably Christian work written toward the end of the
first century C.E. but drawing heavily on Jewish traditions.[85]
When the seer falls prostrate at the feet of his angelic guide "to
worship him" (*proskynēsai autō*), the angel reminds him: "You
must not do that! I am a fellow servant with you and your brothers who hold the testimony of Jesus. Worship God!"[86]

It is against this background that the rabbinic polemic against
the worship of angels must be seen. To begin with, the rabbis
explicitly prohibit the creation and worship of images of angels.
Interpreting Exodus 20:4f., they include the angels in their prohibition of graven images:

> "You shall not make for yourself a graven image (*pesel we-
> khol temunah*), [whether in the form of anything that is in
> heaven above, or that is on the earth beneath, or that is in
> the water under the earth. You shall not bow down to them
> or worship them]" (Ex. 20:4f.). . . .
>
> But perhaps one may make an image (*demut*) of the
> sun, the moon, the stars, or the planets? [Since] Scripture
> says: "And when you look up to the heavens, etc. [and see
> the sun, the moon, and the stars, all the host of heaven, do
> not be led astray and bow down to them and serve them]"
> (Deut. 4:19), [we must conclude that] one shall not make
> an image (*demut*) of any of these.
>
> But perhaps one may make an image of the angels
> (*mal'akhim*), the Cherubs or the Ofannim? [Since]

Scripture says: "Of anything that is *in heaven*" (Ex. 20:4), [we must conclude that one shall not make an image of any of these].

As for "that is in heaven (*shamayim*)" (ibid.), one might think it refers only to an image of the sun, moon, stars, and planets? [Since] Scripture says: "[in heaven] *above*" (ibid.), [we must conclude that one should] not [make] an image of the angels, nor an image of the Cherubs, and nor an image of the Ofannim.[87]

This is an elaborately structured midrash. First, the rabbis include the heavenly bodies—the sun, moon, stars, and planets—in the prohibition of images, using Deuteronomy 4:19 as proof text. Then they ask whether the angels are also encompassed by this prohibition (they are not luminaries in the strict sense of the word). The answer is yes, since they are in heaven and the prohibition refers to anything that is in heaven, including the angels. The third step of the argument implies knowledge of the composition and configuration of several, mostly seven, heavens common to both apocalyptic and rabbinic literature. The anonymous interlocutor presupposes the classical system according to which the heaven called *shamayim* is the first of the seven heavens—the heaven that we see and that contains the sun, moon, stars, and planets.[88] Could it be, our interlocutor asks, that the prohibition in Exodus 20:4 uses "heaven" (*shamayim*) in this technical sense and indeed refers only to the heavenly bodies and not to the angels (who are definitely not in the first heaven)?[89] Answer: Exodus 20:4 speaks of "in heaven *above*"; that is, literally understood, it refers to a heaven *above* the first heaven *shamayim*—and since the angels are in a heaven above the first heaven, we learn that they are included in the prohibition of graven images.

Why was it so important for the rabbis to include the angels in the prohibition of Exodus 20:4? In prohibiting a graven image "of anything that is in heaven above" the Bible in all likelihood has just the heavenly luminaries in mind and *not* the angels— all the more so as we know from the description of Solomon's Temple in 1 Kings not only that the Temple's inner sanctuary contained statues of two Cherubs[90] but also that the walls of the Temple and its doors were decorated all around with carvings of Cherubs (among other things).[91] So the real novelty in our midrash is the inclusion of the angels in the prohibition, as can also be seen from the midrash's structure. Somewhere along the line a perceptual change must have taken place between the angels in Solomon's Temple (seen as purely decorative?) and their being viewed as something potentially dangerous by the rabbis. If we take into consideration the multiplication of angels in the Second Temple literature[92]—with the caveat of the ascent apocalypses against the angels' veneration—it is difficult to avoid the conclusion that the rabbis polemicized against images of angels because such images could be venerated—just as images of the sun, moon, stars, and planets could be and were indeed venerated.

The Mishna, the Tosefta, and a Baraitha in the Bavli explicitly prohibit sacrifices offered in the name of idols. Whereas the Mishna is silent on the subject of angels, simply stating "He who slaughters [an animal] as a sacrifice to[93] mountains, hills, seas, rivers, or deserts—his slaughtering is invalid,"[94] the Tosefta specifies: "He who slaughters [an animal] as a sacrifice to the sun, the moon, the stars, the planets, to Michael, the Great Prince of the Army, or to a small worm—this is meat of sacrifices of the dead."[95] A Baraitha in the Bavli combines both versions:

It [the sacrifice mentioned in the Mishna] is only invalid but it is not regarded as a sacrifice of the dead.
I will point out a contradiction. [It was taught in a Baraitha:] He who slaughters [an animal] as a sacrifice to

mountains, hills, seas, rivers, deserts, the sun, the moon, the stars and planets, to Michael, the Great Prince, or to a small worm—lo, these [sacrifices are regarded as] sacrifices of the dead.

Abaye explained: There is no contradiction. Here [in the Mishna] he declared it to be a sacrifice to the mountain itself, but there [in the Baraitha] he declared it to be a sacrifice to the genius (*gadda*) of the mountain. There is indeed support for this view, for [in the Baraitha] they are all stated together with "Michael, the Great Prince." This is conclusive.[96]

The two lists in the Mishna and Tosefta differ in that the Mishna exclusively mentions sacrifices offered to earthly objects, whereas the Tosefta refers only to heavenly objects (with the exception of the small worm); the former are regarded as merely invalid, the latter as sacrifices to the dead—that is, real idolatry.[97] The Bavli sugya first confirms the ruling of the Mishna but then quotes a Baraitha in which the combined lists of the Mishna and the Tosefta are declared sacrifices of the dead. Abaye—the fourth-generation Babylonian amora (beginning of the fourth century C.E.)—"solves" the contradiction by arguing that the Mishna's sacrifices are offered to earthly objects as such, whereas the Baraitha's sacrifices are offered to the genii (or spirits or deities) of all objects, including earthly ones. This is obviously a weak compromise—if typically Babylonian—since it introduces an essential difference between the same earthly objects in the Mishna and in the Baraitha/Tosefta.

I have argued elsewhere—the difference between "invalid" and "sacrifices of the dead" notwithstanding—that the combined list in the Baraitha may well have been the original version.[98] It follows the prohibition of Exodus 20:4f. (don't make for yourself a graven image of anything that is in the *heaven* above or on the *earth* below), though in reverse order. Starting with the mountains on earth and climaxing in Michael, the Great Prince in heaven, it breaks off with the small worm, the vilest and most futile creature on earth. The clear message, therefore, is that Michael is as worthy of sacrifice as is a small worm. Moreover, a sacrifice offered to him is regarded in all versions as a sacrifice of the dead, that is, the worst case of idolatry.

Again, as was the case with the graven images of angels in the Mekhilta quoted above, the angel Michael seems to be the major concern of the rabbis: as it is forbidden to worship graven images of angels, so too is it forbidden to offer sacrifices to them (it is no coincidence that Michael is given as an example—Michael, the Prince of Israel, who offers the sacrifices in the heavenly Temple).[99] Having said this, I should like to add that these texts don't necessarily imply that angels were actually worshiped in Second Temple Judaism. I clearly overstated this point in *Rivalität*,[100] and Larry Hurtado rightly criticized me for it.[101] But I don't think that this is the main issue. Whether or not the angels were in fact worshiped in ancient Judaism, the rabbis make a forthright effort to include the angels as possible objects of worship—encouraged no doubt by contemporaneous pagan practices as well as by Jewish customs. After all, according to ancient cosmology, the angels govern the heavenly bodies, which in turn govern the years and the festivals. As we have seen, the apostle Paul not only subordinates the Law of Moses to the new law of Jesus[102]; he also warns his fellow Jews against observing the "special days, months, seasons, and years" as well as the "festivals, new moons, or Sabbaths," which are all under the authority of the angels.[103] The Kerygma Petrou—first half of the second century C.E., probably from Egypt—follows the same tradition when it says of the Jews that they "worship angels and archangels, the months and the moon."[104] And no lesser personage than Origen quotes Celsus as claiming that certain Jews "worship the heaven and the angels who dwell therein."[105] That Origen rejected such an accusation is no proof that it is completely unfounded.[106] To reiterate, it makes little sense to attempt to reconstruct Jewish groups that actually worshiped angels; but it makes equally little sense to argue that the Christian "condemnations of Jews as worshipping angels" are but "theologically motivated interpretations of Jewish ritual observances."[107] This is a false alternative. Paul and the theologians following him debased the Jewish law, but this did not mean that what they had to say about it and its customs was invented purely for the sake of theological argument. The rabbis obviously had every reason to fear the Jewish worship of angels, and it would hardly have smoothed their ruffled feathers that the Christians demoted their Torah to a product of the angels and imputed to the Jews worship of these same angels.

Traditionally, one of the major tasks of the angels is to act as Israel's or the individual's advocate before God and to submit their prayers to him. This is common practice in Second Temple and rabbinic Judaism.[108] But whereas the angels as a rule are mere mediators between human beings and God and play no significant role in decision making—that is, in terms of whether or not God grants the prayers—the following midrash goes a step further:

> R. Yudan said in his own name: a human being has a patron. If a bad fate falls upon him, he does not go immediately to him [the patron] but positions himself at the patron's gate and calls [one of his] servant[s] or [one of the] member[s] of his household. He then says [to the patron]: N.N. stands at the gate of your courtyard—shall [I] let him in?
>
> Not so the Holy One, blessed be he. If trouble befalls someone, he should not cry out to Michael or to Gabriel—

to me he should cry out, and I will hear him immediately. This is what is written: "Then everyone who calls on the name of the Lord shall be saved" (Joel 3:5).[109]

This midrash is part of a series of midrashim on patrons, attributed to R. Yudan (the fourth-generation Palestinian amora, circa 350 C.E.).[110] They all attack the Roman system of patronage by pointing out that the Jewish God's patronage is far more beneficial and efficacious than any Roman patron's could be. This particular midrash criticizes the mediators interposed between patron and client—the servants or members of the patron's household who ultimately decide whether or not the client's petition reaches the ears of the patron. True, R. Yudan argues, Michael and Gabriel are God's mediators, but in times of trouble God's creatures should not turn to them but directly and immediately to God himself. It is God who answers their prayers and saves them from trouble, not the angels.

This is the crucial point. Unlike the Roman patronage system, where it might sometimes be better and more useful to know (and bribe) the patron's servant, addressing one's request to Michael or Gabriel—that is, in fact, praying to them—does not quite do the trick. Again these two angels are singled out as the most important among their celestial brethren. As we have seen, the rabbis found it necessary to ensure that Michael and Gabriel did not participate in God's creation[111] and that no sacrifices were offered up to Michael.[112] The angels, particularly Michael and Gabriel, were obviously regarded as potential intruders into a realm strictly reserved for God: creation, revelation, prayer, and worship. The third in league with Michael and Gabriel is Metatron. Whereas the Babylonian Talmud openly polemicizes against worshiping Metatron,[113] the Palestinian parallel has an anonymous "Prince," most likely Michael, as the object of its critique.[114]

To sum up, there can be little doubt that Judaism was well on its way to developing or even institutionalizing an intermediate level of angelic powers between God and his creatures and that the rabbis consciously and quite effectively put a halt to this trend. Evidence in Palestinian sources for this potential danger is rather scanty, but the few surviving texts speak for themselves. Philo's angelic powers and the Christian critique of (alleged) Jewish angel-worship may well have helped the rabbis in their attempts to nip the danger in the bud. But this seems true mainly for Palestine. In contrast to the situation in Palestine, certain Jewish groups in Babylonia must have succeeded in establishing Metatron, the human-turned-angel, as a second divine power next to God. Although an angel, he was superior to all the other angels and was even worshiped by them. In this regard, as I have demonstrated above, he is the only "angel" who can compare to Jesus.

Adam

THE HEBREW BIBLE GIVES TWO VERY DIFFERENT accounts of God's creation of Adam, the first man. In the first creation account (Gen. 1:1–2:3), presumably part of the Priestly narrative (P), Adam's creation comes at the very end of God's creation activity, on the sixth and last day. Having finished with all the creatures inhabiting the newly created earth, God finally says: "Let us make man (*adam*) in our image (*be-tzalmenu*), after our likeness (*ki-demutenu*)" (Gen. 1:26), and then he immediately puts this plan into action: "And God created man (*adam*) in his image (*be-tzalmo*), in the image of God he created *him*, male and female he created *them*" (Gen. 1:27). I have discussed these two verses above and pointed to the strange shift from "created him" (that is, man) to "created them" in Genesis 1:27.[1] Clearly, "man" is not "humankind," as the politically correct translation in the New Revised Standard Version of the Hebrew Bible insinuates, but rather Adam, that single and unique first man created by God. And the shift from "him" to "them" is P's solution to the problem of how Eve, Adam's female partner, was created: Eve's creation is not made explicit—as it is in the second creation account—but only mentioned in passing, indicated solely by the shift from "him" to "them."[2] Now that both Adam and Eve have in fact been created, the next verse can continue, "God blessed *them*, and God said to *them*: Be fruitful and multiply, and fill the earth and subdue it" (Gen. 1:28)—Adam's creation is the climax of God's creational activity, and Eve is somehow included in it.

The second creation account (Gen. 2:4–25), presumably part of the Jahwist's narrative (J), tells a very different story. It explicitly states that Adam's creation took place when the earth was completely empty—with no plants and herbs because there wasn't yet any rain—that is, on the first day of creation, in crass contradiction to P. Moreover, it explains how Adam was created: God formed him from the dust of the ground (*adamah*, a play on words with *adam*) and breathed life into his nostrils (Gen. 4:5–7)—again in diametrical contrast to P's claim that Adam was created in the image and likeness of God. And immediately after Adam's creation God fashioned the Garden of Eden, where Adam was placed and instructed to till and maintain it (Gen. 2:15). Then follows Eve's creation, on which much greater detail is lavished than in P's account. First, God muses that it is unsalutary for Adam to be alone and decides to "make him a helper as his partner" (Gen. 2:18). But before he carries out this plan, he creates all the animals and birds (forming them out of the ground as he did with Adam) and orders Adam to accord them suitable names (Gen. 1:19). It is only after Adam has duly disposed of this task that the narrator remembers that Adam's partner is still missing, and he now has God finally create Eve—in a rather complicated procedure, to be sure: he causes a deep sleep to fall upon Adam, takes one of his ribs, and "made[3] it into a woman" (*ishah*). When Eve is brought by God to Adam, he recognizes her as flesh of his flesh and ultimately gives her a name: "woman" (*ishah*) because she was taken from "man" (*ish*).[4]

Reading these two accounts, one will not be surprised that they gave rise to confusion and worries; but here is not the place to deal with all their implications, and I will limit my considerations to the problem of Adam's relationship with God. Two of the inconsistencies and tensions in the two creation accounts immediately stand out: first, the contradiction regarding the day of Adam's creation (sixth day versus first day), and second, the tension regarding the question of how Adam was created (in the image and likeness of God versus from the dust of the ground). I will discuss the relevant sources in the order of their respective age and provenance (Palestinian or Babylonian).

The earliest text relevant to our subject can be found in Mishna Sanhedrin, where the Mishna, in the context of warning the witnesses, refers to the difference between witnesses in capital cases and in property cases: whereas in trials of property cases the false witness achieves atonement for himself by paying a certain sum of money, in capital cases the "[wrongfully accused's] blood and the blood of all his descendants are held against him [the false witness] forever" (as was the case with Cain).[5] In order to illustrate this principle, the Mishna continues:

Therefore man [Adam] was created alone/singular (*yehidi*), to teach you that whoever destroys a single soul from Israel, Scripture imputes it to him as though he had destroyed a complete world. And whoever preserves a single soul from Israel, Scripture imputes it to him as though he had preserved a complete world.

Furthermore, [Adam was created alone] for the sake of peace among humankind, [namely,] that one might not say to his fellow: "My father was greater than your father."

And that the heretics (*minim*) might not say: "There are many ruling powers (*harbeh rashuyyot*) in heaven."[6]

Why is the blood of the wrongfully accused (and executed) held against the false witness forever? Because the false witness hasn't killed just one man—he has killed a complete world. To make this principle clear, the Mishna argues, Adam was created alone, that is, as a single person and not in several versions, and the world in its entirety is encapsulated in the life of Adam and the lives of all his descendants.

The second explanation adds another dimension: in creating Adam alone or singular, God made sure that all subsequent humankind stemmed from one father so that no one could claim another and greater father for himself. This sets the tone for the third explanation: if there had been several Adams and they claimed different fathers for themselves, the heretics could indeed conclude that there were different gods who created them (as many as the originally created Adams). So, ultimately, Adam's creation as a single and unique person corresponds to the notion of the single and unique God in Judaism.

No doubt, this last statement is a bit of a stretch. Why would one want to suggest in the first place that God created not one Adam but, at the same time, several Adams? And why would one want to conclude from this that different gods created different Adams? There are certainly no grounds for such an assumption in the biblical text. The only conclusion that we may derive from our reference in the Mishna is the fact that some (later?) editor of the Mishna found the heresy of many ruling powers threatening enough to mention it in this rather far-fetched context. Nor can we sustain any meaningful argument for the identity of our heretics,[7] unless we want to take literally the "*many* ruling powers" allegedly creating many Adams and then interpret this phrase—which stands in stark contrast to the much more common "two powers" (*shetei rashuyyot*)—as referring not to certain dualistic heresies but to the Greco-Roman pantheon of multiple gods who do a variety of things. But this is only a vague supposition that cannot be validated.

The next text to be discussed is also relatively early (preserved in the Tosefta) and, unlike the Mishna, definitely refers to the biblical creation narrative:

> Adam was created last. And why was he created last? That the heretics (*minin*)[8] might not say: He [God] had a partner (*shutaf*) [Adam] in his work (of creation).[9]

This exegesis follows the first creation narrative in Genesis, according to which Adam was fashioned on the last, that is, sixth day of creation; the parallel in the Bavli specifies further that he was created on Sabbath eve (*'erev shabbat*)—that is, in that very last moment before God took a rest from his strenuous creation activity.[10] The anonymous Tosefta author argues that the clear reason for this is God's seeking to ensure that the heretics would have no incentive in maintaining that Adam helped God with his creation. This immediately reminds us of the rabbis' effort to keep the creation of the angels away from the first day of creation at any cost—and for very much the same reason: that they could not be God's partners in his work of creation.[11] So some people—called here "heretics"—must have held the view that not only the/some angels but also Adam were divine powers who participated in God's creative activity. The text gives no concrete explanation of just who these "heretics" might have been, but it makes little sense for us to restrict ourselves to a single specific heretical group or sect (e.g., the oft-favored "Gnostics"); as we have seen in other cases, our "heretics" may even have been certain rabbis who ventured to suggest certain bold interpretations of the Hebrew Bible. In postponing Adam's creation to the very last moment, our anonymous author thereby thwarts the possible emergence of a second god next to God (presumably of lower rank because Adam was nevertheless created).

But why, alongside the angels, was Adam a candidate for such a divine or semidivine being? Such speculations are obviously based on the pre-sin Adam, that is, before he ate from the Tree of Knowledge and while he was still an innocent creature fresh from creation.[12] This is precisely what a midrash preserved in Babylonian as well as in Palestinian sources proposes:

> Rav Yehudah said in the name of Rav: The first man (*adam ha-rishon*) reached from one end of the world to the other, as it is written: "Since the day that God created man (*adam*) on the earth, even from one end of heaven to the other" (Deut. 4:32). But when he sinned, the Holy One, blessed be he, laid his hand upon him and diminished him, as it is written: "You have hemmed me in, behind and before, and lay your hand upon me" (Ps. 139:5).
>
> R. Eleazar said: The first man reached from earth to heaven, as it is written: "Since the day that God created man (*adam*) on the earth, even from one end of heaven to the other" (Deut. 4:32). But when he sinned, the Holy One, blessed be he, laid his hand upon him and diminished him, as it is written: "You have hemmed me in, behind and before, etc." (Ps. 139:5).
>
> But these interpretations contradict each other!—(No,) both measurements are identical.[13]

Both interpretations assign to Adam gigantic dimensions, the first (Rav Yehudah in the name of Rav)[14] maintaining that he covered the whole earth (horizontally) and the second (R. Eleazar)[15] suggesting that he reached from earth to heaven (vertically). The Talmud editor notices the tension if not contradiction between these two interpretations—which use the same biblical verse as proof text, although in fact it fits R. Eleazar's interpretation better than Rav's—and he resolves it by arguing that both measurements are virtually identical in rendering Adam's enormous size.[16] Each tradition clearly assumes a gargantuan macro-anthropos,[17] with R. Eleazar's interpretation taking the boldest step in that it envisions Adam's head bursting through the heavenly clouds, as it were, and gazing eye-level with God. One can easily see how such an idea was perceived as dangerous—although, of course, Adam precipitated his own downfall and undermined his special status when he sinned and gave God the (desired) pretext to cut him down to size.

Whereas the midrash of Adam's originally mammoth dimensions gives no hint of a polemical debate (either within the rabbinical schools or with heretics from outside), the following text leaves no doubt that such a debate indeed took place:

> R. Hoshaiah said: When the Holy One, blessed be he, created Adam, the ministering angels mistook him (for a divine being) and wished to exclaim "Holy" before him.
> What does this resemble? A king and a governor (*eparchos*) who sat (together) in a chariot, and the people of the province wished to say to the king "Domine!"—but they didn't know which one was (the king). What did the king do? He pushed him [the governor] out of the chariot, and so they all knew that he was the governor (and not the king).
> Similarly, when the Holy One, blessed be he, created the first man (*adam ha-rishon*), the ministering angels mistook him (for a divine being) and wanted to exclaim "Holy" before him. What did the Holy One, blessed be he, do? He caused sleep to fall upon him, and so they all knew that he

was (but mortal) man. Thus it is written: "Turn away from (mortal) man, who has (only) breath in his nostrils, for of what account is he!" (Isa. 2:22).[18]

Here we have a very clear statement that the newly created Adam could indeed be mistaken for a divine being, and this by no less a group than the angels. It is quite ironic that the angels should have conceived such an idea if we recall how the midrash explains the fact that, according to the second creation narrative in Genesis, God gave Adam the task of naming all newly created creatures: God first gives the angels a chance to come up with appropriate names (a task which they embarrassingly botch), and then he calls in Adam, who knows not only the names of all the creatures but even the name by which God wishes to be praised by his angels. It is the height of irony that the angels are able to praise God properly only after *Adam* has revealed God's name.[19] To emphasize Adam's elevated status, well above that of the angels, in another version of this midrash God calls him by his own name "lord" (*adon*), using a nice play on words (*adam—adon*).[20]

Small wonder, then, that in our Bereshit Rabba midrash the angels draw the conclusion that this superior being deserves to be worshiped: their desire to exclaim "holy" before Adam doesn't mean that they regard him as "holy" in the usual sense of the word but rather that they wish to worship him with the trisagion of Isaiah 6:3 ("Holy, holy, holy is the Lord [*YHWH*] of hosts"), which is nothing short of declaring Adam a divine being, that is, a second god in heaven. Hence, the angels interpret the fact that Adam was created according to the image of God (Gen. 1:26) as meaning that he was indeed equal to God. As the parable demonstrates, Adam is so similar to God that the angels can actually no longer distinguish between the two, and God must take drastic measures—the king pushes the governor out of the chariot,

and God causes sleep to fall upon Adam—both of which immediately produce the desired result: the king's rival is reduced to
his state as a subordinate, and God's rival is unmasked as mortal.
(That sleep defines Adam as mortal is particularly ironic in this
context, since in the second creation narrative God causes a sleep
to fall upon Adam *after* Adam has called all the creatures by their
appropriate names, that is, after he has proven his superiority to
the angels.)

That the angels' worship of Adam must have been an issue in
ancient Judaism can also be inferred from the Vita Adae et Evae
(The Life of Adam and Eve), a kind of midrashic narrative about
the first couple subsequent to their expulsion from paradise. This
text, preserved in Greek and Latin but presumably going back to
a Hebrew original, may well be of Palestinian origin (although
some scholars suggest Alexandria in Egypt) and was probably
written toward the end of the first century C.E.[21] Here, the bone
of contention is precisely the fact that Adam was created in the
image of God. After Adam's "countenance and likeness were
made in the image of God," Michael, by God's order, demands
that all the angels in heaven worship Adam. The only resisters are
Satan and his followers among the angels:

> And Michael went out and called all the angels, saying:
> Worship the image of the Lord God, as the Lord God
> has instructed. And Michael himself worshiped first, and
> called me [Satan] and said: Worship the image of God,
> Yahweh. And I [Satan] answered: I do not worship Adam.
> And when Michael kept forcing me to worship, I said to
> him: Why do you compel me? I will not worship one infe-
> rior and subsequent to me. I am prior to him in creation;
> before he was made, I was already made. He ought to wor-
> ship me.[22]

When Satan continues to refuse, he and his angelic followers are expelled from heaven and cast down to earth, Satan's refusal to worship Adam becoming the reason for the fall of the angels. Interestingly, Satan's argument that he was created before Adam and hence more deserving of worship is quite a "rabbinic" one, since according to the rabbis the angels were created on the second or fifth day, that is, definitely before Adam, who was created on the sixth. It is difficult to determine the *Sitz im Leben* of this narrative in the Vita, but the similarity between the Vita and our rabbinic midrash is striking, the major difference being the fact that God in the Vita *demands* the angels worship Adam, whereas in the midrash the angels *mistakenly* believe—certainly against God's will—that they should worship him. Yet the disturbing message of both sources remains: certain people in the first centuries C.E. maintained that Adam, although created, was a divine or at least semidivine being who deserved to be worshiped, and the rabbis vehemently opposed such a "heretical" idea. But who in fact might these "certain people" have been?

The graphic image of the king throwing his rival out of his chariot has prompted scholars to search for a more concrete historical setting, and it was Alexander Altmann who proposed the following context: When Galerius, Caesar under the Augustus Diocletian, was defeated in Mesopotamia by the Sassanid king Narseh in 296 C.E., Diocletian allegedly humiliated Galerius for this defeat (when the two met in Antioch) by forbidding him to sit beside him in the imperial chariot and instead forcing him to walk in front of him.[23] The historical value of this interpretation is far from proven,[24] but there can be no doubt that the co-rulership of the Augustus and the Caesar was prone to tensions (after all, the Caesar was destined to one day become the Augustus' successor). A "governor," as the parable has it, could hardly be perceived as the emperor's rival, but a Caesar clearly could (after Diocletian's reform). And the time frame fits quite well if we identify the R. Hoshaiah in our midrash not as Hoshaiah I, the first-generation Palestinian amora (living around 225 C.E.), but as Hoshaiah II, the third-generation Palestinian amora of Babylonian origin, who lived around 300 C.E. This brings us strikingly close to Diocletian and Galerius, co-rulers of the East. Furthermore, if we take into consideration that, as I have emphasized above,[25] the imperial hierarchy of the Augustus and Caesar serves also as background or even blueprint for the emerging Christological debates on the relationship between the Father and the Son, we might see in our midrash the echo of precisely this debate—there is no such construct of two equal co-rulers, either on earth or in heaven, our rabbis would argue, since it simply doesn't work; rather sooner than later they will be at loggerheads. Hence we, the rabbis, don't believe in two divine powers in heaven—our God has made this perfectly clear by causing sleep to fall upon Adam, the would-be God, thus revealing his mortality.

Such a Christological interpretation of our midrash makes much more sense than Altmann's gnostic reading, imagining sleep as "synonymous with the entanglement of man in the world of evil, his intoxication with the poison of darkness."[26] This sounds very much like a Hans-Jonas-inspired version of "the" gnostic myth, far removed from the actual evidence.[27] Pace Altmann, the "sleep" in our midrash is of course taken from Genesis 2:21 and has nothing to do with any gnostic ideas about evil and darkness.

The potential Christological background becomes even more evident in looking at Philo and the New Testament. In tune with his fundamental distinction between the archetypal world of ideas discerned only by the mind or the intellect (*kosmos noētos*) and the created world perceived by our senses (*kosmos aisthētos*),[28] Philo also distinguishes between two Adams in Genesis: whereas the Adam of Genesis 2:7 refers to the earthly Adam, Genesis 1:27 in fact refers to the ideal man:

After this he [Moses] says that "God formed man by taking clay from the earth, and breathed into his face the breath of life" (Gen. 2:7). By this also he shows very clearly that there is a vast difference between the man thus formed and the man that came into existence earlier after the image of God: for the man so formed is an object of sense-perception (*aisthētos*), partaking already of such or such quality, consisting of body and soul, man or woman, by nature mortal; while he that was after the (divine) image was an idea or type or seal, an object of thought only (*noētos*), incorporeal, neither male nor female, by nature incorruptible.[29]

Philo makes very clever use here of the major differences between the two creation accounts in Genesis. The man created from the dust of the earth—in using the word "clay" Philo follows the Septuagint translation—is the earthly Adam (in the literary sense of the word), consisting of body and soul, who has a partner (as Gen. 2:21ff. describes in graphic detail, unlike the first creation account where the woman is at most hinted at) and who is mortal (sleep). Quite in contrast, the man of Genesis 1 is incorporeal, not yet male or female, and incorruptible, that is, immortal. The earthly Adam of Genesis 2 is part of the *kosmos aisthētos*, whereas the heavenly Adam of Genesis 1 pertains to the *kosmos noētos*, perceived only by the intellect.

Who then is the heavenly Adam of the first creation account in Genesis 1? If we follow Philo's theological system, the answer is clear. Since the ideal world of the *kosmos noētos* takes shape in the mind of God, which is the divine Logos ("Word"),[30] Philo can even identify the *kosmos noētos* with the Logos:

Should a man desire to use words in a more simple and direct way, he would say that the world discerned only by the intellect (*ton noēton kosmon*) is nothing else than the word of God (*theou logon*) when he was already engaged in the act of creation.[31]

So if Adam represents the *kosmos noētos* thought by the Logos, it is only logical to take the next step and *identify* him with the Logos. And this is indeed what Philo does. He says that the Logos, "God's First-born, who holds the eldership among the angels (*anggelōn presbytaton*), their archangel as it were," is called by many names, among them "the Beginning" (*archē*), "the Name of God" (*onoma theou*), the Word (*logos*)—and "the Man after his image" (*ho kat' eikona anthrōpos*).[32] The "Man after his image" no doubt is the Adam of Genesis 1, who is identical to God's Logos, the "most holy Word," and as Philo further specifies, "the eldest-born image (*eikōn presbytatos*) of God."[33] This is a bold statement that creates an almost insurmountable gap between the heavenly Logos-Adam and the earthly Adam. In elevating the Logos-Adam above the (ordinary) angels, Philo follows the same idea as Vita Adae et Evae, casting it, however, in Platonic garb.

Moving now to the New Testament, we see striking similarities between Philo and certain ideas about the Logos Jesus, in particular in Paul. (I have no intention of making an argument here about any possible relationship between Philo and Paul; I am merely pointing out the structural overlaps.) In his first Letter to the Corinthians, Paul makes the following distinction between the first and the second/last Adam:[34]

45: the first man Adam	the last Adam
ho prōtos anthrōpos Adam:	*ho eschatos Adam*:
became a living being	became a life-giving spirit
psychē zōsa (Gen. 2:7)	*pneuma zōopoioun*

47: the first man	the second man
ho prōtos anthrōpos	*ho deuteros anthrōpos*
was from the earth	is from the heaven
ek gēs	*ex ouranou*
of earth/clay	
choïkos	
48: the man of earth/clay	the man of heaven
ho xoïkos	*ho epouranios*
49: the man of earth/clay	the man of heaven
ho xoïkos	*ho epouranios*

There can be no doubt that the first man/Adam is modeled along the lines of Genesis 2, that is, of the second creation account, and refers to the earthly Adam, created out of earth, and that the second/last Adam is modeled along the lines of the first creation account (Genesis 1) and refers to Jesus, the heavenly Adam. Over and over again Paul makes clear that the first man is made of earth (*xoïkos*) and that the second man is from the heaven (*epouranios*)—presumably not made of heaven but of heavenly origin. Accordingly, the first man becomes a living being by God breathing life into his nostrils (Genesis 2:7), whereas the second man does not receive but rather gives life. Paul doesn't explain here where the second man comes from, but he seems to imply that he is (forever?) with God in heaven. This stark contrast between the first and second man comes surprisingly close to Philo's contrast between the earthly and heavenly Adam.

By calling the earthly Adam "first man" and the heavenly Adam = Jesus "second/last man," Paul certainly does not refer to an ontological or chronological sequence (first Adam and then Jesus); rather, he refers to the soteriological sequence in the course of history: first the earthly Adam entered earth, sinned, and became the progenitor of all humankind; and then Jesus came to earth and saved all humankind through his death and resurrection. Ontologically speaking, Jesus comes first, since he was with God in heaven before the creation of Adam. This is made crystal clear by the author of the Letter to the Colossians (whether Paul or someone else):

> (1:15) He [Jesus] is the image (*eikōn*) of the invisible God,
> the firstborn (*prōtotokos*) of all creation;
> (16) for in him (*en autō*) all things in heaven and on earth were created,
> things visible and invisible . . .
> all things have been created through him (*di' autou*) and for him (*eis auton*).
> (17) He himself is before all things (*pro pantōn*),
> and in him (*en autō*) all things hold together.
> (18) . . . He is the beginning (*archē*),
> the firstborn (*prōtotokos*) from the dead,
> so that he might come to have first place in everything.[35]

In calling Jesus the "image" of God, Paul clearly evokes the first creation account (Gen. 1:26f.) and identifies Jesus with the second/last Adam of First Corinthians. Hence, Jesus is the "firstborn," created before all creation (and certainly before the earthly Adam). This is immediately reminiscent of Philo's Adam as the "eldest-born image (*eikōn presbytatos*) of God." Just as Philo's Logos is the place and origin of the ideal world that in turn serves as blueprint for the visible world, Paul's Jesus, preceding all creation, "contains" in him all things in heaven and on earth that will be created. As such he is "before all things" and the "beginning" (*archē*) of everything, just as Philo's Adam-Logos is called "the Beginning" (*archē*). Only Philo's qualification of the First-born as the "eldest among the angels" is missing here, but it is duly emphasized in the Letter to the Hebrews, where Jesus is explicitly praised as "superior to the angels"[36] and where God—precisely as in the Vita Adae et Evae—demands from the angels worship of his Firstborn Jesus:

> And again, when he [God] brings the firstborn (*ton prōtotokon*) into the world, he says: "Let all God's angels worship him."[37]

What Paul has God saying here is a quotation from Deuteronomy 32:43 according to the Greek translation of the Hebrew Bible (the Septuagint), a line that in fact is missing in the Masoretic text of the Hebrew Bible.[38] The "him" in Deuteronomy 32:43 of course refers to God; so Paul ultimately identifies God's Firstborn Jesus with God himself—having previously quoted Psalms 2:7 ("You are my Son; today I have begotten you") and 2 Samuel 7:14 ("I will be his Father, and he will be my Son"): Jesus, God's Firstborn and Son, has been elevated to a divine being in heaven deserving of worship by the angels and consequently also by human beings.

And hence we come full circle. In view of the background of the Philonic and Pauline passages just discussed, I should like to argue that the rabbinic polemic against Adam as a supernatural and (semi)divine being is aimed at possible Christological interpretations of the Adam myth. I do not claim that our rabbinic midrashim—in particular the one in Bereshit Rabba—are directly responding to Philo or to Paul (there are no such hints in the texts); rather I posit that the rabbis, familiar with the hierarchical structure of the Roman Empire after the Diocletian reform, got wind of the emerging Christological debates centered around Adam-the Logos-Jesus and reacted vehemently against such implications. None of the Adam texts betray sympathy for these ideas; they are generally perceived as dangerous and hence attacked. Yet this does not exclude the possibility that they did in fact gain a foothold among certain rabbis; on the contrary, as I have pointed out above,[39] older Jewish concepts of Wisdom and the Logos could easily lead to such dangerous speculations. After all, Philo is a perfect case in point. Therefore, instead of trying to nail down well-defined circles of "heretics" being attacked by the rabbis, I again opt for the alternative that our Adam midrashim argue against enemies from within, that is, from within a not yet fully established and demarcated rabbinic Judaism.

8

The Birth of the Messiah, or Why Did Baby Messiah Disappear?

PROVING TO BE OF CRUCIAL IMPORTANCE FOR OUR subject is the distinction between Palestine and Babylonia, the two centers of Jewish life in antiquity as reflected in the predominantly Palestinian Midrashim and the Jerusalem Talmud on the one hand and the Babylonian Talmud on the other. These two Jewish communities lived under very different political and social circumstances: the former under Roman rule with the growing influence of a Christian religion that would increasingly dominate and even suffocate Jewish life in Palestine, and the latter under Persian (that is, Sassanian) rule with the *Christian* community increasingly seen as the fifth column of the Byzantine Empire and subjected to a series of persecutions by the Sassanian authorities. These remarkably dissimilar conditions under which the Palestinian and Babylonian Jews lived had a direct bearing on their attitudes toward their Christian sister religion. Whereas the later Babylonian Jews were confronted with a more or less defined Christian *religion*, their Palestinian brethren witnessed Christianity *in statu nascendi*, that is, during its birthing process, which was not marked by a well-defined point in time but took place over an extended period until finally developing into a mature religion of its own. Accordingly, the Palestinian sources are much less direct than their Babylonian counterparts—more restrained—and more often than not even ambiguous.

In what follows I will analyze just a single one of these ambiguous sources, a famous text in the Palestinian Talmud's tractate Berakhot (Benedictions or Blessings). Fittingly the very first tractate of the Talmud, Berakhot deals with prayers and certain blessings that are part of such prayers. One of the two most important Jewish prayers, next to the *Shemaʿ Yisraʾel* or "Hear, O Israel!" prayer, is the so-called Eighteen Benedictions prayer, the *Shemoneh ʿEsreh* in Hebrew. Its fourteenth blessing, called "Who rebuilds Jerusalem," is one of the eschatological blessings of the prayer connected with the messianic restoration and the Messiah from the house of David, and in discussing this blessing the Talmud refers to the various names used for the Messiah. Among the names mentioned is also that of Menahem, which literally means "comforter." This suggestion is made by a certain R. Yudan in the name of another rabbi, R. Aibo (a Palestinian amora of the fourth generation, who flourished in the first part of the fourth century),[1] and to support his claim R. Yudan tells the following story, also in the name of R. Aibo.[2] My English translation tries to follow as closely as possible the Aramaic original:

(1) As it happened, a certain Jew was plowing when his cow lowed. A certain Arab was passing by and heard its voice.

He said to him [the Jew]: "Son of a Jew, son of a Jew, unharness your ox and unharness your plow, for the Temple has been destroyed."

When she lowed a second time, he said to him: "Son of a Jew, son of a Jew, harness your ox and harness your plow, for the King Messiah has been born."

He [the Jew] said to him [the Arab]: "What is his name?"

[The Arab answered:] Menahem.

[The Jew] asked: "What is his father's name?"

[The Arab] answered: "Hezekiah."

[The Jew] asked: "Where is he from?"

[The Arab] answered: "From the royal city, Bethlehem in Judah."

(2) [The Jew] went, sold his ox and sold his plow and became a peddler of swaddling clothes for babies. He went from city to city[3] until he came to that city. All the women (there) made purchases except the mother of Menahem.

He heard the voices of the women saying: "Menahem's mother, Menahem's mother, come, make a purchase for your son." (But) she said: "I would rather like to strangle the enemies of Israel, for on the day that he was born, the Temple was destroyed."

He [the peddler] said to her: "We trust that as it was destroyed in his wake (*be-ragleih*), in his wake it will be rebuilt."

She said to him: "I have no money."

He answered: "What does it matter to me? Come and make a purchase for him. If you don't have any money today, I will come back later[4] and collect it."

(3) Some time later, he came [back] to that city and said to her: "How is the baby doing?"

She answered: "After you saw me, winds (*ruhin*) and whirlwinds (*'al'olim*) came and snatched him out of my hands."

(4) R. Bun said: "Why do we need to learn from this Arab? Isn't there an explicit biblical passage (to this effect)? Namely, 'Lebanon[5] will fall by a powerful (or: mighty, majestic) one' (Isa. 10:34).[6] What is written (immediately) thereafter? 'And a shoot shall come forth from the stump of Jesse' (Isa. 11:1)."[7]

This is a strange story indeed.[8] It is structured in four sequences (marked by the numbers 1 to 4 in my translation): (1) the exchange between the Jew and the Arab in the field, (2) the first exchange between the Jew and the mother of the baby in Bethlehem, (3) the second exchange between the Jew and the mother, and (4) the learned exegesis by another rabbi, R. Bun (which is rendered in Hebrew instead of Aramaic and is clearly an addition that has nothing to do with the story itself). I will briefly point out some of the problems and oddities of the story that immediately catch our eye and then go on to a detailed discussion of the various motifs:

- That the birth of the Messiah is announced by the lowing or mooing of a cow is highly unusual, to say the least, and even more so in that this omen must then be explained by an Arab, of all people. To be more precise, even the motif of the Messiah's birth is not a particularly common one in the Jewish tradition.[9] Typically, the Messiah comes down from heaven, sent by God, as an adult, his birth and childhood being of no particular interest.
- The same holds true for the mother of the Messiah, who plays no significant role in the Jewish messianic tradition. There exists only one much later text in which a mother of the Messiah is mentioned (to which I will return later).

- The name of the Messiah, Menahem son of Hezekiah, is uncommon. Apart from our story, it appears only in a long section of the Babylonian Talmud listing the names of the Messiah.[10]

- The search for the Messiah by the Jewish farmer turned peddler is strange. To begin with, why does the Jew so blatantly ignore the Arab's advice to harness his ox and his plow? After all, the Messiah has been born and everything is fine again. Moreover, if he decides to ignore the Arab's advice so as to return to his job as a farmer, then why does he need to look for the Messiah at all? Hadn't the Arab just informed him that the Messiah had been born in the city of Bethlehem? The only parallel to his search that I know of is the story, again in the Babylonian Talmud, according to which R. Yehoshua b. Levi inquires of the prophet Elijah as to the whereabouts of the Messiah, and Elijah sends him to the city of Rome (of all places), where the Messiah is sitting among lepers and waiting for his big moment.[11]

- The exchange between the Jew and the baby's mother is the most bizarre part of the story. First of all, we are never explicitly told that the baby is the Messiah—following the peddler, we can infer this only from his name, Menahem, and from the fact that the women of Bethlehem call his mother "Menahem's mother"; since we know that the Messiah's name is Menahem, we understand that the peddler has attained his goal (although, to be sure, Menahem happens to be quite a common Jewish name). And what are we to make of the Messiah's mother's weird excuse for not buying diapers for her newborn—that she would rather strangle the enemies of Israel, that is, the Romans?![12] What has her desire to kill the Romans to do with neglecting her child? Obviously we have here a very bad mother and certainly not the exemplary "Jewish mother," whose concern for her children is proverbial. Even when the peddler tries to comfort her by arguing that the birth of the Messiah is connected with the Temple in a double sense—true, it follows the destruction of the Second Temple, but ultimately it will usher in the construction of the third and last Temple—even then the mother comes up with the lame excuse that she has no money. In order to save the poor baby, the peddler has to force the diapers on her. In a much later parallel to our Yerushalmi story the mother, after the birth, even leaves her baby in his birth blood at her front door and idly takes her seat next to him[13]—a very uncaring mother indeed. And sadly, the peddler's concern for the baby obviously does not help. When he comes back to see how baby Messiah is doing, the mother tells him, strangely unmoved, that he has disappeared and that she doesn't know where he is.

- Finally, another odd inconsistency in the story: In the exchange between the Jew and the Arab the Messiah is clearly born *after* the destruction of the Temple, whereas the mother in her answer to the peddler seems to imply that somehow the birth of the Messiah is linked with the Temple's destruction, and the peddler takes this up by arguing that the Temple will also be rebuilt "in his wake."

So much for our first run-through of the story's oddities. Now let us have a closer look at the motifs.

The Arab

The Arab, although unusual in connection with the Messiah, is quite common in the rabbinic literature—and his image is ambiguous.[14] On the one hand we find a number of quite nasty traditions depicting the Arabs not only as the most lecherous—"there is no harlotry (*zenut*) like the harlotry of the Arabs"[15]—but the most obtuse of peoples—"ten portions of stupidity are assigned to the world: nine among the Ishmaelites, and one to (the rest of) the world."[16] (According to both Jews and Muslims the ancestors of the Arab people were the Ishmaelites, descendants of Ishmael, Abraham's eldest son by his wife Sarah's handmaiden Hagar.) A well-known midrash on Exodus 20:2, the beginning of the Ten Commandments,[17] has God asking all the nations whether or not they accept the Torah, and they all reject it for reasons that would appear to be a prime example of ancient stereotypes: The "children of Esau"—that is, the Romans, according to rabbinic taxonomy—reject the Torah because it prohibits murder. Their answer to God's offer is: "The very heritage which our father [Esau] left us was, 'And by your sword shall you live' (Gen. 27:40)." The "children of Amon and Moab" likewise reject the Torah because it prohibits adultery. Their answer to God's offer makes reference to the fact that the daughters of Lot slept with their father and that out of this union (which was actually incest and not adultery, but our midrash isn't troubled by such fine distinctions) were born the forefathers of the Ammonites and Moabites. Finally, when God offers his Torah to the "children of Ishmael," they reject it because it forbids stealing. The biblical proofs for this rejection are remarkable (and very typical of midrashic exegesis):

> They [the Ishmaelites] said to him [God]: "The very blessing that had been pronounced upon our father [Ishmael]

was: 'He shall be a wild ass of a man: his hand shall be upon everything (*yado ba-kol*)' (Gen. 16:12). And it is written: 'For indeed, I was stolen away (*gunnov gunnavti*) out of the land of the Hebrews' (Gen. 40:15)."

Again, the midrash takes both verses very literally. That Ishmael's hand "shall be upon everything" simply means that he is prone to stealing; and the person speaking in the second verse is Joseph, who was "stolen" by the Ishmaelites—that the Ishmaelites did not steal Joseph but bought him from his brothers and actually saved his life (Gen. 37:25–28) is of little concern to the author of our midrash.

These examples may suffice as regards the nasty rabbinic traditions vis-à-vis the Arabs. But on the other hand, and quite in contrast to such unpleasant stereotypes, we also find the Arabs—a group characterized by their peculiar nomadic lifestyle—brought into a close relationship with nature, in particular animals.[18] Their skills make them exceptionally qualified to explain the signs of nature, such as in their "smelling" of sand in order to find the way to the next oasis,[19] or their ability to understand the language of the animals. The rabbis are no doubt adopting here traditions that were common in the Greco-Roman world. According to Cicero, for example, the Arabs—among other nations—were experts in deciphering the language and movements of birds,[20] and according to Pliny, the Greeks Pythagoras and Democritus visited the magicians of Persia, Arabia, Ethiopia, and Egypt.[21] The Greek historian Appian of Alexandria relates that during the Jewish uprising in Egypt (116 C.E.) he escaped being caught up in the massacre of the Jews thanks to his Arab guide, who was able to interpret the triple caw of a crow.[22] Philostratus (ca. 170–247 C.E.), one of the leading Greek sophists of his time, explains that the Arabs gain their knowledge of the birds' language through consuming the heart or liver of large snakes—apparently because snakes are regarded as the wisest and canniest of animals in the Bible (Gen. 3:1).[23]

It makes sense to see just such positive traditions about the divinatory abilities of the Arabs behind the Arab in our story.[24] Understanding the language of the cow, the Arab—and not the Jew—deciphers the omen of the cow's mooing: it means that the Temple has been destroyed and that the Messiah has been born. But the fact remains that the employment of such a tradition deviates considerably from standard Jewish tradition regarding the appearance of the Messiah. For one important element connected to the rabbinic expectation of the Messiah is missing here—the prophet Elijah as his forerunner.

ELIJAH

Scholars have therefore tried very hard to find motifs of the Elijah tradition in our story and to read it as a kind of transformation of the traditional messianic inventory: the Arab-turned-Elijah who announces the advent of the Messiah. The New Testament scholar Anna Maria Schwemer ingeniously directs our attention to the fact that the story distinguishes between the lowing cow and the harnessed ox used for plowing (most translations gloss over this distinction because the two words are almost identical in Aramaic).[25] Did the Jew use an ox and a cow for his plowing or did he use two oxen and the mooing cow just happened to be there as well? Schwemer suggests that the ox entered the story because, when the prophet Elijah called upon Elisha to follow him, Elisha was plowing with oxen.[26] This may seem a bit far-fetched—it also fails to explain the mooing cow[27]—but Schwemer provides some other postbiblical references according to which the prophet Elijah in fact originated in the land of the Arabs.[28]

Whether the Arab in our story has absorbed these and other traditional Elijah elements—or whether such a patchwork of intertextual references is the result of an untamed scholarly mind that in the end renders the passage meaningless—there is *one* Elijah element in the story that we cannot ignore: the whirlwind as the mother's excuse why the baby is gone. It is Elijah, and only Elijah, who did not die but was taken up into heaven by a whirlwind: "As they [Elijah and Elisha, his successor] continued walking and talking, a chariot of fire and horses of fire separated the two of them, and Elijah ascended in a whirlwind into heaven."[29] We don't have the chariot and the horses in our story but we do have the whirlwind, in Hebrew *se'arah*, which, quite conspicuously, is translated in the Targum (the Aramaic Bible translation) with *'al'ola*,[30] precisely the Aramaic word used in our story (*al'olim*). I will return to this motif later, but for the moment let it suffice to note that our story is connected with the (or rather some) Elijah traditions.

THE MESSIAH

Of course there exists no uniform expectation of the Messiah in the Jewish tradition. It begins with the hope for the restoration of the Davidic kingship, that is, the inauguration of a new king from the house of David, who will govern the reunited northern and southern kingdoms of Israel and Judah. Out of this hope evolved the expectation of a Davidic Messiah who would appear as the savior king at the end of time and usher in a new era entailing the ultimate victory over Israel's enemies, the rebuilding of the Temple, the gathering of the exiles, and a period of peace and prosperity. This expectation was augmented or changed by other elements—for example, a priestly Messiah equal or even superior to the Davidic Messiah (so predominant in the Qumran community), or the "Son of Man" from Daniel (so important in the New Testament). We can nevertheless safely assume that the Davidic Messiah had become the major messianic figure in the rabbinic period—as evidenced, for example, by the Eighteen Benedictions prayer or the Bar Kokhba revolt, the second major Jewish uprising against Rome in the first half of the second century (132–135 C.E.). Its hero, Simeon bar Kosiba, clearly assumes the role of the Davidic Messiah, albeit probably accompanied by a priestly Messiah (namely, a certain priest Eleazar who is mentioned on his coins).

A striking example of the need to link any messianic candidate with the house of David is also the genealogy of Jesus in Matthew, which begins with the solemn declaration: "An account of the genealogy of Jesus the Messiah, the son of David, the son of Abraham."[31] The genealogy that follows, however, is very odd. It not only includes several women—despite the common, largely patriarchal structure—but it also climaxes with "Jacob the father of Joseph the husband of Mary, of whom Jesus was born, who is called the Messiah."[32] So Jesus' Davidic genealogy is patrilineal, through his "father" Joseph, Mary's "husband"—although we learn immediately thereafter that his mother Mary was only *engaged* to Joseph and that her child was actually fathered by the Holy Spirit.[33] So, quite ironically, the author of the Gospel of Matthew finds it necessary to "prove" Jesus' Davidic lineage—although the child was in fact conceived by the Holy Spirit, that is, by God himself.

No doubt, therefore, that the Messiah in our story is the Messiah from the house of David. This is also made explicit by the fact that he was born in the "royal city" of Bethlehem in Judah. This, of course, alludes to the biblical verse Micah 5:1: "But you, O Bethlehem of Ephrath, least among the clans of Judah, from you shall come forth for me one who is to rule in Israel, whose origin is from of old, from ancient days"—a verse that, not surprisingly, plays an important role in the New Testament as well.

But what about his name, Menahem son of Hezekiah? "Menahem," comforter, is quite appropriate to a Messiah—but "son of Hezekiah"? We know Hezekiah as one of the kings of Judah who governed at the end of the eighth/beginning of the seventh century B.C.E. (727–698 or 715–687 B.C.E.), but he had no son by the name Menahem. The son of Hezekiah, a notably pious king, was Manasseh, the worst king in Israel's history, who was so wicked that the Book of Kings holds him responsible for the later destruction of the First Temple.[34] Is this then the connection—the destruction of the First and Second Temples? (Although strictly speaking, the enigmatic Menahem son of King Hezekiah would have been born about a hundred years *before* the destruction of the First Temple.) Things become more complicated by the fact that, according to the Babylonian Talmud, Menahem son of Hezekiah is indeed among the many possible names of the Messiah.[35] Other rabbis, also in the Bavli, entertain the possibility that Hezekiah himself may have been the Messiah: "R. Hillel said: 'There shall be no Messiah for Israel, because they have already enjoyed him in the days of Hezekiah.'"[36]

Yet there is still another option. One of the leading zealots during the first Jewish revolt against Rome (66–73 C.E.) was a certain Menahem son (or grandson) of Judas son of Hezekiah. The Jewish historian of the first Jewish war, Josephus Flavius, recounts that this Menahem conquered, along with his followers, the fortress Masada and subsequently played an important role in Jerusalem. The priestly zealots, however, opposed his claim to leadership and killed him when he attended the Temple worship, as Josephus says, in "royal attire."[37] This phrase may well be hinting at Menahem's messianic (that is, Davidic messianic) aspirations—aspirations that the priestly party invariably disliked. Some scholars suggest that with this Menahem we have located the famous "historical core" of our story: it echoes the murder of the historical Menahem, the zealot leader during the first Jewish war. To support this claim they refer to the Jewish peddler's remark, "We trust that as it was destroyed in his wake (*be-ragleih*), in his wake it will be rebuilt," which they read as meaning that the Temple was destroyed *because of him*, that is, the destruction of the second Temple was punishment for the murder of Menahem, which took place on (or rather near) the Temple compound.[38]

Scholars always like to discover the historical core of a story—but this one is too good to be true. To begin with, what has the *murder* of the alleged Messiah Menahem to do with the *birth* of the Messiah in our story? Second (if we accept this link), the fact that the Temple was destroyed "in his wake" does not necessarily mean that it was destroyed *because* of him, the newborn Messiah; it only posits a chronological link between the birth of the Messiah and the destruction of the Temple, not necessarily a causal one. This primarily chronological link is made clear in the mother's statement, "for *on the day* that he was born, the Temple was destroyed," which, in turn, is in keeping with the Arab's interpretation of the lowing cow: the first moo means that the Temple was destroyed, and the second moo refers to the birth of the Messiah (if the birth of the Messiah was the cause of the Temple's destruction, we would expect a reverse order).[39] So, in short, I think that neither the talmudic parallels nor the reference to the historical zealot leader are very helpful. They provide some hints as to the reservoir from which our story drew its inspiration—the collective memory, if you wish—but they don't *explain* the story in the sense that they tell us *why* these and other motifs have been used; in other words, they fail to explain the message of our story.

THE MOTHER OF THE MESSIAH

The only other Jewish text mentioning a mother of the Messiah is the seventh-century apocalypse Sefer Zerubbabel (Apocalypse of Zerubbabel), written against the backdrop of the Byzantine-Persian wars between 604 and 630 C.E.[40] There, the mother of the Davidic Messiah is called Hephzibah, and she plays an important role in the last war between the Jews and the Antichrist Armilos—presumably a reference to Romulus—who was born of the intercourse between Satan and the stone statue of a most beautiful virgin. As it happens, according to the Hebrew Bible,[41] Hephzibah was the mother of Manasseh, King Hezekiah's wicked son; therefore she must have been Hezekiah's wife (or one of his wives). This seems to be another piece of the biblical patchwork from which such stories were stitched together. But the mother of the Messiah in our story is very different from Hephzibah in the Book of Zerubbabel. In the Book of Zerubbabel it is Hephzibah, the mother of the Davidic Messiah, who initiates the "eschatological showdown,"[42] acting as the messianic warrior and slaying Israel's enemies. The first male Messiah to appear is the Messiah from the tribe of Ephraim, who will be killed in battle, and it requires the Messiah from the tribe of Judah, the Davidic Messiah and Hephzibah's son (whose name is Menahem son of Ammiel—another Menahem!) to resuscitate the slain Messiah and finally defeat the wicked Armilos.

The Messiah's mother in our story is just the opposite of the warlike mother in the Apocalypse of Zerubbabel. Not only is she completely impassive—even neglecting her child, as we have seen—but her behavior is much worse. To understand this, we need take another look at her strange statement: "I would rather like to strangle the enemies of Israel, for on the day that he [my son] was born, the Temple was destroyed." The first part of this sentence can also be read euphemistically, in fact meaning: "I would rather like to strangle him, my child, as the enemies of Israel." Such euphemisms are common in the rabbinic literature, in particular in the Yerushalmi,[43] but a closer look at the Yerushalmi text makes clear that the manuscripts are quite uncertain regarding the correct reading of this sentence. The Leyden manuscript (and accordingly the *editio princeps* Venice) reads: "I would rather like to strangle *him* (*mehnequneih*), the enemies of Israel,"[44] and hence reveals the attempt of a later scribe/editor to replace the suspicious "to strangle *him*" with the euphemistic version "to strangle *the enemies of Israel*.[45] It becomes immediately clear that the reading "I would rather like to strangle him" goes much better with the context of our story: the mother doesn't want to buy diapers for her son because she hates him and wishes him dead. This also explains why she comes up with the feeble excuse that she has no money. The problem is not the money but the mother's hatred for her baby. Some scholars even suggest that her concluding statement about the whirlwinds snatching the baby from her hands is just a cover-up for what really happened, namely that she did in fact murder her child.[46]

Christianity

Now I will finally turn to a text that I have deliberately ignored until now—the New Testament, which is, after all, also a Jewish source. The first New Testament text—put forward in the 1920s[47] and gaining increased support over the years[48] as a possible background for our story—is Revelation 12:1–6, the vision of the "woman clothed with the sun, with the moon under her feet, and on her head a crown of twelve stars" (12:1), who is about to give birth to a son "who is to rule all the nations with a rod of iron" (12:5). But the poor child is threatened by a "great red dragon" who wants to devour it "as soon as it was born" (12:3f.). Yet miraculously the child "was snatched away and taken (*hērpastē*) to God and to his throne," while his mother "fled into the wilderness" (12:5f.).

The woman here is plainly the mother of the Messiah and, obviously, her son the Messiah who is destined to rule the nations—hence, the Davidic Messiah—while the dragon is the leader of the nations, presumably the Antichrist. The snatching away of the child, in order to rescue him from the dragon, fits in very well with the snatching away of the infant Messiah in our Yerushalmi story—the Aramaic verb used there (*hataf*) is similar to the Greek verb used in Revelation (*harpazein*)[49]—and one could easily assume that baby Messiah in the Yerushalmi was likewise carried off and taken up to heaven, to God's throne. But that is also where the parallel ends, the major difference being that in Revelation the baby Messiah needs to be protected from his enemies, the foreign nations (presumably Rome)[50]—the Messiah as the opponent and ultimate conqueror of the foreign nations is a very common feature of messianic traditions— whereas baby Messiah in the Yerushalmi needs to be protected from his own mother (a highly *un*common feature of messianic traditions).

A more promising approach has been taken by Galit Hasan-Rokem,[51] who has noticed the conspicuous similarity of our story to Jesus' birth narratives as preserved in Matthew[52] and Luke.[53] The first and most straightforward parallel, of course, is the city of Bethlehem as birthplace of the Messiah. But this theme, with the verse Micah 5:2 attached to it,[54] is a stock motif that belongs to any such birth story making claims to authenticity. Yet there is more. The strange genealogy of the child with his father King Hezekiah may well allude to the Messiah's Davidic origin (so conspicuous also in Mt. 1:9f., where Hezekiah is indeed listed among Jesus' Davidic forefathers). And the plowing Jew with his oxen and lowing cow—could this possibly be a reference to those shepherds in the fields to whom an angel of the

Lord announces the birth of the Messiah,[55] with the angel transformed to an Arab? The Arab reads the omen of a lowing cow,
whereas in the New Testament the wise men from the East, or
magi, read the omen of a rising star.[56] As for the other oddity of
our story—that the Jew goes from city to city to find the Messiah
(although he knows very well that he was born in Bethlehem)—
does this perhaps allude to the same magi, whose search for the
newborn Messiah is perfectly appropriate and who have a star
(actually the very same star that told them of the Messiah's birth)
to show them the exact location of the Bethlehem manger?[57] The
magi bring the precious gifts of gold, frankincense, and myrrh to
the mother,[58] whereas the peddler in our Yerushalmi story
brings . . . diapers. Mary wraps her child Jesus in diapers, [59]
whereas our mother refuses to buy diapers. And finally, the desire
of the mother to kill her child—is this an allusion to King
Herod's plan to murder the Messiah, whom he quite rightly regards as the most dangerous threat to his throne?[60]

Following Hasan-Rokem, I doubt that these parallels to Jesus'
birth narrative in the New Testament are accidental. But I don't
agree with her conclusion, namely:

> These similarities [between the Yerushalmi story and the
> New Testament birth narratives], in details apparently
> lacking any theological significance, suggest that these are
> neither polemics nor imitations but parallels typical of
> folk narrative. Folk traditions were shared by those Jews
> who belonged to the majority and by others belonging to
> a minority group, who believed in Jesus as the Messiah
> and joined the early Christian Church, made up mostly of
> Jews.[61]

"Folk narrative" seems to serve here as some kind of *deus ex
machina*, explaining almost everything—or nothing.[62] In fact, I

don't believe that the similarities between the two narratives are "lacking any theological significance." On the contrary, in my view the Yerushalmi story is a complete and ironical inversion of the New Testament—the lowing cow versus the star; the Arab versus the angel of the Lord and/or the magi; the Jewish peddler versus the magi; diapers versus gold, frankincense, and myrrh; and the murderous mother versus the murderous king. Quite an impressive list, which, summarized in this way, sounds almost comical, like a parody of the New Testament infant story.

And this, I propose, is precisely what our story wishes to do. It is a counternarrative, a parodistic inversion of the New Testament, of the Christian claim that this child Jesus, born in Bethlehem, the city of David, was indeed the Messiah. As such, it is of *great* theological significance. For it undermines the essence of the Christian message by arguing that no, this child Jesus is not the Messiah, at least not the Messiah who you Christians say lived among us on earth in order to teach the new doctrine of the new covenant, and to be crucified and ultimately resurrected and lifted up to heaven. This Jesus cannot be the Messiah for the very simple reason that soon after his birth he was snatched away by whirlwinds and disappeared.

But this isn't yet the end of the story, since we still need to explain the murderous feelings of the mother toward her baby. Martha Himmelfarb has come up with a very intriguing and very different reading of the story in general and the mother's feelings in particular.[63] She wishes to reconstruct an originally *positive* Jewish story of the mother and her child, a story seeking to provide the Jews with a loving mother of the Messiah just as Christians had with their Jesus and his mother Mary. In other words, originally there were certain Jews who were attracted to the Christian message of Mary, the loving and beloved mother of the Messiah, and who tried to appropriate this message for their own purposes—and our Yerushalmi story (this is Himmelfarb's conclusion) *responds* to such efforts by "transforming the mother into a would-be murderer."[64] For Himmelfarb, therefore, the story is directed not only against Jewish messianic expectations tinged by Christian influences but likewise against Jewish messianic expectations as such—at least for the time being and in particular after the failure of the Bar Kokhba revolt in the first half of the second century C.E. "For the Yerushalmi, then," she concludes, "messiahs who have already been born are a bad idea, even without respect to Christianity."[65]

I would put this somewhat differently: Messiahs who have already been born pose a problem *because* of Christianity, or, more precisely, because of the relationship between Judaism and Christianity. For there is only a single community which claims that the (Jewish!) Messiah was born at a certain point in time and which sticks to that claim—the Christian community. Other such claims were made, for example, by Bar Kokhba, but these claims came to an end as soon as political circumstances proved them wrong.[66] The Jewish sect of the Christians not only stood stubbornly by their Messiah Jesus but even maintained that the "other Jews" (the Jewish establishment) had killed him. And here is where the would-be murderous mother in our story comes in. She is the Jewish mother of the newborn Jewish and simultaneously Christian Messiah—a mother who wishes him dead because his birth is inextricably linked to the destruction of the Temple, the most shattering event in Jewish history. This coming of the Messiah at the nadir of Jewish history is a perfectly acceptable idea within the framework of the Jewish messianic expectation. There is nothing at all wrong with it—if only it weren't for this Christian sect, which insists that with the coming of this Messiah the old covenant was superseded by a new covenant for which the destroyed Temple wasn't a disaster at all; on the contrary, for these Christians it was the ultimate proof that God had punished the Jews of the old covenant and was now bestowing his favor on the Jews of the new covenant, who make do without a Temple and its bloody sacrifices.

So what I want to argue is that our Yerushalmi story captures Christianity—literally—*in statu nascendi*, that is, at the very moment it sprang from the loins of Judaism. This "Christianity," with its Messiah born on the very day when the Temple was destroyed, no doubt falls within the realm of Judaism and is a perfectly Jewish form of "Christianity"; however, our Talmud author of course knows how the story of this Messiah continues: that in the end he was murdered by his fellow Jews (at least this is what the New Testament claims). Therefore he tells a different story: no, the Messiah's mother insists, I did *not* kill him (that is, *we Jews* did not kill him); true, I *wanted* to kill him, but I didn't. The mother's feelings, then, are feelings of guilt—guilt toward her son whom she considered killing, which would have necessarily prevented him from becoming Israel's Messiah.

This point needs to be stated more precisely. The mother with her newborn is caught in an ambiguous or—to use that fashionable term—"liminal situation" of in-between. On the one hand, the Messiah has been born and there is no turning back—unless one wants to claim that he was a false Messiah and therefore deserved to be killed. But our story gives no hint of this possibility, which serves as the typical solution for such a dilemma. On the other hand, the mother knew only too well how the story with the Christian Messiah Jesus would end. In fact, and against the grain of historical logic, the story captures at one and the same time *two* Messiahs: the "Christian" Messiah—against whom it polemicizes—and the "Jewish" Messiah, the Messiah who remains within the realm of the traditional Jewish taxonomy. It goes without saying that the labels "Jewish" and "Christian" are completely out of place here. We are still far from drawing that neat distinction between "Judaism" and "Christianity"—to the contrary, "Judaism" is in its very essence intrigued by

"Christianity." So, ultimately, the mother's hatred of her child and her desire to kill him result not only from the fact that he was born on the day of the Temple's destruction; she hates the child also because, in the Christian reading of events, he is destined to become the most dangerous threat to Judaism (at least in the way *she* understands it)—a new Judaism that maintains that it does not require a physical Temple because it itself is the new, spiritual Temple. To go a step further and put it more drastically: in her desire to kill her child, the mother (Judaism) attempts to kill the emerging Christianity within her.

But to reiterate—she did *not* kill her child. The end of our story provides the only appropriate answer to the mother's ambiguous attitude toward her son. For what does one do with a Messiah who has been born prematurely? One cannot simply dispose of him because, after all, he is indeed the Messiah. (As I said, our story never considers the possibility that he is a false Messiah and therefore *deserves* to be killed.) Hence the only viable solution to such an exceptional case is to have him taken away by God and hidden somewhere in heaven until his real time has come. This is the only way to keep him within the taxonomy of the traditional Jewish expectation of the Messiah—and this is why baby Messiah had to disappear.

One final remark: we are talking here about the very early relationship between "Judaism" and "Christianity"—long before they became two distinct communities, let alone religions. Instead of following the old paradigm of the "daughter religion" (Christianity) being born from the "mother religion" (Judaism), I prefer to use the term "sister religion" for Christianity, since, ultimately, I am arguing that once the idea of the Christian Messiah was put forth—with all its ramifications—Judaism could not remain the same. Now Judaism acquires a mother for the Messiah and even entertains the possibility that the Messiah might be killed. Our story finally rejects this possibility, but I have alluded to the tradition of the dual Messiah in Judaism—the Messiah from the tribe of Ephraim, who will be slain in battle, and the Messiah from the tribe of Judah (the Davidic Messiah), who will gain the ultimate victory.[67] It is hard to avoid seeing in such a tradition the Jewish appropriation of the slain Messiah Jesus—albeit trumped by the "real" Jewish Messiah, the Messiah son of David. And even the disappearance of the baby Messiah in our story could be an ironic appropriation of the Christian distinction between the first and second coming of the Messiah. Following his first appearance on earth, when he was rejected by most of his fellow Jews and crucified, Jesus needs to return from his heavenly abode and put in a second appearance. This is the famous delay in the advent of the Messiah, *Parusieverzögerung* in German. Similarly, our Messiah, taken away by God so soon after his birth and waiting in heaven for his return, could be another, Jewish version of this Christian *Parusieverzögerung*.

The Suffering Messiah Ephraim

IN ADDITION TO THE MESSIAH FROM THE HOUSE OF DAVID (the Messiah ben David)—the predominant messianic figure—rabbinic Judaism knows of a Messiah ben Joseph (ben Ephraim), that is, a Messiah from the house of Joseph or Ephraim respectively. Joseph, as one of Jacob's twelve sons, was the progenitor of one of Israel's twelve tribes, the tribe that was later divided into Ephraim and Manasseh (Josh. 17:17).[1] We don't know why Joseph of all people was honored with his own Messiah, nor can we explain or pinpoint the origin of this idea of a Messiah from his house.[2] What is clear, however, is the fact that sometime during the prerabbinic or even the rabbinic period the Davidic Messiah from the tribe of Judah was supplemented with another Messiah from the tribe of Joseph/Ephraim.

Direct evidence about this Messiah ben Joseph/Ephraim is scanty and relatively late. Targum Pseudo-Jonathan (which is notoriously difficult to date) mentions in passing that the Messiah ben Ephraim is a descendant of Joshua and that he will defeat Gog and Magog at the end of time.[3] The Babylonian Talmud weaves traditions about the Messiah ben Joseph into a debate about the evil inclination in such a way that one suspects these traditions were well known.[4] There, R. Dosa—a fourth-generation tanna of the late second century C.E.—mentions rather casually that the Messiah ben Joseph will be killed, proving this fate with the biblical verse Zechariah 12:10: "And they will look at the one whom they have pierced, they shall mourn for him, as one mourns for an only child." The rabbis add that the Messiah ben David, when he sees that the Messiah ben Joseph has been killed, asks God to spare him this fate, and God grants his request. Hence, we may assume that the Bavli presupposes a tradition according to which the Messiah ben Joseph precedes the Messiah ben David and will be killed in (the final?) battle; the Messiah ben David, by contrast, will survive him and presumably emerge as victor in the decisive battle against the nations.[5] The Apocalypse of Zerubbabel from the early seventh century C.E. describes this final messianic battle in more detail: the Messiah ben Ephraim/Joseph is killed in the battle against Armilus, the Antichrist, who personifies the Roman Empire and Christendom; the decisive victory over Armilus is left to the Messiah ben David and his mother Hephzibah.[6]

This notion of a dual messianic expectation—the dying Messiah ben Ephraim and the victorious Messiah ben David—has become the standard Jewish tradition. It stands out against another tradition that knows only one Messiah, by the name of "Messiah Ephraim"—that is, without the "ben" and without his partner Messiah ben David. This tradition is absolutely unique and is found only in the Midrash Pesiqta Rabbati, a homiletical midrash for the festivals and special Sabbaths, dated in its final redaction to the sixth or seventh century C.E. (which doesn't say much, however, about the dating of its respective literary units).[7] I am referring to homilies 34, 36, and 37 in Pesiqta Rabbati, all of these mentioning the Messiah Ephraim and all clearly deriving from a common tradition. Arnold Goldberg has dedicated an important monograph to these homilies.[8] I will now examine the notion of the Messiah Ephraim in these three homilies in greater detail.[9]

PISQA 34

Pisqa 34, a homily about the Haftarah verse Zechariah 9:9, immediately introduces the messianic theme: "Rejoice greatly, O daughter Zion! Shout aloud, O daughter Jerusalem! Lo, your king comes to you; triumphant and victorious is he, humble and riding on a donkey, on a colt, the foal of a donkey." This verse, with its long messianic tradition-history, is applied at the end of the homily to a Messiah with the name Ephraim:

"Humble and riding upon a donkey" (Zech. 9:9).
This is the Messiah.
And why is he called "humble" (*'ani*)? Because he humbly bent down (*nit'aneh*)[10] all these years in prison while the sinners of Israel laughed at him.
And why "riding upon a donkey"? Because of the wicked. . . .[11]
But through the merit of the Messiah, the Holy One, blessed be he, shields them [Israel] (and guides them) in a straight way, and redeems them, as is said: "They shall come with weeping, and with supplications will I lead them; I will let them walk by rivers of water, in a straight way [wherein they shall not stumble; for I have become a father to Israel, and Ephraim, he is my firstborn]" (Jer. 31:9).
What does Scripture teach us by saying "[Ephraim,] he [is my firstborn]" (Jer. ibid.)?[12]

> It is he [Ephraim], (who is the Messiah) in the days of
> the Messiah (as well as) in the world-to-come, and there is
> no one else with him.[13]

The Messiah, having spent a long time in prison, reveals himself
here as "humble" and "riding on a donkey." His enemies are the
"sinners of Israel," that is, Jews who have mocked him and obviously put him in prison. His name, Ephraim, is deduced indirectly from the verse quoted from Jeremiah: Ephraim, Joseph's
favored son (the secondborn-turned-firstborn through Jacob's
blessing), is now the Messiah Ephraim, God's firstborn. The
cryptic conclusion seems to make clear that Ephraim is indeed
the only Messiah, that there is no other Messiah besides him (as
there is no other god besides God). This is presumably a rejection of the idea of two Messiahs, one from the house of Ephraim
and another from the house of David. Hence, the tradition of a
Messiah from the house of David not only plays no role here; it
is explicitly rejected.

The work of redemption carried out by the Messiah Ephraim
is not described in detail, but it is clear that Israel's redemption is
somehow related to the "merit" (*zekhut*) of the Messiah. The
well-attested rabbinic tradition of the "merit of the fathers" (*zekhut avot*)—that "merit" accrued through the selfless acts of Israel's patriarchs (and matriarchs) and which has an effect on all
future generations—has been transferred here to the Messiah. It
is only because the imprisoned Ephraim has humbly borne the
ridicule of Israel's wicked that he is able to become Israel's Messiah and redeemer; or, to put it differently, Israel will be redeemed
only because the Messiah has taken upon himself the ridicule of
his enemies. Elsewhere in the midrash God says of the Messiah's
merit that it outweighs in value all the members of his celestial

court, that is, it is as important and precious to God as his celestial court (i.e., his angels).[14]

The homily elaborates on who precisely are the opponents and who the followers of the Messiah. Right from the beginning it identifies the "mourners of Zion" (*avelei Tzion*) as his followers, a phrase that we encounter for the first time in the Hebrew Bible.[15] Some scholars assume that we are dealing here with an actual ascetic group that was established after the destruction of the First Temple but had its effect well into the rabbinic period.[16] In our homily, the mourners of Zion are distinguished by their active expectation of messianic redemption, and it is for this reason that they are despised and ridiculed by their opponents; hence, the ridicule of the Messiah directly corresponds to the ridicule of his followers. Immediately before the Messiah appears (that is, before he is released from prison), God sends angels into the world to destroy those who mocked redemption, yet he spares the mourners of Zion. Now Israel's wicked realize that they were wrong to ridicule the mourners of Zion and their Messiah.[17]

It is much more difficult to identify Israel's wicked—the opponents of the Messiah and of the mourners of Zion—but the contrast becomes clearer upon closer examination of our text. Immediately after the punishment of the mockers, God turns to the "righteous of the world":

And the Holy One, blessed be he, will proclaim and say to all the righteous men of generation after generation:

O righteous men of the world, even though (your obedience to) the words of the Torah is pleasing[18] to me—that you love (*hibbitem*)[19] (only) my Torah but not love my kingdom, (therefore) I have declared on oath that for him who loves my kingship,[20] I myself shall bear witness on his behalf, as is said: "Therefore wait (*hakku*) for me, says the

Lord, for the day when I arise as a witness" (Zeph. 3:8)—
for the mourners of Zion who grieved with me[21] because
of my House which is destroyed and because of my Temple
which is desolate. Now I bear witness for them, as is said:
"[I am] with the one who is of a contrite and humble spirit"
(Isa. 57:15). Do not read: *with the one* who is of a contrite
and humble spirit, read rather: *with me*[22] is he who is of a
contrite spirit. These are the mourners of Zion who humbled their spirits, listened meekly to abuse of their persons,
keeping silent, yet did not consider themselves particularly
virtuous therefore.[23]

The righteous of each and every generation that God addresses
here are Israel's righteous who distinguish themselves by their
particularly strict adherence to the Torah—hence, they are far
from being a group of wicked evildoers. Yet still, I wish to suggest
that it is precisely these "righteous" who are the opponents of the
mourners of Zion. They are the pious who focus on uncondi-
tional obedience to the Torah and whom God nevertheless rep-
rimands because they have neglected his "kingdom." God's message to the righteous is that Torah obedience is absolutely
necessary and pleasing to him—yet not at the expense of his
kingdom. This is an almost paradoxical statement, since what
else do the righteous do other than take upon themselves over
and over again, through their Torah obedience, the "yoke of
God's kingdom"? But God rebukes them anyhow and accuses
them of forgetting the love of his kingdom for sake of love of the
Torah. Torah obedience alone is not enough; it needs to be com-
plemented by the active expectation of God's kingdom, that is,
active expectation of redemption. This is what God blames the
righteous for (ultimately branding them as wicked): that they are
content with imperfect Torah obedience, a Torah obedience that
lacks the decisive component of messianic expectation.

With this bold statement the author of our homily ventures into new and untrod territory. The extent to which he deviates from the accepted standards and conventions of rabbinic Judaism is demonstrated by the continuation, where the righteous of the world burst into tears because of their failure and God needs to reassure them that the reward for their Torah obedience still remains with them.[24] The homily's author performs a difficult balancing act between the ideals of classical rabbinic Judaism and those of the mourners of Zion. It is certainly not the *substitution* of one ideal (Torah obedience) for another (expectation of God's kingdom) that is at stake here; but still, the homily clearly manifests a decisive shift of emphasis. Predominant rabbinic Judaism, according to our author's critique, has forgotten one crucial component of this Torah obedience; or even worse, it has suppressed it in aggressively persecuting the mourners of Zion—namely, the expectation of imminent redemption. When and wherever the homily's author might be located, one thing is certain: he criticizes his contemporaries—or rather, that socially and politically influential stratum of his contemporaries—for neglecting the messianic expectation. In view of the evident decline of acute messianic hopes after the failure of the Bar Kokhba revolt, the conclusion seems likely that we are dealing here with a countermovement to this trend—either sometime during the peak of rabbinic Judaism, with the mourners of Zion constituting a mysterious fringe group that is difficult to pinpoint historically, or at the end of the rabbinic period, with the resurgence of apocalyptic writings in the seventh century C.E. (I will return to this.)

Pisqa 36

This Pisqa addresses the tension between Torah obedience and messianic expectation right from the start. It contrasts the Haftarah verse Isaiah 60:1 ("Arise, shine; for your light has come, and the glory of the Lord has risen upon you") with Psalms 36:10[25] ("For with you is the fountain of life, in your light we see light"). In a first step the interpreter expounds Psalms 36:10 as referring to the light of the Torah, which is called the source of life, that is, whose fulfillment guarantees life: if we fulfill the Torah as instructed, we will be granted the light of the Messiah of Isaiah 60:1. In other words, Torah obedience leads to salvation. No doubt, this is the traditional rabbinic exegesis.

Yet in its next step the homily takes a very different turn. Having effectively satisfied the norm, the author of our homily interprets the light of Psalms 36:10 as referring to the light of the Messiah: it is the light of which Genesis 1:4 says, "And God saw the light that it was good," and which God has hidden, along with the Messiah, beneath his throne of glory in heaven.[26] The author here takes up the well-known tradition according to which the Messiah is one of those seven things that were created before the creation of the world or the necessity of which God foresaw before he created the world.[27] God hides the Messiah beneath his throne[28] until the time of his revelation has come. This, too, is standard rabbinic theology, but in the combination of his two interpretations of Psalms 36:10—as referring first to the Torah and then to the Messiah—the homily's author strikes an unexpectedly polemical tone. True, he argues, Torah obedience leads to messianic redemption—but equally true is that the light of the Messiah waits beneath God's throne for its appointed time, a time determined by God and ultimately independent of Israel's Torah obedience. One is immediately reminded of the famous debate between R. Eli'ezer (b. Hyrkanos) and R. Yehoshua (b. Hananiah) concerning the question as to whether the time of redemption depends on Israel's Torah obedience (R. Eli'ezer) or whether it has been determined once and for all by God (R. Yehoshua) and remains unaffected by Israel's efforts.[29]

The homily unambiguously accepts R. Yehoshua's opinion, never returning to the subject of Torah obedience; to the contrary, it operates under the assumption that the apocalyptic "week of years" represents the prearranged time of redemption.[30] The Messiah Ephraim was hidden beneath God's throne before the creation of the world and will appear at a time predetermined by God. Although Satan and the "Princes of the kingdoms," who are dependent on him (that is, the kings of the world's nations), try to prevent the Messiah's appearance,[31] their intrigues are to no avail: God has chosen his Messiah and foreordained the time of his appearance.[32]

This more or less follows the traditional rabbinic script—with a difference. To begin with, there is the name of the Messiah that God at first mentions directly and with no reference to Jeremiah 31:9 (as in Pisqa 34) when he addresses the princes of the nations: "He is [the] Messiah, and his name is Ephraim, my Messiah of righteousness."[33] This name alone, as we have seen in Pisqa 34, is anything but typical rabbinic theology.[34] But what the homily's author then has to say about this Messiah Ephraim far exceeds what we can expect from rabbinic Judaism. After he has chosen him as his Messiah, God reaches an agreement with Ephraim, or, more precisely, he negotiates with him the terms that the Messiah must accept if he indeed wishes to become Israel's Messiah:

> At that time the Holy One, blessed be he, began negotiating with him [the Messiah] the terms (*matneh*) and said to him:[35]
>
> "Those[36] that are hidden with you, it is their sins which will bend you some day under[37] a yoke of iron and make you like that calf whose eyes grew dim, and they will choke your spirit as with a yoke.[38] Because of their sins your

tongue will stick to your palate. Are you willing to endure this?"

The Messiah asked the Holy One, blessed be he: "Will this suffering last many years?"

The Holy One, blessed be he, replied: "Upon your life and the life of my head, it is a week (of years) [a period of seven years] which I have decreed for you. But if your soul is sad (at the prospect of this suffering), I shall at this moment banish them (from my presence)."[39]

This agreement between God and the Messiah is unique in rabbinic literature. What does it entail? First of all, that the sins of all those who are hidden together with the Messiah will be a heavy burden for the Messiah. The text does not explain who those hidden together with the Messiah might be, but there can be no doubt that it refers to the "generation" of those who were mentioned earlier as hidden with the Messiah beneath the throne of glory.[40] We are presumably dealing here with those souls who are awaiting their incorporation in a human body, that is, all the future members of the people of Israel from the creation of the world until the coming of the Messiah at the end of time.[41] In other words, God decrees for the Messiah that the sins of all human beings of all generations will be imposed on him like an iron yoke. They will darken his eyes like the eyes of a calf that is on the verge of collapsing under its burden—an image that probably alludes to Jeremiah 31:18 ("Indeed I heard Ephraim pleading: You disciplined me, and I took the discipline; I was like a calf untamed"); the spirit of the Messiah will choke under the burden of the sins, that is, be suffocated; and his tongue will stick to his palate. This latter part obviously alludes to Psalms 22:16:[42] "My strength[43] is dried up like a potsherd, my tongue sticks to my palate."[44]

God explicitly asks the Messiah whether he agrees to take upon himself this heavy burden, but the Messiah first asks in return—in the vein of a talmudic discussion—how long these sufferings will last. God's answer: one week (of years). This is the measurement of the apocalyptic week of years, that is, of seven years. The classical reference that is presumably presupposed here is the Baraitha of the seven weeks of years in the Babylonian Talmud: "The week [the seven year cycle at the end of which] the son of David will come, in the first year . . . , in the second year . . . , in the third year . . . (etc.); in the seventh (year) wars, and at the conclusion of the seventh (year) the son of David will come."[45] Hence, the Messiah must endure a time of suffering of seven years, most likely during his presence on earth, that is, after he has been incorporated as the Messiah and sent to earth. God solemnly reaffirms the duration of this time of suffering with an oath: it will certainly be no longer but also no shorter than seven years. And God gives the Messiah the choice: he can accept these terms or reject them. What happens when the Messiah rejects God's conditions is hinted at in the last cryptic sentence. Apparently God wishes to say: In case you are not prepared to agree to these terms, I will banish them from my presence (presumably the souls of the unborn human beings beneath his throne), that is, I will make sure that they will never be born. If this assumption is correct—that the unborn souls in heaven are in fact all future human generations—then God is conveying an implicit threat to the Messiah: in case you are not prepared to take upon yourself the sins of humankind, I will revoke my decision to create humankind; in other words, creation of humankind depends on the Messiah's assent to take upon himself all the future sins of humanity.

This request of God is unheard of. One is immediately reminded of the extensive midrashic traditions about the angels' opposition to the creation of humankind and God's furious reaction to it: he throws down to earth those angels who have dared to object,[46] or he burns them,[47] because he has long since decided to create humankind—although he knows they will sin. According to classical rabbinic Judaism, the existence of humankind has been made possible, despite their sinfulness, because from the very beginning God built into his plan of creation the crucial corrective of repentance (*teshuvah*): humans can repent and thus expiate their sins.[48] But this is not the route that is taken here. God does not trust in humankind's ability to repent; he relies solely on the willingness of the *Messiah* to take upon himself the burden of sin of all humankind; this alone guarantees that creation will persist and arrive at its happy end during the messianic period. Arnold Goldberg is absolutely right when he writes: "In a unique way the Messiah is put [here] into the center of creation; all future life depends on him."[49] However, in an attempt to harmonize the sources, Goldberg then proceeds to take the sting out of the homily by immediately qualifying his statement in saying that this midrash isn't so exceptional after all, there being many midrashim that are aware of the merit of the fathers (*zekhut avot*) as a prerequisite for the world's preservation. As we have seen with Pisqa 34, the authors of our Pesiqta Rabbati homilies know very well the traditional concept of the merit of the fathers, but the Messiah's merit goes far beyond this. His merit is not one among others; rather, in a certain sense, it abrogates the merit of the fathers. Such things as customary Torah obedience are insufficient and need to be supplemented by messianic expectation; so the merit of the fathers alone no longer suffices and will be ultimately replaced by the merit of the Messiah.

There can be no doubt that the songs of the servant of the Lord ('*eved YHWH*) in Isaiah represent the biblical background of the Messiah's vicarious suffering, in particular the long song of Isaiah 53:

> (3) He was *despised* (*nivzeh*) and rejected by others;
> a man of suffering and acquainted with infirmity;
> and as one from whom others hide their faces
> he was *despised* (*nivzeh*), and we held him of no account.
> (4) Surely *he has borne our infirmities*
> and carried our diseases;
> yet we accounted him stricken,
> struck down by God, and afflicted.
> (5) But he was wounded *for our transgressions*,
> crushed *for our iniquities*;
> *upon him was the punishment that made us whole,*
> *and by his bruises we are healed.*
> (6) All we like sheep have gone astray;
> we have all turned to our own way,
> *and the Lord has laid on him*
> *the iniquity of us all.*
> (7) He was *oppressed*, and he was *afflicted*,
> yet he did not open his mouth;
> like a lamb that is led to the slaughter,
> and like a sheep that before its shearers is silent,
> so he did not open his mouth.
> (8) By a *perversion of justice he was taken away*.
> Who could have imagined his future?
> For he was cut off from the land of the living,
> stricken *for the transgression of my people*.
> (9) They made his grave with the wicked
> and his tomb with the rich,
> although he had done no violence,
> and there was no deceit in his mouth.
> (10) Yet it was the will of the Lord *to crush him with pain*.

When you make his life *an offering for sin*,
he shall see his offspring, and shall prolong his days;
through him the will of the Lord shall prosper.
(11) *Out of his anguish he shall see light*;
he shall find satisfaction through his knowledge.
The righteous one, my servant, *shall make many righteous*,
and he shall bear their iniquities.
(12) Therefore I will allot him a portion with the great,
and he shall divide the spoil with the strong;
because he poured out himself to death,
and *was numbered with the transgressors*;
yet *he bore the sin of many*,
and *made intercession for the transgressors*.

We do not know who was originally meant as the despised servant of the Lord, but this is unimportant for our midrashic context. What is certain is the fact that the song could be and indeed was interpreted as referring to the Messiah. It remains conspicuous, however, that it is *not* quoted in our midrash, although the homily can be read in many details as an exposition of Isaiah 53 (I have highlighted some relevant passages in italics; bear in mind, though, that the Hebrew text is extremely difficult and in part corrupt): the contempt of the Messiah; his suffering for the sins of humankind, imposed on him by God; his imprisonment; he sees the light when his suffering is completed; he is righteous and makes many righteous, and so forth. Only one crucial detail in the song is completely missing in the homily—the death of the servant of the Lord. The Messiah Ephraim doesn't die; on the contrary, through his suffering, he secures (eternal?) life for himself and the people of Israel.

We know of a few prerabbinic texts that mention the vicarious suffering of an eschatological savior figure and most likely allude to Isaiah 53,[50] most prominent among them the Aramaic

Testament of Levi and the so-called Self-Glorification Hymn (both preserved in fragments in the Qumran library). The Testament of Levi says of the eschatological priest:

> (2) And he will atone (*yekhapper*) for all the children of
>   his generation,
> and he will be sent to all the children of (3) his [people].
> His word is like the word of the heavens,
> and his teaching according to the will of God. . . .
> (5) They will utter many words against him,
> and an abundance of (6) [lie]s;
> they will fabricate fables against him,
> and utter every kind of disparagement (*genu'in*) against
>   him.[51]

The eschatological hero presented here is obviously controversial, but he himself claims that God is with him. Although there is no mention of his expiatory *suffering*, he clearly atones—presumably in a cultic act—for the sins of his people.

In the Self-Glorification Hymn, which is preserved in many Qumran fragments,[52] an unknown figure boasts of having been exalted among the angels in heaven and seated on a throne. But this exaltation, uttered in very self-assured words, is oddly combined with a mysterious humiliation:

> (7) I am counted among the gods (*elim*)
> and my dwelling is in the holy congregation;
> [my] des[ire] is not according to the flesh,
> [but] all that is precious to me is in (the) glory (of)
> (8) . . . the holy [dwel]ling.
> [W]ho has been considered despicable on my account
>   (*mi la-vuz nehshav bi*)?

And who is comparable to me in my glory? . . .
(9) Who bea[rs all] sorrows (*tze'arim*) like me?
And who [suffe]rs evil like me?[53]

This figure, exalted among the angels and practically Godlike, is at the same time deeply despised—apparently by his human contemporaries—but ostentatiously takes this contempt upon himself as well as its attendant sorrows. Since the Hebrew root (*buz*) used here for this contempt is the same as in the song of the servant of the Lord of Isaiah 53, it makes sense to assume some influence of Isaiah on the hymn—though it is not explicitly stated that the hymn's hero takes these sorrows *vicariously* upon himself for the sins of his people. The opinions about who this hero might be differ widely in the scholarly literature,[54] but there can be no doubt that he is modeled along the lines of an eschatological savior figure. Israel Knohl has suggested that we are dealing here not only with a suffering qumranic Messiah but more concretely with an immediate precursor of Jesus and one who in fact influenced Jesus and the Christian expectation of the Messiah.[55] This is a bold assumption, but whatever the connection might be between the hero of the hymn and the Jesus of the New Testament, the New Testament presents its Jesus without any ambiguity under the impact of motifs from Isaiah 53.

In the New Testament it is mainly the letters that relate the suffering servant of Isaiah 53 to Jesus of Nazareth.[56] In probably an early formulation, the Letter to the Romans says of Jesus that God has "put forward (him) as a sacrifice of atonement by his blood" (*hilastērion . . . en tō autou haimati*),[57] and according to the First Letter to the Corinthians, "Christ dies for our sins in accordance with the scriptures" (*apethanen hyper tōn hamartiōn hēmōn kata tas graphas*).[58] And the Letter to the Romans alludes directly to Isaiah 53:11:

(18) Therefore just as one man's trespass led to condemnation for all, so one man's act of righteousness leads to justification and life for all. (19) For just as by the one man's disobedience *the many* were made sinners, so by the one man's obedience *the many will be made righteous*.[59]

It is left to the First Letter of Peter to offer the most extensive and direct comment on Isaiah 53:

(21) For to this you have been called, because Christ also suffered for you,
leaving you an example, so that you should follow in his steps.
(22) *He committed no sin*,
and no deceit was found in his mouth.
(23) *When he was abused, he did not return abuse*;
when he suffered, he did not threaten;
but he entrusted himself to the one who judges justly.
(24) He himself bore our sins in his body on the cross,
so that, free from sins, we might live for righteousness;
by his wounds you have been healed.
(25) For you *were going astray like sheep*,
but now you have returned to the shepherd and guardian of your souls.[60]

Verse 22 quotes verbatim Isaiah 53:9, verse 23 alludes to Isaiah 53:7, verse 24 quotes Isaiah 53:5, and verse 25 quotes Isaiah 53:6. It is doubtless Jesus who is the suffering servant of the Lord here; being without sin, he takes upon himself the sins of all humankind and leads them to justice and life.

Rabbinic Judaism does acknowledge the idea of the suffering Messiah, but these occasions are extremely rare. The only reference that provides a direct link between the Messiah and Isaiah

53 can be found in the Babylonian Talmud in a discussion about the names of the Messiah:

> The Rabbis say: His [the Messiah's] name is "the leper (*hiwra*) from the house of Rabbi," as it is written: "Surely he has borne our infirmities (*holayenu/holyenu*) and carried our diseases; yet we accounted him stricken (*nagua'*), struck down by God, and afflicted" (Isa. 53:4).[61]

It is odd that the Messiah is called "the leper"—and even from the house of Rabbi, that is, from the house of R. Yehudah ha-Naśi. Apparently the keyword in Isaiah 53:4 that is used to prove this exegesis is *nagua'*, which can indeed be understood as "leper," but this proof is somewhat clumsy since *hiwra* and *nagua'* have nothing in common linguistically. Interestingly enough, the notorious medieval pamphlet *Pugio Fidei*, authored by Raimundus Martinus, has preserved a much better reading:

> Those from the house of Rabbi say: "The sick (*hulya*)" is his name, as it is written: "Surely he has borne our infirmities (*holayenu/holyenu*)" (Isa. 53:4).[62]

Here the name of the Messiah and the proof text fit perfectly well—as does the reading "those from the house of Rabbi say," which makes much more sense than "the leper from the house of Rabbi." It is with good reason that Abraham Epstein has suggested that the version in *Pugio Fidei* is indeed the original version of our midrash in the Bavli, which was cleansed by the Bavli's censor, who sought to reserve the Messiah's vicarious suffering for Christianity alone.[63]

For further evidence of the suffering Messiah in rabbinic Judaism, scholars usually refer to two other sources from the Babylonian Talmud. In the first text, R. Alexandrai—a second-generation Palestinian amora—applies the verse Isaiah 11:3 to the Messiah:

> "He [God] shall make him [the shoot from the stump of Jesse] of quick understanding (*wa-hariho*) in the fear of the Lord" (Isa. 11:3). R. Alexandrai said: This teaches that he loaded him [the Messiah] with good deeds (*mitzwot*) and suffering as millstones (*rehayim*).[64]

R. Alexandrai derives the difficult word *hariho* (literally "he makes him smell") from *rehayim* ("millstones"): the Messiah is loaded with the burden of good deeds and of suffering as if loaded with millstones. The emphasis here is clearly placed on the *burden* of the good deeds and the suffering resulting from them rather than on the sins of humankind. Hence it is only in a qualified way that this text can be used for the notion of the vicarious expiatory suffering of the Messiah. And this is also true of the second source from the Bavli, the well-known midrash of the Messiah who sits among the sick and lepers at the gates of Rome to wait for the time of his appearance.[65] There is no mention here of the idea that Israel's sins have caused the Messiah's wounds.

This is the meager yield of our inquiry. It demonstrates, as Goldberg suggests, that the notion of the Messiah's suffering and even his vicarious expiatory act was *possible* in rabbinic Judaism; but Goldberg's far-reaching conclusion "that the darshan of PesR 36–37 remains entirely within the boundaries of rabbinic messianism" again overshoots the mark with its harmonizing tendency.[66] On the contrary, in my view everything points to the fact that the author of our Pesiqta Rabbati homilies goes far beyond what we might expect within the framework of rabbinic messianism. And this is also true of the rabbinic references, according to which it is not the Messiah but other figures who are supposedly interpreted as the suffering servant of the Lord. For Goldberg they are further proof of the fact that our homilies still belong to the realm of traditional rabbinic messianism.[67] One could, however, reach just the opposite conclusion, namely, that the rabbis felt much more at ease with other figures taking upon themselves the burden of vicarious suffering than with the Messiah of all figures. Furthermore, the references in question are anything but unequivocal. If, for example, the verse "And he [Phinehas] made atonement for the Israelites" (Num. 25:13) is understood as saying that Phinehas, with his zeal for God, accomplished not just one act of atonement but that his atonement was effective for all subsequent generations until the resurrection of the dead,[68] then this exegesis has certainly nothing to do with the suffering servant of the Lord[69] but is instead part of the traditional idea of the "merit of the fathers" (*zekhut avot*). The same holds true for the midrash in the Mekhilta, where it is said of Moses and David that they "sacrificed their life for Israel": Moses and David did not in fact sacrifice their lives—and least of all as vicarious expiatory suffering for Israel—but Moses does not wish to live if God will not forgive Israel's sin (that is, he effectively blackmails God); and David makes clear that it is he alone who has sinned and that God should punish him alone and not the innocent people of Israel.[70]

Indeed, the Messiah's vicarious expiatory suffering in our Pesiqta Rabbati homilies transcends the boundaries of traditional rabbinic messianism. One cannot but agree with Goldberg when he ultimately—despite all his attempts to harmonize and smooth the evidence—comes to the conclusion:

> The amplification (*Überhöhung*) of the Messiah's expiatory suffering in PesR 36–37 is unique in the rabbinic literature. It expresses itself here all the more forcefully as all this is being said with a high degree of authority, as if there couldn't

be any doubt about it. It is not the opinion of one teacher that is rendered but something that happens in heaven, something that is not qualified by "as if" or "probably."[71]

That is correct—but there remains the crucial question as to why the suffering Messiah in Pesiqta Rabbati is so out of place. Before answering, we need to make a few more observations regarding the homilies 36 and 37. Ephraim accepts God's terms (Pisqa 36) and agrees to become Israel's Messiah:

He [the Messiah] said to him [God]:

> Master of the universe, with joy in my soul and gladness in my heart I take (this suffering) upon myself so that not one person in Israel shall perish.
> That not only those who are alive be saved in my days but also those who are dead, who died from the days of Adam up until now [the time of redemption].[72]
> And that not only these (be saved in my days) but also those who died as abortions.[73]
> And that not only these be saved in my days but also those of whom you thought to create but were not created.
> Such are the things I desire, and for these I am ready to take upon myself (whatever you decree).[74]

The Messiah's main concern is that God reassure him that, when the time of his appearance has come, *all* humans will be redeemed: those happening to be alive at that point in time, those who have died since the days of the first man, all miscarriages, all the souls that God had in mind to create but whose creation couldn't be realized because of the coming of the Messiah—indeed, every last human being, created or not yet created, from Adam and Eve until the appearance of the Messiah and beyond.

Yet, as the Messiah makes unmistakably clear, his redemptive work does not apply to all humankind but only to the people of Israel ("that no person in Israel shall perish"), that is, only to the Jews and not to the Gentiles. This possibility of redeeming *all* Jews is the decisive reason why the Messiah accedes to the expiatory suffering inflicted on him. Furthermore, the Messiah's acceptance of expiatory suffering *is* redemption; nowhere in the homily is an event or an act of the Messiah mentioned that might bring about redemption. At the end, when the Messiah reveals himself,

> he will come and stand on the roof of the Temple and will make a proclamation to Israel, saying: Meek ones, the day of your[75] redemption is come. And if you do not believe me, behold my light[76] which rises upon you, as is said: "Arise, shine, for your light is come, and the glory of the Lord is risen upon you" (Isa. 60:1).

The light of the Messiah is that light promised by God to illuminate Israel and make visible the consummation of redemption—yet it is not the *light* that brings about redemption but solely the expiatory suffering of the Messiah; or, to put it differently, it is not God who brings about redemption—he only determines its exact moment—but the Messiah. Such a statement is unheard of within the taxonomy of rabbinic Judaism.[77]

The Messiah's unprecedented act of redemption finds its unprecedented answer in God's reaction to the Messiah's acceptance of his terms:

> At this hour, the Holy One, blessed be he, will appoint for the Messiah four creatures who will carry the Messiah's throne of glory.[78]

No doubt, the four creatures carrying the Messiah's throne of glory are the four creatures of Ezekiel 1, but the throne that they carry in Ezekiel is God's throne and not the throne of the Messiah. This can only mean that in our homily God has the Messiah take a seat on his own throne or at least on a throne similar to his throne—an assumption substantiated by the throne's designation as "throne of glory" (*kisse ha-kavod*). What makes this statement so egregious becomes immediately clear if we recall the debate in the Bavli about the plural of "thrones" in Daniel 7:9 (with Aqiva's explanation that one of the thrones was reserved for God and the other for the Messiah from the house of David, as well as R. Yose's and R. Eleazar b. Azariah's sharp rebuke).[79] As a reward for his willingness to take upon himself the expiatory suffering, God gives the Messiah not just any throne but a throne identical to his own throne of glory. What remains unclear is only whether this throne of the Messiah is a second throne *next to* God's throne—as is the case in Aqiva's interpretation of Daniel and arguably also in 3 Enoch—or whether God has the Messiah take a seat on his own throne (which God abandons temporarily?).[80] Whatever the correct answer (probably the first option), this concept again goes far beyond what we can expect from classical rabbinic Judaism. It is only in the Similitudes of the Ethiopic Book of Enoch that we learn of a throne of glory for the Chosen (i.e., the Messiah),[81] and this throne is explicitly identified with God's throne.[82] Otherwise, only the New Testament designates the Messiah's throne as "throne of glory."[83]

God has inflicted on his Messiah one apocalyptic week of suffering for the sins of humankind,[84] and this suffering with the Messiah's response to it is described in more detail immediately before the Messiah reveals himself:[85]

During the seven-year period preceding the coming of the son of David, iron beams (*qorot shel barzel*) will be brought and loaded upon his neck until the Messiah's body is bent low. Then he will cry and weep, and his voice will rise up to the very height of heaven, and he will say to him [God]:

> "Master of the universe, how much can my strength endure? How much can my spirit endure? How much can my soul endure?[86] How much can my limbs suffer? Am I not flesh and blood?"
>
> It was because of this hour that David wept and said: "My strength is dried up like a potsherd" (Ps. 22:16).
>
> At that hour the Holy One, blessed be he, will say to him:[87] "Ephraim, my Messiah of righteousness, ever since the six days of creation you did take this (ordeal) upon yourself. Now your pain is like my pain. Ever since the day that the wicked Nebuchadnezzar came up and destroyed my House and burned my Temple and exiled my children among the nations of the world—and this I swear by your life and by the life of my own head—I have not been able to bring myself to sit upon my throne. And if you do not believe me, see the night dew that has fallen upon my head, as is said: 'My head is filled with dew, my locks with the drops of the night'" (Cant. 5:2).
>
> At this hour he [the Messiah] will reply: "Master of the universe, now I am reconciled. The servant is content to be like his master."[88]

The introduction—"During the seven-year period preceding the coming of the son of David"—is a fixed formula and presumably a quotation of similar apocalyptic or apocalyptizing texts from the rabbinic literature;[89] this may well explain, as Goldberg has observed,[90] the reference to the son of David, that is, the Messiah from the house of David, which is quite incongruous in the context of our homily. Now the Messiah Ephraim has been incarnated, that is, has begun his work on earth, but he has not yet been revealed as the Messiah (certainly not to all human beings, at best to the mourners of Zion of Pisqa 34). His opponents put "iron beams" on his neck—apparently the "iron yoke" that God has made a condition for him—that is, wooden beams covered with iron. Again, this torture imposed on the Messiah is unique in rabbinic Judaism. The Messiah, pressed down by this burden, cries out to God that he cannot bear it—being only a human being of flesh and blood. The homily's author connects the Messiah's grievance with Psalm 22, and it seems safe to assume that the psalm verse "My strength is dried up like a potsherd" has been put into the mouth of the Messiah. Beyond that, Goldberg has suggested that the entire lament alludes to the corresponding verses in Psalm 22, namely:[91]

- "He will cry and weep": "O my God, I cry by day, but you do not answer" (Ps. 22:2).[92]
- "His voice will rise up to the very height of heaven": "You are holy, enthroned on the praises of Israel (Ps. 22:4).[93]
- "How much can my strength (*kohi*) endure": "My strength (*kohi*) is dried up like a potsherd" (Ps. 22:16).[94]
- "How much can my soul (*nishmati*) endure": "Deliver my soul (*nafshi*) from the sword" (Ps. 22:21).[95]
- "How much can my limbs (*evarai*) suffer": "all my bones (*atzmotai*) are separated from each other" (Ps. 22:15).[96]
- "Am I not flesh and blood": "But I am a worm, and not human" (Ps. 22:7).[97]
- "My strength is dried up like a potsherd" (Ps. 22:16).

These implicit allusions to Psalm 22 are hardly accidental, particularly as the psalm has a long tradition history—not least in the New Testament (to which I will return).

God reminds the Messiah that he has accepted this unbearable suffering even before the creation of the world (and therefore must not chicken out now), but he comforts the Messiah with the fact that he ultimately takes upon himself God's grief. God has been in mourning since the destruction of the (First) Temple and proves this with Canticum Canticorum 5:2: the "dew" on God's head is, taken literally, the tears that he sheds because of the destruction of his Temple. It is only now that the Messiah finally accepts his suffering—in bearing this suffering, he is like his God. We know numerous rabbinic texts about God's grief and lamentation because of the destruction of the Temple,[98] but here his grief acquires a new dimension: the Messiah suffers like God, but it is only through the *voluntary* suffering of the Messiah—not because of the destruction of the Temple but because of Israel's sins—that this shared suffering gains a soteriological quality; or, to put it differently and more pointedly, God's suffering becomes effective only through the suffering of the Messiah.

Now, with the Messiah enduring his suffering, the time of redemption has come: the Messiah reveals himself on the roof of the Temple, Israel sees its light, the nations remain in darkness, but eventually they acknowledge the Messiah and become Israel's servants.

PISQA 37

The third homily about the Messiah Ephraim takes up the motifs discussed thus far and works them out in further detail. The homily is based on the Haftarah verse Isaiah 61:10 ("Rejoicing I will rejoice in the Lord, my soul shall be joyful in my God; for he has clothed me with the garments of salvation, he has covered me with the robe of righteousness"), which is expounded by means of Jeremiah 31:13.

Now the Messiah Ephraim is presented in a discourse with the "fathers of the world" (that is, the patriarchs Abraham, Isaac, and Jacob), the scene taking place in the Messiah's prison immediately before the onset of redemption. Clearly imitating the terms of the "contract" between God and the Messiah (Pisqa 36), the fathers ask the Messiah:

> "Ephraim, our Messiah of righteousness, even though we are your fathers, you are greater than we because you did suffer for the iniquities of our children, and terrible ordeals befell you, such ordeals as did not befall earlier generations or later ones. For the sake of Israel you did become a laughingstock and a derision among the nations of the earth; and did sit in darkness, in thick darkness,[99] and your eyes saw no light, and your skin cleaved to your bones,[100] and your body was as dry as a piece of wood; and your eyes grew dim from fasting, and your strength was dried up like a potsherd[101]—all these (afflictions) on account of the iniquities of our children. Is it your desire that our children[102] benefit from that goodness which the Holy One, blessed be he, will bestow in abundance upon Israel? Yet it may be because of the anguish (*tza'ar*) which you did greatly suffer (*nitzta'arta*) on their account—for they [your enemies] put you in prison—that you are displeased with them."

And the Messiah responds:

> "Fathers of the world, all that I have done, I have done only for your sake and for the sake of your children, for your glory and for the glory of your children, that they benefit from that goodness which the Holy One, blessed be he, will bestow in abundance upon them—upon Israel."
>
> The fathers of the world answered him: "Ephraim, our Messiah of righteousness, be content with what you have

done, for you have made content the mind of your Maker as well as our minds."[103]

Here the motif of the "merit of the fathers" (*zekhut avot*)[104] is taken up again, and the patriarchs make clear from the outset that the Messiah's merit exceeds their own because he has taken upon himself the sins of all humankind; therefore, the Messiah Ephraim is greater than they are. Once again, they show to him quite plainly all his earthly wretchedness—alluding to various Bible verses, among them Psalm 22 again[105]—and make sure that he is ready to bear these sufferings. The Messiah confirms his readiness, and God rewards him:

> At this hour the Holy One, blessed be he, will lift the Messiah up to the heaven of heavens and will cloak him in something of the splendor of his own glory.[106]

No doubt, this means that the Messiah is taken up to God in heaven, similar to his enthronement in Pisqa 36.[107] Moreover, God prepares seven canopies for him, presents him to the "righteous ones, the pious ones, the holy ones, and the mighty ones of the Torah" in Israel and has the winds "sweep and sprinkle all kinds of spices from the Garden of Eden" before him;[108] and eventually he clothes him with "a garment, whose splendor will stream forth from one end of the world to the other."[109] The Messiah's exaltation concludes with a *makarismos* with which Israel blesses the Messiah:

> Blessed (*ashrei*) is the hour in which he was created,
> blessed is the womb whence he came,
> blessed is the generation whose eyes behold him,
> blessed is the eye which waited for him. . . .

Blessed is the eye which merits seeing him,
since the utterance of his tongue is pardon and forgiveness
for Israel.
His prayer is a sweet savor,
his supplication is purity and holiness.
Blessed are his fathers who merited the goodness of the
world,
hidden for the eternity (to come).[110]

CHRISTIANITY

The central place that the Messiah's vicarious expiatory suffering for the sins of humankind takes in the three homilies of Pesiqta Rabbati is unique in rabbinic Judaism. While rabbinic Judaism reacted very guardedly to this idea, it was developed mainly from Isaiah 53, taken up in a few Jewish sources, and found its culmination in the expiatory death of the New Testament's Messiah Jesus Christ; hence, the anomaly of our homilies can hardly be exaggerated. In what follows I will summarize certain crucial points and relate them to Christianity.

1. We encounter a Messiah who exists even during (if not before) the creation of the world. The homily in Pisqa 36 does not unambiguously state when precisely he was created—it is not even clear whether he has been created at all or isn't preexistent; it merely points out that God "contemplated the Messiah and his works before the world was created";[111] that is, he recognized the Messiah's necessity for history's road to salvation. Yet he is physically with God in heaven during the creation of the world since God talks to him and negotiates his terms with him. Rabbinic Judaism does recognize the idea of the Messiah's necessity

in God's road to salvation as it becomes apparent during the creation of the world,[112] but what is unique is the Messiah's physical presence in this portrayal: the Messiah is with God when he creates the world. Moreover, God asks the Messiah whether he is ready to take upon himself humankind's burden of sins *before* he begins to incorporate the human souls waiting under his throne, that is, before he begins to create man. The most direct parallel to this idea can be found in the early Christian exegesis of Genesis 1:26, where God turns to his Son, the preexistent Logos.[113]

2. It remains unclear who precisely the Messiah is in his premundane existence beneath the throne of glory: a human being or an angel or a quasi-divine being? What is certain, however, is that he is a human being in his prison on earth when he says to God: "Am I not flesh and blood?!"[114] But this means only that he has been incorporated in human form; we still do not know what his previous status was. The midrash keeps us in suspense; or, rather, it doesn't pose the question in such a pointed way.

3. The Messiah's vicarious expiatory suffering brings about salvation, that is, justice and life. To be sure, the Torah is the source of life, but it doesn't suffice—the Messiah's expiatory suffering is necessary to salvation because of Israel's sins. Here we have the New Testament within grasp, above all (as we have seen) Paul's letters and the First Letter of Peter. And we might add the prologue of the Gospel of John: taking upon himself Israel's sins, the Messiah Ephraim brings the light of life to the people of Israel (Pesiqta Rabbati)—the Word that was with God from the beginning and through which everything came into being is life and light of all people (prologue of John).[115] Goldberg, although he has recognized this connection with the prologue of John, immediately neutralizes it when he continues: "Are the boundaries of rabbinic messianism being crossed here? In essence, cer-

tainly not."[116] But they *are* being crossed, or at least expanded, in a manner that is audacious and without precedent.

The idea of the Messiah's vicarious expiatory suffering finds its climax in the New Testament with the Messiah's death on the cross. It is precisely here, however, that our homilies' parallel to the New Testament ends: the Messiah Ephraim doesn't die—he is not the Messiah *ben* Joseph/*ben* Ephraim (who does indeed die, but not an expiatory death). At this point the homilies of the Messiah Ephraim are still squarely within the framework of rabbinic messianism, but one fact remains conspicuous: all commentators point to the central place of Psalm 22 in the description of the Messiah Ephraim's sufferings, yet they ignore the importance of exactly this psalm in the New Testament account of the Messiah Jesus' suffering and death:[117]

- Jesus is mocked and ridiculed before his crucifixion (Mt. 27:29ff.; Mk. 15:17ff.)—a clear allusion to Psalms 22:7f.;
- after the crucifixion "they divided his clothes among themselves by casting lots" (Mt. 27:35; Mk. 15:24; Lk. 23:34)—a literal quotation of Psalms 22:10;
- passersby deride Jesus, "shaking their heads" (Mt. 27:39; Mk. 15:29)—a literal quotation of Psalms 22:8;
- "he trusts in God; let God deliver him now, if he wants to" (Mt. 27:43)—a partially literal adoption of Psalms 22:9;
- "my God, my God, why have you forsaken me?" (Mt. 27:46; Mk. 15:34)—a literal quotation of Psalms 22:2;
- immediately before his death Jesus gets vinegar to drink (Mt. 27:48; Mk. 15:36; Lk. 23:36)—an allusion to Psalms 22:16.

So what we have here is a Jewish Messiah in a rabbinic homily who doesn't die but for whose suffering precisely those biblical images are conjured that we know from the New Testament for the suffering of Jesus. If we presume some knowledge of the New Testament on the part of the author/authors of these homilies—and there is no reason to think that the rabbis of Pesiqta Rabbati would not have known the New Testament or certain parts of it—then the appropriation of such images and associations must have been either very naïve or very bold.

4. If we set aside R. Aqiva's exposition in the Bavli, the Messiah Ephraim's exaltation and enthronement is also unique in rabbinic Judaism. The closest parallel is the exaltation and enthronement of Enoch-Metatron in 3 Enoch, which I have discussed extensively.[118] What otherwise remains—apart from the few earlier references, such as the Similitudes of 1 Enoch and the Self-Glorification Hymn—is again in the New Testament. In the synoptic Gospels, in his interrogation before the Sanhedrin, Jesus quotes Daniel 7:13: "From now on you will see the Son of Man seated at the right hand of the Power and coming on the clouds of heaven,"[119] and after his resurrection he is carried up into heaven before the eyes of his disciples.[120] The ending of Mark explicitly combines the ascension to heaven with Psalms 110:1: "So then the Lord Jesus, after he had spoken to them, was taken up into heaven and sat down at the right hand of God."[121] And, according to the Book of Revelation, all those who follow the Messiah Jesus may eventually expect this very same enthronement for themselves: "To the one who conquers I will give a place with me on my throne, just as I myself conquered and sat down with my Father on his throne."[122] It is obviously these New Testament parallels to which the Pesiqta Rabbati homilies come closest.

5. Certain other parallels to the New Testament catch our eye. When the Messiah Ephraim in Pisqa 36, weighed down by the burden of suffering, prays to God that this agony is beyond his strength, one is reminded of Jesus' prayer in the garden of Gethsemane before his capture: "My Father, if it is possible, let this cup pass from me."[123] And could it be that the strange beams covered with iron that are imposed on the Messiah Ephraim are a faint echo of the wooden cross that Jesus was forced to carry on the way to his execution? Furthermore, Pisqa 36 speaks somewhat cryptically of the "last" redemption brought about by the Messiah Ephraim and distinguished from the "first redemption" by the fact that "following your previous redemption, you suffered anguish and enslavement by the kingdoms,[124] whereas following this last redemption you will have no anguish or enslavement by the kingdoms."[125] What does this oddly dual redemption mean? Could it allude to the expectation of Jesus' reappearance after his ascension because he hadn't yet finished his work of salvation? And finally the *makarismos* at the end of Pisqa 37: We are quite familiar with such *makarismoi* in the rabbinic and not least the Hekhalot literature,[126] but they are unique with reference to the Messiah. The only direct parallel is Mary's blessing by Elisabeth in Luke: "Blessed (*eulogēmenē*) are you [Mary] among women, and blessed (*eulogēmenos*) is the fruit of your womb. . . . And blessed (*makaria*) is she who believed that there would be a fulfillment of what was spoken to her by the Lord."[127] Particularly conspicuous is the blessing of the Messiah's mother in Pisqa 37 ("Blessed is the womb whence he came")[128] and in Luke.

This accumulation of features common to our three homilies and the New Testament/Christianity—not only in terms of individual motifs but fairly central statements—is hardly accidental. But how can it be explained? An answer to this question is closely linked with how we endeavor to locate the homilies chronologically and geographically.[129] We can take for granted that they occupy an exceptional position in Pesiqta Rabbati and that therefore the presumed final redaction of the midrash (which is controversial anyway) offers no clue. As regards the time frame, the range extends from the amoraic period,[130] probably even in the third century C.E.,[131] through the first half of the seventh century (more precisely between 632 and 637)[132] and up until the Karaite period in the ninth and tenth centuries.[133] In favor of the earlier date, scholars invoke the relationship to Christian ideas; later on, they argue, such ideas are inconceivable.[134] The later dating is based on the assumption that the mourners of Zion are identical to a Karaite group that lived in Jerusalem and was famous for its ascetic lifestyle.[135] With regard to the place of origin, assumptions vary among Greece,[136] southern Italy,[137] and Palestine.

It is in Pisqa 36 that we find the sole hint that might shed light on the time of origin. There we read: "In the year in which the King Messiah reveals himself, . . . the King of Persia will make war against a King of Arabia, and this King of Arabia will go to Edom to take counsel from the Edomites. Thereupon the King of Persia will again lay the whole world waste."[138] Bernard Bamberger sees here an allusion to the triangle of power between the Byzantine (Edom) and the Persian empires as well as the emerging Islam (Arabia), and more concretely to the war over Palestine between Byzantium and Persia (Jerusalem was conquered by the Persians in 614 C.E. and reconquered in 629 by the Byzantine emperor Heraclius) and the conquest of Palestine by the Arabs (the Arabs began their advance in 632 and conquered Jerusalem in 638). Although these events are by no means fully congruent with the brief remark in Pisqa 36, the reference to the political balance of power in the triangle between Byzantium, Persia, and Arabia is conspicuous. Günter Stemberger believes that the text might refer to the Roman vassal king Odenat of Palmyra (second half of the third century C.E.), who was waging war against the Persians.[139] Thus we are back again to the third century, but the "King of Arabia" doesn't fit in at all with this proposal. I posit, therefore, that the reference to the King of Arabia as a prominent player in world politics—despite all the uncertainty regarding the dating of Pisqa 36—does not allow any other dating than the period after 632 C.E., and this independent of whether or not one wishes to accept Bamberger's more precise dating between 632 and 637.

There is yet another factor that speaks in favor of dating not only Pisqa 36 but all three homilies to the first half of the seventh century. Goldberg has pointed out that the language of the homilies—pure, fluent Hebrew without any loanwords—sheds no light on their origin.[140] This is certainly correct, but Goldberg ignores here the fact (something that he is well aware of elsewhere) that our homilies have much in common—both stylistically and substantively—with the later apocalyptic literature of the seventh and eighth centuries C.E., that is, with texts such as the Apocalypse of Zerubbabel, the Pirqe Mashiah, and others. It is certainly no accident that precisely these later Jewish apocalypses are not only aware of Christian ideas but adapt them positively (a prime example being the mother of the Messiah in the Apocalypse of Zerubbabel).[141] The eminently Christian coloring of our homilies would then certainly not indicate their early origin—before Christianity became dogmatically differentiated—rather, and quite to the contrary, it would point to the (relatively late) deliberate Jewish reception, or better, reappropriation of ideas that had been usurped by Christianity and had for a long time been regarded as exclusively Christian. We do not know precisely where the homilies originated and were edited, but we encounter here the same phenomenon that we have observed in the Babylonian Talmud and in 3 Enoch: Judaism's self-assured answer to a Christianity that had established itself politically and dogmatically. The point here is not the question of possible Christian "influences" on Judaism—such an approach unnecessarily constricts the attempts at an explanation[142]—but still, the task cannot be to smooth out all the rough edges of the homilies and ultimately explain them by drawing on the repository of the Jewish tradition and circumventing any Christian evidence. If we do not wish to see "Judaism" and "Christianity" as static entities forever confronting each other but rather as vital, dynamic forces in constant exchange with each other, then such demarcations and harmonizations become superfluous. It is true, as Michael Fishbane has noted, that the simplistic model of Christian "influence" on Judaism "impoverishes the Jewish theological tradition";[143] but in appealing to the inexhaustible trove of Jewish theology, we must not forget that Judaism also developed and changed together with an emerging Christianity.

Notes

INTRODUCTION

1. On this, see my *Judeophobia: Attitudes toward the Jews in the Ancient World*, Cambridge, Mass., and London: Harvard University Press, 1997, pp. 34ff.

2. Sometimes other terms are used, such as *tzadoqim* (literally "Sadducees"—of course not identical with the historical Sadducees), "nations of the world" (various "nations" representing various beliefs, also synonymous with "pagans"), or *apiqorsin* ("apostates"). On the latter, see recently Jenny R. Labendz, "'Know What to Answer the Epicurean': A Diachronic Study of the *'Apikoros* in Rabbinic Literature," *HUCA* 74, 2003, pp. 175–214.

3. R. Travers Herford, *Christianity in Talmud and Midrash*, London: Williams & Norgate, 1903; reprint Jersey City, N.J.: Ktav, 2006.

4. Alan F. Segal, *Two Powers in Heaven: Early Rabbinic Reports about Christianity and Gnosticism*, Leiden: Brill, 1977.

5. Daniel Boyarin, *Border Lines: The Partition of Judaeo-Christianity*, Philadelphia: University of Pennsylvania Press, 2004.

6. Daniel Boyarin, "The Gospel of the Memra: Jewish Binitarianism and the Prologue to John," *HTR* 94, 2001, pp. 243–284; id., "Two Powers in Heaven; or, The Making of a Heresy," in Hindy Najman and Judith H. Newman, eds., *The Idea of Biblical Interpretation: Essays in Honor of James L. Kugel*, Leiden: Brill, 2004, pp. 331–370; id., "The Parables of Enoch and the Foundation of the Rabbinic Sect: A Hypothesis," in Mauro Perani, ed., *"The Words of a Wise Man's Mouth Are Gracious" (Qoh 10,12): Festschrift for Günter Stemberger on the Occasion of His 65th Birthday*, Berlin and New York: Walter de Gruyter, 2005, pp. 53–72; and the as yet last incarnation of this article, id., "Beyond Judaisms: Meṭaṭron and the Divine Polymorphy of Ancient Judaism,"

JSJ 41, 2010, pp. 323–365. It is no easy task for the reader to cleave his or her way through Boyarin's rather longish articles to figure out the respective *hiddushim*, all the more so as Boyarin is engaged in an endless debate with the secondary literature rather than with the sources.

7. Moshe Idel, *Ben: Sonship and Jewish Mysticism*, London and New York: Continuum, 2007.

8. Idel, *Ben*, pp. 4f. A variety of Scholem and his school are now "simplistic historicist approaches that anchor specific developments beyond what the evidence shows in particular circumstances" (ibid., p. 5).

9. I have explained my reservations against this methodology in my *Origins of Jewish Mysticism* (Tübingen: Mohr Siebeck, 2009; paperback Princeton, N.J.: Princeton University Press, 2011), pp. 24ff., and I suppose that said reservations would fall under his category of a "simplistic historicist approach."

10. Idel, *Ben*, p. 46.

11. 1 Enoch is a compilation of different books, and the Enoch passages in question belong to the so-called Similitudes, dated by most scholars to the end of the first century B.C.E.; 2 Enoch is usually dated to the first century C.E.

12. Somewhere between the seventh and the ninth century; see Schäfer, *Origins*, pp. 315f.

13. Idel, *Ben*, p. 160; see also p. 120. Without any proof—even without bothering to provide the reference—he dismisses Joseph Dan's claim that the identification of Enoch with Metatron is a later addition (ibid., p. 94, n. 150). I agree, but this is not the point: the point is the dating of 3 Enoch as a book and part of the Hekhalot literature.

14. Following the precedent of Boyarin; see the literature mentioned in n. 6, in particular "Beyond Judaisms."

15. Adiel Schremer, *Brothers Estranged: Heresy, Christianity, and Jewish Identity in Late Antiquity*, Oxford: Oxford University Press, 2010; and see his earlier article, "Midrash, Theology, and History: Two Powers in Heaven Revisited," *JSJ* 39, 2008, pp. 230–253.

16. Schremer, *Brothers Estranged*, p. 22.

17. Ibid., p. x. A similar argument has been launched, yet with a fundamental methodological claim, by Alon Goshen-Gottstein, "Jewish Christian Relations and Rabbinic Literature—Shifting Scholarly and Relational Paradigms: The Case of Two Powers" (in Marcel Poorthuis, Joshua Schwartz, and Joseph Turner, eds., *Interaction between Judaism and Christianity in History, Religion, Art, and Literature*, Leiden: Brill, 2009, pp. 15–43). Goshen-Gottstein makes out "the present paradigm, that favors Jewish-Christian relations as a hermeneutical lens for understanding rabbinic literature," as the culprit behind Boyarin's and similar approaches (p. 19) and offers instead a theoretical model that reads the rabbinic sources as "a hermeneutic response to certain exegetical triggers, rather than a historical response to concrete situations involving other religious communities" (p. 31). I, for one, find his clear-cut distinction between "hermeneutics" and "history" worrisome (as if the rabbis reacted to "exegetical triggers" like the Pavlovian dog, without any connection to historical reality) and, as far as the "present paradigm" is concerned, have always tried to steer clear of the modern Jewish-Christian "dialogue"; in fact, for much of my scholarly career I followed Goshen-Gottstein's third model of Judaism and Christianity in antiquity as two parallel religious phenomena without much interaction (under the influence of my teachers at the Hebrew University such as Ephraim E. Urbach and, not least, Alon Goshen-Gottstein's father Moshe). Only since quite recently have I been able to confront the fake (self-)sufficiency and scholarly sterility of this model. As for Boyarin's response to Goshen-Gottstein, see his "Beyond Judaisms," pp. 360ff.

18. Proven by a sentence such as "[A] careful reading of the rabbinic texts reveals that the connection between the theological and the historical *and the view of the former as rooted in the latter* are suggested by the rabbinic texts themselves" (Schremer, *Brothers Estranged*, p. x, my emphasis). I couldn't agree more, in particular with the emphasized phrase, since this is precisely what I try to demonstrate in my book.

19. I include what is called "Gnosis" or "Gnosticism" in the category of "Christianity," following the trend in recent scholarship that

is reluctant to distinguish between "Christianity" and "Gnosis" as two stable entities that can neatly be separated.

20. Peter Schäfer, *Jesus in the Talmud*, Princeton, N.J., and Oxford: Princeton University Press, 2007; German translation *Jesus im Talmud*, Tübingen: Mohr Siebeck, 2007, 2nd edition 2010 (with a new afterword in which I deal with some of my critics).

21. I do not enter here the debate about the possible impact of Zoroastrianism or Manichaeism on rabbinic sources and the Bavli in particular, not because I think there was no such impact (of course, there was), but because I am not interested in antagonistic and dualistic systems as such. I am dealing with sources that raise the possibility of a second divine power next to God in a positive sense, not as a negative and antagonistic force fighting the supreme God. This is why I "plump for Christianity," as one reader of my manuscript has put it.

22. Geza Vermes, *Jesus the Jew: A Historian's Reading of the Gospels*, London: Collins, 1973.

CHAPTER I: DIFFERENT NAMES OF GOD

1. See Ephraim E. Urbach, *The Sages: Their Concepts and Beliefs*, Jerusalem: Magnes Press, 1975, pp. 396–407.

2. The literature about this contested subject is endless; for some recent publications, see Joel S. Baden, *J, E, and the Redaction of the Pentateuch*, Tübingen: Mohr Siebeck, 2009; Tzemah L. Yoreh, *The First Book of God*, Berlin: de Gruyter, 2010. I am grateful to my Princeton colleague Naphtali Meshel for these references.

3. SifBam § 143, ed. Horovitz, p. 191; cf. Sifra pereq 2, parashah 2:5, fol. 4a, ed. Friedmann, p. 42 (R. Yose); b Men 110a (Shim'on b. Azzai). Jacob Neusner distorts the meaning of the Sifra passage when he translates (J. Neusner, *Sifra: An Analytical Translation*, vol. 1, *Introduction, Vayyiqra Dibura Denedabah and Vayyiqra Dibura Dehobah*, Atlanta: Scholars Press, 1988, p. 79): "R. Yosé says, Any passage in which 'an offering' is stated along with the divine name, lo, it is so as not to give unbelievers occasion to cavil."

4. As for *Shaddai*, it is difficult to judge whether it was seen as singular or plural.

5. Wilhelm Bacher, *Die Agada der Tannaiten*, vol. 1, Strasbourg: Karl I. Trübner, 1884, p. 422.

6. MT: "and all your righteous ordinance endures" (sing.).

7. BerR 1:7 (the translation follows Freedman, with modifications).

8. The literal meaning of *le-'olam*. The author plays here with both meanings of *le-'olam*.

9. The acceptance of God's ordinances as righteous also implies that his creatures don't challenge them, irrespective of whether they show mercy or stern justice—in other words, whether they originate in "*Elohim*" or in "*YHWH*."

10. Although, to be sure, the first parashah of Bereshit Rabba explicitly rejects the notion of preexistent matter that the creator God might have used for the creation of the material world—which does smack of "gnostic" ideas; see in particular BerR 1:5 and 1:9.

11. Verb in the plural.

12. Verb in the singular.

13. Verb in the plural.

14. Verb in the singular.

15. Literally: "where you find (a problem allowing) the *minim* to open their mouth," i.e., to utter a heretical view.

16. Verb in the plural.

17. Verb in the plural.

18. Verb in the singular.

19. BerR 8:9; parallel y Ber 9:1/9–10, fol. 12d.

20. In the parallel version in b Sanh 38b the collection of exegeses is attributed to R. Yohanan; in the Yerushalmi version (Ber 9:1/9–16, fol. 12d–13a) the author is R. Simlai.

21. Presumably from a different source.

22. See Burton L. Visotzky, "Trinitarian Testimonies," *USQR* 42, 1988, pp. 73–85 (74ff.); id., "Goys 'Я'n't Us," in Eduard Iricinschi and Holger M. Zellentin, eds., *Heresy and Identity in Late*

Antiquity, Tübingen: Mohr Siebeck, 2008, pp. 302ff. Visotzky follows, among others, Jacob Jervell, *Imago Dei: Gen. 1.26f. im Spätjudentum, in der Gnosis und in den paulinischen Briefen*, Göttingen: Vandenhoek & Ruprecht, 1960, p. 311, with n. 464; Madeleine Boucher, "Some Unexplored Parallels to 1 Cor. 11:11–12 and Gal. 3:28: The New Testament and the Role of Women," *CBQ* 31, 1969, pp. 50–58.

23. Literally, "authority" (*exousian*), the veil being the symbol of authority.

24. I prefer the translation of *kai* as "also" instead of "now" in the RSV translation.

25. 1 Cor. 11:2–13, following the RSV translation but omitting the parentheses in verses 8–9 and 11–12.

26. It actually runs through 1:16.

27. My emphases.

28. My emphasis.

29. This is the literal translation of the Greek *chōris* ("apart from").

30. Visotzky, "Trinitarian Testimonies," p. 74. Commenting on this passage in a private communication, Burt Visotzky qualifies this argument by stating that the rabbis are not necessarily quoting the New Testament Paul but are making use of Paul as they heard him quoted by contemporary Christians.

31. BerR 8:9 (only in some manuscripts; see Theodor-Albeck, vol. 1, p. 63, *apparatus criticus* on line 5); y Ber 9:1/11–16, fol. 12d–13a (the immediate continuation of the text quoted above).

32. Or: "the name of one."

33. Or: "the name of one."

34. y Ber 9:1/11–12, fol. 12d–13a; BerR 8:9 (some manuscripts); translation according to y Ber.

35. "King" as a generic designation for all kinds of rulers, "Caesar" and "Augustus" as more specific information. Similarly, "craftsmen" as a generic designation for all kinds of trades and "masons" and "architects" as specific information. This skillful parallelism can be developed even further: just as the Caesar is subordinate to the Augustus, so is the mason subordinate to the architect.

36. See ShemR 23:1, where God is compared with a king who has won a war and, as his reward, receives the title "Augustus." The midrash then, asking about the difference between a "king" (*melekh*) and an "Augustus" (*agostos*), responds that the "king" is depicted as standing on a *luah* (presumably a stone frieze) whereas the "Augustus" is depicted as seated. Thus the "Augustus" is clearly superior to the "king" here, and it makes sense to identify the "king" with the Caesar. Cf. also EsthR 1:19—here the subject is not the diarchy of the Augustus and the Caesar but a "king" (that is, a general) who has been proclaimed "Augustus" by his legions.

37. Hans Peter Laubscher, *Der Reliefschmuck des Galeriusbogens in Thessaloniki*, Berlin: Mann, 1975, pp. 69–78 (pp. 76f. with plates 58 and 60/1); Christoph Markschies, *Alta Trinità Beata*, Tübingen: Mohr Siebeck, 2000, p. 13.

38. Markschies, *Alta Trinità Beata*, pp. 14f. with references p. 13, n. 52.

39. Gunther Gottlieb, *Ambrosius von Mailand und Kaiser Gratian*, Göttingen: Vandenhoek & Ruprecht, 1973, pp. 32f.; Markschies, *Alta Trinità Beata*, pp. 14f.

40. Markschies, *Alta Trinità Beata*, p. 16.

41. y Ber 9:1/13–15, fol. 13a; BerR 8:9 (only the first part in some manuscripts).

42. Whether R. Yohanan or R. Simlai is the "original" author of this collection is a question of secondary importance; more important is the fact that they both belong to the late third century C.E.

43. b Sanh 38b.

44. See below, ch. 3.

45. b Sanh 38b.

46. The fuller explains to R. Ishmael that he has heard this interpretation from R. Meir.

47. Segal, *Two Powers in Heaven*, pp. 118f.

48. On him, see Bacher, *Agada der Tannaiten*, vol. 2, pp. 407–411.

49. The exegesis is preceded by a structurally similar problem addressed by a heretic to Rav Idith, presumably a Babylonian amora who lived around 350 C.E.; see below, ch. 4.

50. "Sadducee" (*tzaddoqi*) in the printed editions; "heretic" (*min*) in the manuscripts (Mss. Vatican Ebr. 120–121 and 122; Ms. Munich 95).

51. Rabbi thought the heretic who had argued with him had returned with the answer.

52. So it was another heretic who delivered the good news.

53. b Hul 87a; cf. the parallel in b Sanh 39a (there an exchange between the emperor and Rabban Gamliel).

54. Even Segal is inclined to distrust the attribution of the story to R. Yehudah ha-Naśi (*Two Powers in Heaven*, p. 117).

55. The solution in the parallel b Sanh 39a is much better. It doesn't draw upon the continuation of Amos 4:13 but demonstrates the absurdity of the heretic's argument.

56. See above, pp. 32f.

57. Visotzky, "Trinitarian Testimonies," pp. 76ff.; see also Menahem Kister, "Let Us Make Man," in Yaakov Sussmann, ed., *Sugyot be-Mehqar ha-Talmud: Conference Marking the Fifth Anniversary of the Death of E. E. Urbach*, Jerusalem: Israel Academy of Sciences, 2001, pp. 28–64 (55–57) [in Hebrew]; expanded English version "Some Early Jewish and Christian Exegetical Problems and the Dynamics of Monotheism," *JSJ* 37, 2006, pp. 563ff. And see below, pp. 49f.

58. Visotzky, "Trinitarian Testimonies," p. 80.

59. Barnabas 6:12: "For the scripture says concerning us, how He [God] says to the Son [Jesus]: Let us make man after our image and after our likeness ... (Gen. 1:26)."

60. Irenaeus, Adversus haereses IV, 20:1; cf. also ibid., IV, praef. (4); V, 1:3.

61. BerR 8:4f. and parallels; see below, ch. 6.

62. Although, as Christoph Markschies reminds me (private communication), Philo no doubt belongs to the prehistory of the Christian trinity theology and may even be held responsible for its long and persistent "subordinationist" orientation.

63. My emphases.

64. Augustine, On the Trinity XII 7 (10); English translation Arthur West Haddan, *The Works of Aurelius Augustine: A New Translation*, vol. 7: *On the Trinity*, Edinburgh: T&T Clark, 1873, p. 292.

65. Ibid., VII 6 (12); XII 6 (6f.).

66. Gregory of Nazianzus, Or. 29:2; 31:11. English translation: *A Select Library of Nicene and Post-Nicene Fathers*, in J.N.D. Kelly, *Early Christian Doctrines*, London: A&C Black, 4th edition, 1968, p. 268.

67. Visotzky, "Trinitarian Testimonies," p. 81.

68. See the concise and very useful overview by Christoph Markschies, "'. . . *et tamen non tres Dii, sed unum Deus* . . .': Zum Stand der Erforschung der altkirchlichen Trinitätstheologie," in id., *Alta Trinità Beata*, pp. 286–309 (originally in *MJTh* 10, 1998, pp. 155–179).

69. Justin Martyr, Dial. 56:11; id., Dial. 62:1–4 (exegesis of Gen. 1:26–28): the Logos = Wisdom was begotten of the Father and was with the Father when he said: "Let us make man."

70. Christoph Markschies pointed out to me in a private communication that the distinction between "adoptianist" and "modalist" monarchianism is problematic, since the latter in fact *identifies* Father and Son.

71. See Wolfgang A. Bienert, *"Sabellius und Sabellianismus als historisches Problem,"* in Hanns Christof Brennecke, Ernst Ludwig Grasmück, and Christoph Markschies, eds., *Logos: Festschrift für Luise Abramowski zum 8. Juli 1993*, Berlin and New York: de Gruyter, 1993, pp. 124–139.

72. Tertullian, Adversus Praxean 2 (Ernest Evans, ed., *Tertullian's Treatise against Praxeas*, London: SPCK, 1948, p. 91); cf. Markschies, *Alta Trinità Beata*, p. 296, n. 45.

73. Markschies, *Alta Trinità Beata*, pp. 297ff.; see also id., "Der Heilige Geist im *Johanneskommentar* des Origenes: Einige vorläufige Bemerkungen," in id., *Origenes und sein Erbe: Gesammelte Studien*, Berlin and New York: de Gruyter, 2007, pp. 107–126.

74. On the Cappadocian Fathers, see the excellent summary by Christoph Markschies, "Gibt es eine einheitliche 'kappadozische Trinitätstheologie'?: Vorläufige Erwägungen zu Einheit und Differenzen neunizänischer Theologie," in id., *Alta Trinità Beata*, pp. 196–237 (originally in *MJTh* 10, 1998, pp. 51–94). A case in point is Basil's statement in one of his letters (Basil, ep. 125:1, 42–45, in Yves Courtonne, *Saint Basile: Lettres*, Texte établi et trad., vol. 2, Paris: Les Belles

Lettres, 1961, p. 32), according to which the Son is *homoousios* with the Father (and implicitly the Holy Spirit with the Son and the Father), whereas all three—the Father, the Son, and the Holy Spirit—are at the same time each a hypostasis of their own.

75. See Wolf-Dieter Hauschild, *Gottes Geist und der Mensch: Studien zur frühchristlichen Pneumatologie*, Munich: Kaiser, 1972, pp. 92, 137f., and Markschies' trenchant attack on Hauschild and the use of the term "binitarian" (Markschies, *Origenes und sein Erbe*, pp. 108ff.).

76. On his contribution, see Markschies, *Alta Trinità Beata*, pp. 199ff.

77. Verb in the singular.

78. Verb in the plural.

79. Verb in the singular.

80. Basilius von Caesarea, *Homilien zum Hexameron*, eds. Emmanuel Amand de Mendieta and Stig Y. Rudberg, Berlin: Akademie Verlag, 1997, pp. 159f.; Basil de Césarée, *Homélies sur l'hexaéméron*, ed. Stanislas Giet, Paris: Cerf, 1950, pp. 516–521; quoted also by Kister, "Let Us Make Man," p. 55; id., "Dynamics of Monotheism," p. 589. The translation follows (with some changes) David T. Runia, "'Where, Tell Me, Is the Jew': Basil, Philo and Isidore of Pelusium," *VigChr* 46, 1992, pp. 173f.

81. Basil, ep. 361, 27–29 (Courtonne, *Saint Basile*, vol. 3, Paris: Les Belles Lettres, 1966, p. 221); Markschies, *Alta Trinità Beata*, pp. 199f.

82. That R. Simlai does not refer to the Holy Spirit as the third member of the trinity does not, however, necessarily mean that "the Christian subtleties and fine distinctions within the Trinity were, for them [the rabbis], incomprehensible," as Kister assumes ("Dynamics of Monotheism," p. 590).

83. Prov. 8:29f.

84. Wisdom 7:25f.

85. Sir. 24:23.

86. BerR 1:1.

87. John 1:1–4.

88. "It," of course, is the Word, which is Jesus; accordingly, one could also translate "he."

89. On this, see my monograph *Mirror of His Beauty: Feminine Images of God from the Bible to the Early Kabbalah*, Princeton, N.J.: Princeton University Press, 2002.

CHAPTER 2: THE YOUNG AND THE OLD GOD

1. MekhY, ba-hodesh 5 and shirata 4 (ed. Horovitz-Rabin, pp. 219f. and pp. 129f.; ed. Lauterbach, vol. 2, pp. 231f. and 31f.); the translation follows Lauterbach. Parallels: MekhS, Ex. 15:1 (p. 81) and Ex. 20:2 (p. 146); MHG Ex., pp. 398f.; PesK, ed. Mandelbaum, p. 223; PesR, ed. Friedmann, p. 100b; TanB Yitro 16 (p. 40a); Yalq Yitro 275 (p. 167b); ibid. 286 (p. 172a); Yalq Isa. 463 (p. 797b); ShemR 28:5; b Hag 14a; MidrHakh, p. 16; SekhT, p. 202; LeqT Ex., pp. 66b–67a; We-hizhir, p. 23a; cf. SifDev § 329, ed. Finkelstein, p. 379. On this, see Peter Schäfer, "Israel und die Völker der Welt: Zur Auslegung von Mekhilta deRabbi Yishma'el, bahodesh Yitro 5," *FJB* 4, 1976, pp. 32–62.

2. "I am he who was at Sinai" only in the printed editions.

3. Schäfer, "Israel und die Völker der Welt," p. 32.

4. The parallel in MekhS, ed. Hoffmann, p. 81, corrects the (in my view, original) opposition of war hero versus old man to young man versus old man, whereas PesK, ed. Mandelbaum, p. 223, expands the opposition to war hero (at the sea) versus scribes (Mount Sinai) and old man (Daniel) versus young man (Solomo). PesK clearly reflects a later development.

5. Most recently Adiel Schremer, correctly observing in opposition to Boyarin (see below) that the purpose of Ex. 24:10 in the Mekhilta is to prove that God appears as an old man, has suggested another solution: God appears as an old man because *livnat ha-sappir* in Ex. 24:10 means the whiteness of sapphire and therefore God "is said to have been seen as 'white,'" that is, as an old man (Adiel Schremer, "Midrash, Theology, and History: Two Powers in Heaven Revisited," *JSJ* 39, 2008, p. 246). Schremer gives no proof for such a midrash (in

fact, he creates a new one) and seems unaware of the rabbinic texts about the sapphire brick; nor does he know my article "Israel und die Völker der Welt," in which I discuss them.

6. For the midrashic parallels, see Schäfer, "Israel und die Völker der Welt," p. 40.

7. The warrior God of Ex. 15:3 is the God of justice, and the God of Ex. 24:10 is the God of mercy.

8. The Aramaic word used here (*tehot*) usually means "beneath, under," but the meaning "in place of, instead" is also possible and more appropriate here: the sapphire brick was not placed *under* God's (regular) footstool but was put there instead of it, as a substitute.

9. Thus, explicitly, in a midrash attributed to R. Levi b. Sisi and Bar Qappara, both tannaim of the fifth and last generation; see WaR 23:8; y Suk 4:3/4 (fol. 54c); PRE 48 (fol. 116a/b); ShirR 4:8, § 1; Sif-Zut Num. 10:35 (p. 267); TanB beshallah 11 (fol. 30a).

10. The fact that God doesn't age is taken a step further in the piyyut *Az be-'ein kol* and expressed in the wonderfully paradoxical phrase: "You are ever renewing, / for in the beginning you were aged, / and in the end youthful"; see Michael D. Swartz and Joseph Yaha-lom, eds. and trans., *Avodah: Ancient Poems for Yom Kippur*, University Park: Pennsylvania State University Press, 2005, pp. 96f.

11. Although he speaks of "heretics" and not of "nations."

12. One could also argue that it was not the "nations" that missed their chance to reject God's claim but the other gods; yet this seems un-likely in view of the context and the subsequent exegesis of Isa. 45:19.

13. This question is part of the larger context of our midrash in the Mekhilta, but still needs to be kept separate.

14. See Schäfer, "Israel und die Völker der Welt," pp. 41f.

15. Segal, *Two Powers in Heaven*, p. 50. But when he sees in R. Nathan's exegesis the opposition to "gnostic sectarians" (ibid., p. 57), he is back on that one-dimensional and simplistic "gnostic" track.

16. *Ke-var enash*, literally "like the son of a man."

17. Segal, *Two Powers in Heaven*, pp. 35ff.

18. Without giving Segal full credit for it. This has also been no-ticed by Schremer ("Midrash, Theology, and History," p. 245, n. 41),

but it does not prevent him from presenting the "new" interpretation as if it had been invented by Boyarin—an interesting case of scholarly attribution.

19. Boyarin, "The Gospel of the Memra," pp. 243–284; id., "Two Powers in Heaven," pp. 331–370; id., "Parables of Enoch," pp. 53–72; id., "Beyond Judaisms," pp. 336ff.

20. Boyarin, "Parables of Enoch," p. 59 (italics in the original); and see id., "Beyond Judaisms," p. 337.

21. Boyarin, "Parables of Enoch," p. 59 and pp. 62f.; id., "The Gospel of the Memra," p. 253, n. 35; more explicit in id., "Two Powers in Heaven," pp. 353f.

22. This has also been correctly observed by Schremer, "Midrash, Theology, and History," p. 245: "In a sense, then, instead of reading the midrash, Boyarin in fact re-writes it"; see also id., *Brothers Estranged*, pp. 82ff. In his response to Schremer ("Beyond Judaisms," p. 338), Boyarin now argues that the quotation of Dan. 7:10 in fact includes Dan. 7:13f.—although he admits that this reading is "a bit of a stretch." Indeed, it is a stretch, despite his attempts to convince us otherwise.

23. For b Hag 14a, see below, p. 285, n.2.

24. Christian Gnilka, *Aetas Spiritalis. Die Überwindung der natürlichen Altersstufen als Ideal frühchristlichen Lebens*, Bonn: Peter Hanstein, 1972, pp. 49ff. Among the many biblical individuals who served as models for the late antique Christian ideal, Moses, David, Daniel, and, of course, Jesus figure prominently (ibid., pp. 228ff.). I thank Christoph Markschies for this reference.

CHAPTER 3: GOD AND DAVID

1. b Sanh 38b; see above, p. 37.

2. In the parallel b Hag 14a, the emphasis is slightly different: "One verse reads: 'His throne (sing.) was fiery flames' (Dan. 7:9, end), and one verse reads: 'Till thrones (pl.) were set in place, and the Ancient of Days took his seat' (Dan. 7:9, beginning)."

3. See above, p. 37.

4. *Pamalya shel ma'lah*, a technical term for God's angels.

5. b Sanh 38b.

6. That is, from underneath the throne upon which the Ancient of Days is seated.

7. b Sanh 38b; b Hag 14a.

8. Even if for the attribute of mercy the unusual term *tzedaqah* is used here instead of the standard *rahamim*.

9. See Urbach, *The Sages*, pp. 448ff.

10. BerR 12:15.

11. Cases of Nega'im (leprosy) and Ohalot (the impurities spread by a corpse) are regulated by complicated halakhic stipulations.

12. Not by accident using a similar argument as the Mekhilta passage with its reference to Ex. 24:10.

13. See above, pp. 64ff.

14. Cf. Dan. 10:20f.; 12:1.

15. George W. E. Nickelsburg, *Jewish Literature between the Bible and the Mishnah*, Philadelphia: Fortress Press, 1981, pp. 221–223. John J. Collins, *The Apocalyptic Imagination: An Introduction to Jewish Apocalyptic Literature*, Grand Rapids, Mich./Cambridge: William B. Eerdmans, 2nd edition, 1998, p. 178, now proposes the early or mid-first century C.E., whereas J. T. Milik prefers an even later date: according to him, the Similitudes are the product of a Jew or a Jewish-Christian of the first or second century C.E. (Józef Tadeusz Milik, *Ten Years of Discovery in the Wilderness of Judaea*, Naperville, Ill.: A. R. Allenson; London: SCM Press, 1959, p. 33). Conspicuously, no fragments of the Similitudes have been discovered at Qumran, whereas fragments do exist from all other parts of the First Book of Enoch; on this, see also Geza Vermes, *Jesus the Jew: A Historian's Reading of the Gospels*, London: Collins, 1973 (with numerous subsequent editions), p. 176.

16. 1 En. 46:1–5. All translations from 1 Enoch according to Matthew Black, *The Book of Enoch or 1 Enoch: A New English Translation*, Leiden: Brill, 1985.

17. 1 En. 71:9–17.

18. 1 En. 14:14 and 24f.

19. 1 En. 71:12–15.

20. 1 En. 71:16–17.

21. 4 Ezra 13:3. All translations from 4 Ezra according to Bruce M. Metzger, "The Fourth Book of Ezra," in Charlesworth, *OTP*, vol. 1, pp. 517ff.

22. 4 Ezra 13:10f.

23. 4 Ezra 13:26.

24. 4 Ezra 13:32.

25. 4 Ezra 13:38.

26. Josef Schreiner, *Das 4. Buch Esra*, Gütersloh: Gütersloher Verlagshaus, 1981, p. 397, n. 32a (*JSHRZ*, vol. 5, part 4).

27. 4 Ezra 7:28.

28. Isa. 42ff.

29. Ps. 2:7.

30. 2 Sam. 7:14.

31. Vermes, *Jesus the Jew*, pp. 177ff.

32. Mk. 13:26f.; Mt. 24:30f.; Lk. 21:27.

33. Mt. 26:63f.; Lk. 22:67 ("If I tell you, you will not believe").

34. Mk. 14:62; and see Mt. 26:64; Lk. 22:69.

35. Cf. Arnold Goldberg, "Sitzend zur Rechten der Kraft: Zur Gottesbezeichnung Gebura in der frühen rabbinischen Literatur," *BZ* NF 8, 1964, pp. 284–293 = id., *Mystik und Theologie des rabbinischen Judentums. Gesammelte Studien I*, ed. Margarete Schlüter and Peter Schäfer, Tübingen: Mohr Siebeck, 1997, pp. 188–198.

36. In both cases the Septuagint translation is *kyrios*.

37. See Markschies, "'Sessio as dexteram': Bemerkungen zu einem altchristlichen Bekenntnismotiv in der Diskussion der altkirchlichen Theologen," in *Alta Trinità Beata*, pp. 1–69.

38. See above, pp. 73ff. and below, pp. 85ff.; 214ff.

39. See below, p. 224.

40. Cf. Acts 2:34f.; 1 Cor. 15:25; Eph. 1:20; Heb. 1:13.

41. Through the Diatessaron or the New Testament Peshitta; see Schäfer, *Jesus in the Talmud*, pp. 122f.

42. y Taan 4:8/27, fol. 68d; on this, see Peter Schäfer, *Der Bar Kokhba-Aufstand: Studien zum zweiten jüdischen Krieg gegen Rom*, Tübingen: Mohr Siebeck, 1981, pp. 137ff.

43. Boyarin, "Parables of Enoch," p. 60; id., "Beyond Judaisms," p. 339. Segal, *Two Powers in Heaven*, p. 49, is more optimistic and believes that the messianic controversy could indeed be from Aqiva's time.

44. Boyarin, "Parables of Enoch."

45. See, in particular, Ra'anan S. Boustan, "The Study of Heikhalot Literature: Between Mystical Experience and Textual Artifact," *CBR* 6, 2007, pp. 130–160, and Moulie Vidas, *Tradition and Formation of the Talmud*, Princeton, N.J.: Princeton University Press, forthcoming.

46. In order to move the Mekhilta and the Bavli closer together chronologically, he declares that the Mekhilta is from the fourth century (Boyarin, "Parables of Enoch," p. 58) and the Bavli sugya a "late third-century or so passage" (ibid., p. 60). I still regard it as safer to date the Mekhilta earlier and the Bavli sugya later.

47. Boyarin, "Parables of Enoch," pp. 63f.

48. See the useful volume, edited by Adam H. Becker and Annette Yoshiko Reed, *The Ways That Never Parted: Jews and Christians in Late Antiquity and the Early Middle Ages*, Tübingen: Mohr Siebeck, 2003.

49. Peter Schäfer, *Synopse zur Hekhalot-Literatur*, Tübingen: Mohr Siebeck, 1981, §§ 122–126; see id., *Hekhalot-Studien*, Tübingen: Mohr Siebeck, 1988, p. 215.

50. Schäfer, *Origins of Jewish Mysticism*, p. 258.

51. See Schäfer, *Synopse zur Hekhalot-Literatur*, § 397, where Sasangiel is one of the seventy names of Metatron.

52. According to Mss. B238 and L4730 in place of "He" in Ms. N8128.

53. Literally: "run" (*ratzin*).

54. Mss. B238 and L4730 read "toward David."

55. Classes of high angels.

56. According to Ms. B238 in place of the less meaningful "were made" (*na'asu*) here in Ms. N8128.

57. One of the seven heavens; see below, pp. 88, 116ff.

58. According to Ms. B238; Ms. N8128 here reads "GWZK," the meaning of which is uncertain.

59. Ex. 15:18 has: "The Lord will be king for ever and ever."

60. According to Mss. B238 and L4730 (instead of "angels").

61. According to Ms. L4730 (instead of "great house of learning").

62. The uppermost of the seven heavens.

63. According to Mss. B238, L4730, and a gloss in N8128.

64. Mss. B238 and L4730: "and his family."

65. The four holy creatures of Ezek. 1.

66. All the heavens.

67. And more often, e.g., Ps. 96:10; Ps. 97:1.

68. Schäfer, *Synopse zur Hekhalot-Literatur*, §§ 125f. The translation follows Ms. N8128 with important variant readings and corrections recorded in the footnotes.

69. Ezek. 1:13.

70. Ezek. 1:14.

71. There is no equivalent of the number seven in Ezekiel, but in the Book of Revelation (to which I will soon turn) "flashes of lightning" emit from the throne of the Son of Man, and in front of the throne "burn seven torches of fire" (Rev. 4:5).

72. The variant reading "toward David" in Mss. B238 and L4730 is clearly the *lectio facilior* and hence a later correction.

73. On the taxonomy of the seven heavens, see Peter Schäfer, "In Heaven as It Is in Hell: The Cosmology of *Seder Rabbah di-Bereshit*," in Ra'anan S. Boustan and Annette Yoshiko Reed, eds., *Heavenly Realms and Earthly Realities in Late Antique Religions*, Cambridge: Cambridge University Press, 2004, pp. 233–274.

74. Ezek. 3:12f.

75. Schäfer, *Synopse zur Hekhalot-Literatur*, § 15; for more on Metatron, see below, ch. 4.

76. Dan. 7:9.

77. Schäfer, *Synopse zur Hekhalot-Literatur*, § 13; and see below, p. 109.

78. Anna Maria Schwemer, "Irdischer und himmlischer König. Beobachtungen zur sogenannten David-Apokalypse in Hekhalot Rabbati §§ 122–126," in Martin Hengel and Anna Maria Schwemer, eds., *Königsherrschaft Gottes und himmlischer Kult im Judentum, Urchristentum und in der hellenistischen Welt*, Tübingen: Mohr Siebeck, 1991, pp. 309–359.

79. Ibid., p. 323.

80. Rev. 4 and 5; I have analyzed this passage in greater detail in my *Origins of Jewish Mysticism*, pp. 103ff.

81. Rev. 1:13f.

82. Rev. 3:21.

83. See above, p. 35.

84. Rev. 4:8.

85. Rev. 4:11.

86. As I have suggested in *Origins of Jewish Mysticism*, p. 108, with n. 87.

87. Rev. 4:11.

88. Rev. 5:12.

89. Rev. 5:13f.

90. Schwemer, "Irdischer und himmlischer König," p. 323.

91. Cf., among others, Robert Comte du Mesnil du Buisson, *Les Peintures de la synagogue de Doura-Europos, 245–256 après J.-C.*, Rome: Pontifico Istituto Biblico, 1939, pp. 48–51; André Grabar, "Le Thème religieux des fresques de la Synagogue de Doura," *RHR* 123, 1941, pp. 170–172; Henri Stern, "The Orpheus in the Synagogue of Dura-Europos," *JWCI* 21, 1958, pp. 1–6; Erwin R. Goodenough, *Jewish Symbols in the Greco-Roman Period*, vol. 9, *Symbolism in the Dura Synagogue: Text, i*, New York: Pantheon, 1964, pp. 78–123 ("The Reredos"). Paul V. M. Flesher ("Rereading the Reredos: David, Orpheus, and Messianism in the Dura Europos Synagogue," in Dan Urman and Paul M. Flesher, eds., *Ancient Synagogues: Historical Analysis and Archaeological Discovery*, vol. 2, Leiden: Brill, 1995, pp. 346–366) has emphatically argued against any Jewish-messianic interpretation of this fresco and related scenes. He points to the fact (quite rightly so) that certain important Christian theologians such as Clement and Eusebius identify Orpheus with Jesus (and, in the wake of this interpretation, Orpheus with David) and that the evidence for a Jewish identification of Orpheus with David is particularly scanty (apart from the alleged example at Dura, there is only the mosaic at the synagogue of Gaza from the sixth century C.E.). But when he concludes from this that the Jewish-messianic interpretation of the Dura scene(s) is untenable and

presupposes a "'christianization' of Dura's Judaism" (p. 359), he seems to follow the pejorative German maxim *Es kann nicht sein, was nicht sein darf* ("What you don't want, cannot be").

92. Isa. 11:1.

93. Kurt Weizmann and Herbert L. Kessler, *The Frescoes of the Dura Synagogue and Christian Art*, Washington, D.C.: Dumbarton Oaks Research Library and Collection, 1990, p. 91.

94. Ibid., pp. 91f.

95. Jonathan Goldstein, "The Central Composition of the West Wall of the Synagogue of Dura-Europos," *JANES* 16–17, 1984–1985, pp. 118ff.

96. Mt. 17:2f.; Mk. 9:4.

CHAPTER 4: GOD AND METATRON

1. b Sanh 38b; for the parallel ShemR 32:4, see below, p. 115, n. 44, and p. 195, with n. 114.

2. Literally, "do not exchange me for him."

3. Literally, "faith in their hand."

4. *Parwanqa* is a Persian loanword, derived from Middle Iranian *parwānak* (Middle Persian *parwānag*), and means "guide, messenger, precursor"; see Michael Sokoloff, *A Dictionary of Jewish Babylonian Aramaic of the Byzantine Period*, Ramat-Gan: Bar Ilan University Press, 1990, p. 929.

5. Literally, "face."

6. See the previous interpretations by Herford, *Christianity*, pp. 285ff.; Segal, *Two Powers in Heaven*, pp. 68ff.; Nathaniel Deutsch, *Guardians of the Gate: Angelic Vice Regency in Late Antiquity*, Leiden: Brill, 1999, p. 49; Boyarin, "Parables of Enoch," pp. 66ff.; id., "Beyond Judaisms," pp. 329ff.

7. See above, p. 38.

8. I prefer this interpretation to the traditional one (Rashi ad loc.), according to which it is Metatron who says to Moses "Come up to the Lord." If Metatron invites Moses to ascend to God, we don't have a problem with the name *YHWH*—and accordingly we don't need the

explanation that Metatron's name is like the name of his master. My reading is supported by Ramban ad. loc., who explains that God invites Moses to ascend to Metatron. Ramban's exegesis cannot be neutralized by arguing that it is built upon the (much later) kabbalistic identification of Metatron with the Shekhinah (see Dov Septimus, "Het'o shel Metatron: bisevakh leshonot we-nusha'ot," *Leshonenu* 69, 2007, p. 294, n. 16). I am grateful to Moulie Vidas for referring me to this article.

9. Cf. Ex. 14:19.

10. See also Boyarin, "Parables of Enoch," p. 67; id., "Beyond Judaisms," p. 331.

11. Literally "he" in Hebrew, but "he" refers to "the Lord, your God."

12. 1 En. 37–71.

13. 1 En. 71:11, without saying so explicitly: the book only mentions that Enoch's "spirit was transformed," apparently alluding to his spiritual transformation into an angel (while remaining in his body?). For a more detailed discussion of this, see Schäfer, *Origins of Jewish Mysticism*, pp. 333f.

14. 1 En. 71:14; see above, pp. 76f.

15. 2 En. 22:10.

16. For the (Palestinian) Targum Pseudo-Jonathan to Gen. 5:24 and Deut. 34:6, see below, pp. 115f.; p. 295, n. 54; for SifDev § 338, see below, pp. 111f.

17. Cf. Peter Schäfer and Klaus Herrmann, *Übersetzung der Hekhalot-Literatur*, vol. 1, §§ 1–80, Tübingen: Mohr Siebeck, 1995, pp. liiif.

18. Schäfer, *Synopse zur Hekhalot-Literatur*, §§ 11, 14.

19. Ibid., § 12.

20. Ibid., § 13.

21. Ibid., § 15.

22. Ibid., § 16.

23. Ibid., §§ 17f.

24. Ibid., § 19.

25. See the useful summary in Andrei A. Orlov, *The Enoch-Metatron-Tradition*, Tübingen: Mohr Siebeck, 2005, pp. 92–96.

26. This has been suggested by Saul Lieberman, "Metatron, the Meaning of His Name and His Functions," in Ithamar Gruenwald, *Apocalyptic and Merkavah Mysticism*, Leiden: Brill, 1980, pp. 235–241. I followed this etymology in my *Hidden and Manifest God: Some Major Themes in Early Jewish Mysticism*, New York: SUNY Press, 1992, p. 29, n. 70.

27. Philip Alexander, "3 (Hebrew Apocalypse of) Enoch," in Charlesworth, *OTP*, vol. 1, p. 243; id., "From Son of Adam to a Second God: Transformation of the Biblical Enoch," in Michael E. Stone and Theodore A. Bergen, eds., *Biblical Figures Outside the Bible*, Harrisburg, Pa.: Trinity Press International, 1998, p. 107, n. 31.

28. Alexander, "3 Enoch," p. 243.

29. SifDev § 338, ed. Finkelstein, p. 388. I do not judge as successful Orlov's attempt to detect in chapter 43 of the short recension of 2 Enoch an early reference to the title "governor" (*prometaya* in Slavonic) for Enoch, which connects the names Enoch and Metatron (Orlov, *The Enoch-Metatron-Tradition*, pp. 176–180).

30. Alexander, "From Son of Adam to a Second God," p. 107.

31. As Alexander has made crystal clear earlier, namely in "3 Enoch," p. 229, n. 17: "SifDev 338, ed. Finkelstein, p. 388, does not allude to Metatron the archangel." When he later ponders the possibility that Enoch could indeed be regarded as a *metator* since he showed the people of Israel "how they could escape from the wilderness of this world into the promised land of heaven," I am afraid he goes too far. See Alexander, "From Son of Adam to a Second God," p. 107; also id., "Jewish Believers in Early Rabbinic Literature (2nd to 5th Centuries)," in Oskar Skarsaune and Reidar Hvalvik, eds., *Jewish Believers in Jesus: The Early Centuries*, Peabody, Mass.: Hendrickson, 2007, p. 703.

32. Literally "at the voice."

33. Variant readings in the manuscripts and printed editions (see the *apparatus criticus* in Theodor-Albeck, ad loc.): *mitatron, metator, mitator, mistorin, mistirin, metron, metarton*. The reading *metatron/ mitatron* is attested in Mss. London Add. 27169 (Theodor-Albeck's base text) and Oxford Neubauer 147; the reading *metator/mitator* is suggested by a gloss in Ms. London and a commentary on BerR.

34. BerR 5:4; parallels MidrTeh 93:5 end (*metator*); PesR, ed. Friedmann, Hosafah 1 Pisqa 1, p. 192b (*metartar*, obviously corrupt for *metatar/metator*); the Vilna edition of BerR combines the Metatron of the waters with the Metatron for Moses in SifDev § 338.

35. As Scholem has repeatedly maintained; see his *Major Trends in Jewish Mysticism*, New York: Schocken, 1974 (reprint), p. 69; id., *Jewish Gnosticism, Merkabah Mysticism, and Talmudic Tradition*, New York: Jewish Theological Seminary, 2nd edition, 1965, p. 43. See also Alexander, "3 Enoch," p. 243.

36. Hag 15a (see below, pp. 127f.).

37. Joseph Dan, *The Ancient Jewish Mysticism*, Tel Aviv: MOD Books, 1993, pp. 109f.

38. Preserved only in an Old Slavonic translation, but originally composed in Palestine, sometime after 70 C.E.

39. See Schäfer, *Judeophobia*, p. 52 with n. 128 (p. 232).

40. Alexander, "3 Enoch," p. 244; Schäfer and Herrmann, *Übersetzung der Hekhalot-Literatur*, vol. 1, p. lii.

41. Idith and Idi are apparently variations of the same name.

42. Günter Stemberger, *Einleitung in Talmud und Midrasch*, Munich: Beck, 8th edition, 1992, p. 101.

43. As did the David–Son of Man tradition, also in b Sanh 38b.

44. ShemR 32:4; cf. also Yalq mishpatim § 359.

45. Michael Maher, trans., *Targum Pseudo-Jonathan: Genesis*, Edinburgh: T&T Clark, 1992, p. 36.

46. As has also been suggested by Alexander, "3 Enoch," p. 229, n. 16.

47. O. S. Wintermute, trans., "Jubilees," in Charlesworth, *OTP*, vol. 2, p. 63; see also Jub. 4:17.

48. See the chapter "Enoch as the Scribe," in Orlov, *Enoch-Metatron Tradition*, pp. 50ff.; ibid., pp. 97ff.

49. 1 En. 12:4; 15:1.

50. B 11:2–4 (E. P. Sanders, "Testament of Abraham," in Charlesworth, *OTP*, vol. 1, p. 900).

51. 1 En. 74:2; see also 1 En. 81:6; 82:1.

52. 2 En. 23; see also 2 En. 68:2; 40:13; 53:2; 64:5.

53. 4Q203 8:4 and 4Q530 2:14 (Florentino García Martínez and Eibert J. C. Tigchelaar, eds., *The Dead Sea Scrolls Study Edition*, Leiden: Brill, 1997 and 1998, vol. 1, pp. 410f., and vol. 2, pp. 1062f.).

54. In Targum Pseudo-Jonathan Deut. 34:6 Metatron appears, together with Yofi'el, Uri'el, and Yefefiah, as one of the angels who lay Moses to rest on his deathbed. Here, these angels are characterized as "wise sages" and may well reflect a late "rabbinization" of earlier apocalyptic traditions.

55. Hebrew text in Ithamar Gruenwald, "Re'uyot Yehezqel," *Temirin* 1, 1977, pp. 101–139 (pp. 128–131); English translation in Scholem, *Jewish Gnosticism*, p. 46; David Halperin, *The Faces of the Chariot: Early Jewish Responses to Ezekiel's Vision*, Tübingen: Mohr Siebeck, 1988, p. 267; German translation in Arnold Goldberg, "Pereq Re'uyot Yehezqe'el: Eine formanalytische Untersuchung," in id., *Mystik und Theologie des rabbinischen Judentums: Gesammelte Studien I*, ed. Margarete Schlüter and Peter Schäfer, Tübingen: Mohr Siebeck, 1997, pp. 127f.

56. The latter doesn't make much sense (as has been observed also by Goldberg, *Gesammelte Studien*, vol. 1, p. 127, n. 130).

57. Scholem, *Jewish Gnosticism*, pp. 5, 44f.; Gruenwald, "Re'uyot Yehezqel," p. 102.

58. Halperin, *Faces of the Chariot*, p. 413.

59. See the summary of his findings in his *Gesammelte Studien*, vol. 1, p. 147.

60. Gruenwald, "Re'uyot Yehezqel," pp. 101f.; id., *Apocalyptic and Merkavah Mysticism*, p. 134.

61. See the long treatment in Halperin, *Faces of the Chariot*, pp. 268ff., with the conclusion on p. 277.

62. Ibid., pp. 413f.

63. Seder Rabba di-Bereshit (Schäfer, *Synopse zur Hekhalot-Literatur*, § 772) and others; see in detail my "In Heaven as It Is in Hell," pp. 261ff.

64. Scholem, *Jewish Gnosticism*, p. 46.

65. For other striking similarities between Re'uyot Yehezqel and b Hagiga, see Schäfer, "In Heaven as It Is in Hell," pp. 265f.

66. See above, pp. 113f.

67. Schäfer, *Synopse zur Hekhalot-Literatur*, §§ 390, 399.

68. BamR 12:12.

69. See Stemberger, *Einleitung in Talmud und Midrasch*, pp. 305f.

70. Which is, predictably, what Scholem prefers (*Jewish Gnosticism*, p. 49, n. 20): "*Shiur Komah* [the section in the Hekhalot literature to which he assigns §§ 390 and 399] is, of course, very much older than the medieval *Bemidbar Rabbah*."

71. See above, pp. 109ff, and below, pp. 127ff.

72. See above, pp. 68ff.

73. See above, pp. 104ff.

74. See the list and discussion in Halperin, *Faces of the Chariot*, pp. 269ff.

75. b Yev 16b.

76. ShemR 17:4.

77. Gen. 1:11.

78. b Hul 60a.

79. b Sanh 94a.

80. In the (late) midrash Pirqe de-Rabbi Eli'ezer it is Michael (usually Israel's guardian angel) who obtains the epithet "Prince of the World," another indication of the fact that the functions of Michael and Metatron are interchangeable. See *Pirkê De Rabbi Eliezer*, translated and annotated with introduction and indices by Gerald Friedlander, London: Kegan Paul, Trench, Trubner & Co., and New York: Bloch, 1916, ch. XXVII, p. 193.

81. See above, pp. 70f.; pp. 104ff.

82. Schäfer, *Synopse zur Hekhalot-Literatur*, §§ 3–5; see also § 384 (Hekhalot Zutarti).

83. Ibid., §§ 47 and 56; and see Alexander, "3 Enoch," p. 243. In ibid., § 939, Metatron is called the "Great Prince of the Testimony."

84. b AZ 3b.

85. The tradition of Metatron teaching the small children who died a premature death is again also preserved in 3 Enoch (§ 75), and there with no implicit critique.

86. b Hag 15a.

87. t Hag 2:3f.

88. *Pardes* can also mean "paradise," which is sometimes located in the third or seventh heaven; Paul, too, reports that he was carried up to the "paradise" in the third heaven (1 Cor. 12:1–5).

89. For a more detailed discussion of this, see Schäfer, *Origins of Jewish Mysticism*, pp. 196ff.

90. Most manuscripts read: "What did he see?" See David Halperin, *The Merkabah in Rabbinic Literature*, New Haven, Conn.: American Oriental Society, 1980, p. 167 with n. 84.

91. Most manuscripts add: "one hour a day"; see ibid., with n. 85.

92. "No standing" in most manuscripts (ibid., p. 168, with n. 87), although it is clearly corrupt (the logical conclusion would be that, if there is no standing *and* no sitting, the angels can only fly); see also below, n. 96.

93. "No jealousy (*qin'ah*)" in most manuscripts; ibid., with n. 88.

94. This sentence is missing in many manuscripts and the first printed editions; instead, Ms. Vatican 171 reads "Why, when you saw him, didn't you approve him [as someone who is worthy to enter the *pardes*] before this hour." Septimus ("*Het'o shel Metatron*, pp. 292f.) argues convincingly that this is the earlier and original version. This interpretation that de-emphasizes Metatron's sitting goes well with Boyarin's observation (Boyarin, "Beyond Judaisms," p. 349) that the Bavli version—in remarkable contrast with the 3 Enoch version (see below)—obliterates Metatron's throne.

95. b Hag 15a.

96. That there is no standing in heaven does not make much sense, since the point is that the angels don't sit, not that they don't stand.

97. This aspect actually applies solely to the four creatures of Ezek. 1, not to all the angels in heaven.

98. Schäfer, *Synopse zur Hekhalot-Literatur*, § 15.

99. Ibid., § 20.

100. A variant of the tetragrammaton *YHWH*.

101. Schäfer, *Synopse zur Hekhalot-Literatur*, § 20; I follow (with variations) the translation by Alexander, "3 Enoch," p. 268. See also the parallel in Merkavah Rabbah, *Synopse zur Hekhalot-Literatur*, § 672.

102. Boyarin, while at first making a strong claim for the 3 Enoch version being the source of the Bavli version ("Beyond Judaisms," p. 349)—presumably because he still prefers an early dating of 3 Enoch—ultimately grants a common source (ibid., p. 351).

103. Hence pace Boyarin ("Beyond Judaisms," p. 349), I don't think "that the purpose of the author of 3 *Enoch* was to validate Meṭaṭron speculation while that of the Talmud was to delegitimate that very speculation." Both devaluate Meṭaṭron speculation, but in very different ways.

104. b Ber 7a.

105. See above, pp. 71f.

106. Pace Scholem, *Jewish Gnosticism*, p. 51.

107. Schäfer, *Synopse zur Hekhalot-Literatur*, § 151.

108. Ms. New York 8128 is famous for its later additions; see Klaus Herrmann and Claudia Rohrbacher-Sticker, "Magische Traditionen der New Yorker Hekhalot-Handschrift JTS 8128 im Kontext ihrer Gesamtredaktion," *FJB* 17, 1989, pp. 101–149.

109. Schäfer, *Synopse zur Hekhalot-Literatur*, §§ 130–138.

110. Ibid., § 501.

111. Ms. Jerusalem 5226 (ca. 1300), Ms. Oxford Opp. 495 (Neubauer 1568, beginning of the seventeenth century), and Ms. Oxford Michael 175 (Neubauer 2257, also beginning of the seventeenth century). For the date of these manuscripts, see Schäfer and Herrmann, *Übersetzung der Hekhalot-Literatur*, vol. 1, pp. xii, xiv, xv.

112. See Schäfer and Herrmann, *Übersetzung der Hekhalot-Literatur*, vol. 1, pp. xlff.

113. See the description of the manuscripts and of the macroform's structure in *ibid.*, pp. xxxiv.

114. Alexander, "3 Enoch," pp. 303f.; Scholem (*Jewish Gnosticism*, p. 52) refers to it.

115. *Middot* clearly refers here to God's mysteries.

116. Schäfer, *Synopse zur Hekhalot-Literatur*, § 597, only in Mss. Oxford 1531 and New York 8128; the translation follows Ms. Oxford.

117. See above, pp. 127ff.

118. The confused scribe of Ms. New York even tells us: "I couldn't find the parable."

119. In § 279 (only in Mss. Budapest 238 and Munich 22) and in §§ 309f. as part of the microform Pereq R. Nehunya b. Haqanah (only in Ms. Vatican 228).

120. In § 678 (in Mss. New York 8128, Oxford 1531, and Munich 40).

121. Variant readings "Zekuriel" and "Zeburiel."

122. Schäfer, *Synopse zur Hekhalot-Literatur*, §§ 241ff.

123. Ibid., §§ 25ff.

124. The impressive list in our passage after *YHWH* ("the God of Israel, God of heaven and God of earth, God of gods, God of the sea and God of the mainland") does not mean that Metatron *is* the God of Israel, etc., but that these epithets are attributes of *YHWH*. As soon as the name *YHWH* is mentioned, the attributes are invoked.

125. Also indicated by the use of the Persian loanword *parwanqa* in b Sanh 38b. Alexander calls the choice of this term "precise and surprising" ("Jewish Believers," p. 702); in my view, it is certainly precise but not at all surprising, given the Babylonian background of our story.

126. Hence, while I agree with Boyarin's claim that the "talmudic text cannot . . . be isolated or insulated from the Enoch tradition as represented in *3 Enoch*," I disagree with his conclusion that the Bavli tradition can be taken as evidence for the continuity of the so-called pseudepigraphic literature in rabbinic Judaism (ibid., pp. 352f., 358f.). Despite Boyarin's (and some other scholars') untiring efforts to connect 1, 2, and 3 Enoch, what the Bavli and 3 Enoch here present is very different from the much earlier pseudepigraphic literature.

127. Shaul Shaked kindly sent me a preliminary list of Metatron's occurrences on the bowls. On the still unpublished bowls we find the titles "the Great Prince of the firmament/heaven" (*śara rabba de-raqia'*) (Ms. 2053/252) and "Metatron the Prince of the Countenance" (*śar ha-panim*) (Moussaieff 1:12f.), the latter being the most common title for Metatron in the Hekhalot literature. Interestingly enough, there is also evidence for Metatron being coupled with Lilith, the female demon (Ms. 2053/61:17).

128. Also in two Geniza fragments: G4, fol. 1a/17, 1b/1; G8, fol. 1b/15 (Peter Schäfer, *Geniza-Fragmente zur Hekhalot-Literatur*, Tübingen: Mohr Siebeck, 1984, pp. 69, 101).

129. Gordon D = Cyrus H. Gordon, "Aramaic Bowls in the Istanbul and Baghdad Museums," *ArOr* 6, 1934, pp. 328f., l. 11; Charles D. Isbell, *Corpus of the Aramaic Incantation Bowls*, Missoula, Mont.: Scholars Press, 1975, pp. 112f. (Text 49, l. 11).

130. Gordon L = Cyrus H. Gordon, "Aramaic and Mandaic Magical Bowls," *ArOr* 9, 1937, p. 94 = Isbell, *Corpus*, pp. 127f. (Text 56, l. 12f.). Metatron is followed here by Raphael, who is called "the Prince of all healings" (*isra de-asuta*). On a bowl published by Mark Geller ("Two Incantation Bowls Inscribed in Syriac and Aramaic," *BSOAS* 39, 1976, p. 426), Metatron is listed together with six other "Princes, who are appointed over all [ ]" (unfortunately, the decisive word is missing). One of Shaked's unpublished bowls (Berlin VA 2416:4–7) mentions Metatron among the seven angels who "overturn heaven and earth, the stars, the planets, the moon, and the ocean."

131. b Yev 16b; see above, pp. 123ff.

132. Cyrus H. Gordon, "Two Magic Bowls in Teheran: The Aramaic Bowl," *Orientalia* 20, 1951, p. 307 = Isbell, *Corpus*, p. 129 (Text 57, l. 5).

133. James A. Montgomery, *Aramaic Incantation Texts from Nippur*, Philadelphia: The University Museum, 1913, p. 207, l. 4 (no. 25).

134. Ibid., p. 105.

135. Ibid., p. 207, l. 4.

136. See above, p. 134.

137. Rebecca Macy Lesses, *Ritual Practices to Gain Power: Angels, Incantations, and Revelation in Early Jewish Mysticism*, Harrisburg, Pa.: Trinity International, 1998, p. 358. This link, however, is not very convincing: Lesses refers to Schäfer, *Synopse zur Hekhalot-Literatur*, § 80 (the very end of the larger macroform 3 Enoch) where Metatron appears as the angel who reveals the "mystery" (*raz*) to the chain of transmission starting with Moses and climaxing in R. Zera. The one who knows this "mystery" has the power of "healing," but this does not mean that this power derives from Metatron. Moreover, the Bible

verse quoted as proof text (Ex. 15:26) is very common in those magical incantations which show no particular link with Metatron; see now Dorothea M. Salzer, *Die Magie der Anspielung: Form und Funktion der biblischen Anspielungen in den magischen Texten der Kairoer Geniza*, Tübingen: Mohr Siebeck, 2010, pp. 155f., 212f.

138. Lesses, *Ritual Practices*, p. 358; Martin S. Cohen, *The Shi'ur Qomah: Liturgy and Theurgy in Pre-Kabbalistic Jewish Mysticism*, Lanham, Md.: University Press of America, 1963, p. 159; Philip Alexander, "The Historical Setting of the Book of Enoch," *JJS* 28, 1977, p. 167.

139. Lesses, *Ritual Practices*, p. 359.

140. In the light of these findings it is worthwhile to check the court ritual background employed in the Hekhalot literature. Philip Alexander ("The Family of Caesar and the Family of God: The Image of the Emperor in Early Jewish Mystical Literature," in Loveday Alexander, ed., *Images of Empire: The Roman Empire in Jewish, Christian and Greco-Roman Sources*, Sheffield: Sheffield Academic Press, 1991, pp. 294f.) suggests that the Hekhalot literature is influenced by both the Roman and Sassanian court ritual and that no clear-cut distinction can be made. But it may well be that a text such as 3 Enoch (with its Persian loanwords) betrays more of a Persian than a Roman background.

141. See Schäfer, *Jesus in the Talmud*, pp. 115ff.

142. There is, however, one Palestinian source (BerR 25:1) in which it is said of Enoch (not Metatron) that he was not inscribed in the roll of the righteous, that he was a hypocrite, and that he was condemned on New Year's Day. In a subsequent discussion, R. Abbahu (a Palestinian amora of the third generation, d. around 300 C.E.) and R. Yose (b. Hanina, the teacher of Abbahu) fend off the heretic's assumption that Enoch did not die. Apparently, this midrash reflects rabbinic polemics against the pseudepigraphic Enoch literature as preserved in 1 and 2 Enoch; Enoch's identification with Metatron does not seem to be presupposed here. Yet, not surprisingly, the editor of one 3 Enoch manuscript (Ms. Oxford 1572) incorporates this midrash into 3 Enoch (Schäfer, *Synopse zur Hekhalot-Literatur*, § 8), clearly presupposing that Enoch is indeed Metatron.

143. See the overview in Andrew Chester, *Messiah and Exaltation: Jewish Messianic and Visionary Traditions and New Testament Christology*, Tübingen: Mohr Siebeck, 2007, pp. 45ff., and my discussions in the respective chapters.

144. Chester, *Messiah and Exaltation*, p. 68.

145. Markschies, *Alta Trinità Beata*, p. 309.

146. I am here taking up ideas that I first developed in my book *The Origins of Jewish Mysticism*, pp. 315ff.

147. The Aramaic of the Babylonian Talmud is closely related to Syriac.

148. Herford, *Christianity*, pp. 264f.

149. Heb. 1:1–4.

150. On the late biblical and postbiblical Wisdom tradition, see the chapter "Lady Wisdom" in my *Mirror of His Beauty*, pp. 19ff., and above, pp. 51f.

151. According to 1 En. 42:2, Wisdom returned to her place in heaven among the angels because she did not find a dwelling on earth.

152. *Apaugasma* is "radiance," "efflux," and also "reflection" (as translated in the NRSV translation of Hebrews).

153. Referring to Ps. 2:7; 2 Sam. 7:14.

154. Referring to Deut. 32:43 (only in the Septuagint, not in the Masoretic text).

155. Referring to Ps. 45:6 (the throne there is God's throne!).

156. Referring to Ps. 102:26.

157. Referring to Ps. 110:1.

158. Schäfer, *Synopse zur Hekhalot-Literatur*, § 16.

159. Gedalyahu G. Stroumsa, "Form(s) of God: Some Notes on Metatron and Christ," *HTR* 76, 1983, pp. 282ff.; and see id., "Le couple de l'Ange et de l'Esprit: traditions juives et chrétiennes," *RB* 88, 1981, pp. 42–61; id., "Polymorphie divine et transformations d'un mythologeme: L''Apocryphon de Jean' et ses source," *VigChr* 35, 1981, pp. 412–434.

160. Phil. 2:6–11.

161. Schäfer, *Synopse zur Hekhalot-Literatur*, § 14.

162. Ibid., § 16.

163. See above, pp. 104ff. (b Sanh 38b) and pp. 127ff. (b Hag 15a: Metatron writes down Israel's merits, that is, records Israel's good deeds and sins).

164. Schäfer, *Synopse zur Hekhalot-Literatur*, § 70.

165. The macroform §§ 1–70; on the macroforms of 3 Enoch, see Schäfer and Herrmann, *Übersetzung der Hekhalot-Literatur*, vol. 1, pp. xxiiff.

166. Identical with the macroform Alfa Beta de-Rabbi Aqiva; on this, see Schäfer and Herrmann, *Übersetzung der Hekhalot-Literatur*, vol. 1, pp. xxiiff., 155, n. 1.

167. Schäfer, *Synopse zur Hekhalot-Literatur*, § 70.

168. Ibid., §§ 74 and 76.

169. Ibid., § 74; translation according to Alexander, "3 Enoch," p. 312.

170. Hence coming closest to some kind of Arianism according to the Christian nomenclature.

CHAPTER 5: HAS GOD A FATHER, A SON, OR A BROTHER?

1. y Shab 6:10/14, fol. 8d.

2. Stemberger, *Einleitung in Talmud und Midrasch*, p. 94.

3. MekhY, ed. Lauterbach, vol. 2, pp. 18, 46, 61; BerR 9:5; ShemR 8:2; WaR 18:2; b Hag 13a; b Hul 89a.

4. Johann Maier, *Jesus von Nazareth in der talmudischen Über-lieferung*, Darmstadt: Wissenschaftliche Buchgesellschaft, 1978, p. 81; Schremer, *Brothers Estranged*, pp. 104ff.

5. For Schremer, *Brothers Estranged*, pp. 106f., such a Christian interpretation of our source is a prime example of a "Christianizing scholarly reading."

6. ShemR 29:5.

7. See above, pp. 56ff.

8. Johann Maier, *Jüdische Auseinandersetzung mit dem Christentum in der Antike*, Darmstadt: Wissenschaftliche Buchgesellschaft, 1982, p. 197.

9. Or: "the Lord is one."

10. Or: "the Lord is one."

11. DevR 2:33; see also QohR 4,1:8.

12. Segal, *Two Powers in Heaven*, p. 140.

13. Maier, *Jüdische Auseinandersetzung*, pp. 197f. He refers to the late midrashic compilation Aggadat Bereshit.

14. See above, pp. 55ff.

15. Interestingly enough in Aramaic, which indicates a different layer in the midrash's literary structure.

16. Verb in the plural.

17. Verb in the singular.

18. PesR 21, ed. Friedmann, fol. 110b–101a; English translation William G. Braude, *Pesikta Rabbati: Discourses for Feasts, Fasts, and Special Sabbaths*, vol. 1, New Haven, Conn., and London: Yale University Press, 1968, pp. 421f.

19. See the summary in Maier, *Jesus von Nazareth*, pp. 245f.

20. See Schäfer, *Jesus in the Talmud*, pp. 5ff.

21. Maier, *Jesus von Nazareth*, p. 246.

22. Schäfer, *Jesus in the Talmud*, p. 110.

23. Ibid., pp. 15ff.

24. This is also Braude's translation, "a whoreson" (*Pesikta Rabbati*, p. 422), which he explains (ibid., n. 24) as "'son of heresy,' i.e., a heathen or a renegade Israelite."

25. Pace Maier, *Jesus von Nazareth*, p. 245.

26. Ibid., p. 246.

CHAPTER 6: THE ANGELS

1. Peter Schäfer, *Rivalität zwischen Engeln und Menschen: Untersuchungen zur rabbinischen Engelvorstellung*, Berlin–New York: de Gruyter, 1975, pp. 43ff.; 52ff.; 85ff.

2. See Gen. 16:13; 21:17, 19.

3. See also v. 22.

4. See above, p. 107.

5. BerR 1:3; 3:8. For the numerous parallels, see Schäfer, *Rivalität*, p. 53, n. 82.

6. Play on words with *meqareh* in Ps. 104:3 and *raqia'* in Gen. 1:7.

7. Second century B.C.E.

8. Jub. 2:2f.

9. See below, p. 185 (revelation on Mount Sinai).

10. Also, Targum Pseudo-Jonathan states clearly that the angels were created on the second day; see TPsJ Gen. 1:26.

11. Schäfer, *Rivalität*, pp. 53f.

12. See above, pp. 28ff.

13. BerR 8:3.

14. Literally: "met together," interpreted here as "met together in combat."

15. Literally: "kissed each other," derived here from *nesheq*— "arms" (that is, "took arms against each other").

16. Literally: "earth."

17. Using here the Greek loanword *alētheia*.

18. BerR 8:4f. For the parallels and a more thorough analysis, see Schäfer, *Rivalität*, pp. 91f.

19. As Burt Visotzky reminds me in a private communication, the concluding sentence "Man has already been made (*ne'eśah*)" is a pun on *na'aśeh*.

20. See Schäfer, *Rivalität*, pp. 220ff.

21. This is Theodor-Albeck's interpretation of the Greek *bōlarion* (BerR 8:8, p. 62, n. 1 to l. 2); Friedman translates "clod."

22. The same word as in Gen. 1:26.

23. BerR 8:8.

24. And mentioned also in the Palestinian Targum; see TPsJ on Gen. 1:26.

25. Translated according to the interpretation of the midrash.

26. PesR 14:9, ed. Friedmann, pp, 59bf. For the parallels, see Schäfer, *Rivalität*, pp. 85ff.

27. PesR 14:9, ed. Friedmann, pp, 59bf.

28. b Sanh 38b; for the parallels, see Schäfer, *Rivalität*, pp. 95ff.

29. Segal, *Two Powers in Heaven*, p. 113, n. 11.

30. As has been correctly observed by Jarl E. Fossum, *The Name of God and the Angel of the Lord: Samaritan and Jewish Concepts of*

Intermediation and the Origin of Gnosticism, Tübingen: Mohr Siebeck, 1985, p. 205.

31. See the summary in Schäfer, *Rivalität*, pp. 228ff.

32. Fossum, *Name of God*, pp. 198ff.

33. Philo, De somniis, 140ff.

34. De fuga et inventione, 66; De agricultura, 128f.

35. De fuga et inventione, 68ff.

36. De opificio mundi, 75.

37. De confusione linguarum, 179ff.

38. Ibid., 175.

39. Fossum, *Name of God*, p. 200.

40. See Schäfer, *Mirror of His Beauty*, pp. 40ff.; id., *Origins of Jewish Mysticism*, pp. 155ff.

41. Fossum, *Name of God*, p. 200.

42. Heres, 205.

43. De agricultura, 51; De confusione linguarum, 146.

44. De confusione linguarum, 146.

45. De fuga et inventione, 101.

46. See above, pp. 104ff.

47. De confusione linguarum, 171f.

48. Ibid., 174.

49. Ibid., 173.

50. See below, pp. 188ff.

51. Even death; see BerR 9:5, where according to the "Torah of R. Meir" the phrase concluding the creation of the sixth day "and indeed it was very good (*tov meod*)" actually means "death is good (*tov mawet*)."

52. See TO, TPsJ, and CN on Deut. 33:2.

53. See PesK, ed. Mandelbaum, p. 219f.; PesR, ed. Friedmann, pp. 102bff.; SifBam, § 102, ed. Horovitz, p. 100, and parallels; Schäfer, *Rivalität*, p. 43.

54. Splitting up *tzeva'ot* in *tzava* and *ot*.

55. Interpreting *ata* as *ot*.

56. MekhY Shirata 1, ed. Lauterbach, vol. 2, pp. 10f. For the parallels, see Schäfer, *Rivalität*, p. 46.

57. PesR, ed. Friedmann, p. 103b; PesK, ed. Mandelbaum, p. 200; parallels Schäfer, *Rivalität*, p. 47.

58. DevR, ed. Lieberman, p. 68.

59. ShemR 29:2.

60. PesK, ed. Mandelbaum, p. 266f.

61. ShirR 1:13 (Cant. 1:2 § 2); Schäfer, *Rivalität*, pp. 44f.

62. See, for more detail, Schäfer, *Rivalität*, pp. 48ff.

63. MekhY Shabbata 1, ed. Lauterbach, p. 197; MekhS, ed. Hoffmann, p. 221.

64. ARN, version B, chapter 1, ed. Schechter, p. 2.

65. Avot 1:1.

66. MekhY Pisha, ed. Lauterbach, p. 97; ibid., p. 53; see also SifDev § 325, ed. Finkelstein, p. 376.

67. MidrTann, p. 173; Pesach Haggadah, ed. Goldschmidt, p. 122.

68. SifDev § 42, ed. Finkelstein, p. 88.

69. Jub. 1:27 (God asks the angel to "write for Moses" the course of history); ibid. 2:1 (the angel gives Moses an account of the history and asks him to write it down).

70. See Schäfer, *Rivalität*, pp. 13ff.

71. Ant. 15, 136.

72. See Marcus in his note ad loc. and the literature mentioned there; Schäfer, *Rivalität*, p. 45, n. 38.

73. Acts 6:11.

74. Acts 7:38.

75. Acts 7:51–53.

76. Gal. 3:19.

77. Heb. 1:14.

78. Heb. 2:1–3.

79. Hence, it seems to me more likely that the Babylonian rabbis knew Christian literature/the New Testament rather than the apocrypha and pseudepigrapha. Boyarin's categorical statement "It is simply, then, not the case that the so-called pseudepigraphic literature had no legs in later Judaism and was only preserved within Christian circles" ("Beyond Judaisms," p. 353) is overstated and certainly not warranted by the example on which he bases himself.

80. Martha Himmelfarb, *Ascent to Heaven in Jewish and Christian Apocalypses*, New York: Oxford University Press, 1993, p. 51 (on the basis of the single heaven scheme); O. S. Wintermute, trans., "Apocalypse of Zephaniah," in Charlesworth, *OTP*, vol. 1, p. 500 (on the basis of a quotation by Clement of Alexandria).

81. Apoc. Zeph. 6:11.

82. Apoc. Zeph. 6:15.

83. Chapters 6–11 of the Ascension of Isaiah are of Christian origin and dated to the early second century C.E. (see J.M.T. Barton in his introduction in H.F.D. Sparks, *The Apocryphal Old Testament*, Oxford: Clarendon Press, 1984, pp. 780f.) but may well depend on a Jewish source; see Martha Himmelfarb, *Tours of Hell: An Apocalyptic Form in Jewish and Christian Literature*, Philadelphia: Fortress Press, 1985, pp. 136f., 156, n. 56; ead., *Ascent to Heaven*, pp. 55, 135, n. 30.

84. Asc. Isa. 7:21f. (Sparks, *Apocryphal Old Testament*, pp. 798).

85. John W. Marshall seeks to read the apocalypse as a thoroughly *Jewish* text; see his *Parables of War: Reading John's Jewish Apocalypse*, Waterloo, Ont.: Wilfrid Laurier University Press, 2001.

86. Rev. 19:10; see also 22:8f.

87. MekhY bahodesh 6, ed. Lauterbach, vol. 2, pp. 242f.; see also ibid., bahodesh 10, ed. Lauterbach, vol. 2, p. 276; TPsJ Ex. 20:20.

88. See the overview in my "In Heaven as It Is in Hell," pp. 261ff. Although most of the pertinent rabbinic texts begin the series of seven heavens with *shamayim*—the sole exception is the Babylonian tradition, which begins instead with *welon*—the few texts that explicitly mention an inventory of the seven heavens locate the heavenly bodies in the second heaven *raqia'*. But this poses no problem since the Bible identifies *raqia'* with *shamayim* (Gen. 1:8) and has the heavenly luminaries attached to the *raqia' shamayim* (Gen. 1:14ff.).

89. The inventories of the Bavli and of Seder Rabba di-Bereshit locate Michael in the fourth heaven, the ministering angels in the fifth heaven, and the Ofannim, Serafs, Cherubs, and Holy Creatures in the seventh heaven; see Schäfer, "In Heaven as It Is in Hell," p. 264.

90. 1 Kings 6:23ff.

91. 1 Kings 6:29ff.

92. In the Qumran literature, not only are the angels omnipresent, but also the architecture of the Temple with its engravings of trees and flowers and angels becomes animated; see Ra'anan Boustan, "Angels in the Architecture: Temple Art and the Poetics of Praise in the *Songs of the Sabbath Sacrifice*," in id. and Annette Yoshiko Reed, eds., *Heavenly Realms and Earthly Realities in Late Antique Religions*, Cambridge: Cambridge University Press, 2004, pp. 195–212.

93. Literally, "in the name of. . . ."

94. m Hul 2:8.

95. t Hul 2:18; see also b AZ 42b.

96. b Hul 40a.

97. Cf. Ps. 106:28 (sacrifices to the Ba'al Pe'or are sacrifices offered to the dead).

98. Schäfer, *Rivalität*, p. 69.

99. I herewith correct what I say in *Rivalität*, p. 69 (bottom).

100. Schäfer, *Rivalität*, pp. 68ff.

101. Larry W. Hurtado, *One God, One Lord: Early Christian Devotion and Ancient Jewish Monotheism*, London: SCM Press, 1988, pp. 30ff.

102. See above, pp. 187f.

103. Gal. 4:8–11; Col. 2:16–20.

104. Quoted in Clement of Alexandria, Stromata 6:5,39–41; cf. Edgar Hennecke and Wilhelm Schneemelcher, eds., *Neutestamentliche Apokryphen in deutscher Übersetzung*, vol. 2, *Apostolisches, Apokalypsen und Verwandtes*, Tübingen: Mohr Siebeck, 1964, p. 62.

105. Origen, Contra Celsum 5:6; see also 1:26.

106. Hurtado, *One God, One Lord*, p. 33.

107. Ibid., p. 44.

108. See Schäfer, *Rivalität*, pp. 28ff; 62ff.

109. y Ber 9:1/25, fol. 13a.

110. Whereas the previous ones are attributed to R. Yudan in the name of R. Yitzhaq (bar Nappaha, third-generation Palestinian Amora), this midrash is in Yudan's own name. The patron midrashim follow the midrashim attributed to R. Simlai; see above, pp. 27ff., and Visotzky, "Goys 'Я'n't Us," pp. 309ff.

111. See above, pp. 162ff.
112. See above, pp. 192ff.
113. b Sanh 38b; see above, pp. 104ff.
114. ShemR 32:4; see above, p. 115, and Schäfer, *Rivalität*, pp. 70ff.

CHAPTER 7: ADAM

1. See above, pp. 29ff.
2. The NRSV translation, in line with its translation of *adam* as "humankind," "solves" the problem by correcting the Hebrew text and translating "in the image of God he created them" (instead of "created him"). It does the same with Gen. 5:1, although I must admit that there the problem of the translation of *adam* is more complex, since Gen. 5:2 continues: "Male and female he created them and blessed them and called their name *adam* when they were created." Phyllis Trible has taken this as further evidence that *adam* in Gen. 1:26f. is indeed "humankind"; see her *God and the Rhetoric of Sexuality*, Philadelphia: Fortress, 1978, 3rd edition, 1983, pp. 18f. I owe this reference to Burt Visotzky.
3. Literally "built."
4. Gen. 2:20–23.
5. m Sanh 4:5.
6. Ibid. I am omitting the fourth reason, as it is irrelevant to our subject.
7. This is also Segal's conclusion (*Two Powers in Heaven*, p. 110). Segal's treatment of this mishna and related passages suffers, however, from his overzealous attempt to ferret out the heretics and pinpoint the exact date of the "two powers" heresy.
8. The parallel in b Sanh 38a has "Sadducees" instead of "heretics," an obvious anachronism, presumably due to the intervention of a censor.
9. t Sanh 8:7; b Sanh 38a (a Baraitha).
10. Gen. 2:2f.
11. See above, pp. 162ff.

12. Unless we want to argue, following Gen. 3:5, for a post-sin Adam: having eaten from the tree of knowledge, Adam becomes like God (Burt Visotzky, private communication).

13. This midrash is transmitted in many versions and parallels; the translation is according to b Sanh 38b. Cf. b Hag 12a; BerR 8:1; 12:6; 14:8; 19:8; 24:2; WaR 18:2 and more often.

14. Rav is the Babylonian amora of the first generation (first half of the third century C.E.), and Rav Yehudah is his student.

15. It is unclear which R. Eleazar the text is referring to.

16. Bereshit Rabba has the same tension: according to BerR 14:8, Adam's "golem" reached from earth to heaven; whereas according to BerR 8:1, his "golem" covered the whole world; and BerR 24:8 combines both traditions.

17. For possible influences of an ancient *Urmensch* myth see Nico Oswald, "'Urmensch' und 'Erster Mensch': Zur Interpretation einiger merkwürdiger Adam-Überlieferungen in der rabbinischen Literatur," unpublished dissertation, Berlin: Kirchliche Hochschule, 1970.

18. BerR 8:10.

19. See above, pp. 171f.

20. PesK, ed. Mandelbaum, vol. 1, pp. 60f.

21. See M. D. Johnson, "Life of Adam and Eve," in Charlesworth, *OTP*, vol. 2, p. 252.

22. Vita Adae et Evae 13f.

23. Alexander Altmann, "The Gnostic Background of the Rabbinic Adam Legends," *JQR* N.S. 35, 1944/45, pp. 380f.

24. For a brief evaluation, see Timothy D. Barnes, *Constantine and Eusebius*, Cambridge, Mass: Harvard University Press, 1982, p. 17; David S. Potter, *The Roman Empire at Bay: AD 180–395*, New York: Routledge, 2005, pp. 292f.

25. Above, pp. 33ff.

26. Altmann, "The Gnostic Background," p. 389.

27. In fact, Altmann quotes Jonas' *Gnosis u. Spätantiker Geist* as his main source for this statement.

28. De Opificio Mundi, 16ff. On Philo's philosophical-theological system, see Schäfer, *Mirror of His Beauty*, pp. 41ff.

29. De Opificio Mundi, 134; cf. Legum Allegoriarum, I, 31ff.

30. De Opificio Mundi, 20: "even so the universe that consisted of ideas would have no other location than the divine word (*ton theion logon*), which was the author of this ordered frame."

31. Ibid., 24.

32. De Confusione Linguarum, 146.

33. Ibid., 147.

34. 1 Cor. 15:45–48.

35. Col. 1:15–18.

36. Heb. 1:4.

37. Heb. 1:6.

38. But preserved in the Qumran manuscript 4QDeutq (see Eugene Ulrich et al., eds., *Qumran Cave 4*, vol. 9, *Deuteronomy, Joshua, Judges, Kings*, Oxford: Clarendon Press, 1995, p. 141). The Septuagint equates the "sons of God" (*hyioi theou*) with the "angels" (*anggeloi*), whereas 4QDeutq has just "*Elohim*" (following the well-attested tradition that equates the biblical *Elohim* with the angels).

39. See above, pp. 51ff., 144f.

CHAPTER 8: THE BIRTH OF THE MESSIAH, OR WHY DID BABY MESSIAH DISAPPEAR?

1. "R. Yudan, the son of R. Aibo," in the Yerushalmi is clearly a mistake that should be rendered, "R. Yudan, in the name of R. Aibo."

2. y Ber 2:4/12–14; parallel in EkhaR 1:16 § 51 (ed. Buber, pp. 89f.).

3. Literally: "he entered and exited one city after the other."

4. Literally: "after some days."

5. "Lebanon" serves as the symbolic name for "Temple."

6. This is a literal translation of the biblical verse as required by R. Bun's interpretation.

7. That is, immediately after the Temple has been destroyed, the shoot will come forth from the stump of Jesse. The shoot from the stump of Jesse is David (the Messiah), the son of Jesse.

8. For the most important literature, see Israel Lévi, "Le ravisse-ment du Messie à sa naissance," *REJ* 74, 1922, pp. 113–126; reprint in Israel Lévi, *Le ravissement du Messie à sa naissance et autre essais*, ed. Evelyne Patlagean, Paris-Louvain: Peeters, 1994, pp. 228–241; Anna Maria Schwemer, "Elija als Araber: Die haggadischen Motive in der Legende vom Messias Menahem ben Hiskija (j Ber 2,4 5a; EkhaR 1,16 § 51) im Vergleich mit den Elija- und Elischa-Legenden der Vitae Prophetarum," in Reinhard Feldmeier and Ulrich Heckel, eds., *Die Heiden: Juden, Christen und das Problem des Fremden*, Tübingen: Mohr Siebeck, 1994, pp. 108–157; Galit Hasan-Rokem, *Web of Life: Folklore and Midrash in Rabbinic Literature*, Stanford, Calif.: Stanford University Press, 2000, pp. 152ff.; Martha Himmelfarb, "The Mother of the Messiah in the Talmud Yerushalmi and Sefer Zerubba-bel," in Peter Schäfer, ed., *The Talmud Yerushalmi and Graeco-Roman Culture*, vol. 3, Tübingen: Mohr Siebeck, 2002, pp. 369–389; Hillel Newman, "*Leidat ha-Mashiah be-yom ha-horban—He'arot historijot we-anti-historijot*," in Menachem Mor et al., eds., *For Uriel: Studies in the History of Israel in Antiquity Presented to Professor Uriel Rappaport*, Jerusalem: Merkaz Zalman Shazar, 2006, pp. 85–110 (a thorough and learned evaluation of the relevant research; strangely enough, although Newman's findings are very similar to Himmelfarb's, her article evi-dently escaped his attention).

9. On this, see Hasan-Rokem, *Web of Life*, p. 239, n. 33.

10. b Sanh 98b.

11. b Sanh 98a.

12. For the euphemistic reading of this phrase (referring not to the Romans but to Israel), see below, pp. 227f.

13. Bereshit Rabbati, ed. Albeck, p. 131.

14. On Ishmael/the Arabs in rabbinic literature, see recently Carol Bakhos, *Ishmael on the Border: Rabbinic Portrayals of the First Arab*, Albany: State University of New York Press, 2006.

15. ARN, version A, ch. 28, ed. Schechter, fol. 43a; Hans-Jürgen Becker, ed. (in cooperation with Christoph Berner), *Avot de-Rabbi Natan. Synoptische Edition beider Versionen*, Tübingen: Mohr Siebeck, 2006, p. 214; b Qid 49b: "Ten qab of harlotry (*zenut*) descended to the world: nine were taken by Arabia and one by the rest of the world." But

cf. Esther Rabba 1:16 (17): "There are ten portions of harlotry (*zenut*) in the world, nine in Alexandria and one for (the rest of) the world."

16. EsthR 1:16 (17).

17. MekhY bahodesh 5, on Ex. 20:2, ed. Lauterbach, pp. 234ff.

18. Hasan-Rokem, *Web of Life*, p. 159; ead., "Narratives in Dialogue: A Folk Literary Perspective on Interreligious Contacts in the Holy Land in Rabbinic Literature of Late Antiquity," in Arieh Kofsky and Guy G. Stroumsa, eds., *Sharing the Sacred: Religious Contacts and Conflicts in the Holy Land—First–Fifteenth Centuries C.E.*, Jerusalem: Yad Izhak Ben Zvi, 1998, pp. 122ff.

19. b BB 73b.

20. Cicero, De Divinatione 1:92, 94.

21. Pliny, Historia Naturalis 25:13.

22. Appian, fr. 19 (Menahem Stern, *Greek and Latin Authors on Jews and Judaism*, vol. 2, Jerusalem: Israel Academy of Sciences, 1980, pp. 185f., no. 348).

23. Philostratus, Vita Apollonii 1:20.

24. As has been suggested by Hasan-Rokem, *Web of Life*, p. 159.

25. Schwemer, "Elija als Araber," p. 120.

26. 1 Kings 19:19ff.

27. For the mooing cow she refers to the Golden Calf of Gilgal, which, according to the Vitae Prophetarum, let out a shriek when Elisha was born because he was destined to destroy the idols (Schwemer, "Elija als Araber," p. 121).

28. Schwemer, "Elija als Araber," pp. 138ff.

29. 2 Kings 2:11.

30. TJ 2 Kings 2:11.

31. Mt. 1:1.

32. Mt. 1:16.

33. Mt. 1:18.

34. 2 Kings 24:3f.

35. b Sanh 98b: "Others say: His [the Messiah's] name is Menahem son of Hezekiah, as it is written: 'Because Menahem ('the comforter'), who would revive my soul, is far from me' (Lam. 1:16)." The only other text in which a Messiah by the name of Menahem is men-

tioned is the Sefer Zerubbabel, but there he is called Menahem b. Ammiel, not Menahem b. Hezekiah; see below, p. 227, and cf. Himmelfarb, "The Mother of the Messiah," pp. 383ff.

36. b Sanh 99a; see also b Sanh 98b.

37. Bell. II, 442–448.

38. Schwemer, "Elija als Araber," pp. 118, 132; Martin Hengel, *Die Zeloten: Untersuchungen zur jüdischen Freiheitsbewegung in der Zeit von Herodes I. bis 70 n. Chr.*, Leiden: Brill, 2nd edition, 1976, pp. 301f., 369ff.

39. And the same sequence is maintained in R. Bun's biblical exposition: first the Lebanon = Temple will fall, then a shoot will come forth from the stump of Jesse.

40. English translation Martha Himmelfarb, "Sefer Zerubbabel," in David Stern and Mark Jay Mirsky, eds., *Rabbinic Fantasies: Imaginative Narratives from Classical Hebrew Literature*, Philadelphia: Jewish Publication Society, 1990, pp. 67–90, and John C. Reeves, "The Prophetic Vision of Zerubbabel ben Shealtiel," in id., *Trajectories in Near Eastern Apocalyptic: A Postrabbinic Apocalypse Reader*, Atlanta: Society of Biblical Literature, 2005, pp. 51–66.

41. 2 Kings 21:1.

42. Himmelfarb's apt description ("The Mother of the Messiah," p. 384).

43. One could even translate the phrase in such a way: "I would rather like to strangle Israel"; see also Hasan-Rokem, *Web of Life*, p. 154.

44. So also the manuscripts of Paris and London and the printed edition of Amsterdam; only Ms. Vatican has *mehnoq*, without the suffix, that is, "I would rather (like) to strangle the enemies of Israel."

45. Sokoloff, *Dictionary of Jewish Palestinian Aramaic*, p. 571, s.v. *śana*, interprets our text as plural ("the enemies of Israel"), as is clearly the case in y Hag 2:2/5, fol. 77d. The matter, however, is complicated by the fact that *s/śaneihon* could as well be singular ("the enemy of Israel"), which would fit in perfectly well with "him [my son] as the enemy of Israel"; this is how Jacob Levy (*Wörterbuch über die Talmudim und Midraschim*, Berlin and Vienna, 1924; reprint Darmstadt:

Wissenschaftliche Buchgesellschaft, 1963, vol. 2, p. 85, s.v. *ḥanaq*) understands our text.

46. See Hasan-Rokem, *Web of Life*, p. 239, n. 41; Himmelfarb, "The Mother of the Messiah," p. 378.

47. By Israel Lévi, "Le ravissement du Messie," pp. 113ff.; reprinted in Israel Lévi, *Le Ravissement du Messie*, pp. 228ff.

48. Newman, *Leidat ha-Mashiah*, pp. 105ff.

49. The same verb is used in 2 Cor. 12:1–4, where Paul boasts of being "carried off" (*hērpagē*) into "paradise," the third heaven.

50. Or from King Herod, in his dual capacity as the enemy "from within" and "from without."

51. Hasan-Rokem, *Web of Life*, pp. 154ff.

52. Mt. 2.

53. Lk. 2.

54. Which is quoted explicitly in Mt. 2:6.

55. Lk. 2:8ff.

56. Mt. 2:2.

57. Mt. 2:1ff.

58. Mt. 2:11.

59. Lk. 2:7.

60. Mt. 2:3ff.

61. Hasan-Rokem, *Web of Life*, p. 154.

62. On the problematic scholarly category of "folklore," see now Dina Stein, "Let the 'People' Go? The 'Folk' and Their 'Lore' as Tropes in the Reconstruction of Rabbinic Culture," *Prooftexts* 29, 2009, pp. 206–241. I owe this reference to Moulie Vidas.

63. Himmelfarb, "The Mother of the Messiah," pp. 379ff. She explicitly argues against reading the story as a parody of the infancy narratives in the New Testament (ibid., p. 379).

64. Ibid., p. 380.

65. Ibid.

66. The rabbis made no secret of their aversion to Bar Kokhba's messianic aspirations—*post factum*, that is, after his uprising failed: they don't call him "Bar Koseba" (as he is called in the letters and docu-

ments from the Judean desert) and certainly not "Bar Kokhba" (that is, "son of a star," as the Christian sources address him), but "Bar Koziba" ("son of a liar"); cf. Peter Schäfer, *Der Bar Kokhba-Aufstand: Studien zum zweiten jüdischen Krieg gegen Rom*, Tübingen: Mohr Siebeck, 1981, pp. 51f.

67. To which I will return in the next chapter.

CHAPTER 9: THE SUFFERING MESSIAH EPHRAIM

1. Ephraim was Joseph's younger son, who was blessed by Jacob along with his brother Manasseh. Countervailing Manasseh's right of primogeniture, Jacob laid the (favored) right hand on the younger brother Ephraim and his left hand on the older Manasseh (Gen. 48:14).

2. On this, see Charles C. Torrey, "The Messiah Son of Ephraim," *JBL* 66, 1947, pp. 253–277; Joseph Heinemann, *Aggadah and Its Development*, Jerusalem: Keter, 1974, pp. 131–141 (Hebrew); id., "The Messiah of Ephraim and the Premature Exodus of the Tribe of Ephraim," *HTR* 8, 1975, pp. 1–15; David C. Mitchell, "Messiah ben Joseph: A Sacrifice of Atonement for Israel," *RRJ* 10, 2007, pp. 77–94.

3. TPsJ Ex. 40:11. Interestingly enough, the Messiah ben Ephraim does not die here in the final battle against Gog but defeats him. Cf. also Targum Cant. 4:5 and 7:4, where the Messiah ben David and the Messiah ben Ephraim are compared with Moses and Aaron; no final battle is mentioned. On the other hand, in Targum Tosefta Zech. 12:10 the Messiah bar Ephraim is killed in the final battle against Gog before Jerusalem's gates (Rimon Kasher, *Targumic Tosefot to the Prophets*, Jerusalem: World Union of Jewish Studies, 1996, pp. 223f. [Hebrew]).

4. b Suk 52a.

5. Without mentioning their names, BerR 75:6 contrasts a "Warrior Messiah" with a "King Messiah." According to Tan wayyigash 3 (ed. Buber, fol. 103a), the Warrior Messiah comes from the tribe of Joseph, and his partner is the Messiah from the tribe of Judah, that is, the Davidic Messiah. MidrTeh 60:3 mentions the Messiah ben Ephraim as

the precursor of the Messiah ben David and has Nehemia ben Hushiel (this is the name of the Messiah from the house of Joseph/Ephraim in the Apocalypse of Zerubbabel) die before the gates of Jerusalem; cf. also MidrTeh 87:6.

6. Himmelfarb, "Sefer Zerubbabel," pp. 75ff.; Reeves, "The Prophetic Vision of Zerubbabel ben Shealtiel," pp. 55ff.; and see above, p. 227.

7. See Hermann L. Strack and Günter Stemberger, *Introduction to the Talmud and Midrash*, trans. and ed. Markus Bockmuehl, Minneapolis: Fortress, 2nd edition, 1996, pp. 296ff.

8. Arnold Goldberg, *Erlösung durch Leiden: Drei rabbinische Homilien über die Trauernden Zions und den leidenden Messias Efraim (PesR 34. 36. 37)*, Frankfurt am Main: Selbstverlag der Gesellschaft zur Förderung Judaistischer Studien in Frankfurt am Main e.V., 1978. For earlier references, see Gustav Dalman, *Der leidende und der sterbende Messias der Synagoge im ersten nachchristlichen Jahrtausend*, Berlin: Reuther, 1888; Siegmund Hurwitz, *Die Gestalt des sterbenden Messias: Religionspsychologische Aspekte der jüdischen Apokalyptik*, Zurich and Stuttgart: Rascher, 1958; and more recently, Michael Fishbane, "Midrash and Messianism: Some Theologies of Suffering and Salvation," in Peter Schäfer and Mark Cohen, eds., *Toward the Millennium: Messianic Expectations from the Bible to Waco*, Leiden: Brill, 1998, pp. 57–71. In 2009 Jae Hee Han wrote his Princeton B.A. thesis about Pisqa 36: " 'And His Name Is Ephraim, My True Messiah': Christian Elements in the Pesikta Rabbati Piska 36."

9. Hebrew text in Rivka Ulmer, ed., *Pesiqta Rabbati: A Synoptic Edition of Pesiqta Rabbati Based upon All Extant Manuscripts and the Editio Princeps*, vol. 2, Lanham, Md.: University Press of America, 2009, pp. 816–821; 830–836; 837–845 (quoted "PesR," followed by the number of the Pisqa and of the relevant paragraph); the English translation follows—with considerable changes—Braude, *Pesikta Rabbati*, vol. 2, pp. 662–668, 676–693 (quoted "PesR," followed by page number). I also consult the translation and extensive commentary in Goldberg, *Erlösung durch Leiden*.

10. A play on words with *ʿani*.

11. The text here is unclear or rather corrupt; see Goldberg, ad loc.

12. The "he" is seemingly superfluous.

13. Ulmer, PesR 34, § 8; Braude, PesR, p. 668; Goldberg, *Erlösung durch Leiden*, p. 73.

14. Ulmer, PesR 34, § 7; Braude, PesR, p. 666; Goldberg, *Erlösung durch Leiden*, p. 72.

15. Isa. 61:3.

16. Cf. Goldberg, *Erlösung durch Leiden*, pp. 131ff.; Fishbane, "Midrash and Messianism," pp. 61f., with reference to the Elephantine papyri.

17. Ulmer, PesR 34, § 5; Braude, PesR, p. 665; Goldberg, *Erlösung durch Leiden*, p. 70.

18. So (*ʿarevim*) in Ms. Parma; the *editio princeps* has "necessary" (*tzerikhim*).

19. So in Ms. Parma and in the *editio princeps*. Goldberg, *Erlösung durch Leiden*, p. 71 n. 30, suggests correcting *hibbitem* with *hikkitem*, hence, "that you waited for my Torah but not for my kingdom," because this fits better with the biblical proof text Zeph. 3:8 ("therefore wait for me"). I presume that the original midrash plays with both words: "that, although you loved (*hibbitem*) my Torah, you did not wait (*hikkitem*) for my kingdom."

20. The *editio princeps* has the obviously corrupt reading "forgetting" (*shekhihah*).

21. So with the *editio princeps*.

22. The text in Ms. Parma (*'l*) and in the *editio princeps* (*oti*) is corrupt; I read with Goldberg *itti*—"with me."

23. Ulmer, PesR 34, § 6; Braude, PesR, pp. 665f.; Goldberg, *Erlösung durch Leiden*, pp. 71f.

24. Ulmer, PesR 34, § 7; Braude, PesR, p. 667; Goldberg, *Erlösung durch Leiden*, p. 73.

25. Ps. 36:9 in the NRSV translation.

26. Ulmer, PesR 36, § 1; Braude, PesR, p. 677; Goldberg, *Erlösung durch Leiden*, pp. 147f. This exegesis is based on the distinction be-

tween the "light" of Gen. 1:4 and the "lights in the dome of the sky" of Gen. 1:14: since sun, moon, and stars are mentioned only later in the creation account, the light of Gen. 1:4 must be a very special light.

27. BerR 1:4; strictly speaking it is the *name* of the to-be-created Messiah that entered God's mind.

28. The text is not absolutely clear here and could also be understood as meaning that God hides the *light* for the Messiah (instead of the Messiah himself) beneath his throne; cf. Goldberg, *Erlösung durch Leiden*, p. 148. However, since God afterward negotiates with the Messiah the terms of their agreement, it makes sense to assume that the Messiah himself is (physically) hidden beneath the throne.

29. y Taan 1:1/16f., fol. 63d; b Sanh 97bf.; Tan be-huqqotai 3 end; TanB, ibid. 5 end; on this, see Peter Schäfer, "Die messianischen Hoffnungen des rabbinischen Judentums zwischen Naherwartung und religiösem Pragmatismus," in id., *Studien zur Geschichte und Theologie des rabbinischen Judentums*, Leiden: Brill, 1978, pp. 216ff.

30. Ulmer, PesR 36, § 4; ibid., § 8; Braude, PesR, pp. 679, 681; Goldberg, *Erlösung durch Leiden*, pp. 150, 152. In arguing that "obedience to the Law is exalted here as the means by which one may benefit in messianic glory" ("Midrash and Messianism," p. 65), Fishbane smooths out the homily's tension between Torah obedience and messianic expectation and ignores the polemical tone.

31. Ulmer, PesR 36, § 2, 5; Braude, PesR, pp. 677, 679; Goldberg, *Erlösung durch Leiden*, pp. 148, 151.

32. Ulmer, PesR 36, § 5f., 9; Braude, PesR, pp. 679f., 682; Goldberg, *Erlösung durch Leiden*, pp. 149, 152, 154f.

33. Ulmer, PesR 36, § 3; Braude, PesR, p. 678; Goldberg, *Erlösung durch Leiden*, p. 149. The epithet "of righteousness" is missing in Ms. Parma, and the *editio princeps* has "his righteousness" (*tzidqo*), but I emend *tzidqi* with Ulmer, PesR 36, § 6. Braude translates "my true Messiah."

34. Irrespective of the name Ephraim, the epithet "Messiah of righteousness" is also unusual. As a direct parallel, Goldberg points to the title "teacher of righteousness" (*moreh ha-tzedeq*) in Qumran; cf. Goldberg, *Erlösung durch Leiden*, p. 173.

35. Ms. Parma has *lekha* ("to you"), which certainly needs to be corrected to *lo* ("to him").

36. So with the *editio princeps*.

37. So with the *editio princeps*.

38. So, instead of "with his yoke," in Ms. Parma and the *editio princeps*.

39. Ulmer, PesR 36, § 4; Braude, PesR, pp. 678f.; Goldberg, *Erlösung durch Leiden*, pp. 149f.

40. Ulmer, PesR 36, § 2 (Ms. Parma); Braude, PesR, p. 677 (who mistranslates *uledoro*); Goldberg, *Erlösung durch Leiden*, p. 148.

41. Cf. b Yev 62a, 63b; b AZ 5a; b Nid 13b.

42. Ps. 22:15 in the NRSV translation.

43. "Strength" (*kohi*) is probably to be corrected here to "throat" (*hikki*).

44. For the parallel in Raimundus Martinus' *Pugio Fidei*, see Goldberg, *Erlösung durch Leiden*, pp. 181, 260ff.

45. b Sanh 97a.

46. BerR 8:4f.; see above, p. 167.

47. b Sanh 38b; see above, p. 173.

48. BerR 1:4.

49. Goldberg, *Erlösung durch Leiden*, p. 186.

50. On this, see in detail Martin Hengel, "Zur Wirkungsgeschichte von Jes 53 in vorchristlicher Zeit," in id., *Judaica, Hellenistica et Christiana: Kleine Schriften II*, Tübingen: Mohr Siebeck, 1999, pp. 72–114 (first published in Bernd Janowski and Peter Stuhlmacher, eds., *Der leidende Gottesknecht: Jesaja 53 und seine Wirkungsgeschichte*, Tübingen: Mohr Siebeck, 1996, pp. 49–91); expanded English version, "The Effective History of Isaiah 53 in the Pre-Christian Period," in Bernd Janowski and Peter Stuhlmacher, eds., *The Suffering Servant: Isaiah 53 in Jewish and Christian Sources*, Grand Rapids, Mich.: Eerdmans, 2004, pp. 75–146.

51. 4Q541, fragment 9, col. I, in Florentino García Martínez and Eibert J. C. Tigchelaar, eds., *The Dead Sea Scrolls Study Edition*, vol. 2: *4Q274–11Q31*, Leiden: Brill, 1998, pp. 1080f.

52. See in detail, Esther Eshel, "4Q471B: A Self-Glorification Hymn," *RdQ* 17/65–68, 1996, pp. 175–203.

53. 4Q491c, fragment 1, in García Martínez and Tigchelaar, *Dead Sea Scrolls Study Edition*, vol. 2, pp. 980f.

54. See the summary in Schäfer, *Origins of Jewish Mysticism*, pp. 146ff.

55. Israel Knohl, *The Messiah before Jesus: The Suffering Servant of the Dead Sea Scrolls*, Berkeley and Los Angeles: University of California Press, 2000, pp. 42ff., 75ff.

56. Cf. Otfried Hofius, "Das vierte Gottesknechtslied in den Briefen des Neuen Testaments," in Janowski and Stuhlmacher, *Der leidende Gottesknecht*, pp. 107–127; for the Gospels, see Peter Stuhlmacher, "Jes 53 in den Evangelien und in der Apostelgeschichte," ibid., pp. 93–105.

57. Rom. 3:25; see also Rom. 4:25: "who was handed over to death for our trespasses."

58. 1 Cor. 15:3.

59. Rom. 5:18f.; cf. also 2 Cor. 5:21: "For our sake *he made him to be sin* who knew no sin, so that in him we might become the *righteousness* of God"; Heb. 9:28: "so Christ, having been offered once *to bear the sins of many. . . .*"

60. 1 Petr. 2:21–25.

61. b Sanh 98b.

62. Raimundus Martinus, *Pugio Fidei adversus Mauros et Judaeos*, Lipsiae: Friderici Lanckisi, 1687; reprint Farnborough: Gregg, 1967 (1968), p. 862.

63. Abraham Epstein, "*Hiwra de-be Rabbi*," in id., *Mi-qadmoniyot ha-yehudim: Mehqarim u-reshimot*, Jerusalem: Mosad ha-Rav Kook, 1956–57, pp. 100–103 (Hebrew). He is followed by Fishbane, "Midrash and Messianism," p. 59.

64. b Sanh 93b.

65. b Sanh 98a.

66. Goldberg, *Erlösung durch Leiden*, p. 194.

67. Ibid.

68. SifBam § 131, ed. Horovitz, p. 173.

69. As Goldberg, *Erlösung durch Leiden*, p. 194, suggests.

70. MekhY, Pischa 1, ed. Horovitz-Rabin, p. 4; see also b Sot 14a.

71. Goldberg, *Erlösung durch Leiden*, p. 195.

72. So with Ms. Parma.

73. So with the *editio princeps* (missing in Ms. Parma).

74. PesR 36, § 4; Braude, PesR, p. 679; Goldberg, *Erlösung durch Leiden*, p. 150.

75. So with the *editio princeps*; Ms. Parma has "their."

76. So instead of "his light" in Ms. Parma and the *editio princeps*.

77. Goldberg (*Erlösung durch Leiden*, p. 199: "Essentially, the Messiah does not redeem through an open, liberating act but by creating, through his suffering, the precondition for this act. We are dealing here with a truly redemptive act of the Messiah") has correctly recognized this, but he shies away from drawing the appropriate consequences.

78. PesR 36, § 4 (only in the printed edition and in Ms. JTS 8195, but not in Ms. Parma); Braude, PesR, p. 679; Goldberg, *Erlösung durch Leiden*, p. 151.

79. See above, pp. 70ff.

80. The only (much earlier) reference to God abandoning his throne and having someone else take his seat upon it can be found in Ezekiel the tragedian's *Exagōgē*; there, God asks *Moses* to take his seat on his throne. On this, see Pieter W. van der Horst, "Moses' Throne Vision in Ezekiel the Dramatist," *JJS* 34, 1983, pp. 21–29; Martin Hengel, "'Setze dich zu meiner Rechten!' Die Inthronisation Christi zur Rechten Gottes und Psalm 110,1," in id., *Studien zur Christologie: Kleine Schriften IV*, ed. Claus-Jürgen Thornton, Tübingen: Mohr Siebeck, 2006, pp. 338f. (first published in 1993).

81. 1 En. 45:3; 55:4.

82. 1 En. 51:3.

83. Mt. 19:28 ("At the renewal of all things, when the Son of Man is seated on the throne of his glory" [*epi thronou doxēs autou*]); Mt. 25:31 ("When the Son of Man comes in his glory, and all the angels with him, then he will sit on the throne of his glory" [*epi thronou doxēs autou*]).

84. See above, p. 246.

85. PesR 36, § 6; Braude, PesR, pp. 680f.; Goldberg, *Erlösung durch Leiden*, p. 152.

86. So with the *editio princeps* (missing in Ms. Parma).

87. So ("to him") with the *editio princeps*; Ms. Parma has "to them."

88. The last sentence is corrupt in both Ms. Parma and the *editio princeps*; on this, see Goldberg, *Erlösung durch Leiden*, p. 152 with n. 33.

89. See, above all, b Sanh 97a.

90. Goldberg, *Erlösung durch Leiden*, pp. 212f.

91. Ibid., p. 214.

92. All translations are as literal as possible.

93. Ps. 22:3 in the NRSV translation.

94. Ps. 22:15 in the NRSV translation.

95. Ps. 22:20 in the NRSV translation.

96. Ps. 22:14 in the NRSV translation.

97. Ps. 22:6 in the NRSV translation.

98. Peter Kuhn, *Gottes Trauer und Klage in der rabbinischen Überlieferung (Talmud und Midrasch)*, Leiden: Brill, 1978, pp. 128ff.

99. Cf. Micha 7:8.

100. Cf. Lam. 4:8.

101. Cf. Ps. 22:16.

102. Ms. Parma: "your sons."

103. PesR 37, § 2; Braude, PesR, pp. 685f.; Goldberg, *Erlösung durch Leiden*, p. 268.

104. See above, pp. 239, 247, 255.

105. Another description of the Messiah's humiliation in prison (PesR 37, § 4; Braude, PesR, p. 686; Goldberg, *Erlösung durch Leiden*, p. 270) follows almost exclusively Ps. 22.

106. PesR 37, § 3; Braude, PesR, p. 686; Goldberg, *Erlösung durch Leiden*, p. 269.

107. And definitely not that his *figure* is being enlarged, as posited by Goldberg, *Erlösung durch Leiden*, p. 290.

108. PesR 37, § 5; Braude, PesR, p. 687; Goldberg, *Erlösung durch Leiden*, p. 271.

109. PesR 37, § 8; Braude, PesR, p. 689; Goldberg, *Erlösung durch Leiden*, p. 274. The "garments of salvation" and the "robe of righteous-

ness" (*me'il tzedaqah*) of Isa. 61:10, the latter reminding us of "my Messiah of righteousness" (*meshiah tzidqi*).

110. PesR 37, § 8; Braude, PesR, p. 689; Goldberg, *Erlösung durch Leiden*, p. 274.

111. PesR 36, § 2; Braude, PesR, p. 677; Goldberg, *Erlösung durch Leiden*, p. 148.

112. See above, p. 243.

113. See above, pp. 42ff., 49f., 211.

114. PesR 36, § 6; Braude, PesR, p. 680; Goldberg, *Erlösung durch Leiden*, p. 152.

115. John 1:1–4.

116. Goldberg, *Erlösung durch Leiden*, p. 210.

117. The only author who recognized the significance of Ps. 22 and alludes to the possibility that the Messiah Ephraim "is an internalization of the messianic figure of Jesus" is Israel Yuval; see his *Two Nations in Your Womb: Pereceptions of Jews and Christians in Late Antiquity and the Middle Ages*," Berkeley, Calif.: University of California Press, 2006, pp. 36–38. I thank Israel Yuval for drawing my attention to this passage in his book, which escaped my attention when I prepared the German version of my book.

118. See above, pp. 108ff. Also the garment that the Messiah Ephraim receives—and "whose splendor streams forth from one end of the world to the other"—can be found in a similar manner in 3 Enoch (Schäfer, *Synopse zur Hekhalot-Literatur*, § 15). And, of course, David's enthronement in the Apocalypse of David in Hekhalot Rabbati (§§ 122–126) comes to mind; see above, pp. 85ff.

119. Mt. 26:64; Mk. 14:62; Lk. 22:69.

120. Lk. 24:51; Acts 1:9.

121. Mk. 16:19. Ps. 110:1: "The Lord says to my lord: Sit at my right hand."

122. Rev. 3:21.

123. Mt. 26:39; Mk. 14:36; Lk. 22:42.

124. That is, by the pagan nations.

125. PesR 36, § 8; Braude, PesR, p. 682; Goldberg, *Erlösung durch Leiden*, p. 154.

126. See the summary in Ra'anan Boustan, *From Martyr to Mystic: Rabbinic Martyrology and the Making of Merkavah Mysticism*, Tübingen: Mohr Siebeck, 2005, pp. 139ff.

127. Lk. 1:42.45; see also Lk. 11:27.

128. PesR 37, § 8; Braude, PesR, p. 689; Goldberg, *Erlösung durch Leiden*, p. 274.

129. See the summary in Stemberger, *Einleitung in Talmud und Midrasch*, pp. 295–297.

130. According to Meir Friedmann, the first editor of Pesiqta Rabbati, homilies 34–37 are the oldest part of the midrash (*Pesikta Rabbati: Midrasch für den Fest-Cyclus und die ausgezeichneten Sabbate*, Vienna: Selbstverlag, 1880, introduction, p. 24).

131. Arthur Marmorstein, "Eine messianische Bewegung im dritten Jahrhundert," *Jeschurun* 13, 1926, p. 20; Goldberg, *Erlösung durch Leiden*, p. 142: Pisqa 34 "originated some time in the middle of the third century."

132. Bernard J. Bamberger, "A Messianic Document of the Seventh Century," *HUCA* 15, 1940, pp. 427f. Braude, PesR, pp. 20–26, suggests the sixth and seventh centuries.

133. Leopold Zunz, *Die gottesdienstlichen Vorträge der Juden historisch entwickelt*, Frankfurt am Main: Kauffmann, 2nd edition, 1892; reprint Hildesheim: Olms, 1966, pp. 255f. (second half of the ninth century); Dalman, *Der leidende und der sterbende Messias*, p. 53 note (beginning of the tenth century); Jacob Mann, *The Jews in Egypt and in Palestine under the Fāṭimid Caliphs*, vol. 1, Oxford: Oxford University Press, 1920, pp. 47–49 (first half of the ninth century).

134. Against this argument, see Bamberger, "Messianic Document," p. 429: "A friendly and cordial Gentile-Jewish relationship is not necessary to account for borrowings from Christianity."

135. Thus, above all, Heinrich Graetz, *Geschichte der Juden von den ältesten Zeiten bis auf die Gegenwart*, vol. 5, Leipzig: Oskar Leiner, 4th edition, 1909; reprint Berlin: arani-Verlag (licensed edition Wissenschaftliche Buchgesellschaft), 1998, pp. 269, 507f.; Dalman, *Der leidende und der sterbende Messias*, p. 53 note.

136. Zunz, *Gottesdienstliche Vorträge*, p. 256.

137. Israel Lévi, "La Pesikta Rabbati et le 4e Ezra," *REJ* 24, 1892, pp. 281–285; id., "Bari dans la Pesikta Rabbati," *REJ* 32, 1896, pp. 278–282. Mann, *The Jews in Egypt*, vol. 1, p. 48 with n. 2, suggests that the editor of Pesiqta Rabbati, Homilies 34–37, was an Italian haggadist who settled in Jerusalem in the first half of the ninth century and there joined the mourners of Zion.

138. PesR 36, § 8; Braude, PesR, p. 681; Goldberg, *Erlösung durch Leiden*, p. 154. The Persians are also mentioned in Pisqa 37, § 3; Braude, PesR, p. 686; Goldberg, *Erlösung durch Leiden*, p. 269.

139. Stemberger, *Einleitung in Talmud und Midrasch*, p. 296.

140. Goldberg, *Erlösung durch Leiden*, p. 23.

141. See above, pp. 227ff. Speaking in favor of this assumption is the remarkable (and there, rather surprising) allusion in the Apocalypse of Zerubbabel to the rabbis at first not accepting the Davidic Messiah Menahem ben Ammiel as Messiah but despising him because he looks miserable and appears in ragged clothes; cf. Himmelfarb, "Sefer Zerubbabel," p. 77.

142. For the dubiousness of the category of "influence," see Schäfer, *Mirror of His Beauty*, pp. 217ff.

143. Fishbane, "Midrash and Messianism," p. 70, n. 41. For a critique of Fishbane, see also Yuval, *Two Nations*, p. 37, n. 16.

Bibliography

Alexander, Philip. "The Historical Setting of the Book of Enoch." *JJS* 28, 1977, pp. 156–180.

———. "3 (Hebrew Apocalypse of) Enoch," in Charlesworth, *OTP*, vol. 1, pp. 223–315.

———. "The Family of Caesar and the Family of God: The Image of the Emperor in Early Jewish Mystical Literature," in Loveday Alexander, ed., *Images of Empire: The Roman Empire in Jewish, Christian and Greco-Roman Sources*. Sheffield: Sheffield Academic Press, 1991, pp. 276–297.

———. "From Son of Adam to a Second God: Transformation of the Biblical Enoch," in Michael E. Stone and Theodore A. Bergen, eds., *Biblical Figures Outside the Bible*. Harrisburg, Pa.: Trinity Press International, 1998, pp. 102–111.

———. "Jewish Believers in Early Rabbinic Literature (2d to 5th Centuries)," in Oskar Skarsaune and Reidar Hvalvik, eds., *Jewish Believers in Jesus: The Early Centuries*. Peabody, Mass.: Hendrickson, 2007, pp. 659–709.

Altmann, Alexander. "The Gnostic Background of the Rabbinic Adam Legends." *JQR* N.S. 35, 1944/45, pp. 371–391.

Bacher, Wilhelm. *Die Agada der Tannaiten*, vol. 1. Strasbourg: Karl I. Trübner, 1884.

Baden, Joel S. *J, E, and the Redaction of the Pentateuch*. Tübingen: Mohr Siebeck, 2009.

Bakhos, Carol. *Ishmael on the Border: Rabbinic Portrayals of the First Arab*. Albany: State University of New York Press, 2006.

Bamberger, Bernard J. "A Messianic Document of the Seventh Century." *HUCA* 15, 1940, pp. 425–431.

Barnes, Timothy D. *Constantine and Eusebius*. Cambridge, Mass: Harvard University Press, 1982.

Basil de Césarée. *Homélies sur l'hexaéméron*, ed. Stanislas Giet. Paris: Cerf, 1950.

Basilius von Caesarea. *Homilien zum Hexameron*, eds. Emmanuel Amand de Mendieta and Stig Y. Rudberg. Berlin: Akademie Verlag, 1997.

Becker, Adam H., and Annette Yoshiko Reed. *The Ways That Never Parted: Jews and Christians in Late Antiquity and the Early Middle Ages*. Tübingen: Mohr Siebeck, 2003.

Becker, Hans-Jürgen, ed. (in cooperation with Christoph Berner). *Avot de-Rabbi Natan: Synoptische Edition beider Versionen*. Tübingen: Mohr Siebeck, 2006.

Bienert, Wolfgang A. "Sabellius und Sabellianismus als historisches Problem," in Hanns Christof Brennecke, Ernst Ludwig Grasmück, and Christoph Markschies, eds., *Logos: Festschrift für Luise Abramowski zum 8. Juli 1993*. Berlin and New York: de Gruyter, 1993, pp. 124–139.

Boucher, Madeleine. "Some Unexplored Parallels to 1 Cor. 11:11–12 and Gal. 3:28: The New Testament and the Role of Women." *CBQ* 31, 1969, pp. 50–58.

Boustan, Ra'anan S. "Angels in the Architecture: Temple Art and the Poetics of Praise in the *Songs of the Sabbath Sacrifice*," in id. and Annette Yoshiko Reed, eds., *Heavenly Realms and Earthly Realities in Late Antique Religions*. Cambridge: Cambridge University Press, 2004, pp. 195–212.

———. *From Martyr to Mystic: Rabbinic Martyrology and the Making of Merkavah Mysticism*. Tübingen: Mohr Siebeck, 2005.

———. "The Study of Heikhalot Literature: Between Mystical Experience and Textual Artifact." *CBR* 6, 2007, pp. 130–160.

Boyarin, Daniel. "The Gospel of the Memra: Jewish Binitarianism and the Prologue to John." *HTR* 94, 2001, pp. 243–284.

———. *Border Lines: The Partition of Judaeo-Christianity*. Philadelphia: University of Pennsylvania Press, 2004.

———. "Two Powers in Heaven; or, The Making of a Heresy," in Hindy Najman and Judith H. Newman, eds., *The Idea of Biblical Interpretation: Essays in Honor of James L. Kugel*. Leiden: Brill, 2004, pp. 331–370.

————. "The Parables of Enoch and the Foundation of the Rabbinic Sect: A Hypothesis," in Mauro Perani, ed., *The Words of a Wise Man's Mouth Are Gracious" (Qoh 10,12): Festschrift for Günter Stemberger on the Occasion of His 65th Birthday*. Berlin and New York: Walter de Gruyter, 2005, pp. 53–72.

————. "Beyond Judaisms: Meṭaṭron and the Divine Polymorphy of Ancient Judaism." *JSJ* 41, 2010, pp. 323–365.

Braude, William G. *Pesikta Rabbati: Discourses for Feasts, Fasts, and Special Sabbaths*. New Haven, Conn., and London: Yale University Press, 1968.

Charlesworth, James H., ed. *The Old Testament Pseudepigrapha*, vol. 1, *Apocalyptic Literature and Testaments*. London: Darton, Longman and Todd, 1983; vol. 2, *Expansions of the "Old Testament" and Legends, Wisdom and Philosophical Literature, Prayers, Psalms, and Odes, Fragments of Lost Judeo-Hellenistic Works*. Garden City, N.Y.: Doubleday, 1985.

Chester, Andrew. *Messiah and Exaltation: Jewish Messianic and Visionary Traditions and New Testament Christology*. Tübingen: Mohr Siebeck, 2007.

Cohen, Martin S. *The Shi'ur Qomah: Liturgy and Theurgy in Pre-Kabbalistic Jewish Mysticism*. Lanham, Md.: University Press of America, 1963.

Collins, John J. *The Apocalyptic Imagination: An Introduction to Jewish Apocalyptic Literature*. Grand Rapids, Mich./Cambridge: William B. Eerdmans, 2nd edition, 1998.

Courtonne, Yves. *Saint Basile: Lettres*, Texte établi et trad., 3 vols. Paris: Les Belles Lettres, 1957–1966.

Dalman, Gustav. *Der leidende und der sterbende Messias der Synagoge im ersten nachchristlichen Jahrtausend*. Berlin: Reuther, 1888.

Dan, Joseph. *The Ancient Jewish Mysticism*. Tel Aviv: MOD Books, 1993.

Deutsch, Nathaniel. *Guardians of the Gate: Angelic Vice Regency in Late Antiquity*. Leiden: Brill, 1999.

du Mesnil du Buisson, Robert Comte. *Les Peintures de la synagogue de Doura-Europos, 245–256 après J.-C.* Rome: Pontifico Istituto Biblico, 1939.

Epstein, Abraham. *"Hiwra de-be Rabbi,"* in id., *Mi-qadmoniot ha-yehudim: Mehqarim u-reshimot.* Jerusalem: Mosad ha-Rav Kook, 1956–1957, pp. 100–103 (Hebrew).

Eshel, Esther. "4Q471B: A Self-Glorification Hymn." *RdQ* 17/65–68, 1996, pp. 175–203.

Evans, Ernest, ed. *Tertullian's Treatise against Praxeas.* London: SPCK, 1948.

Fishbane, Michael. "Midrash and Messianism: Some Theologies of Suffering and Salvation," in Peter Schäfer and Mark Cohen, eds., *Toward the Millennium: Messianic Expectations from the Bible to Waco.* Leiden: Brill, 1998, pp. 57–71.

Flesher, Paul V. M. "Rereading the Reredos: David, Orpheus, and Messianism in the Dura Europos Synagogue," in Dan Urman and Paul M. Flesher, eds., *Ancient Synagogues: Historical Analysis and Archaeological Discovery*, vol. 2. Leiden: Brill, 1995, pp. 346–366.

Fossum, Jarl E. *The Name of God and the Angel of the Lord: Samaritan and Jewish Concepts of Intermediation and the Origin of Gnosticism.* Tübingen: J.C.B. Mohr (Paul Siebeck), 1985.

Friedlander, Gerald. *Pirkê De Rabbi Eliezer*, trans. and annot. with introduction and indices. London: Kegan Paul, Trench, Trubner & Co., and New York: Bloch, 1916.

Friedmann, Meir. *Pesikta Rabbati: Midrasch für den Fest-Cyclus und die ausgezeichneten Sabbate.* Vienna: Selbstverlag, 1880.

García Martínez, Florentino, and Eibert J. C. Tigchelaar, eds. *The Dead Sea Scrolls Study Edition*, 2 vols. Leiden: Brill, 1997–1998.

Geller, Mark. "Two Incantation Bowls Inscribed in Syriac and Aramaic." *BSOAS* 39, 1976, pp. 422–427.

Gnilka, Christian. *Aetas Spiritalis: Die Überwindung der natürlichen Altersstufen als Ideal frühchristlichen Lebens.* Bonn: Peter Hanstein, 1972.

Goldberg, Arnold. "Sitzend zur Rechten der Kraft: Zur Gottesbezeichnung Gebura in der frühen rabbinischen Literatur." *BZ* NF 8, 1964, pp. 284–293 = id., *Mystik und Theologie des rabbinischen Judentums. Gesammelte Studien I*, ed. Margarete Schlüter and Peter Schäfer. Tübingen: Mohr Siebeck, 1997, pp. 188–198.

————. *Erlösung durch Leiden. Drei rabbinische Homilien über die Trauernden Zions und den leidenden Messias Efraim (PesR 34. 36. 37).* Frankfurt am Main: Selbstverlag der Gesellschaft zur Förderung Judaistischer Studien in Frankfurt am Main e.V., 1978.

————."Pereq Re'uyot Yehezqe'el: Eine formanalytische Untersuchung," in id., *Mystik und Theologie des rabbinischen Judentums: Gesammelte Studien I*, ed. Margarete Schlüter and Peter Schäfer. Tübingen: Mohr Siebeck, 1997, pp. 93–147.

Goldstein, Jonathan. "The Central Composition of the West Wall of the Synagogue of Dura-Europos." *JANES* 16–17, 1984–1985, pp. 99–142.

Goodenough, Erwin R. *Jewish Symbols in the Greco-Roman Period*, vol. 9, *Symbolism in the Dura Synagogue: Text, i.* New York: Pantheon, 1964.

Gordon, Cyrus H. "Aramaic Magical Bowls in the Istanbul and Baghdad Museums." *ArOr* 6, 1934, pp. 319–334, 466–474.

————. "Aramaic and Mandaic Magical Bowls." *ArOr* 9, 1937, pp. 84–106.

————. "Two Magic Bowls in Teheran: The Aramaic Bowl." *Orientalia* 20, 1951, pp. 306–315.

Goshen-Gottstein, Alon. "Jewish Christian Relations and Rabbinic Literature—Shifting Scholarly and Relational Paradigms: The Case of Two Powers," in Marcel Poorthuis, Joshua Schwartz, and Joseph Turner, eds., *Interaction between Judaism and Christianity in History, Religion, Art, and Literature.* Leiden: Brill, 2009, pp. 15–43.

Gottlieb, Gunther. *Ambrosius von Mailand und Kaiser Gratian.* Göttingen: Vandenhoeck & Ruprecht, 1973.

Grabar, André. "Le Thème religieux des fresques de la Synagogue de Doura." *RHR* 123, 1941, pp. 170–172.

Graetz, Heinrich. *Geschichte der Juden von den ältesten Zeiten bis auf die Gegenwart*, vol. 5. Leipzig: Oskar Leiner, 4th edition, 1909; reprint Berlin: arani-Verlag (licensed edition Wissenschaftliche Buchgesellschaft), 1998.

Gruenwald, Ithamar. "Re'uyot Yehezqel." *Temirin* 1, 1977, pp. 101–139.

Gruenwald, Ithamar. *Apocalyptic and Merkavah Mysticism*. Leiden: Brill, 1980.

Haddan, Arthur West. *The Works of Aurelius Augustine: A New Translation*, vol. 7, *On the Trinity*. Edinburgh: T&T Clark, 1873.

Halperin, David. *The Merkabah in Rabbinic Literature*. New Haven, Conn.: American Oriental Society, 1980.

Hasan-Rokem, Galit. "Narratives in Dialogue: A Folk Literary Perspective on Interreligious Contacts in the Holy Land in Rabbinic Literature of Late Antiquity," in Arieh Kofsky and Guy G. Stroumsa, eds., *Sharing the Sacred: Religious Contacts and Conflicts in the Holy Land—First–Fifteenth Centuries C.E.* Jerusalem: Yad Izhak Ben Zvi, 1998, pp. 109–129.

———. *Web of Life: Folklore and Midrash in Rabbinic Literature*. Stanford, Calif.: Stanford University Press, 2000.

Hauschild, Wolf-Dieter. *Gottes Geist und der Mensch: Studien zur frühchristlichen Pneumatologie*. Munich: Kaiser, 1972.

Heinemann, Joseph. *Aggadah and Its Development*. Jerusalem: Keter, 1974 (Hebrew).

———. "The Messiah of Ephraim and the Premature Exodus of the Tribe of Ephraim." *HTR* 8, 1975, pp. 1–15.

Hengel, Martin. *Die Zeloten. Untersuchungen zur jüdischen Freiheitsbewegung in der Zeit von Herodes I. bis 70 n. Chr.* Leiden: Brill, 2nd edition, 1976.

———. "Zur Wirkungsgeschichte von Jes 53 in vorchristlicher Zeit," in id., *Judaica, Hellenistica et Christiana: Kleine Schriften II*. Tübingen: Mohr Siebeck, 1999, pp. 72–114.

———. "The Effective History of Isaiah 53 in the Pre-Christian Period," in Bernd Janowski and Peter Stuhlmacher, eds., *The Suffering Servant: Isaiah 53 in Jewish and Christian Sources*. Grand Rapids, Mich.: Eerdmans, 2004, pp. 75–146.

———. "'Setze dich zu meiner Rechten!' Die Inthronisation Christi zur Rechten Gottes und Psalm 110,1," in id., *Studien zur Christologie: Kleine Schriften IV*, ed. Claus-Jürgen Thornton. Tübingen: Mohr Siebeck, 2006, pp. 281–367.

Hennecke, Edgar, and Wilhelm Schneemelcher, eds. *Neutestamentliche Apokryphen in deutscher Übersetzung*, vol. 2, *Apostolisches, Apokalypsen und Verwandtes*. Tübingen: Mohr Siebeck, 1964.

Herford, R. Travers. *Christianity in Talmud and Midrash*. London: Williams & Norgate, 1903; reprint Jersey City, N.J.: Ktav, 2006.

Herrmann, Klaus, and Claudia Rohrbacher-Sticker. "Magische Traditionen der New Yorker Hekhalot-Handschrift JTS 8128 im Kontext ihrer Gesamtredaktion." *FJB* 17, 1989, pp. 101–149.

Himmelfarb, Martha. *Tours of Hell: An Apocalyptic Form in Jewish and Christian Literature*. Philadelphia: Fortress Press, 1985.

———. "Sefer Zerubbabel," in David Stern and Mark Jay Mirsky, eds., *Rabbinic Fantasies: Imaginative Narratives from Classical Hebrew Literature*. Philadelphia: Jewish Publication Society, 1990, pp. 67–90.

———. *Ascent to Heaven in Jewish and Christian Apocalypses*. New York: Oxford University Press, 1993.

———. "The Mother of the Messiah in the Talmud Yerushalmi and Sefer Zerubbabel," in Peter Schäfer, ed., *The Talmud Yerushalmi and Graeco-Roman Culture*, vol. 3. Tübingen: Mohr Siebeck, 2002, pp. 369–389.

Hofius, Otfried. "Das vierte Gottesknechtslied in den Briefen des Neuen Testaments," in Bernd Janowski and Peter Stuhlmacher, eds., *Der leidende Gottesknecht: Jesaja 53 und seine Wirkungsgeschichte*. Tübingen: Mohr Siebeck, 1996, pp. 107–127.

Hurtado, Larry W. *One God, One Lord: Early Christian Devotion and Ancient Jewish Monotheism*. London: SCM Press, 1988.

Hurwitz, Siegmund. *Die Gestalt des sterbenden Messias. Religionspsychologische Aspekte der jüdischen Apokalyptik*. Zurich and Stuttgart: Rascher, 1958.

Idel, Moshe. *Ben: Sonship and Jewish Mysticism*. London and New York: Continuum, 2007.

Isbell, Charles D. *Corpus of the Aramaic Incantation Bowls*. Missoula, Mont.: Scholars Press, 1975.

Jervell, Jacob. *Imago Dei: Gen 1,26f. im Spätjudentum, in der Gnosis und in den paulinischen Briefen*. Göttingen: Vandenhoeck & Ruprecht, 1960.

Johnson, M. D. "Life of Adam and Eve," in Charlesworth, *OTP*, vol. 2, pp. 249–295.

Kasher, Rimon. *Targumic Tosefot to the Prophets*. Jerusalem: World Union of Jewish Studies, 1996 (Hebrew).

Kelly, J.N.D. *Early Christian Doctrines*. London: Adam & Charles Black, 4th edition, 1968.

Kister, Menahem. "Let Us Make Man," in Yaakov Sussmann, ed., *Sugyot be-Mehqar ha-Talmud: Conference Marking the Fifth Anniversary of the Death of E. E. Urbach*. Jerusalem: Israel Academy of Sciences and Humanities, 2001, pp. 28–64 (Hebrew).

———. "Some Early Jewish and Christian Exegetical Problems and the Dynamics of Monotheism." *JSJ* 37, 2006, pp. 548–593.

Knohl, Israel. *The Messiah before Jesus: The Suffering Servant of the Dead Sea Scrolls*. Berkeley and Los Angeles: University of California Press, 2000.

Kuhn, Peter. *Gottes Trauer und Klage in der rabbinischen Überlieferung (Talmud und Midrasch)*. Leiden: Brill, 1978.

Labendz, Jenny R. "'Know What to Answer the Epicurean': A Diachronic Study of the *'Apikoros* in Rabbinic Literature." *HUCA* 74, 2003, pp. 175–214.

Laubscher, Hans Peter. *Der Reliefschmuck des Galeriusbogens in Thessaloniki*. Berlin: Mann, 1975.

Lesses, Rebecca Macy. *Ritual Practices to Gain Power: Angels, Incantations, and Revelation in Early Jewish Mysticism*. Harrisburg, Pa.: Trinity International, 1998.

Lévi, Israel. "La Pesikta Rabbati et le 4ᵉ Ezra." *REJ* 24, 1892, pp. 281–285.

———. "Bari dans la Pesikta Rabbati." *REJ* 32, 1896, pp. 278–282.

———. "Le ravissement du Messie à sa naissance." *REJ* 74, 1922, pp. 113–126.

———. *Le ravissement du Messie à sa naissance et autre essais*, ed. Evelyne Patlagean. Paris-Louvain: Peeters, 1994, pp. 228–241.

Levy, Jacob. *Wörterbuch über die Talmudim und Midraschim.* Berlin and Vienna, 1924; reprint Darmstadt: Wissenschaftliche Buchgesellschaft, 1963.

Lieberman, Saul. "Metatron, the Meaning of His Name and His Functions," in Ithamar Gruenwald, *Apocalyptic and Merkavah Mysticism.* Leiden: Brill, 1980, pp. 235–241.

Maher, Michael, trans. *Targum Pseudo-Jonathan: Genesis.* Edinburgh: T&T Clark, 1992 (The Aramaic Bible 1B).

Maier, Johann. *Jesus von Nazareth in der talmudischen Überlieferung.* Darmstadt: Wissenschaftliche Buchgesellschaft, 1978.

———. *Jüdische Auseinandersetzung mit dem Christentum in der Antike.* Darmstadt: Wissenschaftliche Buchgesellschaft, 1982.

Mann, Jacob. *The Jews in Egypt and in Palestine under the Fāṭimid Caliphs,* vol. 1. Oxford: Oxford University Press, 1920.

Markschies, Christoph. *Alta Trinità Beata.* Tübingen: Mohr Siebeck, 2000.

———. *Origenes und sein Erbe: Gesammelte Studien.* Berlin and New York: de Gruyter, 2007.

Marmorstein, Arthur. "Eine messianische Bewegung im dritten Jahrhundert." *Jeschurun* 13, 1926, pp. 16–28, 171–186, 369–383.

Marshall, John W. *Parables of War: Reading John's Jewish Apocalypse.* Waterloo, Ont.: Wilfrid Laurier University Press, 2001.

Martinus, Raimundus. *Pugio Fidei adversus Mauros et Judaeos.* Lipsiae: Friderici Lanckisi, 1687; reprint Farnborough: Gregg, 1967 (1968).

Metzger, Bruce M. "The Fourth Book of Ezra," in Charlesworth, *OTP,* vol. 1, pp. 517–559.

Milik, Józef Tadeusz. *Ten Years of Discovery in the Wilderness of Judaea.* Naperville, Ill.: A. R. Allenson; London: SCM Press, 1959.

Mitchell, David C. "Messiah ben Joseph: A Sacrifice of Atonement for Israel." *RRJ* 10, 2007, pp. 77–94.

Montgomery, James A. *Aramaic Incantation Texts from Nippur.* Philadelphia: The University Museum, 1913.

Neusner, Jacob. *Sifra: An Analytical Translation,* vol. 1, *Introduction, Vayyiqra Dibura Denedabah and Vayyiqra Dibura Dehobah.* Atlanta: Scholars Press, 1988.

Newman, Hillel. "Leidat ha-Mashiah be-yom ha-horban—He'arot historijot we-anti-historijot," in Menachem Mor et al., *For Uriel: Studies in the History of Israel in Antiquity Presented to Professor Uriel Rappaport.* Jerusalem: Merkaz Zalman Shazar, 2006, pp. 85–110.

Nickelsburg, George W. E. *Jewish Literature between the Bible and the Mishnah.* Philadelphia: Fortress Press, 1981.

Orlov, Andrei A. *The Enoch-Metatron Tradition.* Tübingen: Mohr Siebeck, 2005.

Oswald, Nico. "'Urmensch' und 'Erster Mensch': Zur Interpretation einiger merkwürdiger Adam-Überlieferungen in der rabbinischen Literatur," unpublished dissertation. Berlin: Kirchliche Hochschule, 1970.

Potter, David S. *The Roman Empire at Bay: AD 180–395.* New York: Routledge, 2005.

Reeves, John C. "The Prophetic Vision of Zerubbabel ben Shealtiel," in id., *Trajectories in Near Eastern Apocalyptic: A Postrabbinic Apocalypse Reader.* Atlanta: Society of Biblical Literature, 2005, pp. 51–66.

Runia, David T. "'Where, Tell me, Is the Jew': Basil, Philo and Isidore of Pelusium." *VigChr* 46, 1992, pp. 172–189.

Salzer, Dorothea M. *Die Magie der Anspielung: Form und Funktion der biblischen Anspielungen in den magischen Texten der Kairoer Geniza.* Tübingen: Mohr Siebeck, 2010.

Sanders, E. P. "Testament of Abraham," in Charlesworth, *OTP*, vol. 1, pp. 871–902.

Schäfer, Peter. *Rivalität zwischen Engeln und Menschen: Untersuchungen zur rabbinischen Engelvorstellung.* Berlin and New York: de Gruyter, 1975.

———. "Israel und die Völker der Welt: Zur Auslegung von Mekhilta deRabbi Yishma'el, baḥodesh Yitro 5." *FJB* 4, 1976, pp. 32–62.

———. "Die messianischen Hoffnungen des rabbinischen Judentums zwischen Naherwartung und religiösem Pragmatismus," in id.,

Studien zur Geschichte und Theologie des rabbinischen Judentums. Leiden: Brill, 1978, pp. 214–243.

———. *Der Bar Kokhba-Aufstand: Studien zum zweiten jüdischen Krieg gegen Rom.* Tübingen: Mohr Siebeck, 1981.

———. *Hekhalot-Studien.* Tübingen: Mohr Siebeck, 1988.

———. *Übersetzung der Hekhalot-Literatur*, vol. 3, §§ 335–596. Tübingen: Mohr Siebeck, 1989.

———. *The Hidden and Manifest God: Some Major Themes in Early Jewish Mysticism.* Albany, NY: State University of New York Press, 1992.

———. *Judeophobia: Attitudes toward the Jews in the Ancient World.* Cambridge, Mass., and London: Harvard University Press, 1997.

———. *Mirror of His Beauty: Feminine Images of God from the Bible to the Early Kabbalah.* Princeton, N.J.: Princeton University Press, 2002.

———. "In Heaven as It Is in Hell: The Cosmology of *Seder Rabbah di-Bereshit*," in Ra'anan S. Boustan and Annette Yoshiko Reed, eds., *Heavenly Realms and Earthly Realities in Late Antique Religions.* Cambridge: Cambridge University Press, 2004, pp. 233–274.

———. *Jesus in the Talmud.* Princeton, N.J., and Oxford: Princeton University Press, 2007 (German translation *Jesus im Talmud*, Tübingen: Mohr Siebeck, 2007, 2nd edition 2010, with a new afterword).

———. *The Origins of Jewish Mysticism.* Tübingen: Mohr Siebeck, 2009; paperback Princeton, N.J.: Princeton University Press, 2011.

Schäfer, Peter, ed. (in cooperation with Margarete Schlüter and Hans-Georg von Mutius). *Synopse zur Hekhalot-Literatur.* Tübingen: Mohr Siebeck, 1981.

———. *Geniza-Fragmente zur Hekhalot-Literatur.* Tübingen: Mohr Siebeck, 1984.

Schäfer, Peter, and Klaus Herrmann. *Übersetzung der Hekhalot-Literatur*, vol. 1, §§ 1–80. Tübingen: Mohr Siebeck, 1995.

Scholem, Gershom. *Jewish Gnosticism, Merkabah Mysticism, and Talmudic Tradition.* New York: Jewish Theological Seminary, 2nd edition, 1965.

Scholem, Gershom. *Die jüdische Mystik in ihren Hauptströmungen*. Frankfurt am Main: Suhrkamp, 1967.

Schreiner, Josef. *Das 4. Buch Esra*. Gütersloh: Gütersloher Verlagshaus, 1981 (*JSHRZ*, vol. 5, part 4).

Schremer, Adiel. "Midrash, Theology, and History: Two Powers in Heaven Revisited." *JSJ* 39, 2008, pp. 230–253.

———. *Brothers Estranged: Heresy, Christianity, and Jewish Identity in Late Antiquity*. Oxford: Oxford University Press, 2010.

Schwemer, Anna Maria. "Irdischer und himmlischer König. Beobachtungen zur sogenannten David-Apokalypse in Hekhalot Rabbati §§ 122–126," in Martin Hengel and Anna Maria Schwemer, eds., *Königsherrschaft Gottes und himmlischer Kult im Judentum, Urchristentum und in der hellenistischen Welt*. Tübingen: Mohr Siebeck, 1991, pp. 309–359.

———. "Elija als Araber: Die haggadischen Motive in der Legende vom Messias Menahem ben Hiskija (j Ber 2,4 5a; EkhaR 1,16 § 51) im Vergleich mit den Elija- und Elischa-Legenden der Vitae Prophetarum," in Reinhard Feldmeier and Ulrich Heckel, eds., *Die Heiden: Juden, Christen und das Problem des Fremden*. Tübingen: Mohr Siebeck, 1994, pp. 108–157.

Segal, Alan F. *Two Powers in Heaven: Early Rabbinic Reports about Christianity and Gnosticism*. Leiden: Brill, 1977.

Septimus, Dov. "Het'o shel Metatron: bisevakh leshonot we-nusha'ot." *Leshonenu* 69, 2007, pp. 291–300.

Smith, Mark S. *God in Translation: Deities in Cross-Cultural Discourse in the Biblical World*. Tübingen: Mohr Siebeck, 2008.

Sokoloff, Michael. *A Dictionary of Jewish Palestinian Aramaic of the Byzantine Period*. Ramat-Gan: Bar Ilan University Press, 1990.

Sparks, H.F.D. *The Apocryphal Old Testament*. Oxford: Clarendon Press, 1984.

Stein, Dina. "Let the 'People' Go? The 'Folk' and Their 'Lore' as Tropes in the Reconstruction of Rabbinic Culture." *Prooftexts* 29, 2009, pp. 206–241.

Stemberger, Günter. *Einleitung in Talmud und Midrasch*. Munich: Beck, 8th edition, 1992.

Stern, Henri. "The Orpheus in the Synagogue of Dura-Europos." *JWCI* 21, 1958, pp. 1–6.

Stern, Menahem. *Greek and Latin Authors on Jews and Judaism*, vol. 2. Jerusalem: Israel Academy of Sciences, 1980.

Strack, Hermann L., and Günter Stemberger. *Introduction to the Talmud and Midrash*, trans. and ed. Markus Bockmuehl. Minneapolis: Fortress, 2nd edition, 1996.

Stroumsa, Gedalyahu G. "Le couple de l'Ange et de l'Esprit: traditions juives et chrétiennes." *RB* 88, 1981, pp. 42–61.

———. "Polymorphie divine et transformations d'un mythologeme: L''Apocryphon de Jean' et ses source." *VigChr* 35, 1981, pp. 412–434.

———. "Form(s) of God: Some Notes on Metatron and Christ." *HTR* 76, 1983, pp. 269–288.

Stuhlmacher, Peter. "Jes 53 in den Evangelien und in der Apostelgeschichte," in Bernd Janowski and Peter Stuhlmacher, eds., *Der leidende Gottesknecht: Jesaja 53 und seine Wirkungsgeschichte*. Tübingen: Mohr Siebeck, 1996, pp. 93–105.

Swartz, Michael D., and Joseph Yahalom, eds. and trans. *Avodah: Ancient Poems for Yom Kippur*. University Park: Pennsylvania State University Press, 2005.

Torrey, Charles C. "The Messiah Son of Ephraim." *JBL* 66, 1947, pp. 253–277.

Trible, Phyllis. *God and the Rhetoric of Sexuality*. Philadelphia: Fortress, 1978, 3rd edition 1983.

Ulmer, Rivka, ed. *Pesiqta Rabbati: A Synoptic Edition of Pesiqta Rabbati Based upon All Extant Manuscripts and the Editio Princeps*, vol. 2. Lanham, Md.: University Press of America, 2009.

Ulrich, Eugene, Frank Moore Cross, Sidnie White Crawford, Julie Ann Duncan, Patrick W. Skehan, Emanuel Tov, and Julio Trebolle Barrera, eds. *Qumran Cave 4*, vol. 9, *Deuteronomy, Joshua, Judges, Kings*. Oxford: Clarendon Press, 1995.

Urbach, Ephraim E. *The Sages: Their Concepts and Beliefs*. Jerusalem: Magnes Press, 1975.

van der Horst, Pieter W. "Moses' Throne Vision in Ezekiel the Dramatist." *JJS* 34, 1983, pp. 21–29.

Vermes, Geza. *Jesus the Jew: A Historian's Reading of the Gospels*. London: Collins, 1973.

Visotzky, Burton L. "Trinitarian Testimonies." *USQR* 42, 1988, pp. 73–85.

————. "Goys Я'n't Us," in Eduard Iricinschi and Holger M. Zellentin, eds., *Heresy and Identity in Late Antiquity*. Tübingen: Mohr Siebeck, 2008, pp. 299–313.

Weizmann, Kurt, and Herbert L. Kessler. *The Frescoes of the Dura Synagogue and Christian Art*. Washington, D.C.: Dumbarton Oaks Research Library and Collection, 1990.

Wintermute, O. S., trans. "Apocalypse of Zephaniah," in Charlesworth, *OTP*, vol. 1, pp. 497–516.

————. "Jubilees," in Charlesworth, *OTP*, vol. 2, pp. 35–142.

Yoreh, Tzemah L. *The First Book of God*. Berlin: de Gruyter, 2010.

Zunz, Leopold. *Die gottesdienstlichen Vorträge der Juden historisch entwickelt*. Frankfurt am Main: Kauffmann, 2nd edition, 1892.

Index

Aaron, 105, 317n3

Abaye, 192

Abbahu (R.), 152–153, 301n142

Abihu, 105

Abraham, 113, 154–156, 161, 220, 224, 261; covenant with, 187

Adam, 10, 16–18, 20, 28–31, 44, 108, 141, 166–168, 171–172, 197–213, 256, 311n12

Aha bar Ya'aqov (R.), 125–126, 154–155, 171

Aher, 127–130, 134–136. *See also* Elisha b. Avuyah

Aibo (R.), 215, 312n1

Akatriel, 131–139

Alexandrai (R.), 253

Alexandria, 205, 314n15

altar, 119

Amorites, 107

Anafiel, 129–130

Ancient of Days, 37, 60–61, 64–68, 70–71, 73–77, 89, 117, 121, 135, 285n2, 286n6

angels, 7, 10, 14–16, 18, 20, 30, 42, 49–50, 69–70, 73–77, 85–86, 88, 93, 103, 105–110, 112–113, 116–117, 119–121, 123–124, 126–129, 131–132, 134–135, 137, 139–140, 144–145, 147, 150–152, 160–163, 165–174, 177–178, 204–205, 209, 211, 230–231, 246–247, 250–251, 265, 285n4, 292n13; as creators of humanity, 176–177; expelled from heaven,

206; as mediators of Torah, 16, 164, 179–188; veneration of, 188–196

Antichrist, 227, 229, 237

Antioch, 206

apocalypse, 76, 85, 88–89, 91–92, 133, 142, 188, 190, 242, 244, 258, 270, 295n54

Appian of Alexandria, 221

Aqiva (R.), 22, 70–73, 81–82, 84, 90, 127, 258, 267, 288n43

Aquila, 52

'aravot, 88–89

Arius, 46, 303n170

Armilos, 227, 237

ascent, 45, 75–77, 109, 127, 133–134, 136–138, 151–152, 191

attributes of God, 21–22, 71–73, 131, 147

Augustine, 43–44

Augustus, 11, 33–35, 41–42, 45, 48, 206–207, 278n35, 279n36

Babylonia, 5, 7, 10, 12–16, 18, 67, 81–83, 85, 115, 122–124, 126, 131, 138, 140–141, 143, 192, 196, 199, 202, 207, 214–215, 279n49, 307n79, 308n88

baptism, 45

Bar Kokhba, 8, 82, 224, 232, 242, 316n65

Bar Koseba/Kosiba, 224, 316n65

Bar Koziba, 317n65

Bar Qappara, 124, 284n9

Basileus, 33–34, 42, 45

Basil of Caesarea, 46, 49–51
bat qol. See voice of God
Ben Azzai, 112, 127
Benedictions of the Grace, 39–40
Ben Zoma, 112, 127
Bethlehem, 216–218, 224, 230–231
binitarian theology, 3, 9, 26, 48–49, 141, 159, 282n75
bowls. *See* incantation bowls
Bun (R.), 217, 312n6, 315n39
Byzantine Empire, 140, 214

Caesar, 11, 33–35, 41–42, 45, 48, 206–207, 278n35, 279n36
Caesarea, 25, 28, 46, 124, 153
Cain, 199
Canaan, 111
Celsus, 194
chaos, 62–63
Cherubs, 189–191, 308n89
Christology, 7, 12, 15–17, 51, 53, 65, 67, 145, 148, 153, 156, 159, 207, 212
Cicero, 221
Constantine, 8
Constantinople, 44
Constantius, 34
cosmology, 193
Council of Chalcedon, 140, 143
Council of Constantinople, 47–48, 102, 140
Council of Nicaea, 43, 46, 102, 140
covenant. *See* old covenant; new covenant
creation, 18, 28, 32, 174, 208–209, 211, 259; of angels, 15, 201, 305n10; of evil things, 175; of humanity, 15–16, 28–31, 43–44, 49–50, 166–173, 197–203, 246–247, 256, 265; of the Messiah, 243; of the world, 3, 15, 24–27, 39, 49, 52, 72, 77, 110, 117, 124, 144, 162–166, 243–245, 260, 264–265, 277n10

Creed of Constantinople, 49
crown, 85–86, 89, 110, 129, 131, 133, 145, 147, 172, 182, 228

David, 10, 13, 17–18, 20, 69–73, 79–80, 84–94, 101–104, 121, 123–124, 180, 255, 258–259, 285n24, 294n43, 312n7
Decalogue. *See* Ten Commandments
demiurge, 3, 23, 26, 158, 175
Democratus, 221
demons, 138–139
diarchy, 11, 35, 41, 48, 279n36
Diatessaron, 143, 287n41
Diocletian, 34, 206–207; reform of, 11, 16, 33, 48, 206, 212
Dosa (R.), 237
Dura Europos, 13, 94–95, 101–102, 29091n91

Eden, 86, 89, 198, 263
Egypt, 12, 55–61, 124, 185, 193, 205, 221
Eighteen Benedictions, 215, 224
Eleazar, 224
Eleazar b. Azariah (R.), 71–72, 81, 258
Eli'ezer b. Hyrkanos (R.), 111–112, 243
Elijah, 101–102, 218, 222–223
Elisha, 222, 314n27
Elisha b. Avuyah, 127, 134, 136. *See also* Aher
Enoch, 5, 7, 14–15, 75, 77, 83–84, 103, 108–110, 114–116, 138, 142, 274n13, 293n29, 299n126; as scribe, 115–116, 145, 301n142. *See also* Metatron
Ephraim, 18–19, 95, 111, 227, 235, 236–271, 317nn1, 2, and 3, 320n34, 325nn117 and 118
Eremiel, 189
Esau, 220
eschatology, 17, 61, 75, 78–79, 91, 149, 215, 227, 245, 251

Euphrates, 95
Eve, 28–31, 44, 108, 197–198, 256
exile, 120
exodus, 185
Ezekiel, 89
Ezra, 78

Fatimah, 115
festivals, 193, 237
flood, 173
footstool, 58–61, 71–73, 80, 284n8
frescoes, 95, 101–102, 290n91

Gabriel, 59, 75–76, 162, 164, 180–182, 195
Galerius, 34, 206–207
Galilee, 71
Gamliel (R.), 280n53
garden. See *pardes*
Gethsemane, 268
glory, 30, 59, 64, 75, 79, 89–90, 93, 112, 124, 134–135, 144, 146, 243, 245, 250–251, 257–258, 262–263, 265, 320n30, 323n83
Gnosis. *See* Gnosticism
Gnosticism, 3–4, 6, 16, 23, 26, 35, 63, 156, 158, 165, 178, 201, 207, 275n19, 277n10, 284n15
Gomorrah, 38
Gregory of Nazianzus, 43–44, 46
Gregory of Nyssa, 46

Hadarniel, 85–86
Hagar, 161, 220
Hama bar Uqba (R.), 116
Hanina b. Hama (R.), 162–163
Hanina b. Papa (R.), 124, 162–163, 166, 168
hayyot, 87, 88. *See also* holy creatures
heavenly voice. *See* voice of God
Hekhalot, 7, 13–14, 82–83, 85, 94, 103, 113, 118, 120, 122, 130–133, 136–142, 268, 274n13, 296n70, 299n127, 301n140
Hephzibah, 227, 237
heresy, 1, 3–9, 11–14, 18–19, 22–23, 26–29, 32–33, 35, 37–41, 44–46, 53, 55, 57, 61–63, 65, 81, 83–84, 104–107, 127, 134–135, 147, 153, 155–156, 158–159, 165, 169–170, 199–201, 203, 206, 213, 277n15, 279n49, 280nn50, 51, and 55, 284n11, 301n142, 304n24, 310nn7 and 8. See also *minim*
heretics. *See* heresy
Herod, 185, 230, 316n50
Hezekiah, 124, 216, 218, 225, 227, 229, 314n35
High Priest, 11, 79, 88, 116, 119, 122, 132, 186
Hila (R.), 169–170
Hillel (R.), 225
Hiram, 151
Hiyya II bar Abba (R.), 157–158
holy creatures, 87–88, 90, 93, 120, 161, 258, 289n65, 297n97, 308n89. See also *hayyot*
Holy of Holies, 11, 76, 132
Holy Spirit, 3, 42–49, 51, 224, 282n74 and 82
homoousios, 46, 282n74
Hoshaiah (R.), 203, 207
Huna (R.), 167
hypostasis, 45–47, 50, 144–145, 282n74

Iaoel, 113–114, 119, 122
Idi bar Abin I (R.), 114
Idi bar Abin II (R.), 114
Idith (R.), 13, 104, 109–110, 114–115, 279n49
incantation bowls, 14, 138–139, 299n127
Inyanei bar Sasson (Sisson?) (R.), 117
Irenaeus, 42–43

Isaac, 154–156, 261

Ishmael, 220–221

Ishmael b. Elisha (R.), 131–134, 136

Ishmael b. R. Yose (R.), 38, 85–86, 88, 91–92

Ishmaelites, 220–221

Israel, 25, 56, 62, 77, 85–87, 91, 127, 133, 147, 153–154, 156, 181–184, 194, 216, 219, 223–225, 238–243, 254–257, 261–265; house of, 90; land of, 15, 84, 105, 111, 120, 159; people of, 12, 17–18, 57–59, 63, 73, 79, 105–106, 112, 152, 155, 180, 245, 249; twelve tribes of, 101

Jacob, 52, 57, 62–63, 95, 154–156, 262, 317n1

Jericho, 111

Jerusalem, 85, 88, 91, 95, 119, 125, 132, 151, 215, 225, 238, 269, 317n3, 327n137

Jesse: stump of, 101, 217, 254, 312n7, 315n39

Jesus Christ, 36, 45–46, 49–50, 78–79, 92, 101, 143, 145–148, 156, 158–159, 187–188, 196, 209–212, 251, 264, 285n24; ascension of, 79, 231, 235, 267–268; birth of, 229; crucifixion of, 235, 252, 266; genealogy of, 224; historical, 20, 159; resurrection of, 79, 211, 231, 267; as Son of God, 6, 12, 15, 18, 41, 43–51, 144, 152, 159; as Son of Man, 79, 83, 92–94, 141, 267, 289n71, 323n83

Job, 124

Joseph (of Nazareth), 224

Joseph (patriarch), 95, 317n1

Josephus, 185–186, 221, 225

Judah, 90, 223–225, 236

justice, 21, 70–73, 131–132, 166, 168, 277n9, 284n7

Justin Martyr, 45

Kabbalah, 6, 54, 292n8

Lamb of God, 13, 92–94

Lebanon, 217, 312n5, 315n39

Levi (R.), 112, 116, 157, 284n9

Levites, 154–156

Logos. *See* Word

Lot, 220

Luliani b. Tabri (R.), 162–163

Lydda, 28, 155

makhon, 88

Manasseh, 95, 225, 227, 317n1

Mani I (R.), 151

ma'on, 88

Mary, 224, 231, 268

Masada, 115

Maximian, 33–34

Meir (R.), 38, 279n46, 306n51

Menahem, 215–216, 218, 225–226, 314n35, 327n141

mercy, 21, 59–61, 66–67, 70–73, 131–132, 168, 277n9, 284n7, 286n8

Mesopotamia, 206

Messiah, 10, 17–18, 20, 75, 77–79, 83, 124, 148–149; ben Ephraim, 236, 237, 266, 317nn3 and 5; ben Joseph, 236, 237, 266; birth of, 19, 216–235; Davidic, 13, 73, 80–81, 85, 88–92, 101–103, 215, 223–229; priestly, 224; suffering, 18–19, 236–271

Metatron, 5, 7, 10, 13–15, 17–18, 20, 85, 87, 89–90, 93, 103–106, 108–115, 117, 119–130, 133–141, 143, 145–149, 160, 195, 274n13, 288n51, 291n8, 293nn29 and 31, 294n34, 295n54, 297nn80, 83, and

85, 297n94, 298n103, 299nn124
and 127, 300nn130 and 137,
301nn137 and 142, 303n163. *See
also* Enoch
Michael, 14, 16, 73, 75–77, 88,
119–122, 138, 162, 164, 180–182,
191–195, 205, 296n80, 308n89
minim, 3, 5–6, 22, 27, 32–33, 36, 57,
104, 169, 199, 201, 277n15. *See also*
heresy
Moab, 111
monarchianism, 45–46; adoptionistic,
45, 281n70; dynamic, 45; strict/
modalist, 45, 281n70
monotheism, 2, 50
mosaics, 95, 101, 290n91
Moses, 52, 58, 101–102, 104–105, 107,
111, 133, 164, 169–170, 174, 184,
186–188, 193, 208, 255, 285n24,
291n8, 294n34, 295n54, 300n137,
307n69, 317n3, 323n80
Mount of Olives, 91
Mount Sinai, 12, 15–16, 56, 58, 60, 62,
101, 105, 157, 164, 179–188,
283nn2 and 4
Muhammad, 115
Muslims, 220
mysticism, 6, 54; Merkavah, 85, 116,
118, 129, 135, 137

Nadab, 105
Nahman (R.), 104
Nahman bar Rav Huna (R.), 114
Nahman bar Ya'aqov (R.), 114
Nahman bar Yitzhaq (R.), 114,
125–126
name(s) of God, 10, 12, 18, 21–24, 27,
33, 35, 37, 39–42, 48, 55, 62, 68–69,
71, 110, 113, 120, 144–148,
171–172, 204, 209, 276n3, 291n8,
320n27

Nathan, 79, 101
Nathan (R.), 57, 61–62, 284n15
Nebuchadnezzar, 150–152, 259
Nehunya b. Haqanah (R.), 136
Neo-Platonism, 3
new covenant, 19, 156, 159, 187–188,
231–233. *See also* old covenant
Nicene Creed, 46–47, 50–51

Ofannim, 86, 88, 189–190, 308n89
offerings, 22–24
old covenant, 19, 159, 188, 232. *See also*
new covenant
Oriental Orthodoxy, 143
Origen, 46, 48, 194
Orpheus, 101, 290n91
orthodoxy, 1, 4, 9

palace, 169; heavenly, 90, 109
Palestine, 5, 7–8, 10–12, 14–16, 25, 28,
41, 67, 81–83, 85, 102, 111–112,
115, 118, 122–124, 138, 140–141,
152–153, 155, 157, 159, 163, 168,
170, 178, 183, 195–196, 199, 202,
205, 207, 214–215, 254, 269,
294n38, 301n142
pardes, 127, 134, 297nn88 and 94
paradise, 108, 205, 297n88, 316n49
patronage, 194–195
Paul the Apostle, 16, 29–32, 44, 145,
187–188, 193–194, 209–212, 265,
278n30, 297n88, 316n49
Pentateuch, 21
Peshitta, 143, 287n41
Phanuel, 75–76
Pharaoh, 12, 58, 151
Philo, 15–16, 43, 52, 175–178, 196,
207, 209–213, 280n62
Philostratus, 221
Phinehas, 255
Pliny, 221

polemics, 16, 43, 81, 152, 156, 158, 165,
191, 195, 203, 208, 212, 230, 233,
243, 301n142, 320n30
polytheism, 9–10, 45, 49–50, 153, 155,
158
powers in heaven, 8, 10–12, 14–16, 20,
25–26, 32, 41–42, 52–53, 56–57,
62–63, 67, 80, 83–84, 94, 117–118,
121–122, 125–129, 131–132,
135–136, 138, 141, 145, 154–155,
174–177, 196, 199–201, 207, 267,
310n7
prayer, 30
priests, 154–156, 186
Prince of the World, 116–117, 119,
121–125, 195
prophecy, 30
prophets, 186, 218
Pythagoras, 221

Qumran, 116, 142, 223, 250–251,
286n15, 309n92, 312n38, 320n34

Raphael, 75–76, 300n130
raqia'/reqi'im, 87, 88, 90, 134, 163,
299n127, 305n6, 308n88
Rav, 131, 172–173, 202–203, 311n12
redemption, 17–18, 45, 56, 60, 73, 77,
85, 91–92, 94, 102, 133, 147–149,
239, 242–243, 256–257, 261, 268
Red Sea, 12, 58, 60–61, 157
resurrection, 255
Reuben, 150–151
revelation, 18, 60, 195
Roman Empire, 8, 11–12, 14, 33–35,
41, 48, 64, 67, 102, 140, 152, 159,
212, 214, 218–219, 225, 229, 237,
254, 269, 301n140
Rome. See Roman Empire

Sabellianism, 46
Sabellius, 46

sacrifice, 24, 88, 119–120, 191–192,
195, 233, 251, 255
Sadducees, 273n2, 280n50, 310n8
Samuel, 101
Sanhedrin, 267
Sanherib, 151
Sarah, 220
Sasangiel, 85, 288n51
Sassanian Empire, 95, 102, 139–140,
206, 214, 269, 301n140
Satan, 205–206, 227, 244
sects, 4–5, 9, 63, 201
Sepphoris, 28, 123, 163, 167, 170
Serafim, 86, 88, 162, 308n89
Seth, 44
Shadrach, Meshach, and Abednego,
151–152
Shapur I, 95
Shekhinah, 28–29, 70, 129, 229n8
Shema', 2, 181, 215
Shemuel b. Nahman (R.), 123, 169–170
She'ol, 151
Shim'on b. Azzai, 22
Shim'on b. Pazzi (R.), 120, 167–168
Simlai (R.), 11, 27–29, 31–38, 41–42,
44–45, 47–49, 51, 53, 68, 165,
277n20, 279n42, 282n82,
309n110
sin, 43, 78, 106, 127–128, 144, 147,
173–174, 202–203, 210, 239,
244–247, 249–252, 254–255,
264–265, 303n163, 322n59
Sodom, 38, 161
Solomon, 154–155
Son of Man, 64–67, 73–83, 103, 109,
121, 224, 294n43
soul, 174–175, 177, 208, 245–246, 252,
256, 259–260, 265
Stephen, 186
suffering servant, 10, 18, 251–252, 255
synagogue, 13, 95, 101–102, 290n91
Syria, 95

Tabernacle, 120

Tanhum (R.), 117, 124, 162

Temple, 11, 87–88, 120, 132, 151, 191, 257, 312nn5 and 7

—First Temple: destruction of, 225, 240, 259, 261

—heavenly temple, 75, 89–92, 119, 122, 132, 193

—Second Temple, 80, 185, 188, 191, 193–194; destruction of, 8, 79, 85, 125–126, 215–216, 219, 222, 225–227, 232, 234, 315n39

—Third Temple, 219

Ten Commandments, 183, 220

Tertullian, 46

tetragrammaton, 21, 23, 113, 139–140, 182, 297n100

tetrarchy, 11, 34, 41, 48

Thessaloniki, 34

throne, 13, 35, 37, 56, 59, 61, 68–76, 81, 83–84, 87–95, 101, 104, 109, 110, 113, 117, 121, 128–129, 131–135, 145, 151–152, 161, 189, 229–230, 243–246, 250, 257–260, 263, 265, 267, 285n2, 297n94, 320n28, 323nn80 and 83, 325n118

Tiberias, 25, 28, 123, 155, 163, 170

Torah, 12, 22, 24, 26, 52–53, 95, 101–102, 126, 134–136, 169, 193, 220, 241–244, 247, 263, 306n51, 319n19, 320n30; revelation of, 15–16, 25–26, 41, 57, 62–63, 78, 157, 164, 179–182, 184–188, 194

Tree of Knowledge, 202, 311n12

trinitarian theology, 3, 9, 24, 42–45, 47–49, 51, 144, 282n82

trisagion, 90, 93, 154–155, 157, 204

uniqueness of God, 2–3, 5, 8, 21–22, 135, 181

unity of God, 2–3, 5, 8, 21–22, 67

Uriel, 116

Valens, 35

Valentinian I, 35

voice of God, 39, 112–113, 128

Vrevoil, 116

Wisdom, 10, 42–43, 51–54, 109, 141, 144, 174, 176–177, 213, 281n69, 302n150

Word, 10, 16, 42–43, 45–46, 49, 52–53, 141, 144, 176–177, 208–209, 211, 213, 265, 281n69, 283n88, 312n30

Yaho'el. See Iaoel

Yehoshua b. Hananiah (R.), 111–113, 243–244

Yehoshua b. Levi (R.), 218

Yehudah bar Shim'on (R.), 154–155

Yehudah ha-Naśi (R.), 40, 253, 280n54

Yitzhaq (R.), 162–163

Yitzhaq b. Nappaha (R.), 24, 36, 39–40, 117, 309n110

Yohanan b. Nappaha (R.), 28, 37, 68–70, 151, 162–163, 183–184

Yohanan b. Torta (R.), 82

Yonathan b. Eleazar (R.), 123, 169–170

Yose (R.), 22, 70–72, 81, 258, 276n3

Yudan (R.), 194–195, 215, 309n110, 312n1

Zebudiel, 136–137

zevul, 88, 116–117, 119, 121

Ziwutiel, 137

Zutra bar Tobi (R.), 131